Michael Jackson: The Complete Story of The King of Pop

Michael Jackson:
The Complete Story
of
the King of Pop

Lisa D. Campbell

Foreword by Michael Firestone

Apogee Publishing

Copyright © 2012 by Lisa D. Campbell

All rights reserved. No part of this book may be used or reproduced in any manner whatsoever without written permission of the publisher.

All photos from the Lisa Campbell collection except where noted.
Cover design by John R. Campbell

ISBN 978-0-9884130-1-6

Artists perform. Icons amaze.
Artists create. Icons inspire.
Artists are on-trend. Icons set trends.

Kimora Lee Simmons
President/Creative Director of Phat Fashions
The Official Michael Jackson Opus

Dedicated to
Michael Joseph Jackson

and
Prince Michael Jackson Jr., Paris Jackson and
Prince Michael Jackson II (Blanket)
Your father makes the world a better place.

Photo courtesy of Michael Firestone

Michael Firestone is a Michael Jackson Tribute Artist. His intense study of Jackson's every move, gesture and vocal vibration combined with his uncanny ability to duplicate his look transforms him into a very convincing substitute for the original. His performances are a great tribute to the greatest entertainer in the world. I am proud to call him my friend. I love you, Michael.

FOREWORD

My name is Michael Firestone. Music and the arts have always captured my attention; whether it was an artist like Salvador Dali, or Joe Perry from Aerosmith killing a guitar solo. I grew up in the 80's, and unlike today, there were tons of talented, original recording artists and singers. Most of the music out today wouldn't have lasted five minutes back then. But there was one guy. A guy who became king to me the first time I saw him. I watched him slide backwards, and sideways, kick, spin and sing with passion. I watched him turn into a werewolf, maul his date, gain her trust again turn in to a zombie and eat her again. I watched him grab himself in "Bad" while trying not to look at my father who wasn't happy about the new move at all, knowing within fifteen minutes I would be grabbing my cash and prizes in my bedroom mirror. I watched him turn into a car, a cat, gold kitty litter, a robot, a scarecrow, a gangster and a legend. I watched in horror when they took him to the hospital, and listened to the news of his death due to the fact I couldn't watch anymore. I'm talking about "the King of Pop", Michael Jackson.

Michael Jackson means everything to me. He taught me how to sing and dance, write songs, be a nice person and how to be a better father. I was so inspired by him I had decided at an early age, around 13, that if I could be anyone else in the world, I would want to be him.

The public response to me prior to his death was off and on. They thought I was freaky because I admired him instead of them. I didn't want to be like them. I wanted to be - different. After his passing, people loved me due to the fact they missed him, or felt guilty that they judged him. Either way, they inspired me, old fans or new fans of his, to give them a little piece of what they now want, although some hated this perfect being while he was here. I just hope he knows how much everyone really did love him down here.

I watched and studied him so much in my younger years that I had maybe three friends who I may have seen five times outside of school. I would get home and sneak my father's video camera out and record myself until he pulled up in the driveway, hide the camera, wait until he jumped in the shower and then put it back in its case and under the bed the exact way I found it. I would eat dinner, do dishes, go to my room and watch Michael until my family fell asleep; then watch myself, comparing myself to him, which sucks. I

Foreword

was very hard on myself during these years. I would record everything positive or negative. I just loved the way he looked. But hoping there was a clip of him singing or dancing. I loved any footage of him signing acappella. Then I could really hear what he was doing.

    Michael's biggest achievement to me was his charity work. That's what I love most about him: kindness. They tried to make him look like a monster, and even with that, still helped children all over the world. All the records and concerts are awesome, and I'm proud of him for all that, but God gave him that because he really was an angel. An angel whose wings where broken by the same people he helped and by a public who selfishly turned their back on him when he needed them the most. But you could only know what he was really about, the excitement he created if you lived then. Kids today will never be glued to the TV in excitement like we were, then going to school for the next week talking about how awesome his new video was. Those days are over. CGI can't replace someone like Michael, he was real, and he was bad ass.

    I first met Lisa and right off the bat felt a connection with her, like a long lost sister or something. I could feel her positive energy and spirit. Being in entertainment it's hard to come by someone so full of light. I was so interested in everything she talked about and I feel like she felt the same. I love you, Lisa.

Preface

On June 25th, 2009, I was with a small group of friends at a Phoenix restaurant celebrating a birthday when a text message was received; Michael Jackson had been taken to the hospital with cardiac arrest. Phone calls and text messages rolled in from family and friends who had also heard the news. Constant checking of news websites quickly revealed TMZ's initial report that Michael Jackson had died. Various news sites were checked repeatedly and furiously. Reuters was the first site found that confirmed the worst. Then the *Los Angeles Times*. One by one, site after site was reporting that the King of Pop had died. I was devastated. The news hit me like a ton of bricks. Driving home I had the car windows down. It was about 105 degrees in Phoenix that day, and I had chills. Goosebumps ran up and down my arms. It was blazing hot outside and I was suddenly freezing and fairly certain lunch was going to make an encore appearance. The radio was cranked up and I flipped from station to station to find each one was playing Michael Jackson songs exclusively. Stations that that very morning wouldn't have played Michael Jackson's music if you begged them to now suddenly and temporarily adopted an all Jackson format.

I wanted desperately for it not to be true but was terrified it was. I wanted him to show up at the Staples Center that evening as scheduled- with Ashton Kutcher in tow- to let us all know we had been punk'd. My heart ached for his children and his mother. I felt robbed of the comeback performances that were a mere seventeen days away. That very morning I checked my calendar and counted the days until he was to hit the stage in London. I was eagerly anticipating seeing the costumes and the choreography, learning what songs were performed, seeing how he looked and hearing how he sounded. I wanted to learn *every* detail of the This Is It shows.

I felt like I had lost a close friend. Michael Jackson's life and career have played a major role in my life since 1979 and especially since 1983. After years of following his career and researching his life, building an extensive personal Jackson library in the process, my first book was published in 1993. It's follow up was published the following year. Both volumes were met with an overwhelming response from Michael Jackson himself and his office, MJJ Productions. He arranged for his publicist to aid in the promotion of the books, signed a copy for me and even sent me three dozen red roses on my birthday.

Over the years, I have been fortunate to attend many dozens

Preface

of concerts by a wide range of artists. Nobody, *nobody* topped Michael Jackson. Pure and simple. The day following his death, I had tickets to an Eric Clapton and Steve Winwood concert. This was the first concert in approximately two hundred shows that I deliberately skipped. I couldn't tear myself away from the continuous news coverage and was certainly in no condition, physically or emotionally, to attend a concert. I was heartbroken. After a rather quiet, relatively inactive period on the Jackson front, I quickly fell into old habits of watching and recording *everything* MJ related on TV, learning ever more grim details; hearing Jermaine's heartbreaking statement to the press and watching my hero's body being loaded into a helicopter for transport to the coroner's office. In the days and weeks that followed I watched, read and collected everything available on Michael Jackson. And I haven't stopped. I hope to offer here a comprehensive look at the life of the world's greatest entertainer and its kindest humanitarian and share some of my own memories along the way. He enjoyed the highest highs the world could offer and suffered some of the lowest lows. Through it all he maintained the love and admiration of millions of fans from literally every corner of the world.

    It is heartening to see the aura of the rumors and scandal and talk of "Wacko Jacko" that seemed to plague him finally subside. It's gratifying to see him finally accorded the acknowledgement and appreciation of the genius in his artistry and unmatched caring for others.

    Michael Jackson's impact on music history, his fans and the

world cannot be overstated. His effect on my life is profound. I miss him deeply. At a time when we were supposed to be celebrating his record breaking string of shows at the O2 Arena in London, we were suddenly mourning his loss. His brilliant contributions to music and dance, his unending humanitarian efforts and his constant efforts to unify people and heal the world will certainly leave an everlasting impression and continue to inspire others around the world.

Rest in peace, Michael. I love you more.

1

A, B, C it's easy as 1, 2, 3
As simple as do re mi
A, B, C
1, 2, 3
Baby you and me girl

"ABC"
- Freddie Perren, Alphonso Mizell, Berry Gordy, Deke Richards

To celebrate the twentieth-fifth anniversary of Motown Records a TV special was produced that brought together the label's biggest stars to honor the man who started it all, Berry Gordy. *Motown 25: Yesterday, Today and Forever* aired on May 16, 1983. Diana Ross reunited with the Supremes, Smokey Robinson was back with the Miracles, The Temptations and Four Tops performed as did Stevie

Wonder. Then the kid group of the label took the stage, reuniting fourteen years after they were first introduced to the world. Michael Jackson was once again fronting his brothers as lead singer of the Jackson Five. For the first time in eight years, Jermaine was also on stage with his brothers. But this was not what made the show historic. After a medley of Jackson Five hits which included "I Want You Back", "The Love You Save" and "Never Can Say Goodbye", they ended the set with "I'll Be There". Then the brothers then left the stage to Michael. Dressed in black tuxedo pants, cropped up around his ankles so his glittery socks were visible, a silver shirt and black sequined jacket, he addressed the crowd while the stage was cleared, leaving just one microphone stand. Something lay next to it. A hat. A black hat. "Those were the good old days. I love those songs. Those were magic moments with all my brothers, including Jermaine. But, those were good songs, I like those songs a lot, but especially, I like the **NEW** songs."

Michael picked up the hat and perched it on his head, angled down over his eyes and began pumping his pelvis to the opening beats of "Billie Jean" and went on to bring the house down with his moves, unveiling the moonwalk for the very first time. It was magical. He glided backwards while appearing to walk forward. It was something most people had never seen before. He seemed to defy gravity, or the laws of physics, or something. It just didn't seem possible to do what we all saw him doing. TV viewers, the Pasadena Civic Auditorium audience, other artists backstage, including his brothers, were stunned. Michael Jackson, who had already been enjoying uncharted success with his recent album, *Thriller*, and was wowing audiences with his fancy footwork in videos for "Billie Jean" and then "Beat It", just sent his popularity soaring into the stratosphere and changed the music industry in the process.

This is only one magic moment in a career that began when five year old Michael Jackson began singing with his four older brothers in Gary, Indiana. Five of Joseph and Katherine Jackson's nine children began singing at home, then at local talent contests, then they took the world by storm.

Katherine Scruse was born in Alabama on May 4, 1930. Before reaching her second birthday, Katherine was stricken with polio, from which she still walks with a limp. When Katherine was four years old, her family moved from Alabama to East Chicago, Indiana.

Joseph Walter Jackson was born on July 26, 1929, in Arkansas to Samuel J. Jackson and Chrystalee King. Joseph was their first of five children. Samuel Jackson was said to be a very strict and unfeeling man, rarely letting his emotions show even to his family. He would pass these traits onto his oldest son. The Jackson children would grow up in a household where they were not allowed to call their father "dad" or "father". He was Joseph. To this day, they all frequently refer to their parents as "Mother and Joseph".

After living with his father in California, Joe later went to live with his mother in Indiana after his father remarried. There, for a brief time, he became a boxer in the Golden Gloves. He then got a job working as a crane operator in a steel mill. Joe and Katherine married in 1949. They settled in a small two bedroom house in Gary, Indiana, a dark, dingy, industrial town and began to raise a family; a big family. A big musical family. Their five oldest sons developed an early interest in music and soon formed their own group, The Jackson Five. This group's lead singer, the seventh of Joseph and Katherine's nine children would go beyond the group and become the greatest entertainer of the world.

Joseph and Katherine Jackson actually had ten children, Marlon had a twin, Branden, who died about eight hours after birth. Their first child was Maureen Reilette (Rebbie), born on May 29, 1950. She was followed by their first son, Sigmond Esco (Jackie) who shares his mother's birthdate, May 4, 1951. Toriano Adaryl (Tito) followed on October 15, 1953. Jermaine LaJuan was born on December 11, 1954. Their second daughter, LaToya Yvonne, was born exactly six years after their first, on May 29, 1956. Marlon David was next, born on March 12, 1957. On August 29, 1958, Michael Joe took his place in the growing Jackson clan. Michael was followed by Steven Randall (Randy) on October 29, 1961. The youngest Jackson, Janet Damita, was born on May 16, 1966.

The continually growing Jackson family still lived in the same small house in Gary, coincidentally on the corner of 23rd Avenue and Jackson Street, at 2300 Jackson Street. The small house had just two bedrooms. Joe and Katherine had one and the boys shared the other in triple bunked beds. The girls slept in the living room on a pull out sofa bed. Roosevelt High School's football field lay directly behind their house though there would be little time for fun and games.

"ABC"

Music always played an important role in the Jackson household. Early in his marriage, Joe Jackson played guitar in a band called The Falcons. The band played cover versions of songs in local bars and colleges but only enjoyed limited success. As his family steadily grew Joe eventually quit the band. Katherine went to work part-time at Sears.

Father Joe's guitar was strictly off limits to the children. However, when he was away, Tito would get the guitar out and practice playing. Katherine was aware they were playing with the forbidden instrument but didn't enforce the ban figuring it was helping to keep her boys off the streets of Gary. When a string was accidentally broken, Tito had no way to replace it. They simply hoped Joe wouldn't notice. But he did. Joe threatened to punish his son unless he could show that he could play the instrument. Tito surprised his father with his talent. Joe was equally impressed with the talent of his other sons.

Joe eventually bought Tito his own, bright red, guitar. Later, a bass was purchased for Jermaine and microphones were added to the boy's growing equipment collection. The three oldest boys, Jackie, Tito, and Jermaine had formed their own group, with Jermaine as lead singer. Not long after the formation of the group, little brothers Marlon and Michael joined with Michael on bongos. The brothers voted that Michael, who at age five had been imitating Jermaine's lead vocals, should be the group's new lead singer.

Michael made his first public performance at age five for his Kindergarten class at Garnett Elementary School when he participated

5

in a school pageant. His performance of "Climb Every Mountain" was so emotional it moved his teacher and his mother to tears. Michael recalls in his autobiography, *Moonwalk*, how he felt at being able to touch people with his performance.

Living out his dream of making it big through his children, Joe was determined that his sons would be their absolute best. He insisted they put in long hours of rehearsal everyday after school while still completing homework assignments and keeping grades up, leaving very little time for any other activities. In *Moonwalk*, Michael remembers working much too hard for a child, missing out on normal childhood activities we all take for granted.

Michael recalled the strictness with which daily rehearsals were held. According to Michael, if one of them messed up at rehearsal, missed a step or forgot a lyric, they were beaten, often with an ironing cord. While each of the children received their share of the beatings, Michael was the only one who ever fought back, one time heaving a shoe at his father. Because of Joe's need to control the lives of his sons and his strictness, Michael never enjoyed a close relationship with him. It left lasting scars from which he never fully recovered. He continuously longed to be closer to his father and felt strongly that if he had had any closeness with his father, however brief, it would have meant everything to him and changed his life dramatically. He became determined that when he became a father, he would have a much different relationship with his children. And he did.

The group soon began entering local talent contests using their new name, The Jackson Five, suggested by a neighbor, and wearing stage costumes sewn by their mother. They performed cover versions of songs by Motown artists and anything by Michael's idol, James Brown. Joe would visit clubs in Chicago to check out other performers to get ideas for his sons' act. They were soon winning every contest they entered and became quite well known around Gary.

The Jackson Five were performing regularly during the week at a club in Gary, Mister Lucky's, when Michael was six years old. On weekends they began traveling to Chicago, New York, and Philadelphia, entering and winning more talent contests. They traveled in a Volkswagon van with their equipment in a second van that they had borrowed. They would often leave for home late Sunday night and the boys would sleep in the van, and would not return home until 3:00 or 4:00 a.m. They would still be up early Monday morning for school.

In between their club dates, Joe was working on getting his sons a recording contract. The big prize being getting in the door at Motown Records. At nine years of age, Michael Jackson made his very first recording when the group made two records with a local record label in Gary, Steeltown Records in 1968. The first release, "I'm a Big Boy Now"/ "You've Changed", gained a certain level of popularity in the Midwest, but never made it nationally. The second release from Steeltown Records was "You Don't Have To Be Over 21 (To Fall In Love)"/ "Jam Session". This second single was less successful than "Big Boy", but both singles did help increase the group's popularity locally. A few "lost" Steeltown reordings were released years later on *Pre-History: The Lost Steeltown Recordings*.

In 1968 came the group's biggest challenge to date. They were invited to perform at Amateur Night at the Apollo Theater in Harlem. Amateur Night at the Apollo had long been regarded as the proving ground for amateurs. It was common for some acts to be booed by the audience or be literally pulled off the stage by a giant hook. The Jackson Five took the tough crowd by storm, they not only won Amateur Night at the Apollo, they received a standing ovation and were invited back as paid performers.

It was while performing at the Apollo that Michael got to watch his idols perform. He would stand backstage and watch the other acts, like Jackie Wilson and the Godfather of Soul, James Brown. He studied and practiced the steps of James Brown until he could duplicate them perfectly. These two performers, along with Sammy Davis Jr., had an especially strong influence on Michael. He also greatly admired and studied the moves of Gene Kelly and Fred Astaire. He studied these greats, his heroes, and then became even bigger than they were. He would borrow a gesture or move from them and put his own spin on it, both figuratively and literally, to create something new and different, something people had never seen before.

The same year they won the talent contest at the Apollo, the group was signed to appear on *The David Frost Show* in New York, their first television appearance. The boys were ecstatic. On the afternoon after school when they were scheduled to leave, Joe announced he had cancelled their appearance in New York and that they would be going to Detroit instead. The boys were crushed until Joe gave his reason. He had received a call from Motown Records.

"ABC"

This was the big break they had been hoping and praying for. How this call from Motown came to be has three different versions, each crediting someone else with "discovering" the Jackson Five. In any case, the group's television debut was postponed until 1969 when they performed on the Miss Black America Pageant.

Contrary to popular belief, Diana Ross did not discover the Jackson Five. In an attempt to generate stronger, more widespread, attention to the newly signed group Motown chose Diana Ross, their greatest star, to present the group to the public. Motown created the now well known tale of how Diana Ross discovered the Jackson Five at a "Soul Weekend" held in Gary for Mayoral candidate Richard Hatcher. According to the legend, when Diana Ross watched the Jackson Five perform she was so impressed she took them to Motown and introduced them to Berry Gordy, president and founder of Motown Records.

Another often told story credits Gladys Knight with discovering the Jackson Five. After seeing the group perform at the Apollo Theater, she brought them to the attention of Berry Gordy at Motown. Actually, she did see them perform and was impressed, but being new to Motown and yet to have any hits, she carried little clout with Berry Gordy. Gordy then took little, if any, notice. He was also against signing any kid acts. He had his hands full dealing with tutors and all the other special arrangements needed for his then youngest discovery, little Stevie Wonder.

A third story, which is most widely accepted as being the true version, has Bobby Taylor of Bobby Taylor and the Vancouvers discovering the Jackson Five. Bobby Taylor first became aware of the Jackson Five when the two groups were both appearing at the Regal Theater in Chicago, after which Taylor arranged for them to audition at Motown. Tommy Chong, of the comedy duo Cheech and Chong, was a member of the Vancouvers at the time. Tommy Chong and Marlon Jackson have each confirmed this version of how the Jackson Five were discovered. Bobby Taylor told *Rolling Stone*, "This squirt did James Brown better than JB himself. He broke out in 'Cold Sweat'. He sang 'I Got the Feelin'' with feelings you can't fake. He tore up the stage like JB's long-lost love child – the spins, the mic action, the fall-on-your-knees-and-beg-for-it moves. His voice grabbed me by the throat and said, 'Take me to your leader'. So right after the show, I did just that. I jumped up and told his dad, 'Joe, we're off to Detroit.'"

2

You and I must make a pact
We must bring salvation back
Where there is love,
I'll be there

"I'll Be There"
-Hal Davis, Berry Gordy Jr., Willie Hutchison, Bob West

Berry Gordy was not present at the Jackson Five's audition for Motown. He did however have the July 23, 1968 audition taped to view later. They kicked off their performance of a lifetime with the same number that won over Bobby Taylor, James Brown's "I've Got the Feelin'". Michael's early mastery of the moves of James Brown is incredible. He duplicates his idol's steps perfectly. Other acts performing in the same small clubs as the Jackson Five during this time were constantly amazed at Michael's dancing ability and the emotion with which the nine year old sang. Next up in their audition for Motown was John D. Loudermilk's "Tobacco Road". The clincher was Smokey Robinsons' "Who's Lovin' You". Other Motowners, including the song's composer, Robinson, were amazed at the young lead singer's emotional delivery. And he had yet to reach his tenth birthday.

Gordy viewed the tape, which was couriered to him in Los Angeles, and decided to sign the group immediately. Gordy was in the process at the time of relocating the Motown headquarters from Detroit to Los Angeles. It took Motown six months to get the boys released from their contract with Steeltown Records, then Berry Gordy moved the family from Gary to Los Angeles, fulfilling a lifelong dream for both Joe and Katherine. Many sources have said the boys were split up in California with half of them staying with Berry Gordy, and the other half, including Michael, staying with Diana Ross. According to Jermaine, this was made up by Motown to add to the story that Diana Ross discovered the group. The boys all actually stayed with Gordy, though Diana lived next door and the boys did spend a lot of time there.

During this time Michael grew very close to Diana, and although she did not discover him, Diana had a profound influence on Michael's life. She taught him to draw and paint, instilling in him an appreciation for art. He carried a deep love and appreciation for art throughout his life. He also carried a deep love for Diana, describing her as his mother-lover-sister. In *Moonwalk*, Michael describes how hurt he felt when Diana announced she was to marry Arne Naess, "I

"I'll Be There"

have to admit that I was a bit hurt and a little jealous because I've always loved Diana and always will."

After signing the Jackson Five, Motown immediately began grooming the boys for their soon to be success. They were taught how to carry themselves, how to respond to interviewers questions, and they were taught the story of how they were discovered by Diana Ross. To complete the package, two years were shaved off of Michael's age by Motown. A nine year old lead singer with that powerful voice was a bigger phenomenon than if they admitted he was now eleven. And rehearsals continued. Many of the group's early routines were choreographed by a young new Motown executive, Suzanne de Passe. She too became close to the boys, especially Michael.

Early in the group's existence, Joe added two other members to the group, Randy Rancifer and Johnny Jackson who played organ and drums. Wanting to present the group as one big happy family, Motown created another story that these two boys were also part of the Jackson family, reporting that they were cousins of the Jackson brothers. Actually, neither boy was related to the Jacksons.

Berry Gordy formed a songwriting team made up of Freddie Perren, Deke Richards, and Fonce Mizell referred to by Motown as "The Corporation". The Corporation had written a song for Gladys Knight, entitled, "I Want to Be Free". Berry Gordy asked that the song be rewritten to make it more appropriate for kids to sing. They rewrote the lyrics and returned to Gordy with "I Want You Back", the Jackson Five's first single with Motown from their debut album, *Diana Ross Presents the Jackson Five*. The album contains cover versions of

Motown hits, most notably Stevie Wonder's "My Cherie Amour". Michael's soulful deliverance of Smokey Robinson's "Who's Lovin' You" makes it impossible to believe he's only eleven years old. Or nine years old.

"I Want You Back" was released in late 1969 and the week of January 31, 1970, became their first number one hit single on *Billboard's* pop singles chart. It spent one week at number one replacing B.J. Thomas' "Raindrops Keep Falling On My Head". The single also went to number one on *Billboard's* black singles chart. The single had staying power, remaining a favorite hit for decades to come, always being included in the group's live performances, and Michael's solo tours up to and including This Is It. Their debut album peaked at number five on the pop album chart and went to number one on the black album chart. And this was only the beginning.

To promote their new single, the Jackson Five appeared on the *Ed Sullivan Show* in December, 1969, performing "I Want You Back" and "Who's Lovin' You". In 1988, Michael narrated a collection of film clips covering his career for *Entertainment Tonight* which included a clip of this performance. "I remember this was the *Ed Sullivan Show*. As young as I was, I never felt shy while performing. It was what I did and what I came into the world to do." Michael's monologue introducing "Who's Lovin' You" helped to make the rather mature themed song more appropriate for kids. Michael spoke of a girl he met at school, they toasted their love at milk break and he gave her his cookies. Well, they had a falling out during finger painting, and now Michael was wonderin' "Who's Lovin' You". Sullivan was prompted to remark, "those youngsters are amazing and the little one out front is incredible."

For the *Ed Sullivan Show* performance, Michael wore a purple hat. For a live performance later, Michael suggested he wear that purple hat again in concert. He did and it created a frenzy with the fans, something a certain single white glove and black sequined jacket would do for decades.

The group was now professionally known as the Jackson Five. However, the spelling and logo of the group varied between projects. Their name was sometimes spelled out, "The Jackson Five", or the number "5" was used, "The Jackson 5", other times these two were combined, "The Jackson 5ive". However you spell their name, Jackie, Tito, Jermaine, Marlon and Michael were on their way to enormous success.

Jackie was the athlete of the family and was once offered a contract with the major leagues. He has released two solo albums, *Jackie Jackson*, and in 1989, Jackie released his second solo album, *Be The One*. Jackie married Enid Spann in November, 1974. They met through Enid's friend, Hazel Gordy, daughter of Motown chief Berry Gordy and wife of Jermaine. Enid was a fashion designer and had designed costumes for the group. Jackie and Enid divorced in 1987 after Enid filed charges of abuse from Jackie. Enid died of an aneurism in 1997.

Like Jackie, Tito enjoyed sports and has coached little league baseball. At age eighteen, Tito married Delores (Dee Dee) Martes. After several years of marriage, they divorced. Tragedy struck in 1994 when Dee Dee was found dead in a suspicious drowning. Her boyfriend, Donald Bohana, was found guilty of her murder.

Jermaine was the original lead singer of the group when they first began performing at home in Indiana. He was later the brother chosen by Motown to be promoted as the group's sex symbol. Michael was too young to be considered in that light, though he was a favorite of their very young fans. Jermaine married Hazel Gordy in 1973 and they divorced in 1987, after which he returned to the family home in Encino with his girlfriend, Margaret Maldonado. Later he married Alejandra Oaziaza, they divorced in 2004. That same year he married Halima Rashia. Jermaine made several solo albums with Motown before signing with Arista in 1984, where he continued his solo career.

Marlon was the brother who had to work the hardest at mastering the group's choreography. Ironically, he was originally singled out by the press as the brother having great dancing talent. He did contribute to the group's choreography early on but was soon overshadowed by you-know-who. Marlon released his first solo album, *Baby Tonight* in 1988. At eighteen, he married Carol Parker. They supposedly kept the marriage secret for months, without even Joe knowing for sure.

The youngest member of the original Jackson Five was Michael. He quickly took over the position of lead singer from Jermaine and contributed to the group's choreography. After the move from Motown to Epic Records in the mid 70's, Michael began a solo career that made him the biggest selling artist and most awarded artist in the world. He used this global platform to bring attention to his other passion, helping the sick and suffering and healing the world. With his worldwide fame however came many challenges and those who sought to bring him down.

Randy officially joined the group when they moved from Motown to Epic though he had played bongos for the group much earlier. He played on albums and even played with his brothers in concert, but with little or no recognition. In the late 1980's, Randy formed his own band, Randy and the Gypsies. The group released their debut album and single, "Love You Honey" in 1989. This Randy Jackson has never served as a judge on *American Idol.*

Randy married Eliza Shaffe in 1989 and they have one daughter, Steveanna. Eliza filed for divorce from Randy in 1990 charging Randy with abuse. Randy ended up serving one month in jail and an additional month in a psychiatric clinic for the offense. He fathered another daughter, Genevieve, born the same year as Steveanna, with Alejandra Oaziaza.. Alejandra later became Mrs. Jermaine Jackson.

The eldest Jackson is daughter Maureen, nicknamed Rebbie. Rebbie married Nathaniel Brown at age eighteen and moved from Gary to Kentucky. Rebbie has released three solo albums, *Centipede, Reaction,* and *R U Tuff Enuff.*

LaToya has released several albums the first of which, *LaToya Jackson,* includes the single, "Night Time Lover" written by LaToya and Michael, and produced by Michael. LaToya was married to her manager, Jack Gordon, in the early 90's. She has since been featured in a number of realty shows and has written two books, one detailing the years of physical and emotional abuse she endured at the hands of Gordon.

Janet started her career as an actress at age ten playing Penny Gordon on the television series, *Good Times*. She also had roles in *Diff'rent Strokes* and later on *Fame*. Then she moved to the big screen with several movie roles. Janet's recording career was relatively unsuccessful until the release of *Control* in 1986 and *Janet Jackson's Rhythm Nation 1814* in 1989. Only half heartedly committed to a singing career, her first two albums, *Janet Jackson* and *Dream Street* failed. She has continued to have chart topping hits from her albums, *janet.*, *The Velvet Rope*, *All For You*, *Damita Jo*, *20 Y.O.* and *Discipline*. Greatest Hits packages include *Decade* and *Number Ones*.

Janet was briefly married to James DeBarge of the Motown family group DeBarge. She was later married to Rene Elizondo for nine years, during which time they managed to keep the marriage a secret from the public. The union was not revealed until they went through a bitter divorce.

The follow up single to "I Want You Back" was "ABC", off of their second album of the same name. "ABC" became the Jackson Five's second number one single, replacing the Beatles' "Let It Be" at the top of the pop chart, where it stayed for two weeks. "ABC" was also their second number one hit on the black singles chart. The *ABC* album reached number four on the pop album chart and became a number one hit on the black album chart.

The single was nominated for a Grammy award for Best Contemporary Group Vocal Performance, but lost to the Carpenters'

"Close to You". The single was featured in a commercial for Alpha Bits cereal and the box included a cut out cardboard record of the song. (I still have mine.) In February, 1970, the Jackson Five made their first appearance on *American Bandstand*. They performed both of their number one hit singles, "I Want You Back" and "ABC". From there Michael formed a long lasting friendship with the show's host and later the creator of the American Music Awards, Dick Clark.

The week of June 27, 1970, the Jackson Five again topped *Billboard's* pop singles chart and again knocked out the Beatles. "Long and Winding Road" was replaced as the number one song in the country by "The Love You Save" off of the *ABC* album. The single stayed at number one for two weeks and also hit number one on the black singles chart. This third number one single fulfilled the prophesy made to them by Berry Gordy that their first three singles would all be number one hits, the first group ever to do so. But the Jackson Five did him one better.

The Jackson Five's *Third Album* yielded their fourth number one single. It was quite a change of pace from the singles that had been previously released. "I'll Be There" is a touching ballad with Michael and Jermaine trading lead vocals. "I'll Be There" gave the Jackson Five their longest stay at number one, remaining at the top of the chart for five weeks, replacing Neil Diamond's "Cracklin' Rose". It also became their fourth number one hit on the black singles chart. The Jackson Five became the first group ever to have their first four singles become number one hits. A remake of "I'll Be There" by Mariah Carey and Trey Lorenz went to number one on the pop singles chart in

June, 1992.

Other notable tracks on *Third Album* include "Goin' Back To Indiana", "Mama's Pearl", and a cover version of "Bridge Over Troubled Water." The album peaked on the pop and black album charts at numbers four and one respectively.

The Jackson Five were honored in 1970, and again the following year, with the NAACP Image Award for Best Singing Group of the Year. They were also recognized by *Billboard* magazine for their chart success throughout the year. *Billboard's* year end singles chart for 1970 showed the Jackson 5's first four singles all in the top twenty. The number two song of 1970 was "I'll Be There", "ABC was number thirteen followed by "The Love You Save" at fourteen, and "I Want You Back" at number nineteen.

What became abundantly clear was that the group's little lead signer was the standout. David Von Drehle wrote in *Time* Magazine, "And even as the Jackson 5 were blazing to glory, anyone with eyes to see could predict that the group wouldn't last long. There was such an imbalance of talents – four mortals and this freakishly powerful fifth. Typical of Motown acts, the Jacksons were pressed into an ensemble, from their choreography to their lyrical trade-offs to their matched outfits. But whenever young Michael eased out of the spotlight and into formation alongside his brothers, the whole act sagged. It was like hitching a Derby winner to a farm wagon, and you could see him trying to hold himself back until, after a few bars, sanity prevailed and he would burst again to the front where he belonged."

While recording at Motown, young Michael watched and

learned from everyone, soaking up every detail. He would hang around the studio while Stevie Wonder worked his magic. He also absorbed everything he could about the business from the master, Berry Gordy. Besides the training provided by Motown experts, he learned about stage presence and presentation from Diana Ross. *Rolling Stone* described him as "first and foremost a Motown artist, an honor graduate of the most rigorous prep school pop music has ever known."

With their fourth single climbing the charts, the Jackson Five set out on their first American tour in the fall of 1970. To help keep their grades up while on tour, a tutor, Rose Fine, traveled with them. When they weren't touring they attended a private school with other young performers and children of performers. Michael attended Gardner Elementary School for a few months in sixth grade before it became necessary to arrange for private tutoring. Michael remained close with and remembered Rose Fine and her husband for years to come. When her husband died, he left a prized piano to Michael Jackson.

The Jackson family moved into their own home on Hayvenhurst Avenue in Encino, California, in late 1970. The brothers gradually all moved out as they got older and were married. Only Michael and LaToya remained with Michael splitting time between Hayvenhurst and his "hideaway" condo in Los Angeles until he purchased Neverland Valley Ranch.

For the first time since they moved to California, the Jackson Five returned to Gary in January, 1971. They played two benefit concerts for the re-election campaign for Mayor Richard Hatcher. In return, January 31, 1971, was declared "Jackson Five Day" in Gary and a ceremony was held in front of the family's old home to officially rename their street from Jackson Street to Jackson Five Street and Mayor Hatcher awarded the Jackson Five with the keys to the city. As part of the homecoming, a plaque was placed at the University of Indiana stating that the Jackson Five gave "Hope to the Young". Their Congressman then presented them with the flag from the top of the State Capital.

These award presentations and performances were filmed and later used in their TV special, *Goin' Back to Indiana* which aired in September 1971. The Jackson Five performed their biggest hits and acted in skits with their guests. A soundtrack album of the special peaked at number sixteen on *Billboard's* pop album chart and number five on the black album chart.

The day following the airing of their first TV special, the Jackson Five received commendations for "contributions to American youth." On September 20, 1971, the Congressional Record read as follows:

The Jackson Five

Mr. Bayh, Mr. President, I desire to pay tribute to a family of five young black musicians and singers from Gary, Indiana, who have made a large contribution to music in the past few years.

The Jackson Five, young men ranging in age from 12 to 20, have captured the imagination of today's youngsters, especially black youth, as no musical group since the Beatles in 1964. The Jackson Five have become a symbol of pride among black youth, who can readily identify and relate to them. As special tribute, the Grambling University Marching Tigers, a predominately black university in Louisiana, saluted the Jackson Five in their half-time performance during Saturday's Morgan State-Grambling University NCAA football game.

Last year the group had four hit singles, and they have had two more already this year. In the words of 12 year old Michael Jackson, the lead singer:

'We started singin' together after Tito started messin' with Dad's guitar and singin' with the radio. It was Tito who decided we should form a group and we did, and we practiced a lot, and then we started entering talent shows and we won every one we entered.'

On September, 19, the Jackson Five starred in their first television special, 'Goin' Back to Indiana,' on ABC-TV, with athletes Elgin Baylor, Ben Davidson, Rosey Grier, Elvin Hayes, and Bill Russell, and comics Tom Smothers and Bill Cosby as their guests. In addition, the Five were featured on September's cover of 'Ebony' Magazine and this fall will have a Saturday morning animated TV series modeled after them.

Group members include Jackie, who is 20, Tito, 17, Jermaine, 16, Marlon 14, and Michael 12. They started singing for fun and soon became known around Gary. Papa Joe, a crane operator, played the guitar and wrote songs to relax away from the job. Their mother, Catherine [sic], sang blues and as they became old enough, the kids joined in the family music sessions. As Joe Jackson says:

'It was fun, the kids liked it and it was one sure way of keeping

them home and not roaming in the streets of Gary.'

Motown Records recording star, Diana Ross, heard them during a benefit for Gary Mayor Richard Hatcher and the rest is history.

Despite their fantastic commercial success, members of the Jackson Five are continuing their education. Jackie has started college as a business administration major; the rest are still in secondary school and follow a rigorous schedule of homework, group practice, and classes. On weekends, holidays and during vacations the group makes recordings and gives concerts around the country.

I think it is important to recognize and pay tribute to the family unity that has made the Jackson Five the No. 1 soul group in the country. Indiana and the Nation are proud of the Jackson Five.

The Jackson Five set out on their second American tour in the spring of 1971. One noteworthy item about this tour was their opening act, a group of musicians from Tuskegee, Alabama known as the Commodores. Suzanne de Passe was charged with handling the boys on the road and found herself becoming the target of their antics, particularly Michael's, who loved to hide when she entered the room. She gave him the nickname "Casper" and rarely called him anything else after that.

While on tour and staying in one hotel room after another, the older brothers took advantage of the affections of their fans and groupies. They would bring girls back to the hotel room, sometimes while little Michael was in the room pretending to be asleep. It left emotional scars on Michael that he would have to cope with for the rest of his life, instilling him the beginnings of his feelings of distrust toward women and the feeling they were only around for their fame and money. It would make future relationships with women difficult for him.

Joe also indulged in many infidelities on the road and throughout his marriage to Katherine. One such liaison resulted in the birth of a daughter, Joh'Vonnie Jackson. Her existence has rarely been acknowledged by the family.

As the group's popularity soared, so did the need for increased security. For this tour, a retired Los Angeles police officer, Bill Bray, was hired as security chief for the boys. Bray worked with the family and later with Michael for years as his personal security chief. They grew to be very close, Bray often being described as Michael's confidant or as his second father. Fans reaction to the Jackson Five rivaled the frenzy that followed the Beatles. It would be something Michael especially would have to deal with for the rest of his life.

Their next two singles just missed adding to their string of number one hits. "Mama's Pearl", the second single from *Third Album,* peaked at number two on both the pop and black singles charts in the spring of 1971. It was held out of the number one spot by the Osmond's "One Bad Apple" a single which was coincidentally turned down for the Jackson Five by Berry Gordy. "Never Can Say Goodbye" from their next album, *Maybe Tomorrow*, spent three weeks in the number two spot on the pop singles chart, but made it to number one on the black singles chart. *Maybe Tomorrow* peaked at number eleven on the pop album chart. The title song from the *Maybe Tomorrow* album peaked at number twenty on *Billboard's* Hot 100. It did much better on the black chart, making it to number three. The Jackson Five would never have another number one song. They did enjoy a top ten hit with "Sugar Daddy", which peaked at number ten on the pop charts, and number three on the black charts, from their *Jackson 5 Greatest Hits* album, which peaked at number twelve on the pop album charts. Their *Christmas Album,* was also a hit for the holidays.

An animated cartoon series based on the Jackson Five began airing in the fall of 1971. At age thirteen, and a huge fan of cartoons, Michael especially enjoyed being depicted in the series. The speaking voices used in the cartoons were not the Jacksons, but the singing voices were. "Mama's Pearl" was used as the series' theme song. Along with having every episode on tape, I am the proud owner of an original animation cell used in the series.

On the heels of Donny Osmond, Motown prepared Michael to begin a solo career in addition to his role as lead singer of the Jackson Five. Michael recorded his first solo single, "Got to be There" in 1971, from his first solo album of the same name. "Got to be There" is a touching ballad in the same vein as "I'll Be There". The *Got to Be There* album includes Michael's version of "Rockin' Robin", a remake of Bobby Day's hit, and cover of Bill Withers' "Ain't No Sunshine" and Carol King's "You've Got a Friend". "Got to be There" peaked at number four on both the pop and black singles chart. "I Wanna Be Where You Are" peaked at number sixteen on the pop singles chart and number two on the black chart.

Michael recorded his second solo album in 1972. It featured

the theme song from a movie, a tender ballad of friendship. What really made this song different was that it was about a rat. A rat named Ben. *Ben*, the sequel to *Willard*, is a horror movie about a young boy's affection for rats, one named Ben in particular. Don Black, who wrote "Ben" with Walter Scharf, suggested Michael Jackson to sing it. Michael's emotion filled performance of "Ben" makes you forget it is a ballad to a rodent.

"Ben" was released as a single and became Michael's first number one hit as a solo artist. It peaked at number five on the black singles chart. At age fourteen, Michael became the youngest artist to hit number one as a solo artist and as a member of a group. The song went on to earn an Academy Award nomination for Best Song and Michael performed the song at the Academy Award presentation, but it didn't win the Oscar. The song however did win a Golden Globe award. Donny Osmond would recall later that he was actually asked first to record "Ben", but he had to pass as he was on tour at the time.

The *Ben* album cover was originally issued with a photograph of Michael with a horde of rats superimposed on the lower half of the picture. A revised cover with just a close-up photo of Michael was soon used instead when it was decided the rat cover was too graphic for children. The original rat cover of *Ben* has today become a rare collectible among fans.

The Jackson Five set out on a tour of England in 1972, where they gave a command performance for Queen Elizabeth at Kings Hall in Glasgow, Scotland. In addition to the concert tour, the Jacksons made several television appearances. Their second TV special, *The*

Jackson 5 Show, aired in November and Michael made an appearance as a contestant on *The Dating Game.* He was introduced as "the lead singer and youngest member of the Jackson 5. He loves sketching, drawing, playing basketball and candy and bubblegum." Lucky contestant number one ended up being his pick for his date. This second TV special, hit records, TV appearances, and concerts fueled their fans continued fascination with the group and Michael. Shortly after the Jacksons signed with Motown, they met and became friends with the president of their fan club, Steve Manning. Manning later worked as a publicist for the Jacksons. In 1976, he wrote a book about them entitled, *The Jacksons.* He still remains close to the family.

For the year end review of 1972, *Billboard* magazine named fourteen year old Michael Jackson as the Top Singles Artist of the Year and Top Singles Male Artist of the Year. The Jackson Five were again named the Best Selling Group with the NAACP Image Award. By the age of fourteen, Michael Jackson, from that crowded two bedroom house in Gary, Indiana, had become a millionaire began raking in awards. It was only going to get bigger from here.

The Jackson Five set out on their first visit to Africa in 1973 when the group played three shows in Senegal. Documentary footage was shot of the trip that was lost for years, being discovered just after Michael's death. *The Jackson 5 in Africa* was soon available on YouTube.

Although each tour continued to attract hordes of fans, the albums the Jackson Five were turning out weren't matching the sales and chart success of their early releases. *Lookin' Through the Windows* peaked on the pop album chart at number seven, and the later *Skywriter* peaked at number forty-four on the pop album chart. "Itty Bitty Pretty One" and "Lookin' Through the Windows", the singles from *Lookin Through the Window,* peaked at numbers thirteen and sixteen on the pop singles chart respectively. *Skywriter's* "Corner of the Sky" and "Hallelujah Day" peaked at numbers eighteen and twenty-eight respectively. "Get it Together" was a bigger hit, peaking at twenty-eight on the pop singles chart, and becoming a number two smash on the black singles chart.. A third solo album for Michael, *Music and Me* also failed to match the success of his earlier solo albums, peaking at number ninety-two on the pop album chart. The last top twenty hit the Jackson 5 had with Motown was "I Am Love (Parts I & II)". The single peaked at number fifteen on the pop charts and number five on the black chart.

One possible factor contributing to these albums' disappointing sales was that Berry Gordy had become preoccupied. Gordy, who had always taken a personal role in producing the Jackson Five's albums had now become involved in Motown's first movie project, *Lady Sings the Blues*, the story of Billie Holiday starring Diana Ross. This preoccupation kept Gordy from supplying the Jackson Five with the big hits they had been getting from Motown. One bright spot however, was the release of "Dancing Machine" from their album, *Get It Together*. The album had disappointing sales, but the single became the group's biggest hit since "Never Can Say Goodbye" three years earlier, peaking at number two on the pop chart and becoming a number one hit on the black chart. "Dancing Machine" had a more mature sound that their other records lacked, helping to bring the Jackson Five out of the "bubblegum pop" sound. Michael's performance of "the robot" dance for "Dancing Machine" performances helped popularize the 70's dance craze. The single was nominated for a Grammy for Best R&B Group Vocal Performance in 1974 but lost to Rufus for "Tell Me Something Good".

Michael recorded one more solo album for Motown, *Forever, Michael*. Later Motown releases were compilations of earlier recordings. The last Jackson Five album to be recorded for Motown was *Moving Violation*. Later Jackson Five album releases were also comprised of earlier recordings.

In 1974, with no input from Motown, Joe Jackson organized performances for his children at Las Vegas' MGM Grand Hotel. The brothers were joined by their three sisters and youngest brother Randy. Randy and Janet teamed up to do impersonations of Sonny and Cher. While these performances were well received by their audiences, they did not get favorable reviews from critics.

On December 13, 1973, Jermaine Jackson married Hazel Gordy, daughter of Berry Gordy. Gordy spent an enormous amount of money on the wedding which had a winter wonderland theme that included mountains of artificial snow and live doves. Smokey Robinson performed "The Wedding Song" which he wrote especially for the occasion. It appeared as though the Jacksons and Motown were closer than ever before, but just the opposite was true.

3

*Don't you carry nothin' that might be a load
Come on, Ease on down
Ease on down the road*

"Ease on Down the Road"
- Charlie Smalls

As with most Motown artists, the Jackson Five were required to record songs written and produced by Motown's staff of writers and producers. While this formula of producing hits worked for the group initially, Motown's production line methods were no longer as successful as they once were. The Jacksons continually fought to gain more artistic control over their careers which Motown denied. Even though they had grown and matured, they weren't allowed to produce and record their own songs that reflected this growth. Joe also grew unhappy with what he saw as Motown's insufficient promotion of the group, and of Michael.

Another factor of dissatisfaction with Motown was the low royalty rate the group was paid. They were paid just over five to ten cents per album sold, assuming a wholesale price of $2.00 per album. They were also responsible for paying all of their recording expenses for all the songs they recorded, regardless if they were ever issued as a single or included on an album.

The royalty rate paid to the group was low, but not considered unusual for a new group. However, they continued to receive the same royalty rate well after they had several hit records and were a firmly established act at Motown. Michael especially learned from this experience. In later years he would sign several contracts for recording and for commercial endorsements making him the highest paid entertainer in the world.

These objections as to how Motown was managing their careers contributed to the announcement made in July, 1975, that the Jackson Five were leaving Motown when their contract expired on March 10, 1976. In the summer of 1975, they signed a new contract with Epic Records, a division of CBS Records. With the new contract with Epic Records, the group received an advance of $750,000 and a royalty rate of 94.5 cents per album sold.

With the switch from Motown to Epic, the group suffered two emotional and crushing blows. The least of which was the loss of their name. Motown fought back by filing a $20 million lawsuit against Joe Jackson and CBS Records for influencing the group into breaching their contract with Motown. Motown claimed the Jackson Five breached their contract when they signed with Epic before their contract with Motown had expired. The Jacksons countersued for back royalties that Motown still owed them. When the suit was finally settled, Motown received a settlement valued at $600,000. Motown was also awarded the right to re-release Jackson Five songs, and they maintained the right to the name, "Jackson Five". This meant a certain loss of identity for the group. They had become known as the Jackson Five well before signing with Motown. From then on they were known simply as "The Jacksons".

The second, and most painful, loss for the group was the loss of Jermaine. Joe Jackson had each of his sons sign the new contract with Epic Records before even mentioning it to Jermaine. He was then shown that each of his brothers had already signed and was told to do the same. Jermaine had a very difficult decision to make. He was faced with choosing between signing with Epic Records and staying with his brothers, or staying with Motown, his father-in-law's company. Feeling a strong sense of loyalty to the company that gave them their start, Jermaine elected to stay with Motown and pursue a solo career. The loss of Jermaine hit the group hard. He was especially missed by his partner on stage, sharing lead vocals, and his partner off stage, pulling practical jokes and fooling around. Randy officially joined the group after Jermaine's departure.

Shortly before the release of their first album with Epic, the Jacksons had their own TV variety series, *The Jacksons* which aired during the summer of 1976. Michael hated doing the weekly series and generally any TV. He hated not having the time to perfect performances, being forced to sacrifice quality to meet deadlines. He also hated the silly comedy routines that were included in each show.

After the move to Epic Records, Joe Jackson became the group's manager once again. In 1977, he hired Freddy DeMann and Ron Weisner as partners in managing the group. The management team of DeMann/Weisner would manage the group as well as Michael on his solo projects for several years.

While the move from Motown to Epic proved to be successful in regaining control over the management aspect of their careers, the artistic control they longed for was a little longer in coming. They were given little more freedom to record their own music, continuing to record songs written and produced by others. They were assigned producers Kenny Gamble and Leon Huff, who had been very successful in producing hits for other artists, becoming known for producing the "Philadelphia Sound". Their first album for Epic did however include two songs written and produced by the Jacksons.

Their first album with Epic was released in November, 1976, and was titled with the group's new name, *The Jacksons*. Two singles were released from the album. "Enjoy Yourself" went to number six on the pop chart and peaked at number two on the black chart, and became the group's first single to be certified gold. They had had other gold singles, but "Enjoy Yourself" was the first to be certified by the Recording Industry Association of America because Motown didn't participate in the RIAA. They refused to allow the RIAA to audit their books.

"Ease on Down the Road"

The second single didn't fare as well. "Show You The Way To Go" peaked at number twenty-eight on the pop chart, and at number six on the black chart. *The Jacksons* also did much better on the black chart than on the pop chart, peaking at number thirty-six on the pop album chart and at number six on the black album chart.

The two songs included on the album written and produced by the Jacksons were "Blues Away", written by Michael, and "Style of Life", written by Michael and Tito. Neither of these songs were released as singles, but Epic was impressed enough with Michael's song writing abilities to allow them to contribute two more Jackson originals on their next album.

The Jacksons wrote and produced "Different Kind of Lady" and "Do You Wanna" for their next album, *Goin' Places*, released in October, 1977, again produced by Gamble and Huff. Although titled *Goin' Places*, the album went nowhere on the pop album chart, making it as high as number sixty-three. On the black album chart, *Goin' Places* just missed the top ten, peaking at number eleven. The album's two singles did just as poorly on the pop chart. "Goin' Places" went as high as number fifty-two, and "Find Me a Girl" never made the Hot 100. The two singles did significantly better on the black chart, "Goin' Places" became a top ten hit, peaking at number eight, and "Find Me a Girl" reached number thirty-eight.

In between the releases of their first two albums for Epic, the Jacksons gave a special performance in England. In May, 1977, the Jacksons were invited for the second time to perform for Queen Elizabeth II, at King's Hall in Glasgow, Scotland, as part of the Queen's

Michaell Jackson: The Complete Story of the King of Pop

Silver Jubilee.

This time surrounding the group's move from Motown to Epic Records was an especially difficult period for Michael. On one hand he was being forced to grow up much too quickly, having much of the group's business responsibilities put on his shoulders at the age of eighteen. He was representing his brothers in their fight for more artistic input in their music, for the freedom to write and produce their own albums. Yet publicly, their audiences still wanted to see cute, "little" Michael Jackson who was now approaching 5' 10". Michael was waging another battle, this one with his mirror. In *Moonwalk*, Michael reveals how troubled he was by his complexion. His bad complexion through his teenage years caused him to shy away from other people and made him feel extremely self-conscious. He describes in *Moonwalk* how dissatisfied and upset he was at the time with his appearance. He also did not like his nose. While it was really no different than any of his brothers, he was teased about his nose, even by his father, and was given the nickname "Big Nose". Being very sensitive, he took the teasing quite hard.

He was also being plagued by rumors in the press that he and singer/songwriter Clifton Davis, who wrote "Never Can Say Goodbye", were lovers. The tabloids went so far as to claim that Michael was undergoing a sex change operation and the two were planning to marry. These difficult situations eventually did clear up, along with his skin, with the exception of the continued speculation by the press as to Michael's sexual preference.

At age nineteen, Michael helped to change the group's

"destiny". He accompanied his father to a meeting with CBS Records' Ron Alexenburg, who had signed the Jacksons to the Epic label. They convinced him that the brothers should be given an opportunity to write and produce an entire album on their own. Alexenburg agreed stipulating that an executive producer be involved as an overseer of the project. Bobby Colomby and Mike Atkinson were chosen as the album's executive producers. This album, the first to be written and produced by the Jacksons, was *Destiny*.

The Jacksons formed Peacock Productions, their own publishing company, the name being chosen out of Michael's love of animals. Later, Michael set up several different companies to handle his own productions, publishing, copyrights, and other business interests. Michael hired Bob Jones as Vice President of Communications of MJJ Productions. Jones had formerly worked in public relations for Motown and had handled the publicity for the Jackson Five. They went on to enjoy a long time working relationship together which eventually ended abruptly and bitterly.

One significant contribution that the executive producers of *Destiny* would make is in suggesting Greg Phillinganes as keyboardist and to aid in arrangements for the album. Phillinganes would go on to play an important role in future Jackson albums, and especially Michael's solo albums and tours.

Destiny, released in December, 1978, was the most successful album the group had had in several years and became their first album ever to go platinum. A party was held to celebrate the album's success and to present the group with a platinum copy of *Destiny*. Los Angeles mayor Tom Bradley declared "Jacksons Day" and a celebration was held in a bank vault specially equipped with a dance floor at the City National Bank of Beverly Hills. Michael's date for the occasion was Tatum O'Neal, his first real love, as Michael said, "after Diana."

All of the songs on *Destiny,* with the exception of one, were written by the Jacksons, or by Michael and Randy. Michael and Randy wrote together most often because they were the only two brothers still living at home. The only song on the album that was not written by the Jacksons was the first single, "Blame it on the Boogie", which was co-written by Michael Jackson. This Michael Jackson however, who actually goes by Mick Jackson, is white and from England. Despite its catchy disco beat and fun lyrics, "Blame it on the Boogie" reached a disappointing number fifty-four on the pop singles chart, but peaked at number three on the black singles chart. Michael's vocals on the single are a great precursor to his vocal styling that would be more firmly established on *Off the Wall.*

The most successful single from *Destiny* was the second release, "Shake Your Body (Down to the Ground)". This infectious dance tune peaked at number seven on the pop singles chart and number three on the black singles chart.

Other excellent tracks on *Destiny,* and there are plenty, include "Things I Do For You", "Bless His Soul", "That's What You Get (For Being Polite)", and the title track. "Things I Do for You" deals with Michael's feelings of being used, the beginnings of his distrust of others except those very close to him, similar feelings to those he would express in "Heartbreak Hotel" and "Wanna Be Startin' Somethin'" and several tracks on *HIStory*.

> *Always wanting something for nothing*
> *Especially what they don't deserve*
> *Reaching in my pocket*
> *I just got to stop it*
> *Even though they got a lot of nerve*

Michael wrote "Heartbreak Hotel" working with guitarist Paul Jackson Jr. who told *Billboard,* the solo I played on the record is what he sang to me note for note." The *Destiny* album peaked at number twelve on the album charts. The Jacksons set out on a world tour in 1979, to promote the album. In addition to over forty stops in the U.S., the Destiny tour also played in Germany, Switzerland, Holland, England, France, Kenya and the Netherlands.

Just prior to the release of the *Destiny* album Michael's first project without his brothers since leaving Motown was released. Ironically, this project was a production of Motown. Michael first fell in love with movies while visiting Diana Ross on the set of *Lady Sings the Blues.* Michael went on to star with Diana Ross playing the Scarecrow to Diana's Dorothy in *The Wiz*, an updated version of *The Wizard of Oz,* featuring an all African American cast. Directed by Sidney Lumet, *The Wiz* also starred Nipsey Russell as the Tinman, Ted Ross as the Cowardly Lion, Lena Horne as Glenda the Good Witch and Richard Pryor as the Wiz.

While these characters very closely resemble their counterparts in *The Wizard of Oz, The Wiz* does differ in some respects. Instead of Kansas, it takes place in New York. "Follow the Yellow Brick Road" is replaced by the duet with Michael and Diana, "Ease On Down the Road". Released as a single off the soundtrack album, the duet peaked at number forty-one on the pop chart and number seventeen on the black chart.

Michael truly loved portraying the Scarecrow. He spent four hours every morning for five months getting into his costume and makeup to be transformed into his character. He loved being the Scarecrow so much, he often wanted to wear the makeup and costume home at night. It was while portraying the Scarecrow in *The Wiz* that Michael decided films would play a definite role in his future career.

While filming the movie, Michael lived in an apartment in New York for six months. LaToya went to New York and stayed with Michael to keep him from getting lonely. Not one for going out to nightclubs, or anywhere for that matter, Michael would become very lonely living by himself.

The Wiz is much more comical than the original. Instead of being stuffed with straw, the Scarecrow is stuffed with garbage, mostly shredded newspaper. He pulls scraps of newspaper from his stuffing to "lay appropriate quotes" on others to help offer advice with their problems. These quotes are more appropriate at some times than others. After meeting the Lion on their search for the Wiz, and learning that the king of the jungle has no courage, the Scarecrow reaches inside his stuffing, retrieves a scrap of paper and reads, "Uneasy lies the head that wears a crown. W. Shakespeare." This would be rather poignant for Michael a few years later. The Cowardly Lion, thinking Dorothy is dead and that he is responsible, decides to end it all and leap off a rooftop. The Scarecrow quickly pulls out an "appropriate quote" and reads, "Showers expected late tomorrow!"

The Wiz was a tremendously elaborate production costing over $30 million to produce, a staggering sum in those days. The Coney Island Amusement Park was used as the deserted carnival where Dorothy and the Scarecrow discover the Tinman. The 42nd Street library was the location where the Lion is discovered posing as a statue outside the building. The Emerald City scenes were filmed at the World Trade Center, using 650 dancers and requiring 385 crew members. A giant mechanical bust of The Wiz, Richard Pryor, looks much like the robotic head of Michael we would see years later in *Moonwalker*.

Reviewers panned *The Wiz*, criticizing the movie as being over-produced and many felt Diana Ross was too old to play Dorothy. Diana, then thirty-two, played a twenty-four year old Dorothy. The one bright spot most critics mentioned was the acting ability of Michael Jackson. All objectivity aside, he is adorable in the role. While *The Wiz* is generally considered to have been a flop, it did show that Michael had genuine acting talent. The role garnered him a nomination for Best Supporting Actor from the Academy of Science Fiction, Fantasy and Horror Films.

Michael's desire to make more movies was deepened in 1980 when he spent time with Jane Fonda on the set of *On Golden Pond*. During the month he spent on the movie set, he became close with the movie's other stars, Katharine Hepburn and Henry Fonda, who had taken Michael fishing. Later, when Henry Fonda died, Michael spent the evening with the Fonda family.

The main reasons Michael wanted to do *The Wiz* were his love for the movies, *The Wizard of Oz* being one of his favorites, and especially the opportunity to work with Diana Ross. However, it was the musical director of the film that would later join with Michael and together they would make music history. The musical director of *The Wiz* was Quincy Jones.

4

*Life ain't so bad at all
If you live it off the wall*

"Off the Wall"
- Rod Temperton

After completing *The Wiz,* Michael began work on his first solo album for Epic Records. He wanted his solo album to have a different sound than his work as part of the Jacksons, so he first looked for an outside producer. He called Quincy Jones to ask for any suggestions he may have, Jones suggested himself and a great team was formed. Epic was not in favor of Jones producing the album, fearing he was too jazzy and not a good fit. Michael insisted and finally got his way. It is probably safe to say he had an easier time getting his way from here on out.

Quincy Jones was already a legend in the music industry. He had worked with, among several others, Billie Holiday, Frank Sinatra, Ray Charles and Count Bassie. Jones produced Leslie Gore's 1963 hit, "It's My Party".

Michael's first solo album with Epic Records was *Off the Wall*. Greg Phillinganes was recruited as keyboardist and arranger. Phillinganes told how Michael and Quincy, "Q", worked together, "Their ideas just blend into each other. You see, Michael is not like a lot of other singers who come around just to add a vocal. Michael is involved in the whole album. `Q' is basically an overseer, who runs the show without really running the show. The icing he adds to the cake can be the difference between a good tune and a great one."

Another partner who joined what Quincy Jones called "the A team" was recording engineer Bruce Swedien. Swedien, widely regarded as a wizard in the recording studio, worked on the recording sessions for *Off the Wall* and went on to play an integral part of the teams for *Thriller, Bad, Dangerous, HIStory*, and *Invincible*. He described his work on these albums, "I am more proud of the recordings that I have done with Quincy and Michael than any other recordings in my career."

Off the Wall is basically a collection of the best dance songs ever included on one album. Three of the album's tracks were written and co-produced by Michael. "Working Day and Night" told of his suspicions that his girl, "must be seeing some other guy instead of me." "Get on the Floor" has him trying to get his girl to join him on the dance floor:

"Off the Wall"

> *So get on the floor*
> *And dance with me*
> *I love the way you shake your thing*
> *Especially*

"Don't Stop `Til You Get Enough", another of Michael's compositions, was the album's first single and became one of the album's biggest hits. The week of October 13, 1979, it held the number one spot on the pop singles chart, Michael's first number one solo hit since "Ben" in 1972. "Don't Stop" spent one week at the top of the pop chart and five weeks at the top of the black singles chart.

Rod Temperton, a songwriter from Germany who was a member of the group Heatwave, made substantial contributions to *Off the Wall*, as he would later do on *Thriller*. Temperton penned "Rock with You", the album's title track, and "Burn this Disco Out". Although never released as a single, "Burn This Disco Out" measures up splendidly against the latter two, which both became top ten hits. "Rock with You" became the album's second number one single, reaching the top of the pop singles chart the week of January 19, 1980 and remaining for four weeks. "Rock with You" was also the album's second single to reach the number one position on the black singles chart. "Rock with You" isn't as fast paced as "Don't Stop", but the beat is definitely just as infectious:

> *Girl, close your eyes*
> *Let that rhythm get into you*
> *Don't try to fight it*
> *There ain't nothing that you can do*

If someone can listen to this song and not want to move, check for a pulse. "Off The Wall", Temperton's other composition, gave Michael his third top ten hit from the album, peaking at number ten on the pop singles chart and number five on the black chart.

Many other established songwriters contributed to *Off the Wall* in addition to Temperton. "I Can't Help It" was written by Stevie Wonder with Susaye Greene. Greene was a member of The Supremes in one of their many configurations after the departure of Diana Ross. Carole Bayer Sager and David Foster contributed "It's The Falling in Love".

Paul McCartney wrote a song called "Girlfriend" which he thought would be perfect for Michael to sing. He told Michael about the song at a party, but they never managed to get together to record the song. McCartney ended up putting the song on his own album, *London Town*. Quincy heard the song and told Michael he thought it was perfect for him to do. Michael was shocked because Quincy never knew McCartney made the offer earlier. So, Michael finally did record "Girlfriend" and included it on *Off the Wall*.

While most of the album does consist of catchy dance tunes, one song definitely stands out as the most moving and most emotional track on the entire album. Michael himself is so moved, he cries at the end. Michael cried when they first recorded the song. So, they did it again. And again he cried. Quincy Jones later recalled recording the song, "I had a song I'd been saving for Michael called, `She's Out of My Life'. Michael heard it and it clicked. But when he sang it, he would cry. Every time we did it, I'd look up at the end and Michael would be crying. I said, `We'll come back in two weeks and do it again, and maybe it won't tear you up so much.' Came back and he started to get teary. So we left it in." They actually ended up using the very first take.

She's out of my life
She's out of my life
And I don't know whether to laugh or cry
I don't know whether to live or die
And it cuts like a knife
She's out of my life

This would not be the only time Quincy Jones would experience Michael being brought to tears while recording.

"She's Out of My Life" was the fourth single from *Off The Wall* to become a top ten hit, peaking at number ten on the pop charts. The ballad peaked at number forty-three on the black singles chart. Michael became the first solo artist in history to have four top ten hits from one album. In England, where "Girlfriend" was released as a single, Michael became the first artist ever to have five hit singles from one album.

Promotional videos were made of Michael performing his biggest hits from *Off the Wall*. Michael performs "Rock with You" dressed from head to toe in silver sequins, including silver sequin covered boots and his afro is now cut much shorter. He seems to be thoroughly enjoying giving us just a hint of the fancy footwork he would dazzle us all with in his next set of music videos. His demeanor is very relaxed and he seems to be just letting the music move him naturally. Well, naturally for him. For "She's Out of My Life", Michael puts away his dancing shoes and sits solemnly on a stool. In the video clip for "Don't Stop `Til You Get Enough", Michael dons his then trademark tuxedo, as on the album's cover. The idea of having him wear the tux in the album's cover photo was to emphasize that he had grown and matured. The glowing socks were Michael's touch.

Off the Wall became CBS Records' biggest selling album to date. It spent a year and a half on *Billboard's* pop album chart, eight months of which were spent in the top ten, peaking at number three. *Off the Wall* went to number one on the black album chart. The album re-entered the album charts during "Michaelmania" in 1984 and would continue to do so for decades. Total sales worldwide now top 25 million copies.

Despite the album's enormous success, it failed to garner a Grammy nomination for Album of the Year. Michael was crushed when he received only one Grammy nomination, even though he won. Michael's first ever Grammy win was for Best R&B Vocal Performance-Male for "Don't Stop `Til You Get Enough". Feeling that he had been overlooked, and disappointed that he was still being seen as solely an R&B artist, Michael skipped the award presentation and vowed that his next album would not be ignored. It wasn't.

Off the Wall was not overlooked at the American Music Awards. Dressed in a black tux with a sequined shirt, Michael took home the awards for Favorite Soul Album, Favorite Soul Male Vocalist and Favorite Soul Single for "Don't Stop `Til You Get Enough".

Off the Wall also received recognition from music industry publications. *Cashbox* magazine chose *Off the Wall* as the most popular soul album of the year. The year end issue of *Billboard* recapped the year in music with Michael, and his *Off the Wall* album and singles, placing high on several charts, often competing with Jermaine and his hit single and album, "Let's Get Serious". Michael was named the number two Top Pop Male Artist, and the number one Top Black Artist, with Jermaine placing at number eight on the latter chart. *Off the Wall* was ranked as the third Top Pop Album of the Year and as the number one Top Black Album, with Jermaine's *Let's Get Serious* being ranked at number five. "Rock With You" placed at number four for the year on the Top Pop Singles chart and at number two on the Top Black Singles chart, just behind "Let's Get Serious".

Off the Wall earned awards throughout the world. The album was certified triple platinum in Great Britain, seven times platinum in Australia, triple platinum in Canada and it went gold in Holland. *Off the Wall* received the British Phonographic Industry Award for Album of the Year.

This was not the end of the awards. Later, in 1980, the Hollywood Chamber of Commerce honored the Jacksons with a star on Hollywood's Walk of Fame. The Jackson's star is located on Vine Street in Hollywood. Once again the Jacksons were named the Best Singing Group of the Year with the NAACP Image Award. This was just a taste of the increased attention the group, and especially Michael, would receive during the next few years.

With this heightened level of interest in Michael's life and career, his distrust of the press began to intensify. He hated being misquoted and he began to give fewer and fewer interviews, isolating himself from the public. His already extreme shyness began to deepen as his popularity began to soar.

Motown attempted to cash in on this renewed popularity of Michael Jackson, releasing a Jackson Five album in 1979, *Boogie*. Since only a limited number of copies were made, today it is a sought after collectors item. *Boogie* includes several songs which were never before released.

Michael also used his talents at this time to help choose hits for other artists. In 1980, Queen released their album, *The Game*. After hearing the album, Michael suggested to the group's lead singer, Freddie Mercury, that one particular track be released as a single. "Another One Bites The Dust" spent three weeks at number one in October of 1980, and it is one of Queen's biggest hits. Michael and Freddie Mercury had recorded a couple of duets together which have yet to be released.

Then it was back to work on the next Jackson album, the follow up to *Destiny*. Again the Jacksons would write and produce their entire album. As with *Destiny,* the Jacksons struck gold. Then platinum. *Triumph* went to number twelve on the pop album chart and number two on the black album chart. Although *Triumph* matched *Destiny's* chart performance it pales, albeit slightly, when compared to the strong tracks on *Destiny.*

Triumph produced four singles, each of which were only moderately successful on the pop charts, but two of which become top ten hits on the black charts. The album's first single was the album's biggest hit, "Lovely One", written by Michael and Randy. "Lovely One" was the only top ten hit from the album, peaking at number ten on *Billboard's* Hot 100 and going to number two on the black singles chart.

The second single released off of *Triumph* was "Heartbreak Hotel", written by Michael. The song's title was changed to "This Place Hotel" on some copies of the album to avoid confusion with the Elvis Presley song of the same name. Although the songs share the same title they are otherwise very different. Michael had said that he didn't have the Presley song in mind at all when he wrote it. Michael's song is a dark, foreboding tale of impending doom, opening with a blood curdling scream courtesy of LaToya. Michael sings of his feelings that people are after him, watching him and that "hope is dead":

As we walked into the room
There were faces staring, glaring
tearing through me
Someone said `Welcome to your doom'
They all smiled with eyes that looked
as if they knew me
This is scaring me

"Heartbreak Hotel" peaked at number twenty-two on the pop singles chart and number two on the black singles chart.

Michael created and produced a short promotional film based on the single, "Can You Feel It", titled "The Triumph". The video includes some impressive special effects well ahead of its time, including animated images of fire and water symbolizing the creation of the world. One of the first times the film was broadcast was on *American Bandstand*, which didn't normally show films. Despite the elaborate video to promote it, "Can You Feel It" did surprisingly poor on the pop and black singles charts, peaking at numbers seventy-seven and thirty respectively.

"Walk Right Now" was the fourth single released off of *Triumph*. It also had very disappointing chart success, peaking at number seventy-three on the Hot 100 and number fifty on the black singles chart. This was surprising for "Walk Right Now" is a catchy tune telling the story of a girlfriend being told to hit the road.

Triumph, like *Destiny,* was dedicated by the brothers to their mother. "A mother is a gift from God. For ours, we are most thankful and we dedicate this album to our beautiful mother, Katherine Jackson." Michael also dedicated *Off the Wall* to his mother. "I dedicate this to the year of the child & my mother. Love M.J." Conspicuously absent is any mention of their father.

In 1981, the Jacksons set out on a thirty-six city tour to support their *Triumph* album. It was a huge production and was, Michael said, the last time he would tour. (In case you're keeping track, this is his first of six "last" tours.)

The Jackson's 1981 U.S. World Tour was chosen by *Rolling Stone* magazine as one of the greatest live performances of the seventies and eighties. The spectacular lighting, pyrotechnics, and choreography helped to show skeptics that the Jackson boys had grown up to be one the best bands around. Michael, Marlon and Jackie each

"Off the Wall"

contributed to the choreography. Jackie, Tito and Randy directed the band. While each contributed to the production, "Michael, who had just turned twenty-three, was unquestionably the star of the Jackson's `81 shows... For disco dynamite like his *Off the Wall* smash `Don't Stop `Til You Get Enough', Michael literally turned into a dancing machine, executing split-second kicks and dizzying spins with smooth precision." The forty date tour played to 600,000 fans and grossed $5.5 million.

The group performed their greatest hits from their early years at Motown and their hits from *Destiny* and *Triumph* as well as Michael's solo hits from *Off the Wall*. A live album was released following the tour. *Jacksons Live* peaked at number thirty on the pop album chart and at number ten on the black album chart. While it does give a taste of what a Jacksons concert is like, it is a small taste. The spectacular effects, costumes, and especially choreography must simply be seen to fully appreciate a live performance of the Jacksons. The live versions of "Ben" and "She's Out of My Life" are both clear winners.

In 1981, Michael made a TV appearance, something that was becoming increasingly rare. He was a guest on Diana Ross' special "Diana". They performed "Ease On Down the Road" in look-a-like white tuxedos and Michael performed "Rock With You". Concert footage included in the special had Diana calling Michael up to join her on stage at a concert performance. Dressed in jeans and a varsity style jacket, Michael joined in with Diana on "Upside Down" and showed off some of what would become signature moves and told the crowd, "I love you".

Michael Jackson: The Complete Story of the King of Pop

It was around this period that Michael's appearance began to change. His complexion had cleared up, thanks in large part to natural maturity and a drastic change in his diet. He had become a vegetarian. Having always been thin, he was now even slimmer. His facial features became more prominent. And he no longer wore the huge afro hairstyle the Jacksons had become know for. He also had the first of his soon to be widely speculated about nose jobs. He had told his biographer, J. Randy Taraborrelli, he had fallen while dancing and had broken his nose. Surgery to repair it offered an opportunity to have his nose reshaped and eliminate the "Big Nose" remarks from his family.

Triumph didn't have the impact that Michael had with *Off the Wall*, but it did rank as the number ten Top Black Album of 1981 on *Billboard's* year-end charts. The Jacksons also ranked at the number ten position on the Top Black Artist chart of 1981, and at number four for Top Dance Artist. "Can You Feel It"/"Walk Right Now" was number four for Top Audience Response Single for the year. Years later the Jackson's *Triumph* album was named by *Spin* magazine as one of the ten most underrated albums of all time.

After completion of the *Triumph* album and tour, Michael started to work on his next solo album. He was now faced with the pressure of topping the success of *Off the Wall*.

5

Keep on with the force, don't stop
Don't stop 'til you get enough

"Don't Stop ('Til You Get Enough)"
- Michael Jackson

In 1982, Michael released a number of new projects. He wrote and produced a song for Diana Ross, titled, "Muscles"; he narrated a children's storybook album, *E.T.: The Extra-Terrestrial;* and he released his second, moderately successful, solo album for Epic Records, *Thriller.*

It was on a flight returning to Los Angeles from England, after working with Paul McCartney on "The Girl is Mine", that Michael came up with a song that he thought would be perfect for Diana Ross. "Muscles" was named after Michael's pet boa constrictor. Michael wrote the song for Diana because he wanted to do something to thank her for all she had done for him. It was a very big thank you. "Muscles" became a top ten hit for Diana and earned a Grammy nomination.

Steven Spielberg, producer and director of the blockbuster movie *ET: The Extra-Terrestrial,* and Quincy Jones produced a children's storybook album which tells the story of E.T. Michael Jackson was chosen to narrate the story. While recording the narration for the album, Michael became so emotional, he cried at the part where E.T. is dying. Steven Spielberg and Quincy Jones decided to leave it in. Trying it again wouldn't lessen Michael's emotions. Quincy Jones learned that from the recording sessions for "She's Out of My Life."

E.T.: The Extra-Terrestrial was released in November, 1982 on MCA Records. CBS Records, Michael's record company, filed a $2 million lawsuit against MCA for releasing the album before Christmas. The agreement between the two record companies stipulated that RCA was not to release the E.T. album before Christmas, so it wouldn't draw sales away from Michael's newly released solo album with Epic, *Thriller.* The ensuing litigation resulted in the New York Supreme Court prohibiting sales of the album's single, "Someone in the Dark". A few promotional copies of the single were already distributed to radio stations before its release was prohibited. Those promotional copies of "Someone in the Dark" are collector's items today amongst Jackson fans.

Several contributors to the E.T. album had also worked with Michael on his solo projects. The music for "Someone in the Dark"

"Don't Stop ('Til You Get Enough)"

was written by Rod Temperton. Freddy DeMann and Ron Weisner, managers of Michael and the Jacksons, served as production coordinators. The album was engineered by Bruce Swedien, who has also engineered each of Michael's solo albums. Quincy Jones was one of the album's narrative writers. Dick Zimmerman photographed Michael for the album's cover and the included poster, he also photographed Michael for the *Thriller* album cover.

During the time of *Thriller's* release, Michael had the family's Encino home completely razed and rebuilt for his mother. Just one year earlier, Katherine Jackson filed for divorce from Joseph in response to his many infidelities. Eventually, Katherine withdrew her petition for divorce and they separated with Joe taking up residence in Las Vegas while Katherine remained in the family compound in Encino, California.

Michael contributed heavily to the design of the Tudor style mansion. He had virtually everything he needed and wanted built into the house, creating his own private world and giving him fewer and fewer reasons to ever have to leave. He had his own arcade, a private screening room with seating for thirty-five people, a sweetshop with an ice cream fountain, popcorn machine and an impressive variety of chocolate bars – all of which were free of charge to visitors. The trophy room housed many of his awards and the memory room was covered with family photos and keepsakes. Along with rooms filled with things to play with, there were also rooms for Michael to work in. He added his own recording studio and dance studio.

Just as it seemed Michael was trying to seal himself off from the rest of the world, his new album and videos would soon constitute the beginning of the world's renewed and intensified fascination with him to be referred to as "Michaelmania".

Bruce Swedien, in his book, *In the Studio with Michael Jackson*, describes Michael's work ethic, perfectionism and professionalism:

Michael Jackson is the most professional and the most accomplished artist I have ever worked with! And I have worked with the best the music industry has to offer. Michael is a bona fide international favorite, and he has been for a long time! He is unquestionably a survivor. Michael is a gentle soul. He is very polite. Working with him I always hear him use 'please' and 'thank you', and 'you're welcome', in an industry where such courtesies are not usually used...

He is the supreme artist. I have never worked with anyone who is more dedicated to his art that Michael. For instance, when we record a vocal on a song, Michael vocalizes with his vocal coach, Seth Riggs, for at least an hour before he steps up to the microphone to record. I don't mean that Michael vocalizes just once in a while. I mean that he vocalizes every time we record a vocal! To me, that is real dedication. One of the most fascinating things about Michael Jackson is the boundless passion that he has for his music. His enthusiasm for the project at hand is like no one else I have ever worked with.

For the recording of *Thriller*, Michael assembled a team of musicians who he found to be talented and cutting edge and he

"Don't Stop ('Til You Get Enough)"

worked to bring them to a higher level, to create "sounds never heard before." Many have regarded their time in the studio with Michael Jackson as one of the most creative times in their career and have professed a new understanding of him as an artist, musician and singer.

The *Thriller* album was released on December 1, 1982, and was an instant smash, selling one million copies before the end of the year. By November, 1983, it had sold ten million copies and was a hot seller for that Christmas season too. According to those involved in the recording of the album, this may have been a surprise considering how they felt when they initially completed the recording. A listening party was held for the record company, with several members of the A team attending: Michael, Quincy Jones, and Bruce Swedien. Michael was horrified when he heard the album and insisted it could not be released, "... I put my soul, my blood, sweat and tears, into *Thriller,* but I was doing *E.T.* at the same time, the *E.T.* album. And that was a lot of stress. But [when we first] mixed the *Thriller* album, it sounded like crap." Quincy Jones suggested they take time to remix the tracks, taking one track per day. It is a safe bet that the outcome was satisfactory.

After choosing the tracks to be included on the album, Quincy suggested they toss out the weakest songs and replace them. Michael had a song he had been working on, but was not yet ready to play if for Quincy. Quincy pressed him and Michael relented, playing him a little ditty he titled, "Beat It".

The first single off of *Thriller* was "The Girl is Mine", a duet with Paul McCartney. Paul and Michael fought over the affections of the same girl all the way to number two on *Billboard's* Hot 100, and to number one on the black singles chart, replacing Marvin Gaye's "Sexual Healing". It marked the first time one of the Beatles appeared in a number one song on the black charts. This was despite some limited radio airplay as some radio stations refused to air a song that hinted at an interracial romance.

The second single became one of *Thriller's* two number one songs. With "Billie Jean", Michael Jackson became the first performer ever to hit number one on the pop singles and album chart, and the black singles and album charts, simultaneously. The week of March 15, 1983, "Billie Jean" began its seven week stay at number one on the pop singles chart, while *Thriller* topped both the pop and black album charts. "Billie Jean" accuses Michael of fathering her child, which Michael denies:

Billie Jean is not my lover
She's just a girl
Who claims I am the one
But the kid is not my son

A couple of different stories have been circulated about who "Billie Jean" really is. One has it that Michael wrote "Billie Jean", originally titled "Not My Lover", in response to being accused of fathering the child of a woman who had been stalking him. It is most likely a reaction to many such claims he and his brothers endured over the years.

A video for "Billie Jean" was made for the then relatively new

"Don't Stop ('Til You Get Enough)"

music television channel, MTV. The video, directed by Steve Barron, shows Michael being followed by a detective. The detective, however, never succeeds in catching him. Michael doesn't even show up on film when several rigged cameras all snap photos of him at the same time. Michael dances his way to Billie Jean's hotel room, with each segment of the sidewalk lighting up at his touch, showcasing his moves. He performs lightening quick spins and then freezes, poised up on his toes. Director Steve Barron had initially envisioned the video with no dancing. Michael requested a dance segment be added. Barron agreed and used a hand held camera in front of him. A good move on Barron's part.

"Billie Jean" is widely recognized as a masterpiece and is consistently ranked among the greatest of all recordings. In 2011 *Time* magazine named "Billie Jean" was one of the 100 Most Extraordinary Pop Recordings in music history. The video also consistently ranks among the best videos of all time.

For his new album and videos, Michael had a new look. He now had jheri curled hair, and he had had his nose surgically reshaped again. He had also adopted a new style of dress. He appears in the "Billie Jean" video in a black leather suit with a pink shirt and a bow tie. From now on, whatever Michael wore would be copied from elementary school playgrounds to college campuses, except in New Jersey where single white gloves were banned at Bound Brook High School. In response, the student held protests.

The cover shot of *Thriller* has Michael dressed in a white suit with a black shirt. Inside the fold out cover is a full length shot of him reclining with a tiger cub on his knee. Michael brought the tiger cub to the photo shoot. While making him up for the shoot, makeup artist Karen Faye shared with him a quick glimpse of the tiger striped underwear she was wearing that day. Years later in sharing this story, she remembered it completely embarrassed him but she also credits the flashing for the call for her next gig with Jackson.

While "Billie Jean" was one of MTV's most popular and successful videos, CBS Records did have some difficulty in getting the video aired on the music network, as MTV's video play list consisted mainly of white rock bands. CBS Records head Walter Yetnikoff threatened to withhold all videos from their company's artists if MTV refused to play more videos by black artists. While "Billie Jean" was not the first video by a black artist to be aired on MTV, it certainly did help to break MTV's predominately white programming. Michael Jackson was reaching across racial lines and becoming an artist who appealed to all races and all ages. As Quincy Jones once said, "Michael has connected with every soul in the world."

Another interesting note about "Billie Jean" is the way in which it was recorded. To get the exact sound that Quincy and Michael were looking for, the instruments were played and recorded many times over until both were finally satisfied and it was perfect. Michael had said he worked on the bass line alone for three weeks getting it just the way he wanted it. Then it was time for Michael to add the vocals. All of the vocals for "Billie Jean" were recorded in one unbelievable take.

Thriller's third single, and second number one hit, was "Beat It". "Beat It" is the hardest rock song on *Thriller,* featuring a guitar

"Don't Stop ('Til You Get Enough)"

solo by guitar great Eddie Van Halen. Eddie Van Halen's contribution, for which he received no money, brought Michael's music to a whole new audience: white kids who liked hard rock music. It had a similar affect for Van Halen, their latest album, *1984,* made it to the black album charts while "Beat It" peaked at number fourteen on the Mainstream Rock chart. Van Halen later joked that maybe he could barter for some dance lessons one day.

Usually, a record company would wait for a song to peak on the music charts and fall, before releasing another single from that same album. It was generally thought that if another single was released prematurely, it would kill the first single. However, while "Billie Jean" was still at number one on the singles chart, "Beat It" was released as the follow up single, the brainstorm of then Epic Records promotions guru Frank Dileo. A few weeks later, "Beat It" and "Billie Jean" were both in the top five, "Beat It" occupied the number one spot and "Billie Jean" was at number five. In fact, only one week separated the two songs' stays at the top of the charts. When "Billie Jean" fell from number one after seven weeks, "Beat It" became the new number one song the week of April 30, 1983, where it stayed for three weeks. Dexy's Midnight Runners' "Come On Eileen" separated "Billie Jean" and "Beat It" as the country's number one pop single. This was the shortest amount of time between number one singles by the same artist since the Beatles replaced themselves at number one in 1964 when "She Loves You" was knocked out of number one by "Can't Buy You Love". "Beat It" was the third single from *Thriller* to hit number one on the black chart.

In "Beat It", Michael expresses his message of uniting people, that violence is not the answer:

> *You better run, you better do what you can*
> *Don't wanna see no blood, don't be a macho man*
> *You wanna be tough, better do what you can*

The video for "Beat It" was directed by Bob Giraldi and choreographed by Michael Peters. Peters also appears in the video as a gang leader. Genuine Los Angeles street gang members were used in the video along with professional dancers, to make the gang scenes look authentic.

Members of two rival gangs emerge from the streets, pool halls, and even the sewers to face each other. Michael shows up just in time to prevent the possible bloodshed. Instead of battling, Michael brings peace to the opposing sides by having them join him in dance. "Beat It" features some of his most recognizable moves and has become a classic video.

Shortly after "Beat It" topped the charts, Weird Al Yankovic recorded a song parodying "Beat It". Weird Al's version was titled, "Eat It" and was a hilarious reworking of Michael's lyrics:

> *Eat a banana*
> *Eat a whole bunch*
> *It doesn't matter*
> *What you had for lunch*
> *Just eat it!*

Michael enjoyed the parody of himself, giving Yankovic permission to use the music from "Beat It".

"Don't Stop ('Til You Get Enough)"

The follow up single to "Beat It" was "Wanna Be Startin' Somethin'". It peaked at number five on both the pop and black singles charts with no video to promote it. The song emphasizes Michael's hatred of how rumors and lies are made up from nothing. In the song's lyrics, he describes himself as being a vegetable and buffet others eat off of:

I took my baby to the doctor
With a fever, but nothing he found
By the time this hit the street
They said she had a breakdown
Someone's always tryin'
to start my baby cryin', talkin', squealin', lyin'
Sayin' you just wanna be startin' somethin'

The next two singles from *Thriller* both made it to the top ten. "Human Nature" peaked at number seven, and "PYT (Pretty Young Thing)" went to number ten on the pop singles chart. They peaked at numbers twenty-seven and forty-six respectively on the black singles chart. Neither single had a video to promote them.

The seventh single from *Thriller* was the album's title track. "Thriller" features the eerie sound of creaking doors and a ghoulish rap by horror film star Vincent Price. "Thriller" debuted on *Billboard's* Hot 100 at number twenty, making it one of the highest debuting singles to date. It entered the top ten in its second week on the charts, and peaked at number four. It went to number three on the black singles chart. This single didn't just have a video to promote it, it had the granddaddy of all videos.

6

*'Cause this is thriller, thriller night
And no one's gonna save you
From the beast about to strike*

"Thriller"
- Rod Temperton

For the seventh and final single from *Thriller,* Michael went all out to create his most elaborate video to date. Costing $1 million to produce, it was the most expensive video ever. By comparison, most other video productions at this time came in with budgets in the $30,000 to $40,000 range. It was also the longest video, running thirteen minutes, always being broadcast with an opening disclaimer and closing credits.

After seeing the film, *An American Werewolf in London,*

Michael decided he wanted that film's director, John Landis, to direct the "Thriller" video. Rick Baker, who did the makeup for *An American Werewolf in London,* was chosen to do the makeup for "Thriller", transforming Michael into a werewolf right on camera. Michael's co-star was Ola Ray. At first Michael was uncomfortable with having an ex-*Playboy* playmate as his co-star, Landis reportedly convinced him she was the right choice as Michael and Ola had a great chemistry together.

The story for the "Thriller" video was written by John Landis and Michael Jackson. Michael transforms into a werewolf on camera. He is later transformed into a zombie and joins his fellow zombies in a funky graveyard themed dance number destined to be imitated for decades. Michael was dressed all in red, to make him stand out in the dark graveyard dance number. His red leather jacket with the black "V" shape, became the latest Jackson fashion craze. The jacket was designed by Deborah Nadoolman Landis, Mrs. John Landis.

"Thriller" had a limited theatrical release. At the premiere, the film received a standing ovation and a demand for an encore. So, they showed it again. When aired on MTV, the music television network saw dramatic spikes in their ratings – increases of six to eight times their normal viewership.

The "Thriller" video was released on video cassette along with a documentary on the making of the video, the brainchild of attorney John Branca to help cover the high costs of producing the video. Included on the tape are Michael and John Landis discussing how they came up with the ideas for the video, and what each wanted to achieve with it.

Makeup artist Rick Baker shows how he made Michael's face gradually transform into a werewolf. The preparation of the costumes and makeup for the "dead" people emphasizes the painstaking measures taken to make every detail as lifelike, or unlifelike, as possible.

The most enjoyable portions of *The Making of Michael Jackson's Thriller* show Michael at dance rehearsals with Michael Peters and with Ola Ray. Although Michael Peters had worked with Michael before on "Beat It", he was still impressed with his talent while working on the choreography for "Thriller":

Michael is quite amazing to me because he's working with these people that have made a living at this, I mean, have studied this for a greater portion of their lives, and he'll walk into a studio and purely on rhythm, I mean I purely give him a rhythm of a step and he does it. It's fascinating because here are these people who have spent X amount of thousands of dollars training, studying to be dancers all their lives and this kid walks into the room and you say this is the beat - da-dat-da-dat- and he does it. It's really wonderful to watch because it's an innate gift that he has. He's a dancer in his soul.

Ola Ray was said to be quite taken with her co-star and did her best to encourage a romance, advances that were not unrequited. She has allowed since only that they did spend some intimate moments together in his trailer on the set.

The documentary certainly more than paid for the cost of the video. *The Making of Michael Jackson's Thriller* sold one million copies, making it the best selling music video ever. *Making Michael Jackson's Thriller* spent eight weeks in the number one spot on *Billboard's* Top Video sales chart. It was ranked as the third best selling videocassette, of all types, of 1984 by *Billboard* and it was the tenth most rented video cassette of 1984.

The ghoulish hit single almost didn't happen. "Thriller" was initially titled "Starlight", with a very similar melody but very different lyrics. With the recording of "Starlight' nearly complete, writer Rod Temperton rewrote the single and came up with a completely different song, now titled "Thriller". The release of the video was nearly axed by Michael himself. He had received heat from the elders of the Jehovah's Witnesses who objected to the depiction of zombies. Landis had to literary hide the film canisters until they had the idea of adding a disclaimer to address the church's objections.

While each of the singles from *Thriller* stormed the singles charts, the album continued to do likewise on the album charts. When considering all of the "firsts" that were achieved, along with the simple sales figures, *Thriller's* success is truly astounding. Eighty consecutive weeks were spent in the top ten of the pop album chart. It spent all fifty-two weeks of 1983 in the top ten on the pop album charts, thirty-seven of which were spent at number one. *Thriller* spent more weeks at number one than any other album by a solo artist. *Thriller* was the first album to ever start and end a year at number one on the album chart. In March, 1983, *Thriller* topped the album charts in England, and was still number one in the U.S., marking the first time an artist held the number one album in both countries at the same time. Given the widespread and unprecedented success of *Thriller* it is very unlikely its numbers will ever be seen again by any other artist. *Billboard* later reported, "Given the decline in album sales, the rise of digital downloads and the lack of an heir apparent to Jackson, it's unlikely another album will ever dominate radio, video or the collective consciousness the way 'Thriller' did." Michael Jackson reached across barriers of race, age, economic status and to virtually every corner of the world.

Thriller, to date, has sold in excess of 110 million copies, making it the best selling album in history. This is truly an astonishing figure. Sales of one million copies, to be certified platinum, is a milestone for any album. *Thriller* sold over one million copies just in the city of Los Angeles in 1983. At one point, *Thriller* was selling one million copies *every four days.* The August 2010 issue of *Word* reviewed the best selling albums globally. The second best selling album globally was reported to be AC/DC's *Back in Black* with sales of 49 million copies. (The Eagle's *Greatest Hits* which would battle for the top spot domestically, was ranked at number 6 with total sales of 42 million). The issue noted, "But way, way out in front is Michael Jackson's *Thriller*... *Thriller* is, by several country miles, still the biggest album any of us are ever likely to see in our lifetime."

For the year-end recap for 1983, *Billboard* named Michael Jackson the top artist in pop, black, and dance/disco music. *Thriller* was named the number one album for the year on the pop and black charts. "Billie Jean" and "Beat It" shared the number one spot on the dance singles chart for the year. "Billie Jean" was the number two single on both the pop and black singles charts. "The Girl is Mine" was the sixth top black single, and the ninth top adult contemporary single.

Thriller held on to again top the pop album chart for 1984, and it was the number two black album for the year. Michael Jackson was the number two Top Pop Artist and the number six Top Black Artist. "Say Say Say" was the number three top pop single of 1984.

The U. S. and England weren't the only countries swept up in Michaelmania. He received several other titles and awards from around the world. In Japan, *Thriller* was named Album of the Year in 1983, and Michael Jackson was named Best Artist and Best Male Vocalist. Australia named *Thriller* Album of the Year and Single of the Year. Michael Jackson was named Artist of the Year in Italy, he had the Record of the Year in Greece and the Album of the Year in Holland. *Thriller* was named the Most Important Foreign Album of the Year in Spain and Michael was named the International Artist of the Year in Brazil, just to name a few.

Thriller didn't just set sales records, it changed the way people looked at the music business. It showed there could be multiple singles released from one album. *Thriller* was the first album to spawn seven top ten singles, becoming a greatest hits package all by itself. Previously albums generally yielded one to three singles, all other tracks on the albums being considered "B" sides, or filler songs. *Thriller* showed an album could be composed entirely of songs that could stand as hit singles. The two songs that were not released as singles, "Lady in My Life" and "Baby Be Mine" could have easily added to the string of top ten hits. *Thriller* had no filler songs, every track is pure gold.

The videos made for the songs on *Thriller* were equally influential and helped change the landscape of the music video industry. "Billie Jean" and his other videos weren't just popular, they raised the bar and set new standards in music video and helped put a young MTV on the map. Some see his contribution and influence as even more profound. Joseph Vogel, in his book *Man in the Music: The Creative Life and Work of Michael Jackson,* quoted cultural critic Hampton Stevens as saying, "The oft-repeated conventional wisdom – that Jackson's videos made MTV and so 'changed the music industry' is only half true. It's more like the music industry ballooned to encompass Jackson's talent and shrunk down again without him. Videos didn't matter before Michael, and they ceased to matter at almost the precise cultural moment he stopped producing great work."

One of the several factors contributing to the phenomenal success of *Thriller* was Michael's appearance on a TV special commemorating the twenty-fifth anniversary of Motown Records. *Motown 25: Yesterday, Today, and Forever* aired on May 16, 1983 and featured vintage clips of Motown's biggest stars along with reunion performances from the company's biggest groups. All of Motown's greatest performers came together to pay tribute to Motown and to Berry Gordy including of course, the Jackson Five performing some of their biggest hits they enjoyed at Motown. The brothers then left the stage to Michael where he went on to create a historical moment in his career and in all of music with his jaw dropping performance of "Billie Jean". Michael later gave the black sequined jacket, which has been said he borrowed from his mother's closet, to Sammy Davis Jr. after he had admired it. This appearance helped to cement the white shinny socks as a trademark look for Michael. But it was more than a catchy gimmick, it was a visual trick to accentuate movement and bring a viewers eye to his ever dazzling footwork.

It was during this performance that Michael first dazzled America with his now signature dance step, the moonwalk. Even his brothers, watching from backstage, were amazed at Michael's moves. He glided backwards, unveiling the moonwalk, went into a lightening quick spin, then froze for a few seconds up on his toes. He received a standing ovation at the end of his performance. Michael Jackson's performance of "Billie Jean" on the *Motown 25* special stands as a pivotal moment not only in Michael's career, but in pop culture, ranking up there with the Beatles' debut on *The Ed Sullivan Show* and Elvis Presley's appearance on the same program. Since childhood, Michael studied and absorbed everything he could from his idols and mentors; Gene Kelly and Fred Astaire, Sammy Davis Jr., and especially James Brown. But he combined all of these bits and pieces with his own undeniable talents to create... magic. Nobody moved like Michael Jackson and nobody ever will.

With this single TV appearance, Michael managed to reach a whole new audience and sales of *Thriller* were again sent into orbit. The Motown special was seen by an audience of 47 million viewers. People who didn't hear his music on the radio, or see his videos on

MTV, became new fans of Michael Jackson and charged into record stores to buy a copy of *Thriller*.

An issue of *Rolling Stone* devoted to a review of the music industry during the eighties examined the impact of Michael's *Motown 25* performance and that of his *Thriller* album. Record sales in the early part of the decade were down noticeably due in part to the poor economy and to the increasing popularity of video games as an alternate form of entertainment. The review credits Michael's electrifying performance of "Billie Jean" on *Motown 25* as rejuvenating the music industry, sending record buyers back into record stores, where they picked up a copy of *Thriller,* and often a second album or two, giving the record industry a badly needed boost. *Thriller* was deemed by the review as redefining the standards of success.

Considering the tremendous impact of Michael's appearance on *Motown 25,* it seems ironic that he was at first reluctant to appear on the special. While he did want to take part in a tribute to Motown and Berry Gordy, he did not like to make TV appearances. Michael agreed to perform on the special with his brothers only after he was allowed a solo spot to perform "Billie Jean", the only non-Motown song performed throughout the entire show.

His brilliant performance earned him an Emmy nomination. Michael lost the Emmy to Leontyne Price, but the Motown special did win an Emmy for Outstanding Musical Special. Even though award nominations, and especially winning awards were very important to Michael, he was most honored by the phone call he received the next morning from one of his idols, Fred Astaire, commending him on his performance. *Motown 25: Yesterday, Today and Forever* was later released on videocassette and was ranked by *Billboard* as the number two Top Music Videocassette of 1986.

Nine years after it was first broadcast, *Entertainment Weekly* magazine included Michael's performance on *Motown 25* as one of the twentieth century's greatest entertainment moments:

... a delicate young man with a choked voice, a white glove, and magic shoes took the microphone and began to write the next chapter of American music history. The moment Michael Jackson ripped into his single, `Billie Jean' - squealing, moaning, spinning, and finally taking viewer's breath away with his moonwalk -the music industry had to throw away its old yardsticks of success.

"Billie Jean" was of course only one of Michael's many hits he enjoyed throughout 1983, but not all of his hit singles during the year came from the *Thriller* album. Michael's seventh single to reach the top ten in 1983 was "Say Say Say". With "Say Say Say" becoming his seventh top ten single in 1983, Michael broke records previously held by Elvis Presley and the Beatles for the most top ten singles in one year. The single went to number one on the Hot 100 the week of December 10, 1983, and stayed for six weeks. It peaked at number two on the black chart. This duet with Paul McCartney is included on McCartney's album, *Pipes of Peace*. McCartney's album also includes another duet with Michael, "The Man".

Paul McCartney flew to California to film the video for "Say Say Say" with Michael because Michael's schedule wouldn't allow him the time to fly to England. The video was filmed in the Santa Ynez

Valley, about 100 miles North of Los Angeles. Paul and Michael pay con men selling a miracle potion "guaranteed to give you the strength of a raging bull." Paul poses as a salesman and Michael, pretending to be a customer, tries the potion and challenges a burly man, also in on the scam, to arm wrestle. When Michael wins, the gathering crowd rushes to buy a bottle of the magic potion. "Mack and Jack" then give all of the money raised in the scam to an orphanage. Changing their trade from salesmen to vaudevillians, they put on a show in a saloon, where Michael catches the eye of a beautiful saloon girl, played by LaToya. Paul McCartney's wife, Linda, also appears in the video as part of the conning crew. Michael fell in love with the location of the video shoot, the Sycamore Valley Ranch in Los Olivos, California. He had his sights set on it for his next home.

Nineteen eighty three wasn't all hit records for Michael. It was also when his management contract with Weisner/DeMann Entertainment expired. A few months later, the management contract with his father also expired. Neither of the contracts were renewed. Michael had fired his father. Although Michael was never close to his father, he explains in *Moonwalk* that it was a business decision, that he and his father were worlds apart when it came to creativity. Joe would come up with ideas that Michael totally disagreed with. This started an extremely rare public battle between Joe Jackson and Michael, and between Joe and Weisner and DeMann. In the June 25, 1983, issue of *Billboard* magazine, Joe Jackson, in regards to Weisner/DeMann Entertainment, was quoted as saying:

...*They're only in it for the money...Weisner\DeMann were needed* *because there was a time when I felt I needed white help in dealing with the corporate structure at CBS.*

Michael responded to his father's remarks in the same issue of *Billboard*:

I don't know what would make him say something like that. To hear him talk like that turns my stomach. I don't know where he gets that from. I happen to be color blind.

Ron Weisner and Freddy DeMann said of Joe:

The problem seems to be with their father more than anybody...we have no problem with Michael or the Jacksons...I don't think he (Joe) enjoys a good relationship with anyone whose skin is not black.

Until Michael could select a new manager, his personal lawyer, John Branca, aided Michael in handling his business affairs. Michael had always maintained an amazing level of control over his business affairs, down to every decision and detail. He learned every detail of his contracts, and although professionals, lawyers, managers, and accountants were consulted, all decisions were ultimately made by Michael himself. John Branca told *Billboard*:

The genius in his artistry speaks for itself. His business acumen isn't necessarily as obvious because it is conducted behind closed doors. But he is equally brilliant in running his career as he is in recording his music.

CBS Records President Walter Yetnikoff also told *Billboard* of Michael's keen business sense: *He has made observations to me about things like promotion, which indicate he would be totally qualified to run a record company if he so desired. He has assembled a terrific team of advisors, but he makes his own decisions in the end. He's not one those artists who reacts blindly to what the last person tells him. He's got a great sense of where he is going and what he wants to do. But he's also got a way of making things happen. He's reached his goals so many times that I've come to believe that if Michael wants something to happen, it'll happen.*

It was nearly a year later, in 1984, when Michael signed a new manager. He had selected Frank Dileo, who was then vice president of promotion at Epic Records. Dileo was responsible in large part for the promotion of *Thriller*. Michael discussed the choice with Walter Yetnikoff first and got his blessing to hire Dileo away from Epic Records. Frank Dileo and Michael soon became close personal friends as well as manager and client.

While Michael spent most of 1983 enjoying one hit single after another, he spent 1984 collecting one award after another. *Thriller* definitely made up for Michael's feeling that his *Off the Wall* album had been ignored at award time.

7

Get me out into the nighttime
Four walls won't hold me tonight
If this town is just an apple
Then let me take a bite

"Human Nature"
- Steve Porcaro, John Bettis

January 1984 brought Michael an avalanche of awards and it was only a taste of what was to come throughout the year. He received a record breaking ten nominations for the American Music Awards in eight categories. Michael attended the award ceremony accompanied by *Webster* star Emmanuel Lewis and his date for the evening was Brooke Shields. He was dressed in cropped tuxedo pants and military style jacket covered with red sequins with a single black sequined glove and dark sunglasses.

Michael approached the podium eight times that night to accept awards, a new record. *Thriller* was named Best Pop Album and Best Soul Album. "Billie Jean" won as Best Pop Single and "Beat It" was named Best Pop Video and Best Soul Video. Michael took top honors as Best Pop Male Vocalist and Best Soul Male Vocalist.

In addition to these awards Michael was honored for his lifetime career achievements as the year's recipient of the Award of Merit. The Award of Merit was presented to Michael by Diana Ross and by the previous year's winner, Kenny Rogers. Barry Manilow also took part in the tribute, at Michael's request, singing "Ben" and a medley of Jackson Five hits. The presentation featured taped messages from Michael's closest friends, including Liza Minnelli, Katharine Hepburn, and Jane Fonda. Winning the award at age twenty-five, Michael was the youngest performer to ever receive the Award of Merit.

Michael's next armload of awards came the following month at the Grammys. Michael again received a record breaking number of nominations. He was nominated for twelve Grammys in ten categories, he was competing against himself in two categories. Both "Beat It" and "Billie Jean" were nominated for Song of the Year, and "Billie Jean" and "Wanna Be Startin' Somethin'" were both nominated for Best R&B Song. *Thriller* was nominated for Album of the Year, "Beat It" was nominated for Record of the Year. Michael received nominations for Best Pop Male Vocalist for *Thriller*, Best R&B Male Vocalist on "Billie Jean" and Best Rock Male vocalist for "Beat It". Michael shared a nomination with Paul McCartney for Best Pop Vocal Duo or Group for "The Girl is Mine". Michael shared two other nominations with Quincy Jones for Producer of the Year, and for Best Recording for Children for *E.T.: The Extra-Terrestrial* storybook album.

Again, Michael attended the award presentation with Emmanuel Lewis and Brooke Shields. He was dressed in tuxedo pants and a sapphire blue sequined military jacket, this time with a single white glove. Uncomfortable in situations where so much attention was focused on him, he again wore sunglasses so dark you could not see his eyes.

Michael won in eight of the ten categories in which he was nominated. The two categories in which he lost both went to the same group. Song of the Year and Pop Vocal Duo or Group went to The Police for "Every Breath You Take". While it would seem that having two nominations in the same category would increase the chances of winning, actually just opposite is true. Having both "Beat It" and "Billie Jean" nominated for Song of the Year served to divide the Jackson vote. Division of Jackson fans between favorites didn't hurt in the R&B category though, "Billie Jean" was chosen over "Wanna Be Startin Somethin'" for Best R&B Song. All of his other nominations earned Michael another Grammy. This Grammy Award telecast is still the most watched Grammy show with an average audience of 51.67 million.

After winning the first of his awards, Michael ascended the stairs to the stage, said his quick thank yous, and quickly returned to his seat. As the evening went on Michael seemed to become more comfortable and started to enjoy himself more. He began making lengthier acceptance speeches, at least for him. At one point Michael called Walter Yetnikoff to the stage, calling him the greatest record company president. Yetnikoff thanked Michael for making *Thriller* the biggest selling album in history. Michael was especially pleased with the win for Best Recording for Children for the E.T. storybook album:

Of all the awards I've gotten, I'm most proud of this one, honestly. Because I think children are a great inspiration, and this album is not for children, it is for everyone. And I'm just so happy and I'm so proud, and I'd just like to say, thank so you so much.

Michael's seventh Grammy of the night was for Best Pop Vocal Performance Male. This win broke a record for the most Grammys won in a single year, set in 1965 by Roger Miller. Michael was aware he had just set a new record and was visibly elated. He called each of his sisters on stage to share his moment. "When something like this happens to you, you want those who are very dear to you to be with you." Then Rebbie, LaToya and Janet joined their brother on stage. Michael continued:

My mother's very shy, she's like me, she won't come up. I'd also like to thank all my brothers whom I love dearly, including Jermaine. I made a deal with myself. If I win one more award, which is this award, which is seven, which is a record, I would take off my glasses. Katharine Hepburn, who is a dear friend of mine, she told me I should and I'm doing it for her, okay?

Over the deafening screams of the fans, he added, "And for the girls in the balcony." He removed his sunglasses for a few seconds, giving the first glimpse of his eyes all evening. He blew kisses to the girls in the balcony and put his glasses back on where they remained for the rest of the night. His record of winning eight Grammys in a single year still stands though it was equaled in 1999 when Carlos Santana matched the record.

When *Thriller* was named as Album of the Year, Michael became the third youngest artist, at age twenty-five to win the award. Barbra Streisand was wenty-two when *The Barbra Streisand Album* won as Album of the Year, and Stevie Wonder was twenty-three when his album *Innervisions* was given the honor. Michael dedicated his Grammy for Album of the Year to Jackie Wilson, his idol who had recently passed away:

Some people are great entertainers, some people make the path and are pioneers. I'd like to say Jackie Wilson was a wonderful entertainer. He's not with us anymore, but Jackie, where you are, I'd like to say I love you and thank you so much.

Along with eagerly anticipating each award category, the audience was also looking forward to the commercials, but not to run to the kitchen for a snack. The Pepsi commercials Michael had made with his brothers were premiering during the Grammy telecast. The premiere of the pair of Jackson Pepsi ads were promoted as heavily as the Grammy telecast itself. These Pepsi ads were regarded as news items so heavily that several of their first broadcasts were free of charge. They are the first and only commercials to ever be included in the *TV Guide* listings. While it was great knowing which programs would air the Jackson Pepsi ads, it could also be excruciating having to, at times, sit through almost an entire episode of *Hart to Hart* just to see one commercial! It could put Jackson starved fans in the awkward position of leaving the room during a program and rushing back when commercials came on.

A new Pepsi jingle was written for the commercials, putting new lyrics to "Billie Jean". Michael lent his music to "Billie Jean" for use in the commercial, helped write the Pepsi lyrics and agreed to perform the new jingle in the ads but had it stated in his contract with Pepsi that he would not be filmed drinking, or even holding, a bottle of Pepsi. It became a well known fact that Michael didn't even drink Pepsi. He had long been a vegetarian and only ate and drank natural foods. Bottled water, fruit juice, and carrot juice being among the few things he did drink. Michael exercised a great deal of control over the making of the commercials, having a hand in choosing the director and the choreographer. The director was Bob Giraldi, who directed "Beat It", and the choreographer was Michael Peters, who had worked with Michael on the videos for "Beat It" and "Thriller". Michael also had control over the editing. One of the commercials includes a close up of Michael which was edited down to last only three seconds.

The first commercial shows a group of children playing and dancing in the street. One of the kid's is dressed as Michael from his "Beat It" video and is imitating his moves when he moonwalks into the real thing. Young Alfonso Ribeiro looks absolutely astonished as he looks up into the eyes of the real Michael Jackson. The commercial ends with Alfonso and his friends joining Michael and the rest of the Jackson brothers in song and dance.

"Human Nature"

Michael and Alfonso became friends while working together and their friendship continued after the completion of the commercials. When Alfonso released his first single, "Dance Baby" in 1984, he dedicated it to Michael Jackson.

The second Pepsi commercial shows the Jacksons in concert. It begins with scenes of the brothers in their dressing room preparing for a concert. There's a shot of Michael's gloved hand and his sequined socks, while Tito finishes off a Pepsi. They hit the stage singing the new Pepsi lyrics to "Billie Jean" and Michael dances down a flight of stairs, with flash bombs going off behind him, to join his brothers on stage. They finish the song, we see the three second close up of Michael and it's over. Seems simple enough, but it wasn't.

Filming on the second commercial concluded on January 27, 1984, at the Los Angeles Shrine Auditorium. At 6:00 PM, director Bob Giraldi called for another take of the scene with Michael dancing down the staircase. This was the last scene to be shot after four days of filming. Michael stood at his spot at the top of the stairs, and was told to stand there until the flash bombs went off this time, then make his descent. So after the pyrotechnics went off, Michael began to dance down the stairs. Suddenly he cried out in pain. A spark from the lighting effects had set his hair on fire. He pulled his jacket up over his head to try to put out the flames. Fans and extras used in the audience were horrified as were his brothers and the crew. The first to reach Michael to help was his security aid, Miko Brando, who suffered burns on his own fingers trying to put out the flames in Michael's hair. A fan from the audience applied an ice pack on the burn. Video released of the accident showing flames from the back of his head are chilling.

Michael was rushed to the emergency room of Cedars Sinai Medical Center. Having been told a barrage of reporters and photographers awaited his arrival at the hospital, Michael, ever the showman, told the ambulance attendants that he wanted to wear his glove when he was wheeled into the hospital.

He had suffered a palm sized second degree burn on the back of his head with a smaller third degree burn the size of a half dollar at the center. It was a serious burn that reportedly could have burned through his scalp and killed him. Michael at first refused any painkillers due to his strong disapproval of any drugs. Later, he did give in to the extreme pain and accepted medication. This appears to be his first introduction to painkillers.

Shortly after the accident, Michael's personal physician, Dr. Steven Hoefflin arrived and decided then to transfer Michael to the burn center of the Brotman Medical Center in Culver City. Security at the hospital had to be increased, with guards stationed at every entrance of the burn center. The emergency room became packed with fans and the phone lines were jammed. Among the callers were Liza Minnelli and Diana Ross.

Before being released, Michael visited the other six burn patients who, coincidentally, he had visited just one month earlier. He posed for pictures and signed autographs for the burn center staff. After his release, his doctor wanted Michael to rest and not to dance for a while, but, "telling Michael not to dance is like telling him not to breathe."

"Human Nature"

People magazine's next issue featured Michael on the cover. The issue informed worried fans of all the details of Michael's accident and his stay in the hospital. That February 13, 1984, issue of *People* became the publication's third best selling issue to date.

Later in the spring, in April, Michael had laser surgery to burn off the scar tissue on his scalp to allow his hair to grow back. Again, the hospital was deluged with phone calls on the day of his surgery, receiving over five thousand calls. Several other surgeries followed to repair the damage to the back of his scalp, which were very painful, extending Michael's use of painkillers. In a settlement, Pepsi paid Michael $1.5 million in damages. Michael used the money to establish the Michael Jackson Burn Center at the Brotman Memorial Hospital in Los Angeles.

These Jackson Pepsi commercials' success in selling Pepsi and popularity with fans was unprecedented. In *The Other Guy Blinked: How Pepsi Won The Cola Wars,* Pepsi president Roger Enrico told how he saw the enormous impact of these commercials:

Why did Coke decide to change its formula after ninety-nine hugely successful years? In two words: Michael Jackson. And I'm the man who signed him up to make commercials for Pepsi.... On November 11th, 1983- my thirty-ninth birthday- I signed the most expensive celebrity advertising contract in history: $5 million for the privilege of making two commercials and sponsoring a tour featuring a talented but shy young man who sang in a high-pitched voice and danced backward. The signing of Michael Jackson to make commercials for Pepsi's Choice of a New Generation campaign and the *debacle of new Coke are not unrelated events.*

It's interesting that the Jackson endorsements of Pepsi is credited with the New Coke debacle, as Coca Cola was first approached with the idea of a Jackson endorsement deal. After considering it, an offer for $1 million was made. The Jackson's declined and went on to sign a much bigger deal with their competitors.

In February, 1984, CBS Records hosted a party at New York's Metropolitan Museum of Natural History to honor Michael Jackson. There were 1,500 invitations mailed out on white cloth gloves, which were required to gain admittance into the museum. Michael was being honored for earning two entries in the *Guinness Book of World Records*. *Thriller* had surpassed the 25 million mark in sales, making it the most successful album in history. It had outsold the soundtrack album for *Saturday Night Fever* to take over the top spot. Michael's recent domination of the Grammy Awards earned him another entry in the *Guinness Book of World Records* as the artist to win the most Grammys in a single year. His eight Grammys broke the previous record of six Grammys in one year.

At the party, CBS Records president Walter Yetnikoff presented Michael with a new copy of the *Guinness Book of World Records,* who had stopped their presses to include Michael's new record setting feats. Allen Davis, president of CBS Records International, presented Michael with the honor:

Tonight, Michael, your international milestones for the album, ***Thriller*** *are a total of 67 gold awards, 58 platinum awards in 28 countries on 6 continents. And the singles with 9 million in sales have* *earned 15 more awards, bringing the total to 140 gold and platinum awards.*

Then Michael spoke:

> *I've always wanted to do great things and achieve many things, but for the first time in my entire career, I feel like I have accomplished something because I'm in the* **Guinness Book of World Records.**

A letter from an admirer who was unable to attend was read to Michael:

> *I was pleased to learn that you were not seriously hurt in your recent accident. I know from experience that these things can happen on the set, no matter how much caution is exercised. All over America, millions of people look up to you as an example. Your deep faith in God and adherence to traditional values are an inspiration to all of us, especially young people searching for something to believe in. You've gained quite a number of fans along the road since `I Want You Back', and Nancy and I are among them. Keep up the good work, Michael. We're very happy for you. Sincerely, Ronald Reagan.*

Although Michael did not meet President Reagan at this ceremony, they did meet soon after when Michael visited the White House to receive, you guessed it, another award. Michael left the party at the museum a couple of times during the night to go outside and wave to the crowds of fans waiting outside to catch a glimpse of him. For the third award ceremony in less than two months, Michael's date was Brooke Shields.

Michael's wide ranging appeal was illustrated by the results of *Rolling Stone's* annual readers and critics' poll, a publication which then focused primarily on white, hard rock artists. *Rolling Stone* readers voted Michael Jackson as the number one artist of the year, the number one soul artist, the number two male vocalist, and the number four songwriter. "Beat It" and "Billie Jean" were chosen as the number two and number three singles of the year respectively. *Thriller* was chosen as the second best album of the year. Quincy Jones tied for number one producer with Steve Lillywhite. The critics voted Michael Jackson as the number one artist of the year, male vocalist and soul artist of the year. "Beat It" and "Billie Jean" were the critics picks for the number two and number three singles of the year and the first and third best videos respectively. *Thriller* was chosen as the second best album of the year. Quincy Jones was the critics' fifth choice for producer of the year.

Michael met President Reagan in May, 1984. Michael had donated the use of his song, "Beat It" to an advertising campaign aimed against drinking and driving. For his contribution to the campaign, Michael received a Special Achievement Award presented to him at the White House by President Reagan. With Michael's visit, chaos set in at the White House offices. The staff, all eager to meet him, left offices empty with phones ringing. The presentation was held on the White House lawn and a large sound system was set up so the huge crowds gathered at the gates of the White House could hear the ceremony. President Reagan remarked, "We haven't seen this many people since we left China!" The plaque presented to Michael by President Reagan was engraved with these words:

To Michael Jackson, with appreciation for the outstanding

example you have set for the youth of America and the world. Your historic record-breaking achievements and your preeminence in popular music are a tribute to your creativity, dedication, and great ability. The generous contribution of your time and talent to the National Campaign Against Teenage Drunk Driving will help millions of young Americans learn that drinking and driving can kill a friendship.

Michael cleaned up at the Brit Awards too, the British equivalent to the Grammys. He picked up the prizes for Best British Album for *Thriller,* and Michael was named the Best International Solo Artist. In Canada, he was awarded honors by the Canadian Black Music Awards for Top International Album for *Thriller,* Top International Single for "Billie Jean", Michael was named the Top Male Vocalist and Entertainer of the Year.

In between award presentations, Michael still found time to work. He sang background vocals on a single by Kennedy Gordy, aka, Rockwell, a Motown artist and son of Berry Gordy. Michael sang one line, "I always feel like somebody's watching me" repeatedly in Rockwell's hit single, "Somebody's Watching Me". The single peaked at number two on the Hot 100 singles chart.

Michael also lent his magical touch to the recordings of two of his siblings. In 1984, Rebbie released her first album, *Centipede.* Little brother Michael wrote and produced the title track. He also co-wrote "Come Alive It's Saturday Night" with three of his brothers. Jermaine released an album in 1984, *Jermaine Jackson* which included "Tell Me I'm Not Dreamin'", a duet with Michael. According to CBS Records head Walter Yetnikoff, Michael did not want to record this duet with his brother but felt obligated to do it. He later asked Yetnikoff to make it look as though Epic was preventing the single's release. Although it was never officially released as a single because of these contrived difficulties between Michael's label, Epic, and Jermaine's label, Arista, the song did receive a lot of airplay. Besides these projects, Michael spent much of 1984 planning and embarking on a U.S. tour reuniting with his brothers, the Jacksons Victory tour.

8

Girl, close your eyes
Let that rhythm get into you
Don't try to fight it
There ain't nothin' that you can do

"Rock with You"
- Rod Temperton

New York's Tavern on the Green played host to the Jackson's press conference in November 1983, to announce the plans for a major U.S. tour. Tour promoter Don King hosted. The brothers, all wearing sunglasses, sat quietly at a table while King did most of the talking. Michael spoke only to introduce his parents and sisters who were seated in the audience. The tour was to be called Victory and was to be sponsored by Pepsi. The tour would promote the group's new album, also to be called *Victory*.

Great anticipation surrounded the album's July 2nd release and sales were expected to skyrocket. *Victory* is the first album ever to be shipped double platinum. The album was disappointing however, consisting mainly of songs written, produced and performed by each of the brothers individually. Failing to follow their previous format of having Michael and Jermaine sing the lead vocals weakened the album dramatically. *Victory* seems like a thrown together piece of work lacking the great dance tracks that make earlier Jackson albums great. Even the album's packaging seems hurried, with the song titles listed on the back cover in a different order than they appear on the record.

The best offerings from *Victory* are the album's first two singles. "State of Shock" was written by Michael and Randy Hansen, with lead vocals by Michael and Mick Jagger. Originally, the duet was to be with Queen frontman Freddie Mercury, but to date, a final version hasn't surfaced; only demo versions. No video was made to accompany the single, but nothing else was really needed to promote the single any further. Anticipation for anything new from Michael Jackson reached such a feverish pitch, that a Los Angeles radio station, K-IQQ, played the brand new single for twenty-two hours straight. The Jackson/Jagger duet peaked on the Hot 100 at number three.

The second single off of *Victory* was "Torture", the only song on the entire album to feature lead vocals by Michael and Jermaine. While it doesn't measure up to previous Jackson singles from *Destiny* or *Triumph*, "Torture" stands out among the album's other weak selections. "Torture" peaked at a very generous number seventeen on

Billboard's Hot 100.

A video was made for the second single but it has one big problem, it lacks an appearance by either of the two lead singers! All six brothers were in New York to film the video when a disagreement broke out between them, and Michael and Jermaine each refused to be a part of the video. Michael took off for Disney World, leaving the others to finish the filming without him. While Michael does not appear in the video at all, there are still many strong references to him.

The third single from *Victory* was Marlon's contribution, "Body". Even though the single features background vocals by the Jackson brothers, it is not enough to help this indistinct dance song. "Body" peaked at number forty-seven on the Hot 100.

The video for "Body" does not have an appearance by Michael or Jermaine either though there is a big tease that Michael may show up. The story has the brothers holding auditions for dancers. Each brother arrives at the studio one by one. Marlon arrives first, riding in on a motorcycle. Driving closely behind Marlon is Tito. Randy drives up next in a Jeep. Jackie arrives a bit late, rushing in the doors of the studio. Suddenly, a huge crowd of fans gather outside as a helicopter makes it landing. Those viewers expecting Michael's arrival were disappointed to see the rest of the brothers disembark, dressed in stage costumes, ready for their performance with the chosen dancers. Michael's contribution to *Victory,* "Be Not Always" was never released as a single.

Michael did not want to do the Victory tour. He did not feel it was a wise choice following the success he had enjoyed with his

Thriller album. He wanted to concentrate on his other love, films. He was persuaded to join his brothers on the tour by his parents, especially his mother who he adored. It was reported that some of the brothers were having financial problems and needed the income from the tour. Having Michael participate in the tour would dramatically increase the tour's earning potential.

From the very beginning, the Victory tour was greeted by as much anticipation and excitement as bitter criticism and controversy. Because Michael didn't tour with his *Thriller* album, the Victory tour would be his fans' first chance to see Michael perform live his monster hits from *Thriller*. The criticism of the tour arose from its poor management and disorganization. Michael quickly became dissatisfied with the leadership of tour promoter Don King, who was not his choice. He wrote King a letter informing him that he had no authority to speak or deal for him. It stated that:

King did not have permission to approach any promoters, sponsors, or any other persons on Michael's behalf,
that King was not to hire any personnel, any local promoters, book any halls or, for that matter, do ANYTHING without Michael Jackson's personal approval.

Shortly thereafter, King was fired as tour promoter and replaced by Chuck Sullivan. King remained on the tour as a figurehead only. The entire tour was marked by constant management changes. One promoter lasted only three weeks.

Ticket prices, set at $28.00 with a $2.00 service charge, were among the first items to come under fire from the press and from fans,

"Rock With You"

all claiming Michael was greedy and wanted to squeeze as much money from the tour as possible. Only Michael was mentioned in this charge, not any of his brothers, his parents or the tour's managers or promoters. Actually, Michael vehemently fought to keep ticket prices down, wanting them no higher than $20.00, the current going price for concert tickets. With each brother and possibly their parents and promoters each having equal say in how the tour was managed, Michael was outvoted. He even offered to perform on the entire tour for free to keep ticket prices down. Again, he was outvoted and ticket prices were set at $30.00. But only Michael took the heat for the high prices, everyone forgot it was a Jacksons tour, not a Michael Jackson tour.

The system by which tickets were sold also came under fire. The tickets were sold by a mail order system and only in lots of four. A lottery system was used to determine which orders were filled first, and which ones would be filled at all if orders exceeded the quantity of tickets available for sale. Regardless of how many tickets were wanted, you had to order four, for a total cost of at least $120.00, with no guarantee of even receiving any tickets. If orders exceeded the number of tickets for sale, you could very well end up empty handed after mailing in $120.00. This money was then held for long periods before being returned with promoters pocketing the interest made on short term investments.

To request tickets, a coupon order form was needed from the local newspaper. For the tour's first stop, Kansas City, the *Kansas City Times* printed an additional 20,000 copies to meet the expected demand for the Victory tour ticket order forms. Again Michael, and only Michael, was unjustifiably the aim of an avalanche of criticism against the ticket order system.

Michael stepped in to correct the situation after an open letter appeared in a Dallas newspaper from a young fan, Ladonna Jones, complaining the ticket order system was unfair and that she couldn't afford $120.00. Michael then had the mail order system abolished. It was ended after the first three cities on the tour.

In an interview in 1985, Michael opened up about the problems on the Victory tour and how he felt it was unfair that he be the sole target of the criticism:

I never really wanted to use a lot of the people we had, but it was a voting thing. It was unfair to me, you know? I was outvoted a lot of times. I never liked doing things that way. I always liked using A-1 people who are considered excellent in their field. I've always tried to do things first class. Use people who are the best. But it was a different story with the family. And the fact that it was the biggest tour that ever happened, and my success has been so overwhelming, it's as if they're waiting to throw darts at you too... He also addressed the controversial lottery system that was initially used to sell tickets:

You know, that wasn't my idea. None of that was my idea. I was outvoted. I mean, mail order... I didn't want that I didn't want the ticket price the way it was... our production was so big, it had to pay for itself, but still. And it's tough, especially when it's your family.

Besides rehearsing their performances the brothers worked behind the scenes in bringing Victory to the stage. Tito and Randy chose the band for the tour. David Williams and Gregg Wright were each chosen as guitarists. Pat Leonard and Jai Winding were chosen as keyboardists along with Rory Kaplan, who would also play on Michael's Bad tour. Jonathon "Sugarfoot" Moffett was hired as the drummer for the Victory tour. Moffett had played with the Jacksons before on their 1981 concert tour. Jackie, Marlon and Michael choreographed the show. The Victory tour concerts were written and designed by Michael. Michael served extra duty as the tour's stage designer.

  Meanwhile, cities around the country were hopeful they would be chosen to host the Victory tour and tried to improve their odds. *The Boston Herald* printed coupons for fans to fill out asking the Jacksons to perform in Boston which were then forwarded on to the Jacksons. Iowa State University collected signatures on petitions urging the Jacksons to include Iowa on their tour. The Governor of Iowa even contacted then tour promoter Don King to urge him to have the Jacksons perform in his state. Detroit Mayor Coleman Young tried to attract the Jacksons to his city's Joe Louis Arena. The largest and most impressive efforts to attract the Jacksons came from their home town, Gary, Indiana. The Mayor of Gary circulated "please come back" letters from school children. The city even sponsored a "Michael Jackson Come Home" event which included Michael Jackson look-a-like contests.

  The day before opening night of the tour, Michael held a press conference to announce the changes being made to the ticket mail order system. He also made one other important announcement:

We're beginning our tour tomorrow and I wanted to talk to you about something of great concern to me. We've worked a long time to make this show the best it can be. But we know a lot of kids are having trouble getting tickets. The other day I got a letter from a girl in Texas named Ladonna Jones. She'd been saving her money from odd jobs to buy a ticket, but with the current tour system she'd have to buy four tickets and she couldn't afford that. So I've asked our promoter to work out a new way of distributing tickets, a way that no longer requires a $120.00 money order.

There has also been a lot of talk about the promoter holding money for tickets that didn't sell. I've asked our promoter to end the mail order system as soon as possible so that no one will pay money unless they get a ticket.

Finally, and most importantly, there's something else I am going to announce today. I want you to know that when I first agreed to tour, I decided to donate all the money I make from our performances to charity.

Three charities benefited from Michael's extraordinary generosity. The United Negro College Fund used Michael's contribution to establish the Michael Jackson Scholarship fund. The other two recipients were Camp Good Times for terminally ill children, and the T.J. Martell Foundation for Leukemia and Cancer Research. Today, the interest earned on Michael's gifts to the United Negro College Fund finances music scholarships for students. Ronald McDonald House built Jackson Pond, for kids with cancer to play and fish. It is still in use and is popular among the kids.

"Rock With You"

On July 6, 1984, all of the tour planning and management problems disintegrated before a sold out crowd of 45,000 fans packed into Arrowhead Stadium in Kansas City. This opening of the Victory tour was one of three sold out shows in Kansas City and was included in all major newscasts that evening. ABC's *Nightline* even broadcasted two songs live from the concert, "Human Nature" and "Off the Wall". Jackie appeared live on the program as he was unable to join his brothers for the tour due to recent knee surgery. Biographer J. Randy Taraborrelli revealed since was that Jackie had suffered a broken leg just prior to the tour, courtesy of his wife, Enid. Enid discovered Jackie was having an affair with choreographer Paula Abdul. The story is that she followed them to a drive in movie theatre, confronted them, jumped in the car and drove into Jackie, breaking his leg.

After what seemed like an endless wait, stairs slowly rose up from beneath the stage. The five brothers descended the stairs in unison, to the pounding beat of "Wanna Be Startin' Somethin'". Michael was in the middle, dressed in black and white stripped pants, a white sequined military jacket with a red sash across his chest, white sequined socks and black loafers and one white sequined glove.

Michael's solo hits were intermixed with Jackson hits, with "Things I Do For You" sandwiched between "Wanna Be Startin' Somethin'" and "Off The Wall". "Human Nature" was next, followed by "Heartbreak Hotel". Michael really tore the house down with "She's Out of My Life", complete with the tears at the end. Then Michael left the stage for a solo set by Jermaine. Initially, an argument was staged between Michael and Jermaine over what to perform next, ending with

Michael leaving the stage. This argument was dropped after a few performances when fans took the cue that Michael was leaving the stage, and headed to the restrooms and snack counters during Jermaine's solos. Jermaine performed "Let's Get Serious" and "Dynamite" then Michael joined him for their duet, "Tell Me I'm Not Dreamin'".

The concert continued with Jackson Five oldies, "I Want You Back", "The Love You Save" and "I'll Be There". "Rock with You" followed the J5 medley, then "Lovely One". Michael changed into a bright red jumpsuit for "Working Day and Night", at the end of which Randy chased Michael around the stage, Michael fell to the ground, and was engulfed by a huge brightly lit spider-like contraption. His body was covered with a cloth and raised up on a pedestal. When Randy jerked away the cloth, Michael disappeared. Seconds later, Michael reappeared on a platform, dressed now in black pants and red sequined zippered jacket as the first distinctive sounds of "Beat It" rang out. Screams rose from the audience as they recognized the choreography from the song's video.

Following "Beat It" in the show was "Billie Jean", for which Michael recreated his unforgettable performance from *Motown 25*. His moonwalking during "Billie Jean" brought the loudest cheers of the night. After singing the song's last words, "Billie Jean is not my lover", Michael whipped his fedora into the crowd to the delight of that single fan who managed to snatch up the prized hat. Inside each fedora was a label that read, "Made Expressly For Michael Jackson by Maddest Hatter/100% Genuine Fur". The concerts closed with "Shake Your

Body (Down to the Ground)". No encore was performed. The tour wound up with six shows at Dodger Stadium in Los Angeles. During the closing number, "Shake Your Body" the crowd was treated to plenty of moonwalking with the famous shiny socks, glove and jacket all on display. Michael announced to the crowd that this was their "last and final tour", with LaToya and Janet joining their brothers on stage for the final good-byes.

Conspicuously absent from the show containing several of Michael's solo hits from *Off The Wall* and *Thriller* was one of his biggest hits, "Thriller". The elders of the Jehovah Witness' thought the song was offensive and endorsed a belief in the occult. Even though Michael included a disclaimer at the beginning of the song's video stating that the video, "in no way endorses a belief in the occult", the Witnesses still objected to it. Michael decided not to include the song in the Victory tour performances to placate the church elders. Also conspicuously absent were any songs from the *Victory* album. It seemed strange that a tour named "Victory" after their latest album contained no songs from that album. Although it was said more songs would be added later, no songs from *Victory* were ever performed on the Victory tour.

While the Victory tour may have been haunted by management, organizational and planning problems, the performances themselves were nothing short of spectacular. The special effects, lighting, and especially choreography and singing were unsurpassable. Even the staging was impressive. Weighing in at 375 tons, it stood five stories high and was 160 feet wide, and ninety feet deep. It used seven computers, several elevators, 120 speakers and 2,200 lights and required twenty two men to operate it. All of this equipment was carried in twenty-two semi trailers. Actually, there were two stages, with one being set up in the tour's next stop.

Two chefs traveled with the Victory tour. Cy Kosis furnished food for the brothers. Mani Khalsa traveled as Michael's personal chef. After a performance, Michael would eat watermelon to replace water lost while performing. He would lose as much as four to ten pounds after one performance.

For their performance in Dallas on July 14, Eddie Van Halen joined the Jacksons on stage to perform his guitar solo on "Beat It". Another superstar Michael met while on the road was Elton John. Both were in Denver for concerts. Michael tried on one of Elton's jackets, an elaborate gold number, and asked if it was one of his stage costumes. Elton replied, that it wasn't, it was just for everyday!

While Victory was in Detroit, Michael had video shot of himself with the Pontiac Police Department. Dressed in a dark blue sequined military jacket, shades, and the single glove, the footage shows Michael running with a large group of police officers behind him. The footage later was included in a video of a live performance of "Billie Jean". He came to like this look and had similar footage shot of himself with groups of uniformed officials behind him over the years.

In between performances, Michael would study tapes of the concerts and fine tune his performance. He carried a portable dance floor with him to practice on to get every detail "perfect." He also attended services at the Jehovah Witness' Kingdom Hall regularly, but he mostly waited for the next performance. He loved to be on stage. Frank Dileo said at the time, "Michael is very happy when he's on stage. Every night before the show, he's the first one dressed and ready to go."

There were also awards to be accepted along the way. Michael and Tito accepted an award from the NAACP, the 1984 Dr. H. Claude Hudson Medal of Freedom Award. They also accepted the 1984 Olympic Medal of Friendship Award on behalf of the entire Jackson Family.

It was while the brothers were still on the road with Victory that they learned of Janet's marriage to James DeBarge. They were married on September 7, 1984, in Grand Rapids, Michigan. None of the Jackson family attended the ceremony. This news hit Michael especially hard. He had always been very close to Janet, who he had nicknamed Dunk, short for Donkey. This made him feel as though he had lost one of his best friends. The couple filed for an annulment, and eventual divorce, four months later.

With *Thriller* breaking all previous sales records and with the Victory tour playing to unprecedented crowds, a flood of Michael Jackson merchandise hit the market. There were numerous books published on Michael and the Jackson family, along with t-shirts, posters and replicas of his jackets. Four Michael Jackson dolls were marketed, authorized by Michael. They came in four different, supposedly "authentic stage outfits", from the videos of "Beat It" and "Thriller", and from the American Music Awards and the Grammys. The Barbie sized dolls each came with a stand, a microphone, a glove, and a tiny pair of sunglasses.

During this period of "Michaelmania" there was, to say the least, a great deal of publicity about Michael. During the first eight months of 1984, Michael appeared on the covers of over 170 magazines. *Time, Newsweek, Ebony, Life, Rolling Stone,* and several issues of *People* all featured Michael Jackson on their covers during the year. *Time* broke a long standing policy of not featuring a person on the cover without an interview. The portrait of Michael that appears on the March 19, 1984 issue of *Time* was painted by Andy Warhol. There was no interview with Michael for the accompanying article, though the author of the article, Denise Worrell, did talk with Joseph and Katherine Jackson, and she did meet Michael briefly.

Besides covering the tour and his music, the tabloid press, which would become his archnemesis, was buried in stories accusing Michael of being gay, having extensive plastic surgery and taking hormones to maintain his high voice. After these stories persisted for some time, with no response from Michael, he finally decided to answer the accusations with a press statement released through his manager, Frank Dileo:

For some time now, I have been searching my conscience as to whether or not I should publicly react to the many falsehoods that have been spread about me. I have decided to make this statement based on the injustice of these allegations and the far-reaching trauma those who feel close to me are suffering.

I feel very fortunate to have been blessed with recognition for my efforts. This recognition also brings with it a responsibility to one's admirers throughout the world. Performers should always serve as role models who set an example for young people. It saddens me that many may actually believe the present flurry of false accusations:

No! I've never taken hormones to maintain my high voice.

No! I've never had cosmetic surgery on my eyes.

Yes! One day in the future I plan to get married and have a family. Any statements to the contrary are simply untrue.

I have advised my attorneys of my willingness to institute legal action and subsequently prosecute all guilty to the fullest extent of the law.

As noted earlier, I love children. We all know that kids are very impressionable and therefore susceptible to such stories. I'm certain that some have already been hurt by this terrible slander. In addition to their admiration, I would like to keep their respect.

When the Victory tour winded down it had grossed $90 million and had played to over three million fans, setting a record for the largest audience for a tour. This record was short lived however, being surpassed by the Boss, Bruce Springsteen's "Born in the USA" tour. The record however set by the Victory tour for the most consecutive sold out stadium dates still stands today. The spectacular performances of Michael and his brothers overshadowed all of the surrounding controversy and management problems, and was definitely worth the $30 price tag. Mark Bego, author of *On the Road With Michael*, which followed the Victory tour, was also truly impressed with Michael:

Throughout these past two years of intense Michael Jackson-mania, I can honestly say that I have nothing but admiration for his talent, his creativity, and his indefatigable energy. On these pages I feel I have faithfully paid tribute to the number-one superstar of the decade and the most successful personality in the history of show business. As a journalist, I have also presented many of the negative aspects of the Victory tour. These tour-planning troubles have in no way altered my respect or admiration for Michael Jackson. My respect for him is not only intact, it has been enhanced. Anyone who would donate 100 percent of his profits from the Victory tour to charity truly has to have a heart as golden as his hit records.

After the conclusion of the Victory tour it was time Michael got on with what he was doing before the tour, winning awards and receiving honors. On November 20, 1984, The Hollywood Chamber of Commerce honored Michael with the 1793rd star to be placed on the Hollywood Walk of Fame. The star was placed, at Michael's request, directly in front of Mann's Chinese Theater on Hollywood Blvd. About five thousand fans turned out, the largest crowd to ever attend such a presentation. Michael appeared at the unveiling of the star for a full three minutes, then he was advised by security to leave as the crowd grew out of control.

Visitors to the Walk of Fame in Hollywood may have noticed another star for Michael Jackson. This second star is for another Michael Jackson, a radio broadcaster. Actually, this other Michael Jackson started in broadcasting before Michael Jackson from Gary started singing. The broadcaster is registered with the performers union as Michael Jackson. Since no two people can be registered using the same name, singer Michael Jackson is registered as Michael J. Jackson.

"Rock With You"

By the end of 1984 and early 1985, Michael was once again dominating award shows. For the American Video Awards, Michael had a whopping twenty-four nominations in eight categories. Randy Newman's "I Love LA" was the only non-Michael Jackson video nominated for Best Pop Video with "Beat It", "Billie Jean", "Thriller" and "Say Say Say" comprising the rest of the nominees in the category. Michael won four awards out of the eight categories.

Michael's nominations for the MTV Video Music Awards included "Thriller" being nominated six times and taking the prize for Best Overall Performance, Best Choreography and the Viewers Choice Award. Michael was further honored with four Black Gold Awards; for Top Male Vocalist, Best Video Performance for "Beat It", Best Single of the Year for "Billie Jean" and Best Album, *Thriller*. And he walked away with the People's Choice Award for Favorite All-round Male Entertainer and "Thriller" was named the Favorite Video of the Year. He didn't attend any of these award presentations.

On top of all of these, he was also awarded eight Cashbox Awards. Michael Jackson was named the Number One Male Artist, Top Male Singles Artist, Top Black Male Artist and Top Black Male Singles Artist. "Billie Jean" was named the Top Pop Single, and Top Black Single. *Thriller* was named the Top Pop Album and Top Black Album.

These awards were only a fraction of the recognition Michael's videos received. At year end, *Billboard's* America's Top 10 Videos compiled the top videos of the year. Not surprisingly, Michael Jackson dominated the chart. In fact, his four videos placed at the very top of the chart, one through four; "Beat It", "Thriller", "Billie Jean" followed by his duet with Paul McCartney, "Say Say Say". These videos continued strong throughout 1985, two years after their release, they again topped the year end video charts. "Billie Jean" was the sixth favorite video of 1985. "Beat It" and "Thriller" remained the top two favorites, with "Beat It" being replaced at number one by "Thriller".

Besides the many awards and honors, there were also problems. A man named Fred Sanford wrote a song titled, "Please Love Me Now" which he claimed CBS Records stole from him. Sanford claimed his song was later recorded by Michael with the new title, "The Girl is Mine". Michael had to testify in a Chicago court that the idea for the song was that of Quincy Jones', and that he wrote the song himself. The jury found in favor of CBS Records.

Around this same time, Michael had to answer charges that he had stolen the sketches that appear on the inside sleeve of *Thriller*. An artist had accused Michael of using the sketches without his permission. Michael had drawn the pictures himself. One is a sketch of Michael and Paul McCartney each pulling on the arms of a girl depicting a scene for "The Girl Is Mine". The other sketch depicts the single, "Thriller".

In March, 1985, Michael traveled to London for the unveiling of his wax likeness at Madame Tussaud's Wax Museum. The street was packed with eight thousand fans each trying to catch a glimpse of Michael as he entered the building. The path from his car to the museum entrance was lined with rows of bobbies to help him gain entry to the museum without being harmed by the massive crowd.

Michael stood next to his likeness and checked it out amid dozens of camera flashes.

An updated likeness of Michael was added to the museum's collection in the summer of 1990. This version copies Michael's costume from the Bad concerts, black pants and jacket lined with buckles. Over the years, the museum continued to keep up with Michael's look. Following the announcement of his This Is It shows at London's O2 arena, the artists began work on the thirteenth wax model of Michael Jackson.

One of two recordings Michael contributed to in 1985 was "Eaten Alive" by Diana Ross. Michael stayed at Barry Gibb's home in Florida while he worked with Barry and Maurice Gibb in writing and producing the title song for Diana Ross' album, *Eaten Alive*. He also provides the background vocals on the song. Written on the back cover of the album is a note to Diana from Michael in his own handwriting: "You are truly supreme, good to be with you again. I love you, Michael". An arrow and "1998" followed his signature as it frequently did.

The other recording Michael contributed to in 1985 was recorded on January 28, 1985, with forty-four other recording artists, comprising USA for Africa.

9

We are the World
We are the children
We are the ones who make a brighter day
So let's start giving

"We are the World"
- Michael Jackson, Lionel Richie

Following the Victory tour, Michael intentionally avoided the limelight. After two years of constantly being in the public eye, he stayed home. He released no new albums or videos and very rarely ventured out of Hayvenhurst, his Encino home. The awards, however, kept rolling in from the continued success of *Thriller*. In early 1985, *Making Michael Jackson's Thriller* captured the Grammy for Best Video Album. Michael also picked up two American Video Awards for Best Home Video and Best Long Form Video both for *Making*

Michael Jackson's Thriller. He didn't attend either of the award presentations. One recording Michael did contribute to in 1985 was "We are the World".

Harry Belafonte first contacted Ken Kragen, an entertainment manager, about starting a project for the relief of famine in Africa. After considering many different ideas, including an all-star concert, they finally decided on a recording involving several major artists. Kragen contacted two of his clients, Kenny Rogers and Lionel Richie, both of whom agreed to be involved. Lionel Richie then contacted Stevie Wonder. Quincy Jones was asked to produce the record. Jones told Michael about the project and Michael readily agreed to contribute, even volunteering to write the song with Lionel Richie.

When they first began work on the project, they didn't get much done, they had dinner at each others homes, and reminisced about the early days. Then they got serious. LaToya told *People* magazine, "I'd go into the room while they were writing and it would be very quiet, which is odd, since Michael's usually very cheery when he works. It was very emotional for them. Some nights they'd just talk until two in the morning."

With the deadline for the song approaching, they finally got down to business. Lionel had taped two melodies. Michael took it from there and came up with music and words that same night: "I love working quickly. I went ahead without even Lionel knowing, I couldn't wait. I went in and came out the same night with the song completed- drums, piano, strings, and words to the chorus. I presented the demo to Quincy and Lionel, and they were in shock- they didn't expect to see something this quick. They loved it."

We are the World, the book that chronicles the making of the famine relief single, reveals that the next meetings between Michael and Lionel didn't produce any additional lyrics. Everything was funny and no work got done. The rest of the song's lyrics didn't get written until the night before the all-star recording session was scheduled. They got down to work and in two and one half hours, the song was completed.

On January 28, 1985, Michael was the second artist to arrive at A&M's Lion Share Studios for the recording of "We are the World". He arrived after Steve Perry of Journey, with manager Frank Dileo and his bodyguard, Bill Bray. Michael arrived at the studio early so he could record the chorus to be used as a guide for the other artists.

Most of the other artists were scheduled to arrive at the studio following the American Music Awards. Michael skipped the awards where he had four nominations. For the second consecutive year, *Thriller* had been nominated for Favorite Album and Favorite Black Album. Michael had been nominated for Favorite Black Male Vocalist, and the Jacksons were nominated for Favorite Group. It was just as well he didn't go, he would have gone home empty handed.

We are the World: The Video Event shows Michael leading the all-star group through the song, and offering individual help on the lyrics to Huey Lewis, a last minute soloist chosen when Prince failed to show up. He offered later to provide a guitar solo, to which organizer Bob Geldof reportedly replied, "Fuck him, he should have been here." Michael's shyness and discomfort around crowds is evident in this

"We Are the World"

documentary. When he's not directly involved in the activity at the moment, he can often be spotted standing alone quietly in the background.

Before the actual recording began, Ken Kragen, one of the organizers, spoke to the group about distributing the proceeds from the record sales and the steps being taken to insure the money went directly to where it was needed. Bob Geldof, organizer of Band Aid and Live Aid, also spoke to the group of artists. Finally, Michael addressed the group. He described the song he and Lionel Richie had written as "a love song to inspire concern about a faraway place close to home." The recording session began at 9:00 p.m., and lasted the entire night. Michael didn't leave until 8:00 a.m. the next morning.

Quincy Jones had posted a sign outside the studio reading, "Leave your ego at the door." The forty-five artists who comprised United Support of Artists for Africa, and who left their egos at the door, included a wide range of actors and music artists, with representatives from various genres of music; Dan Aykroyd, Harry Belafonte, Lindsey Buckingham, Kim Carnes, Ray Charles, Bob Dylan, Sheila E., Bob Geldof, Daryl Hall and John Oates, Huey Lewis and the News and James Ingram were all part of USA for Africa. Perhaps the most widely represented music in USA for Africa was Jackson music, with Jackie, Tito, LaToya, Marlon, Michael and Randy all contributing to the famine relief single. The balance of USA for Africa was made up of Al Jarreau, Waylon Jennings, Billy Joel, Cyndi Lauper, Kenny Loggins, Bette Midler, Willie Nelson, Jeffrey Osborne, Steve Perry, the Pointer Sisters, Lionel Richie, Smokey Robinson, Kenny Rogers,

Diana Ross, Paul Simon, Bruce Springsteen, Tina Turner, Dionne Warwick, and Stevie Wonder.

The song was produced by Quincy Jones and the associate producer was Tom Bahler, who wrote "She's Out of My Life" from Michael's *Off the Wall* album. Keyboards on "We are the World" are handled by another often time Jackson associate, Greg Phillinganes.

The recording session resulted in a single, a video and a video cassette documenting the making of the single, *We are the World- The Video Event*. A double album made up of the "We are the World" single and previously unreleased material from some of the participating artists was also released. Michael did not have a song included on the album. The proceeds from the sale of these items along with proceeds from sales of books, shirts, buttons, posters and other merchandise all went directly to the famine relief fund. *We are the World - The Video Event* was the ninth best selling video cassette of 1985.

All members of the press were barred from reporting the happenings surrounding the history making recording session with the exception of *Life* magazine, which featured a cover story on USA for Africa. Seven members of USA for Africa were pictured on the cover of the April, 1985, issue; Willie Nelson, Bob Dylan, Tina Turner, Cyndi Lauper, Bruce Springsteen, and the song's composers, Lionel Richie and Michael Jackson. Inside were photos of the participants working and taking breaks. One photo was particularly surprising, Mr. Health Food and Bottled Water holding a can of Budweiser! Michael had his representatives tell the press that he was just moving the can when the picture was snapped. The shot does not look like he was moving the can, it looks like he is holding the can. Not a big deal, he was old enough to drink it was just outside the image most people had of him.

"We are the World" became the first single ever to go multi-platinum. The single had an inititial shipment of 800,000 copies. They sold out the first weekend. It eventually sold 20 million copies. It debuted on *Billboard's* Hot 100 at number twenty-one and three weeks later, the week of April 13, 1985, it was the number one song, where it stayed for four weeks.

As a promotional event, on Good Friday, April 5, 1985, at 10:25 am, "We are the World" was broadcast simultaneously on thousands of radio stations around the world. This event was repeated one year later when thousands of stations again simultaneously aired the famine relief single. To date the charity single has raised $60 million toward the fight against famine in Africa.

USA for Africa was possible because of the concern and dedication of all those who contributed. A few critics, however, singled Michael Jackson out as the sole artist who was unable to leave his ego at the door. These accusations were based largely on the shot of Michael in the video with the camera following him from a close up of his feet, with his sequined socks, up past his glove to his face. These few critics concluded that Michael didn't leave his ego at the door because of his wardrobe choices. It seems they only considered what he chose to wear to the recording session rather than recognize the tremendous contribution he made to the entire project. They certainly didn't have any first hand knowledge of the session, because no press was allowed with the exception of *Life* magazine. Michael co-wrote the song with Lionel Richie and worked on his own to come up with the music and words to the chorus. He recorded guide vocals for the other artists to use to learn the song, and he served on the board of directors of USA for Africa. Just like everyone else involved in the project, Michael received NO compensation for his contribution of his time and talent. On the back cover of the *We are the World* book are comments made by some of the members of USA for Africa, included are Michael's thoughts and feelings about the song, "When I was asked to write the song, I put my soul into it. That's really my statement." Michael also describes in *Moonwalk* how honored and proud he felt to be a part of USA for Africa.

USA for Africa took top honors at the American Music Awards and at the Grammys. In 1986, the American Music Award of Appreciation went to the person who first conceived of the idea to create a project for the relief of famine in Ethiopia, Harry Belafonte. In accepting his award, Belafonte had these words:

I would like to take this opportunity to acknowledge four people who really made a great difference in this project. Two for moving it forward. One is our leader, Ken Kragen. Quincy Jones, who made us all leave our egos at the door. And the two artists who, without their great gift would not have inspired us in quite the same way as we were inspired, Mr. Lionel Richie and Mr. Michael Jackson.

These four were then called up on stage to share the award. Michael, who had showed up half way through the show with Elizabeth

"We Are the World"

Taylor, ascended the stairs to the stage of the Shrine Auditorium dressed in a green khaki uniform that looked like a cross between a Canadian Mountie and a school crossing guard. The show concluded with many of the stars reuniting together on stage to sing "We are the World."

A few weeks later, USA for Africa was again honored at the Grammys with four wins out of five nominations. "We are the World" lost in the race for Best Album to Phil Collins' *No Jacket Required,* but won with each of the other four nominations. Three of the awards went to the single, the remaining one was for the song's video, as "We are the World" took top honors as the Best Short Form Video. Among the single's awards, was the prize for Best Pop Group Performance.

Record of the Year and Song of the Year are considered two of the most prestigious honors of all the Grammys. Record of the Year goes to a record's artist and producer. Song of the Year goes to the songwriter. "We are the World" was chosen as both the Record of the Year and Song of the Year. Quincy Jones was joined on stage by Michael Jackson, Lionel Richie, Stevie Wonder and Dionne Warwick to accept the Grammy for Record of the Year. Jones thanked, among others, Richie and Jackson for writing the song.

Michael and Lionel accepted the award for Song of the Year together, with Lionel speaking first to thank the artists involved and the public for responding when the world needed their help. Michael then stepped to the podium, dressed in a black uniform jacket over a red shirt with several gold pins. After the cheers from the audience subsided, he spoke:

First, I'd like to thank God. I'd like to say thank you for choosing Lionel and myself to write `We are the World'. I thank Quincy Jones who is the greatest producer to me. I'd also like to say when you leave here tonight, remember the children. Thank you.

"We are the World" was chosen as the Favorite New Song at the People's Choice Awards. The award was accepted by Kenny Rogers, neither Lionel Richie nor Michael Jackson attended the ceremony.

For the Hands Across America project, which followed the USA for Africa event, Michael favored use of "We are the World". He was out voted by the other board members and a new song was specially written for the event, "Hands Across America", with "We are the World" as the B-side. "Hands Across America" didn't achieve near the degree of success that "We are the World" had achieved. Michael's disagreement with the other board members is assumed to be what contributed to his decision in December, 1986, to resign from the board of directors of USA for Africa.

A second version of "We are the World" was produced by George Duke with children singing the lyrics. Michael preferred this version feeling the song was meant to be sung by children.

"We are the World" would end up being re-recorded in 2010, twenty-five years after the original, in an effort to raise funds for the victims of an earthquake in Haiti. Quincy Jones gathered a new group of artists for the re-recording that included Janet Jackson now sharing lines with her brother, the only voice and video footage used from the original. Undoubtedly Michael would have been one of the first artists to step up to offer whatever aid he could in the face of such a disaster.

The copyright to the "We are the World" single is owned by Brockman Music and Mijac Music, Michael's own music publishing company. By this time, Michael had become intrigued by the publishing aspect of the music business. But co-owning the "We are the World" copyright was not his most significant venture into the music publishing business.

In mid 1985, Michael purchased the ATV Music Publishing Company for $47.5 million. ATV held the copyrights to approximately four thousand songs at the time, including works by Pat Benatar, the Pointer Sisters, the Pretenders, and two of Michael's idols, Little Richard and Sly and the Family Stone. Most significantly, ATV also includes a 251 song catalog of Lennon-McCartney Beatle songs.

After making this investment, Michael wished to arrange for the rights to Little Richard's songs to be returned to him. Michael and John Branca visited Little Richard to let him know of their intentions. Unfortunately due to the complex nature of the rights catalog, the details could not be worked out.

Through ownership of these copyrights, royalties are earned each time one these songs is used in a TV show or film, a record is sold, the song is recorded or aired on the radio. It was estimated at the time of his purchase that Michael would recovered his investment within five years, or possibly sooner with the introduction of Beatle albums on compact discs.

For their help in the negotiations for the ATV Music purchase, Frank Dileo and John Branca were both handsomely rewarded with a

$120,000 Rolls Royce Silver Spur. Branca played a critical role in negotiating the deal for the catalog, which was financed by Columbia Records, a subsidiary company of CBS Records. Branca is widely regarded as brilliant and very accomplished, being credited with helping to create much of Michael's wealth.

Although there are several ways in which to earn money through music publishing, selling a song for use in advertisements tends to be one of the most profitable. It can also be one of the most controversial as Michael soon discovered when he granted permission to Nike to use "Revolution" in their ads for sport shoes, for $250,000. Claiming Nike did not have the right to use the original recording of their song in the commercial, The Beatles and their record company, Apple Records, sued the Nike Corporation.

Many others criticized Michael for only being interested in earning even more money and not being concerned with preserving the integrity of the Beatle's work. *Rolling Stone* magazine reported, "But confidants of the singer stress that Jackson went into that deal with John Lennon's widow Yoko Ono's consent and that his primary goal is to bring the Beatle's music to a new generation, not to turn a quick buck." John Branca added, "Michael is the world's number one Beatles fan, and he wanted to protect and cherish these songs just as the Beatles would. We're in constant touch with the representatives of Paul McCartney, and the estate of John Lennon, and nothing is done without their knowledge." A representative of the company that administers Michael Jackson's publishing holdings reported to *Rolling Stone,* "that while Jackson is certainly interested in the financial aspects of owning the rights to the Beatles catalog, he is more concerned with the artistic value of the songs." According to John Branca, Michael did not want to bid on the catalog against McCartney or Yoko Ono. Branca asked both Ono and McCartney's attorney, both said they were not bidding on it.

Gaining control of the Beatle song catalog cost Michael more than $47.5 million, it also cost him the friendship of former Beatle Paul McCartney. At best, it strained their relationship. While working together on duets for each others albums, the two had become very close friends. Michael learned that Paul had the only cartoon collection larger than his own. They discovered many other common interests as well, one of them being the music publishing business. It was estimated that at the time McCartney was earning $40 million a year from ownership of other artists' songs. Paul taught Michael about the business and Michael became an eager to learn student. Michael even told Paul he would someday buy his stuff. When Michael actually did buy the Beatle catalog, Paul resented it. According to John Branca, Michael had the blessing of Yoko Ono and McCartney's attorneys advised he was not bidding on the catalog. Michael was frustrated by McCartney's attitude given that McCartney was one of the wealthiest entertainers in the world and could have easily afforded to buy the rights to his own music. Michael not only outbid McCartney, but Coca Cola, CBS and Warner Brothers who were all said to be bidding on the catalog.

They were not enemies though and even posed for a picture together in 1990 to help show they were still friendly, if not friends.

McCartney later recalled there being no big blow out, but he did ask Michael for a raise in the royalty rate he was being paid. Michael responded only, "it's just business" and Paul did not get the raise.

McCartney could have been out bid by anyone. It seemed to have attracted so much attention because he happened to have been out bid by Michael Jackson, who he introduced to the music publishing business. Ownership of the rights to the Beatle catalog had been out of the hands of Lennon and McCartney for many years. Lennon and McCartney, early in their careers, signed over ownership of their copyrights to publisher Dick James. James' Northern Songs made millions off of the copyrights, then, in 1967, he sold Northern Songs to Sir Lew Grade. Grade subsequently sold the song catalog to Robert Holmes ã Court. The songwriting royalties are separate from the publishing rights and they still belong to McCartney and the estate of John Lennon.

When unauthorized copies of Beatle movies began to be sold in early 1989, Michael had his attorneys prosecute those distributing the bootlegged tapes. *The Beatles in Tokyo, The Beatles in the Magical Mystery Tour,* and *The Beatles at Shea Stadium* were being sold and distributed by Video Wholesalers, Inc. of Neptune, New Jersey. Michael was successful in obtaining a court order preventing further sales of the videos until the lawsuit was settled. The suit was filed by attorneys for Michael Jackson and the Beatles. It was the first time Michael Jackson and the Beatles joined together to protect the material of the Beatles. In the suit, Michael claimed he actually owned the copyrights to the songs performed in the movies and the video distributors had no right to produce or distribute the tapes. Michael also claimed that the poor quality of the tapes could turn off fans, lowering his potential profits if he should decide to release the movies himself. The suit was settled in October, 1989, Michael Jackson was awarded $130,000 and Video Wholesalers were permanently barred from any further sales of the video cassettes.

Michael greatly expanded his publishing holdings ever since obtaining the coveted ATV catalog. In the spring of 1989, Berry Gordy offered for sale Jobete Music, the publishing division of Motown Records. Estimates of the price were as high as $120 million. Among the parties interested were Warner Communications, Sony and Michael Jackson. Jobete Music holds the copyrights to most of Motown's biggest hits by Motown's biggest stars, such as Stevie Wonder, the Supremes and the Jackson Five.

Later, in 1995, Sony offered Michael $90 million for a 50% stake in the ATV Music catalog. Michael, in need of cash, accepted the offer and made a cool profit. Sony's catalog was merged with ATV, giving an equal share to Sony and Michael Jackson. The new company was named Sony/ATV and became the third largest music publisher in the world. Michael Jackson was a company director and regularly attended board meetings. The catalog has continued to expand and now holds the rights to 500,000 songs including works by Elvis Presley, Eminem, Akon, Bob Dylan, Taylor Swift, the Jonas Brothers, John Mayer and Willie Nelson. Years later the catalog, the world's leading music publisher, was estimated to be worth as much as $2 billion.

10

We're sendin' out a major love
And this is our message to you
The planets are linin' up
We're bringin' brighter days

"Another Part of Me"
- Michael Jackson

Following his work with USA for Africa, Michael went to work on another project, one that involved two of his greatest loves; Disneyland and movies. When Walt Disney Company chairman Michael Eisner asked Michael Jackson if he would like to be involved in a special film project for Disney, Michael accepted, asking that one of his favorite directors also be involved. According to Eisner, "Well, you know Michael Jackson is a Disney aficionado, knows more about

"Another Part of Me"

Walt Disney than anybody. He surely knows more than I do. We called up and said, 'Michael, would you like to do something for the parks?' He said, 'Definitely, but only if you can get George Lucas to direct me.'" Done. George Lucas, director of *Star Wars,* would direct. Francis Ford Coppolla, of *The Godfather,* would produce. Anjelica Huston would co-star. The movie would star Michael Jackson as Captain EO.

Specially constructed theaters were built at Disney World and Disneyland to house *Captain EO* to accommodate the movie's extravagant special effects. Jam packed with 3-D effects; asteroids float out of the screen and throughout the theater and, during a shoot out, lasers are shot from the action on the screen into the audience. At seventeen minutes in length, the movie cost $1 million per minute to produce.

Having bungled their last mission, EO and his crew of misfits need to redeem themselves in the eyes of their boss, Commander Bogg, played by Dick Shawn. EO's new assignment calls for him to use his powers of music and dance to bring beauty and happiness to the evil Witch Queen, played by Anjelica Huston.

EO's crew of misfits magically transform themselves into musical instruments giving EO the power to break free from the clutches of the Witch Queen's troops who surround him and attack him with whips. Genuine whips were used, so exact timing was crucial in filming the scene to avoid any injuries. While filming the scene, Michael was accidentally struck in the face with one of the whips. Fortunately, it was not too serious and he was able to continue filming.

Finally, EO is able to present the Queen with a gift that she "can not only see, but hear". EO and a group of back up dancers perform "We Are Here to Change the World", written by Michael Jackson with John Barnes. The dance routines are especially impressive when seen in 3-D. At one point, Michael goes into a moonwalk and glides out of the screen. After the transformation of the evil Witch Queen into a beautiful woman, EO and crew perform "Another Part of Me":

> *We're sending out a major love*
> *And this is our message to you*
> *The planets are linin' up*
> *We're bringin' brighter days*
> *They're all in line, waitin' for you*

Despite his crew's comedic ineptness, Captain EO is successful in his mission and saves the Dark Planet from the evil Witch Queen. With their mission completed, they say goodbye.

Disney's new *Captain EO* movie premiered at Walt Disney World's Epcot Center in Florida on September 12, 1986. It premiered at Disneyland in California the next day. The premiere at Disney World was celebrated by a TV special which featured sneak peeks at the movie and showed the arrival of many of the celebrities who attended the premiere. The traditional ribbon cutting ceremony to the theater entrance was held with George Lucas, Francis Ford Coppola, and Anjelica Huston. Conspicuously absent from the festivities was the film's star. Michael did not attend the film's premiere.

Six years after *Captain EO* opened at Disneyland and Disney

"Another Part of Me"

World, Euro Disney was opened in France. One of the biggest attractions at the new park was reported to be *Le Captain EO*. The Disney attraction continued to be a top draw until it was eventually pulled from the parks in 1994. Disney brought *Captain EO* back in 2010 for a limited engagement at Disneyland and Disney World. The film was added to Disneyland in Paris and Tokyo as well.

The same year, the follow up album to *Thriller* was anticipated, a few merchandising deals were underway to coincide with the release of this new album. Magic Beat Perfume, endorsed by Michael Jackson, was introduced in 1986. There were three different scents, Unwind, Heartbeat, and Wildfire. This line of perfume, planned to coincide with the release of Michael's new album, failed to reach the expected level of success, for there was no new Michael Jackson album. The follow up album to *Thriller* was delayed.

A line of stuffed toys based on Michael's private zoo was also marketed. Bob Michaelson helped develop the line of toys with Michael Jackson. Michaelson told one publication, "He's (Jackson) very instrumental in the designing of the toys. And he's very instrumental in how it should be programmed. He might not always be right, but he's right 90% of the time. That's pretty good for a 29 year old. He's got tremendous intuition." There are ten Michael's Pets in all. One of which, Cool Bear, is based on Michael himself. Cool Bear is dressed in a black suit, red shirt and black tie. He's also wearing a fedora and sunglasses. A frog is named Uncle Tookie, Michael's nickname for Frank Dileo.

In the spring of 1986, the British Virgin Islands announced

plans to release postage stamps featuring Michael Jackson. Shortly before their release, in fact after a few hundred sets were already printed, the production of the stamps was cancelled due to regulations stating that stamps bearing the likeness of living persons must be members of the Royal family, not the Jackson family. Stamps with Michael's picture were subsequently issued however by the Caribbean Island of St. Vincent. The stamps, and accompanying collector sheets, feature pictures of Michael from the Victory tour. St. Vincent issued a set of stamps in 1992 featuring eight entertainers. Included in the set was Madonna, Elvis Presley, David Bowie, Prince, Frank Sinatra, George Michael, Mick Jagger, and of course, Michael Jackson. Grenada issued a set of stamps featuring entertainers in their Gold Record Award set. Featured in the collection, in addition to Michael Jackson, were stamps with Cher, Elvis Presley, Dolly Parton, Johnny Mathis, Madonna, Nat King Cole, and Janis Joplin. Michael Jackson has also been featured on stamps issued from the Republic of Guinea and Tanzania, as part of a series honoring Famous Black Entertainers.

In 1987, singer Kenny Rogers published a collection of photographs he had taken of some of his famous friends titled, *Your Friends and Mine*. In the introduction to the book, Rogers relates the story of how the idea for the book came about, and the first person he photographed for it:

The first person I shot for the book was Michael Jackson. In 1986, I hosted the Grammy Awards telecast in Los Angeles. That night, my son Christopher met Michael backstage. Christopher had always loved Michael. He would even dress like him at home-

probably because he doesn't have silver hair and a beard, so he could look like me. As it happened, Marianne [Rogers' wife] *sent me some flowers with a little plastic Grammy attached. Unbeknownst to me or anyone else, Christopher took the plastic Grammy, walked into Michael Jackson's press conference, and handed it to him.*

The next day, Michael called to tell Christopher how much he appreciated it. He also invited him out to his house to see his animals, so Marianne and Christopher went out to Encino. Michael knew I was a photographer, he mentioned that he'd like it if I took a picture of him and Christopher together. I called Michael the next day to set up an appointment, and he agreed to come down to my studio.

I told Michael during our first session that I was thinking about doing a book of portraits and calling it Your Friends and Mine. I had heard about his chimpanzee, Bubbles, and we did a shot with the chimp. Later on Michael and I did another session alone, at his request. That was the start. Michael Jackson's agreeing to be part of the book was, in fact, the jumping off point for the whole project.

The photo of Michael holding Bubbles on his hip that was included in Rogers' book is a great black and white shot with Michael dressed very casually. No fedora, no glove, no sunglasses. He's dressed in worn jeans and a simple shirt. Bubbles is also dressed casually in a long sleeved shirt and overalls. The relaxed and casual feeling of the photo may not be only due to their attire, as Rogers tells in the brief description that appears next to the photograph in the book:

There were maybe twenty-five people in the studio that day, and the chimp was the center of attention. That meant the focus was off

Michael, and I think the relative anonymity gave him a chance to relax...

In June, 1987, Michael was in the news and again stories arose concerning him becoming increasingly eccentric. Michael had supposedly offered the London Hospital Medical College $500,000 for the remains of John Merrick, the elephant man. Merrick, who died in 1900, suffered from neurofibromatosis, a disfiguring disease. The hospital refused Michael's offer, saying the remains were not for sale. Michael, as the story went, doubled his offer but was still refused.

Another story generating scrutiny and wisecracks surrounded Michael purchasing a hyperbaric chamber. Michael reportedly felt that by sleeping in the chamber, with purified air pumped in, it would be healthy for him and possibly prolong his life. According to the story, Frank Dileo and Michael's doctor advised him against purchasing it, but Michael insisted and purchased it anyway. Almost immediately, a photo of Michael lying in the chamber hit the cover of the *National Enquirer*.

It has since been suggested who sent the photo to the magazine: Michael Jackson. Actually he saw the contraption, which is used to treat burn victims, while visiting burn patients in a hospital. He then supposedly made up the story and posed for the picture which was "leaked" to the *National Enquirer*. The picture was provided to the *National Enquirer* with the condition that the word "bizarre" be used in the caption. Michael and/or Frank Dileo have since been exposed as the source of the elephant man story too. Michael realized the value of publicity. Good or bad, it is essential to remain in the public's mind, besides he had a new album due for release soon. He learned the value of publicity from his early days at Motown, and had since become a master at the game. All of the talk, jokes, and controversy that surrounded his efforts to buy the elephant man's bones and his wishes to prolong his life by sleeping in the oxygen chamber helped to increase the mystique around him. He purposely harvested an image of mystery and intrigue about himself. He once said he wanted to be on the cover of the *National Enquirer* everyday. Talk about being careful of what you wish for!

Rumors about Michael's weirdness included his extensive plastic surgery. Some said he wanted to look like Diana Ross, others said he wanted to look like his sister, Janet, and still others said he wanted to look like LaToya. Some charged he underwent the surgeries to look less like his father, that he wanted to erase any resemblance of himself to his father. Other stories told of a shrine Michael had built to Elizabeth Taylor in his home, in which her movies played twenty-four hours a day. Michael had also reportedly proposed marriage to Taylor. Some others declared Michael to be weird because one of his companions was often times his chimp Bubbles.

Before the release of *Thriller's* follow up album, Michael was spotted in public wearing a surgical mask over his face. This started reports that Michael had become a second Howard Hughes, afraid of any germs. The stories even went so far as to say that he was going to perform behind a plexi-glass shield while on tour to protect himself from germs. Michael tells in *Moonwalk* that the mask was given to him by his dentist to keep out germs when he had his wisdom teeth removed. Michael grew to like the bit of privacy the mask offered in addition to his sunglasses and he continued to wear it. He was actually not germophobic at all, he just didn't like people staring at him. Covering his face with glasses and now a surgical mask helped provide a bit of privacy while fueling the mystique around him.

Perhaps the most hurtful stories circulating about Michael Jackson concerned him undergoing a variety of extreme treatments in an effort to lighten his dark skin. As usual, when factual information was not available stories were just made up. The media had him undergoing skin peels, having acid applied to his skin, and the ever popular, skin bleaching to make his skin appear lighter. Some assumed this indicated Michael was ashamed to be a black American and was denying his race. It was undeniable that his skin was significantly lighter. It would be years later when he would reveal that he had been diagnosed with vitiligo, a disease which kills the pigmentation of the skin. The loss of pigmentation randomly on the body makes the skin appear blotchy. There is currently no cure, no way to bring the color back to the affected areas. The only options then are to live with it, or kill the pigmentation in the rest of the skin so the color is more uniform. Michael's dermatologist, Dr. Arnold Klein, prescribed a cream, Benoquin, which helped even out his skin tone. Exposure to sunlight decreases the effectiveness of the cream, hence the umbrellas.

The rumors claiming that Michael might be gay persisted then eventually gave way to the idea that he was asexual. Rumors speculating as to Michael's sexual preference have always bothered his mother and the rest of his family. Marlon said in a *People Magazine*

"Another Part of Me"

TV special interview, "I'll tell you right now that I know he's not gay because ...I know!"

All of these rumors were eventually answered by Frank Dileo, Quincy Jones, and Michael himself. Dileo denied many of the rumors in the September 14, 1987 issue of *People Magazine*. Michael's photo was on the cover with the caption, "Is This Guy Weird or What?" Dileo told the magazine that Michael had no shrine to Liz Taylor in his home and that he never proposed to her. Dileo also told *People* that Michael definitely never took hormones to keep his voice high. Michael is the only Jackson singled out as taking hormones to artificially maintain his high voice, even though all of the Jacksons, male and female, have very soft, high voices. Although he did not take anything to maintain a higher pitched voice, he did use a softer tone in public than in private. It would be years before he would use his lower register voice in public and it can be heard throughout *This Is It*.

The article continued with Dileo denying Michael had any cosmetic surgery on his eyes or cheekbones. He admitted that Mike did have his nose reshaped and he did have a cleft put in his chin. "Why?" "He wanted one." Dileo called the claim that Michael had his skin lightened by chemical or surgical means, "preposterous." Dileo continued with the farce of Michael purchasing the hyperbaric chamber, making it clear he advised against it and didn't know for sure if he actually slept in it.

Quincy Jones responded to these claims in an interview with *USA Today*:

The public perception of what Michael is as a human being

has been highly exaggerated. Those articles are hard for me to relate to. For instance, Bubbles is more fun than a lot of people I know. I saw Bubbles at a wedding in a tux. He has great table manners.

Jones went on to say:

The bottom line, after all the rhetoric, all the talk about plastic surgery, is that Michael is still one of the best entertainers America has ever seen. He's not accessible and doesn't do interviews, so people tend to fill in the blanks.

Jones also spoke to *US Magazine* about Michael's so-called strange behavior:

When you start in this business as young as he did, at age five, it's hard to get a realistic point of view on life. Considering his background, and what happened to him in recent years, he's surprisingly sane. I've seen dudes with one record go absolutely nuts. You've got to have a strong center to handle it, and I think Michael has that.

In commenting on Michael's private zoo, Jones replied:

That's not so bizarre. It could be cocaine. But I'm not crazy about it when Michael brings the python to the studio. The reason Michael loves animals and children is he likes the idea of the truth involved with them. He trusts children more than adults.

Jones told *Rolling Stone* magazine:

I'd rather have a kid who's talking about the Elephant man's bones than with a pound of cocaine. Any day. Send me the bones. Oxygen tank too. I wish he were my little brother.

Michael himself even responded to a story claiming he had had several cosmetic surgeries done on his face. The news magazine program, *20/20* did a story on plastic surgery, calling Michael Jackson a "plastic surgery addict". Angry with the story, Michael later phoned one of the programs hosts, Barbara Walters. He told her of his change in diet over the last several years, that he had became a vegetarian, and this change in diet contributed to the change in his appearance. Michael then only ate healthy foods. Snacks were natural foods such as raisins and nuts, or popcorn, one of his favorites. This diet, he claimed, produced a pronounced changed in his build and facial appearance. He told Walters he had his nose and chin cosmetically altered and *nothing* else. He also explained many of the conclusions that he had several alterations to his face are based on comparisons of photos of him when he was very young to photos of him as an adult.

He actually ate very little, leaving his mother to wonder at times what kept him alive. Standing 5'9" to 5'10", he weighed approximately 125 pounds. It was reported that by the end of the Bad tour he had dropped ten pounds. (Frank Dileo, who obviously dealt with the pressures of the road in quite a different manner, gained forty pounds.) On Sundays, he would eat even less than usual, fasting the entire day, taking in only water and fruit juices. And he danced. He danced until exhaustion.

Michael's so-called eccentricities were becoming the subject of an increasing number of press reports and rumors. However, his talent always prevailed over whatever wild story was currently circulating about him. In a not so flattering cover story focusing primarily on his eccentricities, *Rolling Stone* conceded, "Whatever can be said about him, Michael Jackson sings with a shimmery soulful voice and dances like a swirling comet, as an entertainer he has no peer."

Many of these wild stories spread about Michael were based only on a fragment of truth. In some cases the initial seed may have been planted by Michael himself, as with the hyperbaric chamber and possibly the shrine to Elizabeth Taylor in his home. While the stories of the oxygen chamber and the elephant man's bones may have gotten out of control, Michael realized the value of such publicity and had become a master at creating and maintaining the public's interest and curiosity.

Michael's extreme shyness made it almost unbearable for him to talk with reporters. Around people he knew and was comfortable with, Michael relaxed and was something of a prankster with a wonderful sense of humor. In large crowds, especially with people he didn't know well, he was painfully shy and uncomfortable, an almost different person from the Michael Jackson seen in videos or in concert performances. When Silvya Chase interviewed Michael in 1980 for the TV news program *20/20,* Michael talked about his intense shyness, "Being around everyday people and stuff, I feel strange, I do. That's something I work on. A lot of my family's like that." Silvya Chase asked Michael, "There are some people who feel that having always been on stage, you've never had to deal with the real world."

"Yeah, that's true in one way. That's true in *one* way. But it's hard to in my position. I try to sometimes, but people won't deal with me in that way because they see me differently. They won't talk to me like they will a next door neighbor. So, it becomes difficult."

Before pasting a "weird" or "eccentric" label on Michael Jackson, consideration must be given to the circumstances under which he grew up. Michael was a performer for his entire life. He could not remember a time when he wasn't performing. He grew up being constantly sought after by fans and the press to a much greater degree than his brothers experienced. In an interview in 1983, Michael told *Rolling Stone's* Geri Hershey, "Being mobbed *hurts*. You feel like you're spaghetti among thousands of hands. They're just ripping and pulling your hair. And you feel that any moment you're just gonna break." Michael's early memories weren't of classroom buddies and schoolyard playgrounds, but of private tutoring sessions between concert dates, late-night rehearsals and recording sessions.

Probably the strongest center in Michael's life wasn't being caught up in being the world's greatest entertainer, but his belief in God. Michael believed his talent truly came from God and he thought of himself as merely a courier bringing the music to earth. Michael's mother is a devout Jehovah's Witness. Only two of her children were baptized as Jehovah Witness', Rebbie and Michael. Michael would dress in disguise to participate in selling the Witness' religious magazine, the *Watchtower,* door to door. While he was on top of the music charts with *Thriller*, some were slamming doors in his face, failing to recognize him.

In mid 1987, Michael left the Jehovah Witnesses. It was a shocking and unexpected departure. But Michael did chose to leave the church, he wasn't asked to leave as many papers reported. William Van De Wall, a spokesman of the Brooklyn headquarters of Jehovah

Witnesses, told *Ebony* magazine, "He took the initiative. We didn't take any action. We were informed his wishes." In guarding his privacy, Michael never expressed his reasons for leaving the Witnesses. It does seem reasonable to assume, however, that disagreements with the elders over the "Thriller" video and similar disagreements over his career contributed to the split.

Offstage, his greatest inspirations were children and animals. He became friends with both of his co-stars from each of his Pepsi commercials, Alfonso Ribeiro and Jimmy Safechuck. Other friends of Michael's were child stars, such as Emmanuel Lewis and Sean Lennon, the son of John Lennon and later Macaulay Culkin. Michael also grew fond of Ryan White, a young student who was driven from his school when it was learned he had AIDS, contracted from a blood transfusion. During one phone conversation with Michael, Ryan mentioned one of his favorite cars was a Mustang. So, it was no mystery later as to who had anonymously purchased a bright shiny red Mustang for Ryan. Ryan and his mother had also been invited to spend weekends at Michael's ranch.

Many of Michael's other friends were fellow performers. His closest friends seemed to be entertainers who, like Michael, had also grown up in the spotlight. He seemed attracted to those who survived childhood fame and managed to continue in their careers. Michael shared friendships with Elizabeth Taylor, Liza Minnelli, Jane Fonda and Brooke Shields. One former child star he was especially excited to meet was Shirley Temple. He once described in a conversation with Rabbi Shmuley Boteach, what made her special in much the same terms many would use to describe Michael:

Her innocence, how she made me feel good when I was so sad. It wasn't so much her dancing and signing. It was her being. She was given a gift to make people feel good inside. All children have that but, man, she is so angelic to me, and every time I see her, it can be on a film or a picture, I feel so good. I have her pictures all in the room there. It makes me so happy.

In the early 80's Michael met Dominic Cascio, who worked at the Helmsley Palace in New York City. Cascio later owned a restaurant in New Jersey. Michael grew very close to Dominic and his wife Connie and their five children. Frank, Eddie and their sister Marie would frequently travel with Michael on his concert tours and Michael would spend extended periods at their home enjoying the home cooking. Frank eventually worked with Michael as one of his business managers and Eddie worked with him in their home recording studio in New Jersey in 2007 and 2008. The Cascio's became a surrogate family, with Michael and his kids even spending Christmas with them.

Frank Cascio shares in his book, *My Friend Michael: An Ordinary Friendship with an Extraordinary Man*, many fun and personal memories of his time with Michael. Cascio tell of being with Michael during happy times and some of the toughest periods of his life. He and Michael would drink white wine, Michael's favorite, and smoke pot on the grounds of Neverland. Not the memories he probably would like Frank to share, but it's a fun glimpse into his personal life.

As well as working with Michael, Frank Dileo and Quincy

Jones had both formed close relationships with Michael. Jones' nickname for Michael was "Smelly". Jones came up with a nickname for each member of the "A Team". Different explanations have been given as to how he got the nickname. Michael shied away from using profanity and supposedly wouldn't even use the word "funky", preferring instead to use "smelly", even though he included the word "funky" in the lyrics of "Beat It". ("Show 'em how smelly and strong is your fight" must not have sounded quite right.) Somehow, the nickname stuck. The other version of how he inherited the nickname is in what Quincy Jones referred to as Michael's ability to smell out a hit song, saying a song had to have the "smelly jelly" to be a hit.

Other of Michael's friends were performers he had admired for most of his life and strived to match their level of talent and showmanship. The performers Michael watched when he was growing up and who inspired him include James Brown, Jackie Wilson, Fred Astaire, Sammy Davis Jr., Smokey Robinson, and of course, Diana Ross. While Michael saw these entertainers as the best, they in turn were impressed with Michael's talents and longed to match his accomplishments.

James Brown was a tremendous influence on Michael beginning when he was a very young child. During the early stages of Michaelmania, he attended a James Brown concert. Brown introduced him as a "new inspiration and new motivation", and urged him to come up on stage. Michael, seated with Bill Bray, resisted at first then rose from his seat and made his way to the stage shaking many hands along the way. Dressed in black jeans, a blue and gold military style jacket

"Another Part of Me"

and aviator sunglasses, you could imagine the two Michael's duking it out as he approached the stage. When he finally made it, the shy retiring Michael lost out to the dancing and singing whirlwind. He sang briefly, "I love you" to the crowd and sprang into some classic James Brown footwork with his own lightening spin and moonwalking thrown in. He then rather shyly left the stage.

A long time favorite movie star and dance idol and inspiration of Michael's was Fred Astaire. Sarah Giles put together a collection of remembrances about Fred Astaire from his friends in a book entitled, *Fred Astaire: His Friends Talk.* Michael was one of the many people contributing his thoughts and feelings about Fred Astaire:

I could only repeat what has been said and written about Fred Astaire's perfectionism and enormous, one-of-a-kind artistry. What I can reflect on is the inspiration he afforded me personally, being privileged as I was to see him work his magic. Nobody could duplicate Mr. Astaire's ability, but what I never stop trying to emulate is his total discipline, his absolute dedication to every aspect of his art. He rehearsed, rehearsed, and rehearsed some more, until he got it just the way he wanted it. It was Fred Astaire's work ethic that few people ever discussed and even fewer could ever hope to equal.

Another admirer of Michael's dancing style was Fred Astaire himself. Astaire told *People Extra:* "My Lord, he's a wonderful mover. He makes these moves up himself and it's just great to watch. Michael is a dedicated artist. He dreams and thinks of it all the time."

There was mutual admiration between Michael and Sammy Davis Jr. as well. Davis told *People Extra:*

Michael Jackson: The Complete Story of the King of Pop

> *He takes a step that you've been doing and then by the time he switches it around, you don't even recognize it. There is nothing new about thrusting your hips out, but when he does that with quick moves, the high kick out and that slow back-up step he does, people say, `Jeez, what is he doing?' And he never lays on a move long enough for you to figure it out. I'm sure if he worked with Nureyev or Baryshnikov, he would come close to that level. Can he tap dance? I don't know. But then again I'd hate to leave my dancing shoes in his vicinity.*

Smokey Robinson was an idol of Michael's before the Jackson Five signed with Motown. Michael recalls in *Moonwalk* the first time he met Smokey Robinson. He describes vividly how it felt to meet one of his idols and shake his hand. Robinson was also impressed with Michael's career. In his autobiography, *Inside My Life,* Smokey Robinson stated, "I could ego-trip about my big concert dates, but all I have to do is look over at Michael Jackson's tour to put myself back in line."

In addition to these entertainers who inspired Michael and whom he learned he also studied those at the pinnacle of their fields in other avenues, Berry Gordy and Walt Disney for their business acumen and Bruce Lee for his command of martial arts. He long admired Charlie Chaplin and you could see his study of the movements of Marcel Marceau in his dance.

Michael's other great passion was animals. He loved virtually all animals and kept a private zoo at the Neverland Valley Ranch with elephants, giraffes, big cats, llamas and exotic birds. The most popular of Michael's zoo was of course his chimp, Bubbles. In 1985, Michael saved Bubbles from a cancer research center in Texas. Bubbles was one of Michael's favorite companions. Bubbles accompanied Michael on his solo tour in Japan, was featured in magazine articles (although I don't think he gave interviews either), and he appeared on TV talk shows. With the help of trainer Bob Dunn, with whom Bubbles sometimes lived, Bubbles was taught several tricks, including his own special version of his dad's famous moonwalk. Like his giraffe, Jabbar, who appeared in Pee Wee Herman's *Big Top Pee Wee,* Bubbles was also a movie star, appearing briefly in Rodney Dangerfield's *Back to School.* Michael had even gotten Bubbles his own agent to help with his budding acting career.

A bit later in his life, after a bad experience, he developed a fear of large dogs. It seems odd that someone who thought nothing of letting a python wrap its twenty foot body around him or letting a tarantula take a stroll on his hand, would be fearful of a German Shepard. Smaller breeds were okay though, after much begging, he did relent and allow his children to get a dog.

In 1985, Joan Howard Maurer, daughter of Stooge Moe Howard, wrote a biography of her uncle, *Curly.* She asked one of Curly's, and the Three Stooges', biggest fans to write the book's Foreword. This one page Foreword appears in the book opposite full page photo of Michael's dressing table from the Victory tour that appeared in the *People Extra.* Among the carefully arranged items on the table is a snapshot of the Three Stooges.

Michael paid tribute to his other comic hero, Charlie Chaplin, on the comedian's birthday in 1983. Several photos of Michael and actor Samir Kamoun have been published with them each dressed as Charlie Chaplin.

In addition to collecting cartoons and watching old Three Stooges reruns, Michael's other hobbies included reading and art. He was a voracious reader. He read the *Wall Street Journal* regularly and loved history books. On shopping trips to book stores he would often buy thousands of dollars of books, so many his bodyguards would need to return to the store with a truck to collect them all. He would instill this love of books in his children. He read virtually everything available on John Merrick and Walt Disney. His favorite book, however, was *Peter Pan*. It was reported repeatedly that Michael would play the little boy who refused to grow up in a movie of Peter Pan, but nothing ever came of it.

While growing up, Michael gained an appreciation of art, thanks in part to Diana Ross. Michael was a talented artist in his own right and enjoyed drawing since he was very young. He completed an impressive portrait of Charlie Chaplin at age nine that would hit the auction block decades later. He had said that he wished to complete a painting that he was happy with. It would not be widely known until after his death the amount of time he spent on the hobby, creating a collection worth hundreds of millions of dollars in a secret art studio housed in an airplane hangar.

Apart from the stage, Michael longed to help the sick and suffering of the world and make the world a better place. His charitable efforts were heartfelt, not part of a crafted public persona. He genuinely cared about people and the Earth. He used his global

"Another Part of Me"

fame as a platform to spread positive messages and to inspire people.

Of course Michael's main love was his music and performing. And nobody had greater expectations or set higher goals for him than he set for himself. Before *Thriller* was released, Michael told LaToya that it would become the biggest selling album of all time. While working on *Bad,* Michael's goal was to sell 100 million copies. He had a note to himself on his bathroom mirror reading simply, "100,000,000", to remind him of his goal. While in Japan for the start of the Bad tour, Michael was seen wearing a diamond pin reading, "100,000,000".

Michael was a perfectionist in everything he did, especially in his work. He would practice a small dance step until it became second nature. He refused to settle for less than perfection in his dancing as well as his recording. He was very interested in taking an idea as far as possible and creating something new and different, being a leader in his field rather than a follower. This goal had been achieved and surpassed many times over throughout his career. In a 1979 interview Michael revealed, "I'm interested in making a path instead of following a trail and that's what I want to do in life - in everything I do." Michael had also said, "I love to create magic, to put something together that's so unusual, so unexpected that it blows peoples heads off. Something ahead of what people are thinking. So people can see it and say, `Whoa! I wasn't expecting that.'"

His greatest joy came from performing. Michael told *Ebony* magazine, "My main love for what I do is the fans. I love the fans. When I'm out there doing a show and I see the fans there dancing and screaming, excited, and we're bringing that joy to them, that's what I love the most. And it's the greatest feeling in the world." Michael was about to bring that kind of joy to his fans once again as he released an arsenal of songs, videos and performances to continue to show his fans "who's bad".

11

*Well they say the sky's the limit
And to me that's really true
But my friend you have seen nothin'
Just wait 'til I get through*

"Bad"
- Michael Jackson

The follow up album to *Thriller* was originally scheduled for release in the spring of 1986. There were delays and this date was pushed back to the middle of summer. Then fall. Then it was announced the album would be out before Christmas or early 1987. Christmas and the New Year came and went with no new Michael Jackson album. May 1, 1987 was the next date given, one year later than the original date announced. It wasn't out then either.

There were a variety of reasons given for the delays. Some sources speculated Michael was waiting for his sister Janet's *Control* album to peak before releasing his own album, so as not to hinder her success. Others suggested a much more selfish motive, that Michael wanted to be the only Jackson on the charts. Still others focused on the insurmountable pressure they imagined Michael was facing to top *Thriller*. They suggested that Michael didn't want to release its follow up album, demanding that songs be re-recorded several times with the final cut being no different than earlier takes.

Whatever the actual reasons were for the delays, it certainly wasn't due to a lack of material. Michael had written over sixty songs from which to choose the ones to finally make it on the album. More of Michael's own compositions were included on the new album than were included on either of his earlier solo albums. Three songs on *Off The Wall* were written by Michael and four of *Thriller's* nine songs were penned by Michael. Having his own compositions become the biggest hits from these earlier albums perhaps bolstered his confidence in his own songwriting talents. Eight songs on the new album would be written by Michael.

While recording Michael turned out the lights in the studio and almost always danced. A wooden stage was built into Studio of Westlake Audio Studios in Los Angeles where Michael was recording the album. Recording engineer Bruce Swedien would mic his feet to pick up the sounds of the dance. He would also dance during classes with his vocal coach, Seth Riggs. He would try to convince Michael not to use so much energy, but Michael insisted on dancing during vocal exercises.

Those Michael worked with commented on his amazing talent in the recording studio. Keyboardist Steve Porcaro, said, "Michael has strong melodic ideas and can come up with things I'd never think up in a million years." Quincy Jones added, "He has, even more important than playing an instrument, a concept of the colors of music, of rhythmic, percussive sounds and secondary melodic instruments. He hears it in his head and hums the line."

In July, 1987, the first single was finally released. "I Just Can't Stop Loving You", a duet with Siedah Garrett, was the public's first taste of the new album. A New York radio station jumped the single's release date, playing the song two days early, prompting legal action against the station. Without a video to promote it, the single went to number one on both the pop and black singles charts. The week of September 19, 1987, "I Just Can't Stop Loving You" knocked one of the summer's biggest hits, "La Bamba" by Los Lobos, out of the number one spot on *Billboard's* Hot 100. It held the top spot for one week.

A special edition twelve-inch single of "I Just Can't Stop Loving You" was released in Spanish with the translation by Ruben Blades. The B-side was the English version of the song. Because there was only a limited number of the singles made, they are now a much sought after prize of Michael Jackson fans. In the rehearsal footage for This Is It Michael sings the first lines of the song in Spanish.

"I Just Can't Stop Loving You" was chosen as the album's first single from its very inception. Originally, however, it was intended as a duet with Michael and an established female singer. Barbra Streisand was asked and she refused. She didn't like the song. Whitney Houston was also asked. She had to turn the project down because of scheduling conflicts.

Meanwhile, Quincy Jones had come up with another song for the album, "Man in the Mirror", written by Glen Ballard and Siedah Garrett. Siedah Garrett met Michael in the studio when she was adding background vocals to "Man in the Mirror". He was impressed with her voice and decided to do the duet with her. In fact, their voices blend together so well it is sometimes difficult to distinguish between them.

During recording sessions, Siedah told one interviewer, Michael would get playful. While Siedah was trying to be very serious and put a lot of emotion into her lines, Michael would make faces and throw raisins and peanuts at her to make her laugh.

The much anticipated album finally hit record stores on August 31, 1987, and it was *Bad*. A television special aired on CBS that same evening, *Michael Jackson: The Magic Returns*. The thirty minute special began with a short retrospective of his career and concluded with the premiere of the seventeen minute extended length video for "Bad". A very short teaser ad was shown at the conclusion of the special for Michael's new solo Pepsi commercials with the ending line, "The Magic Continues..." And it did.

Thirty percent of the approximately 85 million TV households in the U.S. tuned in to see Michael Jackson's latest video effort, making it the sixth highest rated show for the week. The "Bad" video was filmed in Brooklyn, New York, at the Hoyt Schermerhorn subway station, and took six weeks to make. The story, written by Richard Price, was based on a real life story. Edmund Perry was a student at a private school. He was a good student and planned on attending college. During winter break he returned home, to Harlem, where he was shot to death by his old friends he had left behind.

In the video, Michael plays Daryl, a kid from the ghetto, who attends a private school, away from his friends. Daryl returns home on break and finds he doesn't fit in with his old friends anymore. Daryl's friends realize he has changed and kick him out of the gang, "You ain't down with us no more, you ain't down, you ain't bad!" Daryl yells back, "You ain't bad, you ain't nothin'. You ain't NOTHIN'!" Suddenly the scene changes to color, the action up to now being in black and white, and instead of worn jeans and a sweatshirt, Michael is now dressed entirely in black, with rows of buckles lining his boots, pant leg, sleeves and fingerless gloves. Michael's character is not killed, instead, with a snap of his fingers, Daryl and his magically appearing backup dancers sing and dance eventually uniting the two opposing sides. Through his performance, Michael/Daryl convinces his friends that he is indeed bad, really, really bad.

"Bad" was choreographed by Gregg Burge, Jeffrey Daniel, and Michael Jackson. Martin Scorsese was chosen to direct the video. Scorsese was suggested by Frank Dileo, and was eventually chosen over Michael's first choice, Steven Speilberg. It is Scorsese's photo on the WANTED poster that is ripped from the subway station wall. Daryl's mother, whose voice is heard reading a note Daryl finds when he returns home, is Roberta Flack.

With the new album came a new look for Michael. Now he was seen in tough guy duds, all in black with rows and rows of buckles, and his hair was longer. There were other recent changes too, his nose had been reshaped again and he had added a cleft to his chin.

The photo that appeared on the *Bad* album cover was the second choice. The original photograph was a close up shot of Michael's face with black lace superimposed over it. The photo is included in a book of celebrity photographs by Greg Gorman and in Michael's second book, *Dancing the Dream*. Walter Yetnikoff objected to the picture being used as the album's cover. A photo by Sam Emerson, Michael's personal photographer, taken during a break in the filming of the "Bad" video was used in its place.

Michael Jackson impersonators also began to surface again. The most notable was a young man from Los Angeles, E'Casanova. Casanova made himself look startling similar to Michael Jackson. He duplicated Michael's costumes, hair and makeup, but even more impressive was Casanova's skill in duplicating Michael's moves. Casanova performed in full Jackson attire at a Las Vegas nightclub. He claimed his likeness to Michael Jackson was the work of Mother Nature and not a plastic surgeon, unlike Valentino Johnson, another Michael Jackson impersonator, who spent thousands on plastic surgery to look like Michael Jackson.

The *Bad* album was an instant smash. *Rolling Stone* gave the album a glowing review, declaring that Michael "proves that he can out funk anybody anytime." Another reviewer concluded, "The Bad news is, Michael J. has never sounded better." Immediately after the album's release, record dealers said that its first few days of sales surpassed all of their greatest expectations. By its third day out, Epic reorders of *Bad* had reached one half million copies. The preorders for *Bad,* at 2.25 million, were the largest ever in CBS Records history.

Bad entered *Billboard's* pop album charts in the number one spot and stayed there for six weeks. Coincidentally, *Bad* kept Def Leppard's *Hysteria* album out of the number one spot, just as *Thriller* had done to Def Leppard's *Pyromania* album. Bad spent its first thirty-eight weeks of release in *Billboard's* top five, breaking the record of twenty-six weeks set by the Eagles with *Hotel California.*

The second single released off of the *Bad* album was the title track. Originally intended as a duet with Prince, who refused saying it would be a hit without him. He was right. "Bad" it became the album's second number one single the week of October 24, 1987 staying at the top of the Hot 100 for two weeks. "Bad" also went to number one on the black singles chart. The extended version of the "Bad" video aired on MTV for weeks with the air times announced each day. Later, an edited version of the video was aired.

Following the release of *Bad,* Michael did his first interview in almost five years. He chose to do a televised interview on a syndicated program, *Ebony/Jet Showcase.* He talked with one of the program's hosts, Darryl Dennard:

"The **Bad** album is Michael's most artistically ambitious work to date. He tried several different music styles with his personal favorite being a fast paced tune with a heavy metal/rock and roll beat."

"I love `Dirty Diana'. That's one of my favorites because it's the life

story of a groupie. I hate to say the word 'groupie', but that's what it is. And it's something that I've experienced and a lot of people who grew up on the road, like me, I don't remember not performing."

"Do you feel as though you've missed out on a lot by not remembering not performing?"

"Of course, but I've gained a lot too. A lot of people never get out of their home town and get to see other wonderful places. A lot of kids read about things that I get to see in person, all over the world. I'm so happy about that, I mean, you never can have everything."

The interview concluded with:

"Of all the songs on the album, I think the one I enjoy the most is 'Man in the Mirror'".

"It's my philosophy too, if you want to make the world a better place, take a look at yourself and then make a change. I'm never totally satisfied. I always wish the world could be a better place. Hopefully, that's what I do with my music, bring happiness to people."

       The next single from *Bad* was "The Way You Make Me Feel". It became the album's third consecutive number one single, replacing George Harrison's "Got My Mind Set On You" at the top of the pop singles chart, where it stayed for one week. The single spent four weeks at the top of the black singles chart. "The Way You Make Me Feel" became Michael's seventh number one solo single of the eighties. This broke a three way tie between himself, Madonna and Whitney Houston for the most number one hits in the eighties. Michael Jackson was now the most successful solo artist of the decade.

       The video for "The Way You Make Me Feel" premiered on

MTV on October 31, 1987. In it, Michael chases after a girl who continually gives him the brush off though he finally does get the girl at the end. The video was directed by Joe Pytka and choreographed by Michael Jackson and Vince Patterson, with some of Michael's most suggestive moves to date capped off with an exploding fire hydrant spouting off high in the air.

Michael's co-star for the video was Tatiana Thumbtzen. When she was first told of the role, she was told only that it was a video for a "mysterious artist", someone of Michael Jackson's or Prince's status. When she arrived for the audition "Beat It" was playing, only then did she know it was a video for Michael Jackson. The initial audition had several hundred girls, only four of which were later called back. Tatiana met Michael at this second call. As a guest on *Hour Magazine*, she recalled filming the video and getting her foot caught in the car's upholstery:

The moment where we broke the ice was when my foot got stuck in the car upholstery. Michael put his hand on my leg to try and help me and I thought I'd die. I thought `Oh my God, he's actually touching me.' I got so excited and the director, Joe Pytka, was screaming, `Keep going, keep going', so I pulled away and landed outside the car on my butt. My face was beet red, Michael was cracking up and I gave in and started laughing too, because it was quite funny. And as I got up he was wiping me off. It was great!

Host Gary Collins asked what it was about Michael that turned her to jelly like that and she replied, "I don't know, it's magic. It really is. Michael has a power that you just *feel* when he's in a room". He's the most beautiful person I've ever met and I wish there were more like him, I really do". Asked if she and Michael were dating, she gave a shy smile, lowered her eyes and answered, "We're friends". Years later she admitted to a year long affair.

Bad ended 1987 as the year's biggest selling album, even though it was only out for three months of the eligible period. It reached number one on the album charts in a record setting twenty-five countries throughout the world. Worldwide sales to date top 35 million copies.

With the close of 1987 came more awards and honors. Michael was honored at the British Phonographic Industry Awards as the Best International solo artist of 1987. Michael accepted his Brit award via satellite from Los Angeles. Sweden also honored Michael. In a poll conducted by one of Sweden's largest newspapers, *Aftonbladet,* Michael Jackson was voted as the Best Vocal Artist of 1987.

Michael started off 1988 with some more good news. A judge had dropped a $150 million paternity suit that had been filed against him by Lavon Powlis, who called herself Billie Jean Jackson. Powlis claimed that Michael fathered her three children. At least one of these children was supposedly conceived outside Michael's home in a blue Rolls Royce after he invited her to Los Angeles and they had a date in his car. Powlis claimed this date was in May, 1975, making Michael sixteen years old at the time. Even though the paternity suit was dropped, she continued to harass him. A restraining order was placed against her, forcing her to stay one hundred yards from his Encino home. She violated the order, was convicted, and in January, 1989, she was sentenced to two and one half years in jail. Michael Jackson is not the only celebrity she has claimed to be the father of her children.

At the 1988 Winter Olympics, in Calgary, Canada, Michael Jackson's international appeal was once again illustrated. At the closing ceremonies, German gold medalist figure skater Katarina Witt donned a black leather jacket and fingerless gloves and skated to "Bad". Her performance even included an ice skating version of the moonwalk. At the 2012 Oympic Games in London, the Russian synchronized swim team wore swimsuits bearing the likeness of the King of Pop.

In July, 1989, France celebrated their bicentennial. As part of the celebration, a parade was held which featured representations from several different countries. A snow machine was used to symbolize Russia's winters, and a rainmaker was used to represent Scotland. Representing the United States was a performance by the Florida A&M Marching Band imitating Michael Jackson.

Bad went quintuple platinum in Canada in just a few weeks. In the year end issue of *Billboard, Bad* was called the most eagerly anticipated album of the year. *Billboard's* year end charts named Michael Jackson the ninth Top Hot Crossover Artist of 1987.

In January, 1988, MTV aired a Michael Jackson special, *From Motown To Your Town*. Film footage spanned Michael's career from the early days of the Jackson Five to Bad tour dates in Japan and Australia. Scenes of the Jackson Five performing "I Want You Back" at the very beginnings of their careers are blended into scenes of

Michael performing the same song on his Bad tour. A peek backstage has the band, dancers, singers, Frank Dileo and Michael gathered backstage for a prayer and group holler before hitting the stage.

The fourth single off of *Bad* was one of two songs on the album not written by Michael. "Man in the Mirror", written by Siedah Garrett and Glen Ballard, is a song with a strong message about changing the world, and starting with yourself in making those changes:

If you wanna make the world
a better place
Take a look at yourself and
make a change

The video for "Man in the Mirror", with only one brief shot of Michael, brings out the message of the song with a montage of film clips showing sad and unfortunate situations and those who have made an effort to make a change and make the world a better place. Shots of starving children and homeless people are intermixed with shots of individuals who have made contributions toward helping them. Bob Geldof, organizer of Band Aid and Live Aid for the relief of famine victims, and Willie Nelson, organizer of Farm Aid which benefited farmers are included with shots of Ghandi, Sister Theresa, Dr. Martin Luther King, Bishop Tutu, and President Reagan with Soviet leader Mikhail Gorbachov. Tragic events such as the assassinations of Martin Luther King, John F. Kennedy, and John Lennon are also included.

A few critics charged that the "Man in the Mirror" video, exploited the unfortunate people that were shown in the video for

Michael's own purposes, to sell records and make money. The song has a very strong, positive message, the video only enhances that message and does exactly what Michael wanted it to do, it touches people. Michael accomplishes two objectives with the song and its video, he motivates others to make a change for the better, and he makes a real difference himself, with the donation of his royalties from the single to Camp Ronald McDonald for Good Times, a camp for children with cancer. This anthem to help make the world a better place is still one of the songs most strongly identified with him.

The week of March 26, 1988, the number one song on *Billboard's* Hot 100 was "Man in the Mirror", bringing the total of number one singles from the *Bad* album to four. It stayed at number one for two weeks. Michael became the first artist to ever have four number one singles from the same album. "Man in the Mirror" was also the album's fourth number one single on the black charts. These four solo hits and the Jackson Five's first four number one songs made Michael Jackson the only artist to ever have four consecutive number one singles as a solo artist as well as a member of a group.

With "Man in the Mirror" reaching the top of the charts, Michael also became the first artist to have four singles reach the top ten from three consecutive albums. Four singles from *Off the Wall* reached the top ten, seven singles from *Thriller* reached the top ten, and four singles thus far had reached the top of the charts from *Bad*.

To mark the special achievement of being the only artist to have four number one hits from one album, CBS Records congratulated Michael with an in *Billboard*. Appearing opposite the

Hot 100 chart, the congratulatory ad featured a full page color photo of Michael and proclaimed, *"IT'S NEVER BEEN THIS "BAD" BEFORE!..."* In the same issue of *Billboard,* Michael was named the third most successful songwriter of the year. He had written three number one singles; "I Just Can't Stop Loving You", "Bad" and "The Way You Make Me Feel."

The video for the fifth single from *Bad* premiered on MTV on April 14, 1988. "Dirty Diana" was filmed in Long Beach, California, and is Michael's first performance video. Michael performs dressed in black pants with buckles and a white shirt with long tails. He has several studded belts around his waist, and long black fingerless gloves. White tape covers three fingertips on his right hand. Featured in the video is an appearance by Steve Stevens on guitar, who also plays on the record. Stevens is best known for his work with Billy Idol.

While Michael performs, a girl with long sexy legs in a very short skirt and high heels walks slowly from one car to another and gets inside. When Michael ends his performance of "Dirty Diana", about a girl who will "be your everything if you make me a star", he leaves the stage and heads for his waiting car. Opening the door, he finds that "Diana" is waiting for him in his car.

"Diana's" legs belong to model Lisa Dean. She was chosen over one hundred other girls, all of whom were auditioned and filmed. When Michael reviewed the film, he chose the first pair of legs that appeared on the screen, and Lisa Dean became "Dirty Diana".

In June, 1988, U.S. sales of *Bad* exceeded six million copies. Of course this became another "first". Michael Jackson became the only artist to have three consecutive albums with U.S. sales over six million copies each. *Bad* even sold well in China, were it was difficult to get albums released. In its first few weeks, *Bad* sold in excess of 250,000 copies, which was phenomenal considering the very limited market for records in China.

The number one pop song in America the week of July 2, 1988, was "Dirty Diana". Michael topped his own record set just a couple of months earlier with "Man in the Mirror", making him the first artist to ever have five number one singles from one album, something even *Thriller* couldn't manage. Again, Epic congratulated Michael with a full page ad in *Billboard*. A full page color photo of Michael was accompanied with the words, *"NO ONE'S EVER BEEN THIS BAD..."*

"Dirty Diana" spent one week at the top of the pop singles chart and peaked at number five on the black singles chart. Michael also became the first artist to have five or more top ten hits from two consecutive albums.

Another single Michael had on *Billboard's* Hot 100 was "Get It", a duet with Stevie Wonder, that is included on Wonder's album, *Characters*. "Get It" received extremely little airplay on most pop radio stations and only went to number eighty on *Billboard's* pop singles chart. The single received much more airplay on black radio and peaked at number four on the black singles chart. The single's poor showing on the pop chart is not indicative of the song's quality. It is an up tempo tune with Michael and Stevie trading vocals on which one will eventually capture the heart of a girl they both have their sights set on. It is actually a better song than their duet, "Just Good Friends" from the *Bad* album. Michael recorded another song with Stevie Wonder. "A Pretty Face" was not included on either of their albums, and to date, has not been released.

On July 30, 1988, Michael had his own TV special. *Michael Jackson: Around the World* was a ninety minute special featuring concert footage of the Bad tour, with Michael, as usual, having final approval of the footage to be included. While the concert footage of the Bad tour was impressive, it still only gives a small taste of the excitement of seeing Michael Jackson perform live.

Bad tour band members speak of the excitement of playing London's Wembley Stadium. Frank Dileo adds, "Playing Wembley is one of the biggest honors any artist could have. It's a status symbol within artists themselves, whether or not they can sell out Wembley Stadium, and of course Michael set a new record. He sold it out seven times. You can't get any bigger than that."

The program also featured the premiere of Michael's latest video, for "Another Part of Me". Filmed at London's Wembley Stadium on July 15, 1988, the video is of an actual performance of the song from the Bad tour. Too frequent cuts, however, detract from Michael's fancy footwork performed during the song. *Michael Jackson: Around the World* was the highest rated summer special ever in its time slot attracting twenty-seven percent of the television audience.

"Another Part of Me" peaked on *Billboard's* Hot 100 at number eleven. This broke a string of top ten hits for Michael seventeen songs long. The single, however, reached number one on the black singles chart, his fifth single from *Bad* to do so. This tied the record for the most singles from one album to reach number one on the black singles chart. He tied the record with Janet and her *Control* album. "Another Part of Me" was Michael's ninth number one single on the black chart in his career, making him the artist with the most number one singles ever on the black chart.

MTV premiered the video for Michael's seventh single off of *Bad* on October 13, 1988. A white pinstripe suited MJ renders gangsters helpless and performs one of his most impressive dance sequences. It is taken from a mini-movie of "Smooth Criminal" to be found on his then upcoming movie, *Moonwalker*. The single, recounting the grizzly murder of Annie and using a recording of Michael's own heartbeat, became the sixth top ten single from *Bad*, peaking at number seven on the pop chart and number two on the black chart.

The choreography for "Smooth Criminal" was done by Michael Jackson and Vincent Paterson, who worked with Michael on the video for "The Way You Make Me Feel" and Jeffrey Daniel, who had worked on the "Bad" video. One of the coolest moves has Michael and his group of dancers doing about a forty-five degree lean. This was done for the video using wires and special effects. Then it was done live on stage in concert performances. No wires this time. No nailing their shoes to the floor. Nobody fell flat on their face. Special shoes were developed for the move to help the dancers defy gravity. The anti-gravity shoes were developed by Michael Jackson for which he was granted patent number 5,255,452 in 1993 for the "Method and Means for Creating Anti-Gravity Illusion" shoes, aka Smooth Criminal shoes! The patent expired in 2005 after a government fee went unpaid.

As 1988 came to a close, several year end music charts were being compiled, with *Bad*, its singles and videos, and Michael being recognized on all of them. Those considered here are charts compiled by *Rolling Stone*, MTV's Top 100 Videos of 1988 and *Billboard* magazine. On the year end chart ranking the year's best albums, *Rolling Stone* named *Bad* the seventh top album of the year.

Michael was the artist with the most videos making MTV's Top 100 Videos of 1988. All five videos he released during the year made the top 100 with "Man in the Mirror" being his highest entry at number five.

The biggest impact was on *Billboard's* year end charts, with Michael Jackson making twenty of their charts at least once:

Top Pop Artist- #4- Michael Jackson
Top Black Artist- #1- Michael Jackson
Top Pop Album- #5- Bad
Top Pop Album Artist- #3- Michael Jackson
Top Pop Singles- #21-"Man in the Mirror", #61- "Dirty Diana"
Top Pop Album Artist-Male- #2- Michael Jackson
Top Pop Singles Artist-Male- #2-Michael Jackson
Top Pop Singles Producer- #3- Quincy Jones
Top Hot Crossover Singles- #18-"Man in the Mirror", #20- "The Way You Make Me Feel"

"Bad"

Top Hot Crossover Artist- #2- Michael Jackson

Top Black Singles- #36-"Man in the Mirror", #58-"Another Part of Me", #77- "Get It", #98- "Dirty Diana"

Top Black Singles Artist- #1- Michael Jackson

Top Black Album- #2- Bad

Top Black Album Artist - #2- Michael Jackson

Top Dance Sales Artist- #8-Michael Jackson

Top Dance Club Play Singles- #19 "The Way You Make Me Feel"

Top Dance Club Play- Artist- #9- Michael Jackson

Top Adult Contemporary Artists- #19- Michael Jackson

Top Compact Disks: #9-Bad

Top Pop Singles Publishers- #24- Mijac, BMI

Top Black Singles Publishers- #21- Mijac, BMI

Bad ended 1988, just as in 1987, as the year's biggest selling album. *Bad* was also the biggest selling album of 1988 in England. As the 80's were coming to a close, a columnist for *Adweek* wondered who would be remembered as the superstar of the decade, "the defining figure of our age", Ronald Reagan or Michael Jackson?

Another list Michael was topping at the end of 1988 was *Forbes* magazine's list of the year's highest paid entertainers. Michael moonwalked past the previous year's highest paid entertainer, Bill Cosby, by $5 million and was ranked number one on the list with estimated earnings for 1987 and 1988 of $97 million

For now, more awards were headed his way and he was gearing up to give one of the most memorable TV performances since *Motown 25*.

12

If you wanna make the world a better place
Take a look at yourself
Then make a change
You gotta get it right, while you've got the time
'Cause when you close your heart
Then you close your mind

"Man in the Mirror"
- Siedah Garrett, Glen Ballard

Amid the record breaking success of the *Bad* album and the Bad tour came award time. In January, 1988, Michael was nominated for two American Music Awards. He lost in his nomination for Best Pop/Rock Male Vocalist to Paul Simon. He won however with his second nomination with "Bad" being chosen as the Best Soul/R&B Single. Michael did not attend the award presentation.

"Man in the Mirror"

For the Grammys, Michael had earned four nominations and was scheduled to perform at the award presentation. *Bad* was nominated for Album of the Year, Michael Jackson and Quincy Jones were nominated for Producer of the Year, and Michael was nominated for Best Male Pop Vocal and Best Male R&B Vocal. Bruce Swedien was nominated for Best Engineered Recording for *Bad*. Epic Records congratulated Michael on his Grammy nominations with another full page ad in *Billboard*. The ad featured a photo of Michael from the waist down. But the black loafers and white sequined socks showing below the short black pants, and the taped up fingertips, left no doubt who it was.

Major publications, in reporting their Grammy picks and predictions, generally had Michael winning in three of the four categories. *The Los Angeles Times* and *USA Today* had Michael picking up the prizes for Best R&B Vocal Performance, Best Male Pop Vocal Performance, and sharing the Grammy with Quincy Jones for Producer of the Year. Both papers predicted U2's *The Joshua Tree* as the winner of Album of the Year, but by a very close margin. *The Los Angeles Times* even predicted a possible upset by Jackson's *Bad* album, and Michael possibly going home with all four Grammys for which he was nominated.

Michael's performance on the 30th Annual Grammy Awards was his first TV performance since the *Motown 25* special five years earlier. *TV Guide*, in its preview of the Grammys stated, "The Grammys are worth watching any year, but especially so this year: tonight's Grammy telecast from Radio City Music Hall is slated to include a live performance by Michael Jackson, his first live TV performance since 1983's `Motown 25...Yesterday, Today, Forever' show." Grammy producer Pierre Cossette, when asked what the night's big moment would be, replied, "It would be very difficult to say anything other than Michael Jackson."

About half way through the Grammy telecast the lights dimmed and a silhouette appeared from behind a scrim. The audience roared as they recognized the familiar figure. Michael stood, poised very still, with a hat perched on his head, down over his eyes. He slowly glided from one position to another as the screen slowly rose revealing Michael wearing short black pants, well above his ankles, and a blue shirt over a white t-shirt. He also had a white strip of fabric tied around his waist, and one around his wrist, looking he just stepped from the set of the video for "The Way You Make Me Feel".

He descended a small staircase and sang very slowly the opening lines of "The Way You Make Me Feel", putting out an imaginary cigarette on the floor. In a special cameo appearance, Tatiana crossed the stage in front of him. As the music assumed its usual up tempo beat, Michael tossed the hat, pulled his shirttails out and was joined by four dancers. The dazzling choreography borrowed from the song's video and showcased Michael's new step, gliding around in a circle.

After the performance of an abbreviated "The Way You Make Me Feel", the dancers left the stage to Michael. After a pause for applause, he began "Man in the Mirror". He was joined on stage by the New Hope Baptist Church Choir, all in blue gowns. Michael's other

"Man in the Mirror"

background singers included Siedah Garrett and Andre Crouch, who at one point went out to Michael to help him up from his knees and wipe his forehead, a gesture reminiscent of James Brown's performances. Michael poured his heart and soul into an outstanding performance, spinning and falling to his knees giving full emotion to the song's moving lyrics.

Michael was given a standing ovation for his performance that evening, but no Grammys. In the biggest surprise, shock and disappointment of the evening, Michael was shut out in all four categories in which he was nominated. Immediately following his performance, the award for Album of the Year was presented. It seemed a good omen for Jackson fans that one of the presenters was Diana Ross and he was standing just off stage having just finished his stunning performance. It seemed he couldn't lose. But he did lose, to U2's *The Joshua Tree*.

In the category of Best Producer, which many Grammy predictors said the team of Jackson and Jones were unbeatable, Narada Michael Walden won for Whitney Houston's album, *Whitney*. Sting was named Best Male Pop Vocal over Michael Jackson and Bruce Springsteen. Another surprise came later when Smokey Robinson won as Best Male R&B Vocal over Michael Jackson and the seemingly most popular second choice, Stevie Wonder. The *Bad* album did win the Grammy for Best Engineered Recording, which went to *Bad* engineer, Bruce Swedien. Following his performance, Michael sat out the remainder of the show seated next to Quincy Jones in the front row of Radio City Music Hall.

A small amount of consolation came from the news coverage of the Grammy awards the following day. *USA Today* ran the headline, "U2 big winner, but Jackson steals show." The article went on to say, "Despite his shutout, Jackson won over the audience with a performance recalling his 1983 Motown special stunner." MTV's report on the Grammys spotlighted the winners, but they also gave a considerable nod to Michael Jackson:

The evening's highest highs and lowest lows belonged to one man, Michael Jackson. His all stops out performance of 'Man in the Mirror', complete with full gospel choir was an eye-popping triumph. But by evening's end when the final tally was made, Jackson, who had been nominated for four Grammys, had won none. And his album, **Bad***, had garnered only a lonely engineering award. But Jackson's minimal showing in the statuette sweepstakes hardly diminished his uncontested talents.*

Other reviews said, "In a night when rock put on the dog, the evening's top cat of all, without a doubt, was Michael Jackson. Not only was his performance a show stopper, it stopped interviews in the press room. 'Let's watch Michael', said presenter Herbie Hancock, mid answer, 'you can talk to me later.'" *Jet* magazine wrote, "Even though he won no awards during the ceremony, Michael Jackson virtually stole the show with his performance. The singer, who had not appeared on television in 3 years, [sic] mesmerized the audience and television viewers on 'The Way You Make Me Feel', and poured out his heart in song with 'The Man in the Mirror'".

His performance did indeed win over the television viewers.

"Man in the Mirror"

This was reflected in the increase in album sales following the award telecast. Sales of Michael Jackson's *Bad* album rose higher than U2's *The Joshua Tree,* despite them winning the Grammy for Album of the Year.

Another highlight of the Grammy telecast was the network debut of Michael's new Pepsi commercials. For that story, lets go back to the beginning. In the spring of 1986, Roger Enrico, president of Pepsi, received a message. "It was from Frank Dileo and John Branca- Michael Jackson wanted to make more Pepsi commercials!" In *The Other Guy Blinked: How Pepsi Won the Cola Wars,* Enrico recalls flying to Michael's Encino home to discuss ideas for the commercials:

He sparks to it. It's an enormously difficult idea to pull off. It needs Michael Jackson, and an absolutely first rate director, to have a chance of succeeding. But no one has ever done anything like it before, and if we can make it happen, it will be gangbusters. Michael's reaction to the idea? `Roger', he says, `this time were going to set the world on fire!' He didn't, I assure you, mean that literally.

One of the ads, made up of four parts, follow Michael's efforts to elude a horde of paparazzi stalking him. The second commercial features a young Michael Jackson fan who wanders into Michael's dressing room looking for him, calling, "Mr. Jackson?" The room is empty. He looks around, seeing Michael's jackets, a half full bottle of Pepsi and Michael's sunglasses lying on a table. Meanwhile, Michael is on stage performing "Bad" with new Pepsi lyrics. The young admirer tries on Michael's sunglasses. He dons one of Michael's sequined jackets and the fedora. He does a spin like his idol and pushes the hat down over eyes, as he does, he hears, "Looking for me?" He looks up, very startled, at seeing Michael Jackson in the doorway, and he starts to giggle.

Michael's co-star for this commercial was Jimmy Safechuck. Jimmy was a big Michael Jackson fan and was very excited to be chosen to be in the commercial. However, when Jimmy showed up on the set for filming, he was told that Michael Jackson wouldn't be there. He would have to pretend that Michael was standing in the doorway. When Jimmy did the scene, wearing Michael's jacket and hat, he spun around, and heard "Looking for me?", Michael was really standing there. The surprised look on Jimmy's face in the commercial is genuine.

Michael and Jimmy subsequently became friends. Jimmy accompanied Michael to London with the Bad tour where he joined Michael on stage with other children at the end of the concerts. Years later Safechuck married on the grounds of Neverland Valley Ranch.

In these Pepsi commercials, Michael performed "Bad" with new "Pepsi" lyrics. Like just about everything else with Michael Jackson, these commercials too drew criticism and stirred controversy. Paul McGuinness, manager of U2, criticized Michael for his endorsement of Pepsi. "What's the point of going to all the trouble of being Michael Jackson and achieving so much musically and creatively if you are then prepared to place all that credibility at the disposal of a soft drinks manufacturer for a fee?"

Michael also came under fire from Neil Young. Young made a video, which MTV refused to show, that attacked rock stars for doing

"Man in the Mirror"

endorsements. "This Note's For You" is a tasteless attack on all pop/rock stars who make commercial endorsements, most notably Michael Jackson for Pepsi and Whitney Houston for Diet Coke. The video used look-a-likes for Michael Jackson and Whitney Houston with Jackson's hair catching fire and Whitney Houston putting it out with a Diet Coke. The classless spoof of a serious, potentially fatal, accident jumps over parody and lands squarely in tastelessness.

Michael did not place his credibility as a musician at the hands of Pepsi, probably seeing it as another frontier to conquer. And he did. Michael, as in everything he did, oversaw the entire project, and made certain his high standards of excellence were upheld. As with the Jackson Pepsi ads, Michael had approval power over the lyrics of the song, editing and he was again not filmed drinking or holding a bottle of Pepsi. For this second set of Pepsi commercials, Michael received the highest fee ever paid for a commercial endorsement. At a press conference announcing the deal with Pepsi, Michael received an award recognizing the record breaking fee. Michael accepted the award, speaking a total of sixteen words: "This is a great honor. Thank you Mr. Enrico, Pepsi associates, ladies and gentlemen. Thank you."

Whatever Pepsi's investment in Michael, it definitely paid off. When the Bad tour was in Japan, Pepsi sales doubled. When Michael arrived in Australia for his performances there, Pepsi sales rose immediately sixty percent. During the U.S. leg of the Bad tour, Pepsi sales tripled.

Michael's Pepsi commercials then became the first American advertisements to be shown on Soviet television. A spokesman for

Pepsi stated that the Soviet officials asked specifically for Michael Jackson's commercials. The endorsements were seen by approximately 150 million people in the Soviet Union.

Even if Neil Young disapproved, a lot of other people did approve. They were the most popular commercials, exposing Michael's music to an even wider audience. Pepsi sponsored the Bad tour and Mike picked up a hefty paycheck. Some joke.

With these commercials, Michael seemed to have set precedents for other pop stars to follow. Again. Madonna was the next pop star signed to endorse Pepsi. Her new Pepsi ads were scheduled to coincide with the release of her new album, just as Michael's commercials were scheduled to do. Diet Coke countered in the cola wars by signing George Michael as their spokesman. While these soda pop commercials continued to be very much opposed by some, to others it became almost a status symbol to be asked to do Pepsi or Coke ads. These Pepsi commercials changed the celebrity endorsement scene.

Later, Michael appeared in another TV ad, well, sort of. A new California Raisin commercial that first aired in theaters in July, 1989, and later on TV, featured a claymation Michael Jackson. The claymation Michael Jackson dreams of being Michael Raisin, who performs "Heard It Through The Grapevine". Michael's singing voice isn't used in the ad, but his speaking voice is. When claymation Mike wakes up, he figures the strange dream he had must have been due to, "something I ate". Because of his exclusive contract with Pepsi, Michael's own singing voice could not be used in the ads. He received

"Man in the Mirror"

a $25,000 fee for his contribution to the ads, which he donated to charity.

The weekend following the Grammys and the debut of Michael's Pepsi commercials, was Michael Jackson Weekend on MTV. The music video network devoted the entire weekend to Michael Jackson videos, reports and specials. Interviews with Frank Dileo and members of the band, Jennifer Batten, Greg Phillinganes, dancer Dominic Lucero, and backup singer Sheryl Crow all gave insight into how very much in control Michael was over the show. Sheryl Crow told MTV, "I learned so much from him, just by watching him. He's a perfectionist. I like that. I like the fact that he's completely aware of what's going on as we're doing it." Greg Phillinganes, music director and keyboard player on the Bad tour, said, "He definitely knows what he's doing and what he wants and the elements that he would like to put together to give the best show that he can." Guitarist Jennifer Batten added, "He's very aware of everything, which is incredible because he's got seventeen people on stage including himself."

As well as admiration for his attention to every detail of the show, the tour's cast also had a great deal of praise for Michael's talent. Sheryl Crow told how she found herself watching him, wondering, "How does he do that?" She added, "He has resonance that goes on forever. It's so bright and so clear sounding. The fact that he dances while he's singing, that to me is amazing." Greg Phillinganes also commented on Michael's singing voice, "He's a very strong singer and performer. He's got pipes of plutonium." The greatest praise came from Frank Dileo. Michael's manager described Michael as "extremely creative, he's probably the greatest entertainer of our day. I've been lucky to see the Beatles, and see Elvis, and been able to see Frank Sinatra and Sammy Davis, and by far this is probably the best entertainer of them all."

The second stop on the U.S. tour was New York. Michael performed at Madison Square Garden on March 3, 4, and 5th, with the first performance being a benefit concert for the United Negro College Fund (UNCF). On March 1, Michael appeared at a press conference to preview his new four part Pepsi commercial and to present a check to Christopher Edley, president of the United Negro College Fund, for $600,000, the proceeds from his first concert at Madison Square Garden. Michael, dressed in a red blazer with the familiar crest, spoke a total of eighteen words: "Thank you very much. I am very honored. I am very thankful. I love you all. Thank you."

Michael's benefit concert at Madison Square Garden, combined with his earlier donations, made him one of the UNCF's largest contributors. Michael's donations have been used to establish the Michael Jackson Scholarship Fund. In return for his very generous donation, Michael was honored by the UNCF at their forty-fourth anniversary dinner with their highest honor, The Frederick D. Patterson Award. Michael was also awarded with an honorary doctor of humane letters degree from Fisk University. The degree was presented by Henry Ponder, the president of Fisk University. Approximately 2,000 people attended, many of whom were Michael's guests; Frank Dileo, John Branca, Walter Yetnikoff, Elizabeth Taylor, Liza Minnelli, Yoko Ono, and Michael's parents. Whitney Houston performed at the award

"Man in the Mirror"

presentation, singing "Lift Ev'ry Voice and Sing" and "America the Beautiful". Diana Ross was invited but didn't attend. Long time friend and producer Quincy Jones did attend, and made a speech honoring his friend:

I would just like to say this tribute tonight is about growth as a human being, as a songwriter, as a singer, as a dancer, as a choreographer, as a mind, as a record producer, as a business magnate...and most important of all, as a humanitarian.

Michael was also congratulated by President Ronald Reagan via a taped message:

Michael, I'm sorry that Nancy and I could not be with you for this very special day, but I want to congratulate you for the honors you are receiving tonight from the United Negro College Fund and the honorary degree awarded you by Fisk University. Let me be the first to call you the new Dr. J.

Michael made an uncharacteristically lengthy speech, well at least longer than the usual, "Thank you. I'm very honored. I love you all."

I can't believe I'm nervous, but I really am embarrassed. I appreciate everybody coming... First, I do want to thank God, who makes everything possible. Then my dear mother and father who are in the audience, thank you for all you have done for me. I really appreciate it from the bottom of my heart.

I would like to say this about the United Negro College Fund. An education opens a person's mind to the entire world, and there is nothing more important than to make sure everyone has the opportunity for an education. To want to learn, to have the capacity to learn, and not to be able to, is a tragedy. I am honored to be associated with an evening that says this will never happen. Thank you. I love you all.

Just after receiving these honors from the UNCF, Showtime aired a special on Michael Jackson, *Motown on Showtime: Michael Jackson...The Legend Continues.* Motown's Suzanne dePasse served as executive producer on the special along with Michael Jackson. The program covered Michael's entire career, concentrating on his earlier years with Motown. Almost his entire performance from *Motown 25* is shown with Martin Scorsese calling it, "One of the best performance things I've ever seen." Hermes Pan, a choreographer who worked with Fred Astaire, added that he was dying to know how he did that walk!

In the spring of 1988, Michael finally moved out of the home in Encino. Janet had moved out of the family home some time before and LaToya had just moved to New York. Michael had purchased a 2800 acre ranch in Los Olivos, California from golf course tycoon William Bone. Neverland Valley Ranch is located at 5225 Figueroa Mountain Road in Los Olivos, California. The purchase price for his new home was reported as $28 million, though other sources said the price was closer to $17 million. On the grounds of the ranch, about 100 miles Northwest of Los Angeles, is a mansion, guest house, tennis courts, lakes, streams, thousands of oak trees, and plenty of room for his animals. To celebrate the purchase of his new home, Michael threw a spectacular house warming bash. He had several guests, his parents, however, were not among them. In fact, his father found out about his son's new home on the television news.

He then spent an additional $35 million remaking the grounds into his own private Disneyland. An amusement park, a miniature car race track, a railroad with a train station, a private zoo and elaborately manicured gardens were all added to the grounds. The train station was named Katherine Station, and one of the hills on the grounds was dubbed Mt. Katherine out of his respect and love for his mother. Neverland also has a fifty seat movie theater and two helicopter landing pads. At the peak of Neverland's development, the ranch had a staff of 150 employees and cost $10 million per year to maintain.

March ended with Michael picking up two Soul Train Music Awards out of three nominations. *Bad* was chosen as Best Album, Male, and the single "Bad" won as Best Single, Male. "The Way You Make Me Feel" was nominated for Best Video, but was beaten by Janet's video for "Control". Neither Michael or Janet attended the award presentation.

The next month, "Weird Al" Yankovic released his second parody of a Michael Jackson hit. His follow up to "Eat It" was "Fat", a parody of "Bad". It is included on Yankovic's album, *Even Worse,* the cover of which hilariously duplicates *Bad's* album cover.

In order to parody an artist's song, permission by that artist must be granted. Michael had a great sense of humor and not only granted Yankovic permission to parody his song, he also helped the film crew gain access to the "Bad" set for the "Fat" video. Michael enjoyed the "Fat" video so much he ordered twelve copies to give out to friends. Yankovic told one interviewer, "He doesn't have to let me do this kind of stuff. He doesn't need the additional royalties. The only reason he would let me is that he has a sense of humor. It is heartening to find somebody that popular, talented and powerful who can really take a joke." Weird Al was later one of the many celebrities doing cameo appearances in the video for "Liberian Girl".

The single, "Fat" and its accompanying video are hilarious. "Weird Al's" comical reworking of Michael's lyrics went like this:

Your butt is wide...well mine is too
Just watch your mouth...or I'll sit on you
The word is out...better treat me right
`Cause I'm the king...of cellulite
Ham on, ham on, ham on whole wheat...all right.

In the video for "Fat", "Weird Al" is dressed in a costume very similar to what Michael wears in "Bad", only about forty-two sizes bigger with him padded to look enormous. "Fat" didn't match the chart success of "Eat It", but the "Fat" video did receive heavy airplay on MTV.

On April 20, 1988, after four years in the works, Michael Jackson's autobiography was finally released. *Moonwalk* was published by Doubleday and was edited by Jacqueline Onassis. Bookstore displays, full size cut outs of Michael, featured a note in Michael's handwriting:

One of the reasons that I haven't given interviews over the years is because I've been saving what I have to say for my book. Love, Michael.

In *Moonwalk*, he discusses his childhood, his start with the

"Man in the Mirror"

Jackson Five, winning talent contests in Gary and eventually signing with Motown. He describes how very happy and proud he felt when *Thriller* became the biggest selling album in history and when he won a record breaking eight Grammy awards. He admits to having cosmetic surgery on his nose twice and having a cleft added to his chin. All other claims of his "extensive plastic surgery" he says, are untrue. He also denies the charges that he had his skin lighted either by a skin peel, acid or whatever new means have been dreamed of. Michael describes himself as being one of the loneliest people in the world. He wrote that he was unsure if he was happy being famous, he simply didn't know any other way.

The most poignant portions of *Moonwalk* deal with his strained, cold relationship with his father. He describes being beaten after messing up at after school rehearsals. Even years later, they rarely spoke to each other.

In a special television edition of *People Magazine*, Joe Jackson attempted to answer the things Michael stated about him in his book. He denied the beatings Michael said he received as a child, and refers to them as "little spankings". Marlon, who also appeared on the special, agreed with Michael, saying that they did get hit, and a lot. Marlon added, "My father is a person who loves to control your destiny. By him being your father, he feels he has the right to do that."

Despite criticisms that *Moonwalk* actually revealed very little about Michael, the autobiography, in true Jackson form, entered the *Los Angeles Times* Best Seller List and the *London Times* Best Seller List at number one. *Moonwalk* debuted on the *New York Times* Best

Seller List at number two, moving into the number one spot in its second week on the list. Within a few months, *Moonwalk* had sold over 450,000 copies in fourteen countries. MTV held a contest in which viewers could win autographed copies of the book.

Choreographer Jeffrey Daniels, who choreographed the "Bad" video with Michael, was reportedly disappointed that he wasn't mentioned in *Moonwalk*. Michael writes that he had been practicing the moonwalk for a long time before finally performing it for the first time in public on *Motown 25*. What he doesn't reveal is that Daniels is the one who originally showed him the step. Daniels claims he was the one who first showed him the step though others have also taken credit for it.

After the release of *Moonwalk* there were reports that Michael may write another book revealing more about his relationship with his father. It was said this second book would possibly be published after his father's death. That of course would never come to be.

LaToya, feeling more of the real story should be told sooner, released her own book in the fall of 1991 dealing with the Jackson clan, *LaToya: Growing Up in the Jackson Family*. The publication of LaToya's book coincided with her second photo layout for *Playboy*, appearing in the November, 1991, issue. LaToya's decision to pose nude for *Playboy* and the charges made in her book, which the other members of the family claimed were false, alienated her from the rest of the family. She no longer had phone conversations with her mother like she always used to, Jermaine spoke out publicly against her, and it was reported that Michael changed his phone number and refused to take any calls from his sister. She stated one of her reasons for posing for the magazine was to assert her independence. If these pictures did little to strengthen her independence, they would certainly put an end to the rumors that she and Michael were the same person! LaToya revealed years later in her book, *Starting Over* that these career decisions were made exclusively by Jack Gordon during a period of many years when she was under his total control, enduring years of physical and emotional abuse. She was forced into projects she disagreed with and found distasteful. Gordon died in April 2005.

There were other problems too. Two men from Gary, Indiana, Reynaud Jones and Robert Smith, who knew Michael in his childhood, and a third man from Chicago, Clifford Rubin, filed a $400 million lawsuit against Michael Jackson claiming that he and Lionel Richie had stolen "We are the World" from them. They claimed further that Michael had also stolen "Thriller" and "The Girl is Mine" from them. Quincy Jones was also named in the suit. After only three hours of deliberation a federal jury decided the songs, were the works of Rod Temperton, Michael Jackson and Lionel Richie.

For the MTV Video Music Awards, Michael had two nominations with both "Bad" and "The Way You Make me Feel" garnering nods for Best Choreography. The award went to Barry Lather for his work on Janet's video for "Pleasure Principle".

The MTV Video Vanguard Award is presented each year to an artist for career achievements in video. The 1987 recipient of the award, Peter Gabriel, presented the award to 1988's recipient, Michael Jackson. After a montage of clips from Michael's videos, the award was presented to Michael live via satellite from London, just before one of Michael's performances there. In presenting the award to Michael, Gabriel joked, "I sincerely hope this award will rescue this artist from obscurity and set him on the road to fame and fortune and it gives me great pleasure to give the Video Vanguard Award to Michael Jackson." In an extremely quiet voice, Michael accepted saying only, "Thank you. Thank you very much." The award was renamed the Michael Jackson Video Vanguard Award in 1991.

Following this lengthy acceptance speech, a special taped performance of "Bad" was shown. The performance featured Michael's new version of the moonwalk, gliding sideways instead of backwards. He also executed the original moonwalk, just as fascinating as ever

Seventeen years after the Jackson Five cartoon series first aired, Michael was a cartoon again. Michael lent his song, "Beat It" to be used in a Flintstone Kids cartoon special encouraging kids to say no to drugs. *The Flintstone Kids* aired in September, 1988. In it, little Fred, Barney, Wilma, and Betty work odd jobs to earn enough money for tickets to a Michael Jackstone concert. They finally make it to the concert and see Michael Jackstone singing new lyrics to "Beat It" about not needing drugs. In the cartoon, Stone Age Michael wears one glove and dons sunglasses. He moonwalks, and even grabs his crotch while dancing.

The November 19, 1988, issue of *Billboard* celebrated the 101st anniversary of CBS Records. Several congratulatory ads to CBS Records comprised the special section of the issue devoted to the record company. One ad carried a congratulatory message from the record company's biggest selling artist. A full page photo of Michael Jackson accompanies Michael's words:

The joy of music...

to inspire the young

and the old...

To make the world

a better place.

-Michael Jackson

Congratulations

The portion of the extensive article on CBS Records' history pertaining to the Epic label begins with these words:

*...any overview of the EPA labels must begin with this universally popular performer. It seems safe to predict that **Thriller's** 33 million worldwide sales record will not be topped in this century; indeed it seems the only artist capable of such a feat would be Michael Jackson himself.*

Within two weeks of the release of *Bad,* Michael hit the road with his first ever solo tour. If it didn't work out, he may of had an alternate career as a toy designer. Michael had presented an idea for a new toy to Matel, a transformer type toy that looked like an animal. Michael enjoyed his visit to the factory and enjoyed meeting the company's toy designers, "He was intrigued to meet the designers and see how they worked. It was total role reversal, they were stars in his eyes." They rejected his idea however. Oh well, maybe this touring business would pay off after all.

13

The way you make me feel
You really turn me on
You knock me off my feet
My lonely days are gone

"The Way You Make Me Feel"
- Michael Jackson

Helping to boost sales of the *Bad* album throughout the world was Michael's first ever solo tour. The Bad world tour kicked off shortly after the album's release, on September 12, 1987, in Japan. Nine concerts scheduled for Tokyo, Osaka and Yokohama sold out within hours. Due to the heavy demand, five more shows were added. With these fourteen shows, Michael played to a record breaking crowd of 450,000 fans.

"The Way You Make Me Feel"

With each stop on the Bad tour, Michael seemed to inherit a new nickname. In Japan, he was referred to as "Typhoon Michael". Australian fans dubbed him "Crocodile Jackson". In England, he became known as the "Earl of Whirl". The Europeans christened Michael "The Peter Pan of Pop". It wasn't all flattering, the London tabloid press, in exploiting his so-called eccentricities, called him "Wacko Jacko".

The performances on this first leg of the Japanese tour closely resembled the Victory concerts with some songs from *Bad* added. Songs performed in the Victory tour, "Things I Do For You", "Shake Your Body", "Lovely One", and "Off the Wall" were performed with "I Just Can't Stop Loving You" and "Bad". "Thriller" was also performed in the shows in Japan.

While his first solo concerts in Japan broke attendance records, stories about Michael ran rampant in the press. Rumors of his extensive plastic surgery, his "weird" relationship with Bubbles, and lingering wisecracks about his offer to purchase the remains of the elephant man were only a few of the wacky stories appearing in newspapers and tabloids. Michael responded by sending a letter to the press. He wrote the note in his hotel room at the Tokyo Capital. It later appeared in *People* magazine in Michael's handwriting complete with misspellings:

like the old Indian proverb says do not judge a man until you've walked 2 moons in his Moccosins. Most people don't know me, that is why they write such things in wich most is not true I cry very often because it hurts and I wory about the children all my children all over the world, I live for them.

If a man could say nothing against a character but what he can prove, history could not be written. Animals strike, not from malice, but because they want to live, it is the same with those who criticize, they desire our blood, not our pain. But still I must achieve I must seek truth in all things. I must endure for the power I was sent forth, for the world for the children. But have mercy for I've been bleeding a long time now. M.J.

This was an unexpected move on Michael's part, he rarely communicated with the media. On those isolated occasions when he did respond to the press, his statements were carefully prepared, unlike this one. He later spoke out against the "Wacko Jacko" nickname the tabloids loved to propagate. He told one interviewer the name hurt, "I'm not Jacko, I'm Jackson... I have a heart and I'm human."

After completing the month long tour of Japan, Michael donated approximately thirty personal items to an auction the proceeds of which went toward educating children in third world countries. Among the items Michael donated were sunglasses, T-shirts, and a windbreaker. He also gave $20,000 to the family of a young Japanese boy who had been recently kidnapped and killed.

The second stop on the Bad tour was Australia. In Brisbane, Australia, "Crocodile Jackson" was joined on stage by Stevie Wonder, who was also touring in Australia at the time. The Bad tour played to 120,000 Australian fans at five sold out shows.

Following Australia, the Bad tour finally hit the United States. For the U.S. and European dates, a whole new show was created. In

"The Way You Make Me Feel"

January, Michael attended a performance of Siegfried and Roy at the Frontier Hotel in Las Vegas. He met Siegfried and Roy after the show and spent the next day at their home where they worked on illusions to be included in Michael's new performances. In return, Michael wrote "Mind is the Magic", the theme song for Siegfried and Roy's performances at the Las Vegas Mirage Hotel.

Every detail of the show was Michael's concept. The staging, lighting, sound, costumes, illusions, choreography, everything was conceived by Michael. The staging and equipment was transported in twelve semi-trailers. He personally chose the band, dancers, singers, and crew members, choosing "the best and the brightest and the most fun." Technicians worked on developing special effects especially for the tour. Michael was interested in patenting these newly developed techniques to limit their use by others.

On February 23, 1988, Michael performed his first ever U.S. solo concert in Kansas City's Kemper Arena. The newly revised shows included more songs from the *Bad* album than did the shows in Japan. For the first few shows, there were surprise appearances by Tatiana Thumbtzen for "The Way You Make Me Feel". It was also a surprise for Tatiana, who was contacted by Michael's secretary only one week before the tour's opening. She was glad to be a part of the show, describing it as being like Christmas in February.

After the debut performance, a Kansas City Star arts and entertainment writer said Michael, "left the sold out house of about 17,000 spellbound with moves that weren't around until he invented them. When not dumbfounded the fans cheered and waved their arms in response to the Gifted One's world-class talent and showmanship."

The second stop on the U.S. tour was New York. The day following the Grammy's, where he also performed, Michael performed a benefit concert for the United Negro College Fund at Madison Square Garden. The reviews in New York echoed the sentiment in Kansas City. A New York Daily News critic's review read, "Michael's act has already gone well beyond a pop music concert. He uses music the way other performers from the Nicholas Brothers to Liza Minnelli have used it: his body is every bit as much an instrument as his voice." Another reviewer, from *Newsweek* magazine, declared, "...for sheer virtuosity as a contemporary songwriter and song and dance man, Michael has no peer. Even when he seems to have taken a bite from Bob Fosse or borrowed a gesture from Marcel Marceau, he makes it uniquely his own. The sight of him standing under a single spotlight, his fedora shoved down over his eyes as he slides into a moonwalk, has become as familiar an image in American popular culture as Charlie Chaplin's wobble. That's a rare kind of showmanship."

With the first U.S. dates, thirty in all, the Bad tour played to one half million fans. After a couple weeks off, the tour moved on to Europe. The European tour kicked off on May 23 in Rome, Italy. Michael played three concerts in Italy, two in Rome and one in Turin. Together, these dates drew 123,000 fans. These dates in Italy are the sources of two bootleg live albums that were being found in record stores in the States. Epic officials were furious to learn of the two unauthorized tapings. *Michael Jackson Live* purports to be a taping of a Bad concert in Italy on May 29, 1988. *My Way* is a taping of another concert on May 23, 1988.

The Bad tour attracted the largest audience ever for a European tour, playing forty three concerts in twelve countries to over three million people. The tour kept *Bad* at the top of the album charts in Europe and started a renewed surge of *Thriller* album sales. *Thriller* went back to the top ten albums in West Germany, six years after its release. While *Bad* was the number one album on *Billboard's* Pan European charts, *Thriller* wasn't far behind, ranking at number eleven.

By far the most successful of the European dates were those in London, England, at London's Wembley Stadium. Tickets for the July dates went on sale in January. Ticket demand exceeded 1.5 million, enough to fill Wembley's 72,000 seats twenty times! Michael ended up selling out seven nights at Wembley, shattering the previous record. Madonna, Bruce Springsteen, and Genesis had each sold out four nights. More shows would have been added, but Wembley had reached their quota of live performance licenses.

The third concert at Wembley Stadium, on July 16, was attended by Prince Charles and Princess Diana. Michael met with the Prince and Princess before the show where he gave them Bad tour jackets for Prince William and Prince Harry. He also presented them with a framed set of cassettes and compact discs of *Off the Wall, Thriller,* and *Bad.* Michael Jackson was said to be Princess Diana's favorite pop star. Michael was equally happy to meet her.

It had been reported earlier that Michael would not perform "Dirty Diana" that evening so as not to offend the Princess, a request made by Prince Charles. According to Taraborrelli, Diana then made a visit to Michael's dressing room prior to the show and told him, "I want you to sing that song like you have never sung it before". So, "Dirty Diana" remained in the set list. It was reported that she enjoyed the song and danced along. Michael later shared with Rabbi Shmuley Boteach that he would have liked to have dated Princess Diana following her divorce. He was much too shy to ask though. He said he had never asked a girl on a date, they have always done the asking. He added that each time he and Brooke Shields were seen out together, it was her idea.

With Pepsi, Michael made a $450,000 donation to the Princes' Trust, a charity for disadvantaged children. Michael also made a donation to the Wishing Well Fund, established to help finance the construction of a new building for London's Hospital for Sick Children. Michael toured the hospital and visited with some of the patients.

August was spent doing concerts in other cities throughout England. On his thirtieth birthday, Michael performed in Roundhay Park in Leeds. He told the crowd of 90,000 fans, "Thank you", after they sang "Happy Birthday" to him. The concert was a benefit performance for a British charity, Give for Life.

CBS hosted a lavish celebration for Michael at London's historic Guildhall building. The party, held at the time of his birthday, was also to celebrate the success of the *Bad* album and tour. Before the British concerts, *Bad* had sold nearly two million copies and was expected to return to the number one spot on the album charts. There were further predictions that *Bad* would possibly exceed *Thriller's* British sales of three million copies. This would be quite a feat since

"The Way You Make Me Feel"

Thriller had returned to the British album charts and was selling like hot cakes itself.

The final concert of the European tour took place in the hometown of the Beatles, in Liverpool, at the Aintree Racetrack. The site of this last concert held a special meaning for Michael, "I have always considered Liverpool the home of contemporary pop music by virtue of it being the birthplace of the incomparable Beatles. I intend my Liverpool performance to be a tribute to rock's four greatest songwriters." His concert attracted the largest audience ever by a single artist at the Aintree Racetrack. It was also the site of an unfortunate incident. Over 125,000 fans crammed into the raceway for the show. At the start of the performance the massive crowd pushed forward crushing fans against the stage. Over 3,400 people were injured, forty of which needed to be hospitalized.

The Bad tour played to over 800,000 people in England and grossed £13 million, making it the biggest tour ever in England. A special ad was placed in *Billboard* magazine by U.K. concert promoter Barry Clayman Concerts, Ltd. congratulating Michael on setting a world record on U.K. admission figures.

The most sold out shows at London's Wembley Stadium, total attendance of 504,000.
One sold out show at Cardiff Arma Park, 55,000.
One sold out show at Roundhay Park, Leeds, 90,000.
One sold out show of 60,000 at Milton Keynes Bowl and one sold out show of 125,000 at Aintree Liverpool.

Readers of *Blues & Soul* magazine, in the publication's annual reader's poll, named Michael Jackson as the 1988 Outstanding Artist of the Year. Michael was also given honors for Best Live Show for 1988. He also picked up honors from the NAACP, receiving the Image Award for Best Male Artist for "Bad" and for Best Album for *Bad*. The NAACP further honored Michael with the Leonard Carter Humanitarian Award.

Just before returning to the U.S., Frank Dileo held a press conference to announce that this was Michael Jackson's final tour. Dileo announced Michael would continue to record, but wanted to make films rather than tour. This announcement was met with a great deal of skepticism by the press, fans, and even Michael's family and friends. The press doubted Michael would retire from the stage permanently, pointing out that if he wanted to match his earlier record sales figures, he would need to tour with new albums. But for now, the tour headed back to the United States.

14

This magic music grooves me
That dirty rhythm fools me
The devil's gotten to me
Through this dance

"Blame it on the Boogie"
- Michael "Mick" Jackson, David Jackson, Elmar Krohn

Tickets for the second set of U.S. dates went on sale in June, four to six months in advance of the shows. As the first announced dates sold out in each city, more shows were added, having three concerts scheduled in most cities. The second leg of the U.S. tour kicked off with three shows in Frank Dileo's hometown, Pittsburg, Pennsylvania who honored Dileo by declaring September 22nd as "Frank Dileo Day".

Ticket sales for many acts touring in the summer of 1988 were lower than expected. The unusual heatwave being experienced in the U.S. was partially blamed for low ticket sales for acts playing outdoor venues. Another factor contributing to the disappointing concert crowds were the early sales of tickets by concert heavyweights Elton John and Michael Jackson. Music fans spent their concert budget on these early sales of tickets then couldn't afford to attend many, if any, other concerts. Luckily, they made excellent choices. Elton John's tour in support of *Reg Strikes Back* was among his best.

The return of the Bad tour to the U.S. included only eight cities. After Pittsburgh, it was on to East Rutherford, New Jersey, then dates were made up in Cleveland, Ohio. The Bad tour played in Largo, Maryland on October 13, and 17-19.

Then the Bad tour moved into Motown- Detroit, Michigan., with shows at the Palace of Auburn Hills on October 24-26. The first of the three night stand in Detroit was a benefit concert for Detroit's Motown Museum. The two story house, Hitsville USA, where Berry Gordy originally started Motown, had been declared a historical landmark earlier in the spring. Since Motown relocated to Los Angeles, the building had been turned into a museum, organized by Berry Gordy's sister, Esther Edwards. Michael told Edwards that he "would love to make the museum known all over the world."

The day before his first concert in Detroit, Michael Jackson presented a check for $125,000 to Esther Edwards and Berry Gordy in a ceremony held in front of Hitsville USA, the Motown Museum. Several blocks of West Grand Boulevard were closed to all traffic with

"Blame it on the Boogie"

mounted police lining the street. In spite of low temperatures, thousands of fans stood outside to catch a glimpse of Michael Jackson. Even though he wasn't scheduled to arrive until late afternoon, fans started gathering outside early in the morning. They waited. And waited. Then it started to rain and it got colder.

Huge speakers placed outside played Motown hits for the crowd, classics from Smokey Robinson, Stevie Wonder, and the Supremes. Conspicuously absent were any hits of Michael Jackson and the Jackson Five. Until 3:30 that is. At Michael's planned arrival time, Jackson Five and Michael Jackson solo hits with Motown were played back to back. The excitement continued to build as limos appeared and dropped off guests. Finally, over an hour late, a police escort made its way down West Grand Boulevard, going the wrong way down the one way street, leading two black limousines. Michael was barely visible to the crowd as he made his way up the steps surrounded by guards, one of whom held an umbrella over him. Michael was dressed in a red shirt and a black military jacket and sunglasses.

Detroit Mayor Coleman Young started off the presentation singing the praises of Berry Gordy and Michael Jackson. He then introduced Berry Gordy who spoke next. With each mention of Michael's name, a thunderous cheer rose from the crowd, "Michael Jackson knows that success in life is not merely confined to fame and fortune and material gains, but it's also found in a continual awareness our roots. These are Michael Jackson's roots, right here. You are the first people that bought Michael Jackson's records and he loves you, and he loves you for it." Gordy went on, calling Michael, "not only the biggest star to come out of Motown, but the biggest star to come out of any town!" He then introduced Michael. "I give you my pupil, my protégé, my son, even my big brother at times, and my friend all of the time, and I love him ...MICHAEL JACKSON !!!!!!"

Michael, who had been standing next to Berry, stepped to the podium, his first words were almost impossible to decipher due to the cheering of the fans, "I just want to briefly say I'm honored to be here, to give back to the soil from which I came. And Berry Gordy is the man who made it all possible for me. I'd like to say thank you Berry, and I love you."

In addition to the check for $125,000, Michael also donated to the museum a black fedora, a white beaded glove and the costume he wore in 1972 on *American Bandstand* when he performed "Ben". Michael's donation of money and memorabilia made up the largest contribution ever by one person to the museum.

Following the brief presentation, Michael, Berry, Esther and crew toured the museum. He was pleased with the museum's Michael Jackson room, the only room in the museum dedicated solely to one artist. A mirrored sign over the door read, "Michael Jackson - Magic". The walls were filled with photos and posters of Michael tracing his entire career. Two glass showcases hung side by side on one wall. One housed the costume Michael donated along with a platinum copy of the "Dancing Machine" single. The other housed a poster of Michael and a concert t-shirt from the Bad tour. One corner of the room was enclosed behind a full length glass door. Inside was Michael's sequined glove and black fedora. Michael Jackson and

"Blame it on the Boogie"

Jackson Five music play continuously.

After about an hour and a half visit, Michael and Berry headed for a dinner held at Gordy's Detroit mansion. About twenty- eight people attended, including museum staff and volunteers.

The next day Michael performed the first of three sold out shows at the Palace of Auburn Hills, in Auburn Hills, Michigan. The crowd waited restlessly until Michael hit the stage at 9:00. When the lights went down the crowd forgot their wait and looked forward to seeing the most dazzling performance ever. And that's exactly what they got.

A billboard sized bank of small lights, like a giant Lite Brite, flashes on showing the image of Michael's feet as they walk slowly across the screen, moonwalk back, go into a spin and freeze up on his toes, bringing deafening cheers from the fans. Slowly the bank of lights rises above the stage, revealing the band, singers, dancers and Michael all on stage, frozen in their poses. Michael is dressed in short black pants up to his ankles, a silver shirt with straps and buckles lining each sleeve, a black jacket with silver badges along the front. His hair is pulled back in a ponytail and his first, third, and fourth fingertips of his right hand are wrapped with white tape.

With a flip of a wrist from Michael they begin "Wanna Be Startin' Somethin'". Michael excites the audience with lots of fancy footwork and crotch grabbing. "Heartbreak Hotel" is highlighted with synchronized dance moves with Michael and his dancers, and pyrotechnics. It ends with Michael being circled with green laser light beams. Then it's dark. Out of the darkness Michael calls out to the audience, "How ya doin'? I said, how ya doin'?" To the thunderous approval of the crowd, "Another Part of Me" is performed by Michael alone, without the dancers. The pounding beat of the song emphasized with green laser lights shot rapidly at the stage and ricocheting off in different directions.

"Human Nature" is also performed without the dancers. Michael invites the audience to sing along, "Everybody sing! If they say why, why tell them that it's human nature, why, why does he do me that way?" At the end of "Human Nature" Michael displays some of his incredible moves, walking slowly in place. These steps are blended with mime movements. This is a small taste of the incredible moves yet to come, as the dancers return for the next song.

The stage is darkened and three white screens are lowered. Michael stands behind the center one, preparing for the next song. Someone hands him a white blazer. He takes a few seconds to adjust the white fedora he's also just been handed. He gets into position. He's ready. One dancer stands behind each of the other two screens, also with jackets and hats. Spotlights hit the three screens and their silhouettes move slowly from one pose to another. The three screens are raised and Michael runs to center stage for "Smooth Criminal" with much of the choreography taken from the song's video. At the end of "Smooth Criminal", Michael shoots his dancers with an air machine gun. The stage is dark except for a single spotlight on Michael. The four dancers, or criminals, fall to the ground to their death. Michael pushes his fedora down over his eyes and slowly walks across the stage and steps into a tiny white tent that just popped up on the corner of the

"Blame it on the Boogie"

stage.

He emerges a few seconds later having removed the jacket and hat. The stage is still dark and surrounded by tiny white lights resembling stars. Michael sings his first lines of "I Just Can't Stop Loving You" as a single spotlight hits him. A second spotlight hits Sheryl Crow as she steps forward on the opposite side of the stage to join Michael for the duet. Slowly they walk towards each other meeting in the middle of the stage. Michael draws wild cheers from the crowd as he reaches out and caresses Sheryl's thigh. They end the song abruptly with the line "And if I stop!" Sheryl leaves the stage to Michael. He shields his eyes, weeping, and begins "She's Out of My Life", bringing some of the night's loudest cheers. He finishes the last line, "She's out of my...", hesitating before the last word, weeping again. When he finally sings the last word, "...life", it brings the house down, leaving no doubt Michael Jackson was a well-studied showman who knew exactly how to get the biggest response from his audience.

For the first two performances in Auburn Hills, Michigan, Michael dedicated the next songs, "to a man who is in the audience tonight, Mr. Berry Gordy, who gave me my first big break in show business." The final show used the usual introduction, "Now we're gonna give you the old stuff the old fashioned way." Michael and his four dancers perform "I Want You Back" and the "Love You Save" with the same choreography the Jackson Five performed nearly twenty years earlier. "I'll Be There" completed the Jackson Five medley. Michael had the entire crowd waving their arms in the air. At the end of "I'll Be There", Michael again pauses before singing the last word.

In slow motion, he crouches down, putting his arm over his eyes. He raises up just as slowly and lets out the last word, "...there!" Again, it's a tremendous crowd pleaser, proving once again he can build excitement like no one else can.

"I THINK I WANNA ROCK!" kicks off "Rock With You". Michael displays even more of his fancy footwork while hitting each high note perfectly. After "Rock With You", he returns to the tiny tent which just popped up again. He emerges wearing a long flowing white shirt, white knee pads and long black fingerless gloves with rows of buckles, and he literally lets his hair down, the ponytail is now down. The familiar guitar sounds of "Dirty Diana" begin. Michael belts out the story of Diana with deep emotion, spinning and landing on his knees, (thus the knee pads). At the conclusion of "Dirty Diana", it's back to the tent.

Michael climbs out of the tent wearing a red and white varsity jacket and a werewolf mask. Eerie creaking sounds confirm "Thriller" is next. This is especially thrilling because it is the first tour in the U.S. in which "Thriller" has ever been performed, having been left out of the Victory tour performances due to the objections of the Jehovah Witnesses. He roams across the stage, becomes frightened, and runs back into the tent which explodes and immediately flattens. Instantly, Michael reappears on the opposite side of the stage and pulls off the mask. His dancers, all in zombie attire, join Michael in recreating the choreography from the song's video. Michael changes into a sequined version of the red jacket he wears in the video, the lights go out and the dancer's costumes and Michael's jacket light up.

"Blame it on the Boogie"

Michael changes into a white jumpsuit with several black belts, the rest of the cast are all in black for a grand production of "Working Day and Night". Everybody takes part in the dancing, all lining up across the stage with Michael in the middle. There are several stops where the entire cast instantly stops in position and freezes for a few seconds before starting right up again. At one point, everybody on stage is frozen in their positions. Michael walks among them, waving his hands in their faces and snapping his fingers. They don't even blink. The finish of "Working Day and Night" features a second illusion where Michael climbs a short set of stairs and stands on a small platform while a silver tube is lowered over him. The tube is slowly raised and Michael is gone. BOOM!!! There's an explosion on the opposite side of the stage and Michael appears now wearing black pants and a red sequined multi-zippered jacket.

Michael stands in the box of cherry picker. The huge crane slowly raises out of the floor of the stage and swings slowly out over the first few rows of the audience. Holding onto the railings on either side and hooking his toes on the bottom edge of the platform, he leans forward, out of the box, over the audience. Slowly the crane swings back to the stage. As Michael and his dancers perform "Beat It" the crowd goes wild seeing live the choreography they had seen dozens of times from the song's video.

With the stage darkened, Michael goes to the rear of the stage, where someone waits with another costume. He puts on a black jacket which is covered with sequins. And a black hat. And one white glove. He positions himself in front of the microphone stand, knees bent, one foot out, toes pointed. One hand is on the hat, the other on his crotch. A spotlight hits Michael in this pose that only means one thing: "Billie Jean". Michael recreates his magical performance from the *Motown 25* special. He flawlessly brings that performance back to life, saving most of his moonwalking for this song. The crowd is hysterical. Michael goes back to the microphone stand, retrieves his hat, and unleashes an incredible arsenal of moves. He sings the last line of the song, "Billie Jean is not my lover" and whips the fedora into the audience. A spotlight follows the hat into the audience and remains until it is grabbed up by one of a frenzied crowd. (One of the several semis used to carry the tour's equipment must have been completely stocked with black fedoras!) Michael stands alone on stage watching with everyone else to see who gets the hat.

The stage is then darkened as the huge Lite Brite is lowered again, spelling out one letter at a time, B- A- D. Then it flashes alternately, "BAD" "WHO'S BAD". The excited crowd calls out each word as it appears, "BAD" "WHO'S BAD" "BAD" "WHO'S BAD". The sign is slowly raised and Michael is center stage, wearing a black jacket with several buckles, and black fingerless gloves, also with several buckles. The entire crowd seems to know every word as they sing along, "Your butt is mine, gonna tell you right, just show your face in broad daylight..." For "Bad" Michael unveils his latest step, new sideways moonwalk just as he performed it on the MTV Video Music Awards.

At the end of the song, he introduces each singer, dancer, and band member. He takes singer Sheryl Crow's hand and leads her to the front of the stage and they all too briefly dance together- which is adorable. He leads her back and introduces the other singers, Kevin Dorsey, Dorian Holley and Darryl Phinnesse. He introduces each band member, Chris Curell and Rory Kaplan on keyboards, pausing at keyboards and singing, "Greg ... Phillinganes". They perform synchronized moves and Michael rubs the top of Greg's head and Greg pokes Michael in the belly. Michael giggles and moves on to the drums. The friendly teasing between Greg and Michael seems to be the only non-scripted few seconds of the entire show, until he does the exact same thing the next night, and the night after that, and the night after that... . Michael calls out "Rick, Rick, Rick" in between the beats of drummer Ricky Lawson. After introducing bass player Don Boyette he takes guitarist Jennifer Batten center stage for a brief solo and then guitarist Jon Clark. The dancers that accompanied Michael on the Bad tour are Randy Aelaire, Evaldo Garcia, Dominic Lucero, and LaVelle Smith.

Michael then brings out several children on stage. These children are usually chosen at each stop from local hospitals or charitable organizations, such as the Make-a-Wish Foundation. The children dance and Michael joins in, dancing just like them. He leads them off stage, waves to the crowd, and tells the crowd, "Goodnight, I love you."

After several minutes of screams, whistles, and "We want Michael" chants, out of the darkness Michael calls out, "You knock me off of my feet now baby!" Sheryl Crow takes Tatiana's place for "The Way You Make Me Feel". Michael, now dressed in a blue shirt over a t-shirt and a white belt tied around his waist, chases Sheryl around the stage before joining his dancers. They recreate the steps seen in the song's video, bringing wild cheers from the crowd as they all hit the deck, lay flat on their stomachs and get a little funky with the stage floor.

The stage is then left to Michael for the second encore, "Man in the Mirror". Each performance is just as passionate as his performance on the Grammys, spinning around and falling to his knees, this time he wears knee pads under his pants. The crowd sings along and seem to know every word. Michael finishes with his arms held out and his head back, eyes closed. He seems to be exhausted and genuinely emotional.

He brings out all of the singers, dancers and band members to the front of the stage to take a final bow. The band returns to their places and continues to play. Michael walks from side to side of the stage waving and saying goodnight. While the band still plays, he leaves the stage and exits the stadium, driving off before the house lights come on. Two hours have never flown by so quickly. Being familiar with the shows, I knew he was leaving the stage- and the building- while the band continued to play. I raced outside and got a broad smile and wave as Michael exited the premises. He was likely back in his hotel and in his jammies before the house lights came on.

Dates in Washington and California were cancelled due to swollen vocal cords. After a few weeks of rest and recuperation, the tour headed back to Japan, where it all started over one year earlier. Nine concerts were scheduled between December 9 and 26 in the

"Blame it on the Boogie"

Tokyo Dome. All 405,000 seats sold out months in advance. Michael returned to Japan to end his tour because, "I appreciate the support that my Japanese friends and fans have shown me." The 405,000 fans who attended Michael's second set of concerts in Japan, combined with the 450,000 who saw his first set of shows there, made Michael Jackson's 1987-1988 World Tour the largest tour ever in Japan. The total attendance of 855,000 fans was said to be four times greater than that of any other Japanese tour.

At one of these last concerts in Japan, Michael met backstage with two young fans and their parents. Nine year old Ayana Takada was the four millionth fan to attend the Bad tour. Michael met with her and her brother and presented her with a certificate to commemorate the now record breaking attendance figure. The Bad tour had played to the largest audience ever, four million people. At these final concerts in Japan, farewell concert T-shirts and hats were sold. But it was not really his farewell concert, he still had dates to make up in Los Angeles. So, it was back to the U.S. again.

January 27, 1989, was Michael Jackson's final performance of the Bad world tour. Los Angeles mayor Tom Bradley declared it "Michael Jackson Day" and presented Michael with the proclamation. Many of Michael's friends were there; Suzanne dePasse, Sophia Loren, Jane Fonda, and Smokey Robinson. Rebbie, Jackie, Jermaine, Janet and his mother, Katherine, were all there for Michael's final concert performance as were Elizabeth Taylor and Diana Ross and of course, Bubbles.

For this performance, Berry Gordy was again in the audience.

Michael dedicated the Motown medley to Gordy, and at the end of the show he told the audience, "Ladies and gentlemen, there is a man here tonight who helped my career. He is Berry Gordy. Stand up Berry!"

When the Bad tour finished in Los Angeles that night, after sixteen months, 123 performances in fifteen countries, it had played to 4.4 million people and grossed $125 million. This made the Bad tour the largest grossing tour in history and also the tour to play to the most people ever. Michael Jackson had just earned himself two more places in the *Guinness Book of World Records*. The Bad tour was the sixth largest grossing tour of the year in the United States. Playing in only nineteen U.S. cities, the tour grossed $20.3 million. BET presented Michael with an award in recognition of the tour's success while he was winding up the tour in Los Angeles.

Doubts still remained that this would actually be the end of live performances for Michael Jackson. These doubts seemed to be confirmed when Frank Dileo avoided stating that Michael would never perform live again, only that he wouldn't embark on a tour of such an enormous scale again. Although Michael set new standards in video and had given two of the best television performances ever, on *Motown 25* and the 1988 Grammys, nothing could match the magic and excitement of seeing him perform live. Only Michael's love of performing and love of his fans would bring him back. There were simply no other reasons for him to ever tour again; he hated most of the things that went along with touring, at the time he certainly didn't need the additional income, and there were no other records to top. He set out to put on the biggest, best tour ever, and he did just that.

15

*Ain't no mountain
That I can't climb, baby
All is goin' my way*

"Leave Me Alone"
- Michael Jackson

The seventh video from *Bad* premiered on MTV on January 2, 1989. "Leave Me Alone", a unique blend of live action and animation, combines an animated carnival setting with Michael cruising around in a small aircraft. A precursor of "Tabloid Junkie" and "Privacy", Michael confronts the press and the ridiculous stories that had been printed about him with special effects and humor. Tabloid newspapers land on a doorstep all having outrageous and humorous headlines:

MICHAEL'S SPACE AGE DIET

Michael Jackson: The Complete Story of the King of Pop

BUBBLES THE CHIMP BARES ALL ABOUT MICHAEL
MICHAEL AND DIANA SAME PERSON
JACKSON'S 3RD EYE STARTS SUNGLASS FAD
MICHAEL WEDS ALIEN

Michael delivers lyrics aimed at the media, "leave me alone, stop doggin' me around" while coasting by a proposed image of his "shrine" to Elizabeth Taylor, lying in his hyperbaric chamber, and dancing along side the skeleton of the elephant man. At the video's conclusion, Michael frees himself from ties binding his wrists where an amusement park is built around him. He stands up, a Gulliver sized figure, destroys a roller coaster and towers over the tiny carnival.

The "Leave Me Alone" video was included in the music video release, *Moonwalker*. After the usual delays incurred before the release of any new Michael Jackson product, the video cassette was finally released in the United States on January 10th. Gift certificates were issued in major record and video stores in mid December so Christmas sales wouldn't be lost. *Moonwalker* was released earlier in Europe with a theatrical release. It opened Christmas week in France and was the week's largest grossing film. It was released on cassette in Japan in early December and was sold at his last set of concerts there on the Bad tour.

In Japan, a music video was considered to be very successful if sales exceed 20,000 copies. *Moonwalker* was shipped out at 120,000 copies and sales were expected to reach 200,000. In the U.S., 300,000 copies were initially shipped, the largest first shipment ever for a home video. This made *Moonwalker* automatically the second most

"Leave Me Alone"

successful home video ever, behind *Making Michael Jackson's Thriller* which still held the number one spot. For now.

For the presentation of "Man in the Mirror" on *Moonwalker*, at least two different live performances are blended with scenes from the song's video. Michael's energy filled and emotional delivery of the song's inspirational lyrics demonstrate how touching the song's message was to him.

Brandon Adams, who also appears in "Smooth Criminal", portrays a miniature Michael Jackson for "Badder", a humorous version of "Bad" with a cast of children. Adams lip syncs to Michael's voice and does an excellent job of recreating his moves. One of the young dancers in "Badder" is Jermaine Jackson Jr. The WANTED poster ripped from the subway wall in "Badder" has Michael's picture on it reading, "Wanted For Questioning". This must make Michael the first artist to spoof his own video.

"Speed Demon" is a fun mix of claymation and live action with lots of fun MJ references ending in an amusing dance challenge between Michael and a claymation rabbit, Spike. The competition is ended when Michael is issued a citation for performing a prohibited dance step.

Next up on *Moonwalker* is the video for "Leave Me Alone" in which Michael tells the media just that, leave me alone. This is followed by the forty-two minute mini movie of "Smooth Criminal". Jerry Kramer produced the "Smooth Criminal" mini movie. Kramer worked with Michael before when he directed *Making Michael Jackson's Thriller*. In the mini movie Michael and his young friends stumble upon an evil plan to turn children into drug users, in an effort to gain control of the world. This is the scheme of the diabolical Frankie Lideo, a reference to Frank Dileo. Michael teams with his friends to foil Lideo's plan. Rick Baker, who transformed Michael into a werewolf in "Thriller" now transforms him into a robot for "Smooth Criminal". Michael destroys Lideo, and saves the world. The role of Lideo was played by Joe Pesci, but was originally written for a friend of Michael's, Marlon Brando.

"Smooth Criminal" leads directly to Michael's performance of the Beatles' classic "Come Together" where he is joined by his band from the Bad tour. Michael wears shiny black pants, a huge ornate gold belt and yellow shirt over a white t-shirt. During the performance, obviously made up of several takes, his t-shirt goes through various stages of being torn down the middle to his waist, and then back up again. He delivers the lyrics in a voice lower than usual with almost a raspy quality, in a performance that is nothing less than brilliant, sexy and too short.

The ninety-four minute video concludes with Ladysmith Black Mombazo performing "The Moon is Walking". The song was written especially for Michael after the group met him on the set of "Smooth Criminal". Michael enjoyed the song so much he included it on the *Moonwalker* video.

At least one feature Michael wanted to include on *Moonwalker* never made it. Michael was disappointed when he was refused permission to use footage of Fred Astaire from one of his movies. Michael had wanted to superimpose himself onto the film, creating the

"Leave Me Alone"

dance team of Astaire and Jackson. It is unfortunate it couldn't have been done, it would have been a great tribute to Fred Astaire and a thrill for Michael.

After *Moonwalker's* first two weeks in release, it was announced that in this very short time it had outsold the now former number one best selling music video of all time, *The Making of Michael Jackson's Thriller*. Michael Jackson now had the number one and number two best selling music video cassettes of all time. *Moonwalker* debuted on *Billboard's* top music video cassette chart at, where else, the number one position. It held the top spot for twenty-two weeks before being knocked out by the only one who could- Michael Jackson himself, with his latest release, *Michael Jackson: The Legend Continues*.

On *Billboard's* top video cassette sales chart – of all genres - *Moonwalker* took over the top spot in three weeks, outselling *ET: The Extra Terrestrial*. It was knocked out of number one by U2's *Rattle and Hum*. *Moonwalker* soon returned to number one on the sales chart and remained there until Michael again replaced himself on the list of best selling video cassettes. The week of June 17, 1989, *Moonwalker* slipped to number two on the chart, while the number one best selling video cassette in the U.S. was *Michael Jackson: The Legend Continues*.

Michael Jackson: The Legend Continues was released on video cassette in May. *The Legend Continues* is the retrospective of Michael Jackson's career that was broadcast in March, 1988, on Showtime. The video cassette was released earlier in England, where it became the best selling video cassette ever. *The Legend Continues* sold over 400,000 copies in Great Britain and U.S. sales were expected to at least match its British sales, giving Michael Jackson the top three best selling music video cassettes worldwide. The Video Software Dealer Association named *Moonwalker* as the Favorite Musical Video. *Moonwalker* earned further honors with an award nomination from the National Association of Recording Merchandisers.

Doubleday published three accompaniments to *Moonwalker*. A Michael Jackson Moonwalker calendar had been published earlier in the fall featuring photos from *Moonwalker* and from the Bad tour. The other two items were geared toward children, a Moonwalker coloring book and a storybook.

A press conference was held in Los Angeles in September, 1989, where LA Gear announced they had just singed a new multimillion dollar endorsement deal with Michael Jackson. Michael signed a two year deal to design and market a line of sport shoes and sportswear for the company. Michael worked with Randy Philips in making the deal. At the press conference, Michael wore, instead of the usual black loafers, a pair of black and silver LA Gear sneakers. As usual, Michael was very brief with his comments: "I am very happy to be part of the LA Gear magic and I hope we have a very rewarding, successful career. Thank you." The deal was said to be for double what Pepsi had paid him, the highest corporate association ever. The company's stock responded strongly, rising four points in the three days following the announcement.

The line of shoes and sportswear was scheduled to be in stores in summer 1990. Ads began airing in movie theaters in July, 1990, and the next month on television. Michael dances down a dark, deserted street when a street lamp suddenly explodes. As Michael shields his head from the flying glass, he hears the sole applause of a little girl watching him from her window. The young girl appearing in the ads is Brandi Jackson, Jackie's daughter. Brandi also appeared in the print ads for the shoes with Uncle Mike.

The MJ line of shoes featured Michael's Moonwalker logo on the tongues, soles, and on a tiny gold stud on the side. Three commercials were scheduled to be completed by December, 1991. An added bonus for the shoe company was that Michael Jackson actually did wear the shoes in the ads, unlike the Pepsi ads where Michael would not drink or hold the soda.

The LA Gear shoes and sportswear were scheduled to hit stores the same time as the new album. When the new album didn't happen, sales of the shoes failed to meet expectations. Despite reports that the shoe line bombed, LA Gear officials allowed that profits from Japanese sales alone would recoup their investment in Jackson.

Three years after signing the deal, LA Gear filed a $10 million lawsuit against Michael Jackson charging him with fraud and breach of contract. LA Gear claimed that as part of the contract, Michael was to deliver to LA Gear videos featuring him wearing the shoes. Failure to deliver any of these videos and failure to release an album to coincide with the newly available line of shoes were given as the grounds for the legal action. In November, 1992, Michael filed a $44 million countersuit against L.A. Gear.

The announcement of this deal with LA Gear was made

shortly before *Forbes* magazine compiled its annual list of the world's highest paid entertainers. Again Michael Jackson was ranked number one with a two year total income estimated at $125 million. The magazine estimated Michael Jackson's 1988 income to be $60 million with the remaining $65 million being earned in 1989.

In November, 1989, Michael joined with several other stars at the L. A. Shrine Auditorium in celebrating the 60th year in show business for Sammy Davis Jr. Jessie Jackson appeared on the program and spoke briefly about how Davis had helped to ease racial tensions and break down the walls separating the different races. This lead directly to Michael's performance. With no introduction, Michael stepped from the glare of several spotlights to perform, "You Were There", which he wrote with Buz Kohan especially for the occasion. Michael's touching lyrics brought tears to Sammy Davis Jr.:

Thanks to you, there's no door we all can't
walk through
I'm here because you were there

It was certainly one of the more stationery performances Michael has ever given. With very few of his customary moves, Michael stood relatively still behind the microphone stand delivering the song only a few feet away from Davis. Afterwards, Michael walked over to Sammy and hugged him warmly. His performance netted him an Emmy nomination. The special was awarded the Emmy for Outstanding Music Special.

The program aired in February, 1990, with all proceeds being donated to the United Negro College Fund. On May 16, 1990, Sammy

Davis Jr. died of throat cancer. At the funeral services, Frank Sinatra, Dean Martin, Bill Cosby and Michael Jackson were named as honorary pallbearers.

Just a month before Davis died, Ryan White was near death in an Indiana hospital. Among the thousands of callers and well-wishers was Michael Jackson. When Michael called, a speaker phone was taken to Ryan's bedside. Michael told Ryan he loved him and that God was with him. "Hang in there buddy and get better."

Following his visit to Washington DC to accept the Entertainer of the Decade Award, Michael planned to visit Ryan in the hospital. Ryan died before he got there. On Sunday, April 8, 1990, Ryan White lost his five year battle with AIDS. Michael arrived at Ryan's house early the next morning with Donald Trump. Ryan's mother, Jeanne, met Michael at the door of her home and broke down sobbing, "He really wanted to see you." "I know", Michael replied. He stayed through Wednesday, the day of the funeral. Michael comforted Jeanne at the funeral which was attended by several other celebrities including Elton John who had spent many hours at Ryan's bedside.

After the ceremony, Michael and Elton John joined Jeanne White in a final viewing of the body before the casket was closed. Ryan was buried in jeans and denim jacket with a watch Michael had given him.

The inscription on Ryan's six foot, eight inch headstone was written by Ryan's friends Elton John and Michael Jackson:

Turn me loose from your hands. Let me fly to distant lands. Fly away Sky Line Pigeon fly.

From all things you left so very far behind.
Love
Elton John

Gonna make a difference
Gonna make it right
Forever Friends
Michael Jackson

Later Michael paid $1,000 for a step inside a restored war monument, the Indiana Soldiers' and Sailors' Monument in Indianapolis to honor Ryan White. On the step is a bronze plaque inscribed with the words:

In honor of Ryan White,
His spirit lives on in us all
We miss you. Michael Jackson.

Earlier in the year, Michael had two nominations for the 1989 American Music Awards. He was nominated for Favorite Pop/Rock Male Vocalist and Favorite Soul/R&B Male Vocalist. George Michael won in both categories.

Michael Jackson did not go home empty handed however. He was honored for his ground breaking artistry and technology in video, and for the record breaking success of his *Bad* album and tour. *Cashbox* magazine awarded Michael the Video Pioneer Award in recognition of his excellence in video as captured in the *Triumph* video for "Can You Feel It", *Thriller*, and *Moonwalker*. The inscription on the Video Pioneer Award read:

"Leave Me Alone"

For his pioneering efforts in the field of music videos epitomized by `The Triumph', a pre 1980's breakthrough in concept and special effects, and `Thriller', an innovative combination of drama, music and dance. This Video Pioneer Award is given to Michael Jackson on the occasion of his new feature length film anthology, `Moonwalker' becoming the largest selling music home video of all time.

The second special award Michael received was an American Music Award of Achievement inscribed:

Because his album, `Bad', is the first ever to generate five number one singles, because it has been a number one best seller in a record breaking twenty five countries around the world, and because it has been the largest international seller in each of the last two years, the American Music Award of Achievement is presented to Michael Jackson on January 30, 1989.

Both of these special awards were presented to Michael by Eddie Murphy, at Michael's request. Before introducing Michael, Murphy narrated a tribute to Michael Jackson showcasing his international tour and recapping the *Bad* album's five number one hit singles. Walking shyly toward center stage to gather his awards, the audience greeted Michael with deafening applause and a standing ovation. Michael was dressed in black and red and lots and lots of buckles.

As the applause subsided and Michael began to speak, his soft voice could barely be heard over the microphone, which was on a very low stand. He had to bend over and speak directly into the mic to be heard. Holding his awards, he asked Eddie to adjust the mic stand for him, "Could you lift that up please?" Eddie tried to adjust it but it wouldn't budge. "You do it" Eddie told Michael. Michael replied, "I can't, I need your help." It became a joke when Eddie told the audience what was happening. (Their conversation was barely audible.) "He said, `Pull it up Eddie', like I was working for him! And I do it! Yes Michael!" So, bent over, Michael spoke briefly as always:

I'd like to thank God, who makes all things possible. I'd like to thank my mother and father, Katherine and Joseph Jackson. I'd like to thank Berry Gordy, who gave me my first professional start in show business, the Epic family, Walter Yetnikoff, Larry Stessel, Glen Brunman, Frank Dileo, Quincy Jones, and Bruce Swedien. I love you. And the public. Thank you.

While he was very shy, Michael appeared to be enjoying himself and seemed to be genuinely honored with the awards, the tribute and the overwhelming response from the audience.

The week of January 21, the cover of *TV Guide* featured photos of Elvis Presley, Bruce Springsteen, Madonna, and Michael Jackson. In the accompanying article, the authors searched for the greatest live television performances. They ruled out videos because they felt they don't show the true performer because they are able to re-shoot and use special effects to make everything perfect:

Nothing validates that decision as much as the case of Michael Jackson, who has poured untold time and money into video. Jackson is responsible for the genre's most elaborate and expensive works -- mirco-epics like `Thriller' and `Bad'. His `Moonwalker' cassette, *released last week, is the most ambitious, grandiose use of music video to date.*

Yet his most unforgettable moment on TV was only three minutes in the making and required no other props than a hat and a single glove. It was, of course, his performance of `Billie Jean' on the 1983 NBC special `Motown 25: Yesterday, Today, Forever.'

After singing a medley of old Jackson 5 hits with his brothers, Michael took the stage alone, donning a single gold-lame glove and an old fedora. As the pumping rhythm of `Billie Jean' took hold, he unleashed the inimitably bold whiplash dance style that has since become his trademark. Jackson took the stage that night an aging child prodigy. He left it an emerging superstar.

That was probably the flashiest TV performance ever. The most spirited? It's Jackson again. At last year's Grammy Awards ceremonies, he worked his way through a gospel-influenced rendition of `Man in the Mirror' like a man possessed. That performance, which drove the singer to his knees at several points, may have been the most passionate appearance ever televised.

In February, Michael was named Artist of the 80's at the World Music Awards, held in Monte Carlo. Michael did not attend the award presentation. His award was accepted for him by Barry White.

With the lengthy tour finished it would seem Michael would be content to stay at home on his new ranch venturing out only to pick up his latest award. But he did make a rare public appearance on February 7, 1989. He visited the Cleveland Elementary School in Stockton, California. A few weeks earlier, the school's playground was the scene of a massacre. A gunman shot and killed five children and wounded several others before killing himself. Michael visited two children who were still hospitalized and met with the other children at a nearby church. Michael Jackson's visit to the school helped spur the kids' emotional recovery. Some said Michael Jackson's visit finally made them feel safe again.

Then it was on to pick up more awards. Michael was again named the Best International Male Artist at the 1989 British Phonographic Industry Awards. Footage of the Bad tour was shown with scenes of Michael receiving the Excalibur Award in London at a very elaborate presentation. Michael stood on a small platform with Bill Bray, Frank Dileo and Jimmy Safechuck. A marching band played while a knight on a white horse pranced up to the platform and pulled a sword from a stone. He dismounted and presented the long golden sword to Michael. Michael saluted the knight and the band resumed playing, now switching songs. Michael, looking very serious up to this point, broke out in a big smile and laughed recognizing "Billie Jean".

Michael did not attend the "Brits", but he was shown live via satellite from California to accept the Best International Male Artist Award. He spoke briefly, "Thank you very much to all the fans in the United Kingdom. I look forward to seeing you again in the near future. The tour was a wonderful experience. I love you all. Thank you."

Michael won another "Brit" with his second nomination for Best Video for "Smooth Criminal". The award was accepted for Michael with thank yous given on behalf of Michael and Bubbles.

Just following these award presentations, on February 14, 1989, Michael's publicist, Lee Solters, made a shocking and unsuspected announcement on Michael's behalf. Michael Jackson and Frank Dileo were parting ways. Described as an amiable break, it took most people by total surprise. Frank Dileo and Michael Jackson had formed a close personal relationship as well as their professional relationship. Dileo was often described as Michael's sole confidant, a second father. In the statement read by Solters, Michael said only, "I thank Frank for his contribution on my behalf during the past several years." The media could only speculate as to the reasons for the abrupt split. Among the possible causes given was that Michael may have been disappointed that the sales of *Bad* didn't match *Thriller's,* not to mention his personal goal of 100 million copies.

Dileo's high profile media image was given as another possible cause for the abrupt split. While Michael was well aware of Dileo's manner before hiring him, he had become angered that Dileo continued to feed stories to the media about him. After giving stories to the tabloids about Michael sleeping in the hyperbaric chamber and bidding on the elephant man's skeleton, Dileo reportedly continued to create new stories about Michael for the press, much to Michael's chagrin. These stories, instead of keeping Michael in the public's mind as intended, served more to foster the conception that Michael was weird, feeding the image of him as "Wacko Jacko".

Speculation on the firing of Dileo included the notion that Michael was unhappy with the handling of his *Moonwalker* video cassette. The release of the video in January undoubtedly cost valuable

Christmas sales. Also, Michael had wanted *Moonwalker* to have a theatrical release in the U.S., as in Europe, before being released on video cassette. The blame for these blunders fell on the shoulders of Frank Dileo. Others claimed Dileo's dismissal was due to Michael's feeling that he took too much credit for his success.

Whatever the reason for the split, it was sad to see the long friendship end. At the time of the news, Frank Dileo was adding a room on to his new home in Ojai, California especially for Michael's visits. Their long term relationship was all ended with a cold phone call from Michael's lawyer. Frank threatened to sue Michael for breach of contract. They reached a settlement without going to court, the amount of which was estimated at $5 million. They did end up mending fences shortly thereafter and remained friends for decades with Dileo re-joining team MJ many years later.

In professional and personal relationships, Michael would abruptly drop someone from his life. Bob Jones, John Branca, and Frank Dileo would find this out personally. His friendship with Diana Ross and actor Corey Feldman and even Elizabeth Taylor at times have all been said to have been a roller coaster, with them being on the outs at several points.

Soon after firing Dileo, Michael hired Mike Ovitz, the head of Creative Artists Agency to look for a suitable movie script for him. Frank Dileo, however, was the first one to land a movie role. He signed to play a Mafia boss in *Goodfellas*. Having had worked with the film's director was undoubtedly an advantage in getting the role as well as being friends with the film's star, Joe Pesci. The movie was directed by Martin Scorsese, who was Dileo's choice to direct the "Bad" video. Dileo's second film role was a bit part in *Wayne's World* portraying a record producer. Dileo was later named co-president of Savage Records in New York while continuing to manage other musical acts.

For the thirty first annual Grammy Awards, Michael's sole nomination was for Record of Year for "Man in the Mirror". Given all of the hit singles he had released during the year it seemed Michael had been overlooked by the Grammys. However, because of the complicated rules of the Grammys, Record of the Year was the only category in which Michael was eligible.

The Grammy for Record of the Year goes to a record's producer and the performer. If chosen as Record of the Year, the Grammy for "Man in the Mirror" would go to Quincy Jones and Michael Jackson. Jones did attend the ceremony, Michael did not. Well, he did sort of. Michael watched the Grammy telecast on TV in his limo, parked behind the Los Angeles Shrine Auditorium. If "Man in the Mirror" won, Michael planned to go inside and accept the award. The award went to Bobby McFerrin for "Don't Worry, Be Happy". The Grammy for Best Concept Recording however went to "Weird Al" Yankovic for "Fat".

"Smooth Criminal" was chosen as the Favorite Music Video at the People's Choice Awards. Michael was nominated for Favorite Male Musical Performer which went to country singer Randy Travis. Michael did not attend the award presentation.

The third annual Soul Train Music Awards were presented in

April. As with the American Music Awards, Michael was again presented with two special honors. He was the third recipient of the Heritage Award for career achievement. The two earlier recipients were Gladys Knight and Stevie Wonder. Michael also received the first ever Sammy Davis Jr. Award for outstanding stage performance. The award is to be presented each year to the artist whose live performances have had the greatest impact on audiences during the year.

Eddie Murphy walked on stage joined by Elizabeth Taylor. She introduced a tribute to Michael consisting of video clips and concert footage. She then introduced Michael as "the true King of Pop, Rock and Soul, Mr. Michael Jackson".

Finally, Michael walked out on stage dressed in red, black, and buckles. He did not wear sunglasses, but he did have his latest two trademarks, taped fingertips and an armband. While he stood at the podium, waiting for the screaming crowd to quiet before speaking, Eddie Murphy adjusted the microphone for him, recalling the trouble Michael had had with the mic stand at the American Music Awards. Murphy continued the joke, brushing off imaginary lint from Michael's shoulders and holding a hand up the audience to quiet them so Michael could speak. Then Michael spoke, "Thank you. Thank you very much, Elizabeth Taylor." "Thank you Eddie Murphy." Michael then gave almost the exact same speech he had given at the American Music Awards, leaving one person out of his list of people to thank, Frank Dileo.

Michael had three nominations in addition to these special

honors and he took home two of them. After Michael was presented with the two special honors, the next award presented was for the Best R&B Urban Contemporary Single by a Male which went to "Man in the Mirror". Michael was still backstage when he was announced as the winner. Michael accepted the award saying, "Again, I say thank you. Thanks to God. Thank you Quincy Jones and Bruce Swedien and Siedah Garrett and everyone who worked on the project. I love you. Thank you."

The next award category, for Best R&B Urban Contemporary Song of the Year, for which "Man in the Mirror" was nominated, went to Anita Baker's "Giving You The Best That I Got". Michael's third nomination was for Best R&B Urban Contemporary Music Video, which went to "Man in the Mirror". Michael remembered the children from the Cleveland School he had visited a few weeks earlier:

Thank you again. I want to thank the entire public. I want to thank everybody who worked on these wonderful projects. I'd like to thank all the children at the Cleveland School in Stockton, California. I love them very much. And the public, thank you very much. I love you.

Michael was also being honored this same spring for his charitable and humanitarian efforts. In a ceremony held at the Universal Amphitheater in Universal City, California, Michael was presented with the Black Radio Exclusive Humanitarian Award. One of the presenters of the award was Tatiana Thumbtzen, his co-star from the "The Way You Make Me Feel" video. Further honors were bestowed on Michael on behalf of the "Say Yes to a Youngsters

Future" program. For his participation in the program, Michael received the National Urban Coalition Artist/Humanitarian of the Year Award. The program encourages kids to study math and science.

While 1989 started out with Michael winning more awards and setting more records, the *Rolling Stone* 1988 Readers Poll had very different results. Evidently the twenty million people who bought *Bad* and the record four million people who attended his concerts and spent $125 million on tour merchandise, didn't read *Rolling Stone*. They certainly didn't respond to the magazine's poll. The poll, which was based on the responses of only 24,289 readers, named Michael Jackson as the number one worst male singer, the most unwelcome comeback, and the worst dressed male singer. *Bad* placed fourth for both worst album and worst album cover. Two of Michael's videos made the worst video list, "Bad" placed at number three and "Smooth Criminal" placed at number five. Michael Jackson's tour was voted as the second worst tour of the year. *Us* magazine's reader poll had similar disappointing results. Michael Jackson was voted as the most unwelcome comeback, *Bad* was voted as the worst album, and "Bad" was named the second worst single.

The May 1989 issue of *Ebony* magazine featured the results of a readers poll also, "Who's Hot, Who's Not in 1989". It offered more favorable results. "Thriller" was voted by the magazine's readers as their favorite video of all time, with 37 percent of the vote. In second place, with 23 percent of the vote was Janet Jackson's video for "Control".

In late April, Michael was at work in Los Angeles filming the eighth video from the *Bad* album. "Liberian Girl" features model Beverly Johnson as the Liberian Girl and cameo appearances by forty other celebrities, including Bubbles who makes his second video appearance with his master. The "Liberian Girl" single and accompanying video were only released in England, but have since been included in various DVD collections. Michael has only a brief shot at the end of the video and one line, "Okay everybody, that's a wrap."

A new Jackson album was released on June 23, 1989, titled *2300 Jackson St.*, their former address in Gary, Indiana. The new album featured only four Jackson brothers, Jackie, Tito, Jermaine, and Randy. Marlon and especially Michael are conspicuously absent, except for the title song. The "2300 Jackson St." single reunites all of the Jackson brothers as well as Rebbie and Janet and several nieces and nephews. "2300 Jackson St." is a tribute to their parents and their roots, one of the best tracks on the album, which frankly isn't saying much.

While the "2300 Jackson St." single seemingly reunited the Jackson brothers for the first time in five years and marked the first time ever that their sisters joined the brothers on one of their records, actually most of their individual lines were recorded separately in several different studios with Michael recording his portion at the Encino home studio.

If recording the single didn't really reunite the family, filming the video did. The video was filmed at "Family Day", a special day when the whole family makes a point to get together. Joseph and Katherine appear briefly in the video along with several of their grandchildren. Each of the Jacksons were there except for LaToya and Marlon.

Included in the video are shots of the Jacksons tossing a football and gathering around a pool table with Michael evidently just winning some money off of Rebbie and being quite proud of it. A group shot of the whole clan has Katherine and Joseph each holding a grandchild on their laps. Janet also has a little one, and Jackie's daughter, Brandi, sits on Uncle Mike's lap.

The *2300 Jackson St.* album is a stronger effort by the brothers than their previous album, *Victory,* but that is not exactly high praise. Without their former lead singer, Jermaine takes over the lead on most of the songs, giving the album a much more consistent feel than *Victory.* The album's title song, "Nothin' (that Compares 2 U)" and "Maria" are among the best tracks on the album. In "Harley" there is an obvious reference to Michael. The song, describing a motorbike, includes the line, "She's bad, She's bad, bad" repeatedly. The album peaked at number fifty-nine on the Hot 100 album charts, the title track became a top ten R&B hit, peaking at number nine on the black chart.

A reunion tour was supposedly in the works to support the album, said to include *all* of the brothers plus Janet. This seemed doubtful at best. Janet had just released her follow up album to *Control, Janet Jackson's Rhythm Nation 1814,* and was at work planning her first solo tour. Michael had just come off of a tour that kept him on the road for sixteen months. He badly needed rest, his weight had reportedly dropped dramatically, something he could ill afford. Also, considering the problems, frustration, and public

"Leave Me Alone"

embarrassment of the last Jackson tour, it was an easy bet that Michael would not be touring with his brothers again, ever. They also wouldn't be recording together. With the completion of *2300 Jackson Street,* the Jackson's contract with Epic Records expired. It was not renewed.

A Jackson tour with the remaining brothers didn't seem probable either. Without Michael, demand for tickets would be next to nothing and the brothers were also working on solo projects at the time. The tour never did materialize.

Janet told *Rolling Stone* in an interview following the release of her *Rhythm Nation* album that her biggest inspiration for recording her first successful album, *Control,* was her brother Michael and his success with *Thriller*. She described Michael as her idol and model and said that they are the closet of all the Jackson children. Michael gave Janet, or "Dunk", a key on an earring, which became her trademark at the time. The key Michael gave Janet belonged to some animal cages on their Encino estate. A key is also her logo for her company, JDJ Entertainment.

In September, the MTV Video Music Awards were presented with Michael Jackson dominating the nominations with "Leave Me Alone" garnering six nominations and "Smooth Criminal" earning three. The outcome was disappointing with the only award for Michael's videos going to Jim Blashfield for Best Special Effects for his work on "Leave Me Alone". Michael did not attend the award presentation.

Around this same time, as part of the World Music Video Awards, Michael received the Lifetime Achievement Award for Video.

The award was presented to Michael at his home by Whitney Houston. After the presentation of the award, Michael gave Whitney Houston and the crew a horseback tour of his ranch.

In October, 1989, Michael paid a visit to his former elementary school, Gardner Elementary School, in Los Angeles where he attended sixth grade for a short time. The school's auditorium had been recently refurbished and was renamed the Michael Jackson Auditorium. Michael's former sixth grade teacher, Mrs. Gerstin, and Mrs. Rose Fine, his tutor when he was on the road with the Jackson Five, both attended the dedication. Epic official Larry Stessel, Bob Jones and Bill Bray accompanied Michael.

After several speeches by the school superintendent, PTA representatives and teachers, Michael's former sixth grade teacher introduced Michael and presented him with a plaque: "It's an honor to present this plaque to you on behalf of the parents and faculty, past and present, of Gardner School as a token of our respect and our love for you not only as a performer, but as a fine human being." Dressed in black pants and a red shirt covered with buckles and long black fingerless gloves, Michael accepted the honor and spoke briefly as always:

First of all I'd like to thank my teacher, Mrs. Gerstin, Mrs. Rose Fine, she's another one of my teachers, she's here also and I'd like to thank her. I am deeply touched and honored that the PTA, principal, faculty members and students have been so kind as to dedicate the auditorium where I sat as a child, in my honor. We must all never forget that the children are our future and without them mankind would become extinct. I thank Mrs. Gerstin, I love you, and Mrs. Rose Fine, I love you, the Gardner Street School associates, and all the children. I love you. Thank you.

Following the presentation of the plaque, a very happy student presented Michael with a key to the school. Michael then joined the student choir in singing "We are the World." A small crowd then moved outside as Michael unveiled the new letters on the face of the building identifying it as the Michael Jackson Auditorium. Michael was given a tour of his former school, he visited his old classroom and autographed the wall with a marker, "Michael Jackson Love the Children".

As the year and the decade came to a close, various media outlets prepared a look back at both the year and the closing decade. Michael Jackson would of course figure prominately in both.

16

Do you remember back in the spring
Every morning birds would sing
Do you remember those special times
They'll just go on and on in the back of my mind

"Remember the Time"
- Teddy Riley, Michael Jackson, Bernard Bell

As 1989 came to a close it was time for numerous TV programs and seemingly every magazine publication to begin compiling a look back at not only the past year, but at the closing decade. Not surprisingly, Michael Jackson dominated the various countdowns and charts compiled to reflect both the past twelve months and the last ten years.

On *Billboard's* year end charts for 1989 "Smooth Criminal"

placed at numbers ninety-three and fifty-eight on the year end pop and black singles charts respectively. Michael was ranked as the nineteenth Top Pop Male Singles Artist and as the eighty-third Top Pop Singles Artist. The Jacksons placed at numbers forty-nine and forty-one on the Top Black Artist and Top Black Singles Artist charts respectively. *2300 Jackson St.* was ranked at number sixty on the Top Black Album Chart for the year.

The December 23, 1989 issue of *Billboard* recapped both the past year and decade. Reviews of the decade in general and of the decade's pop and black music all began by focusing on the artist making the biggest impact of the eighties. An overview of "The Decade in Charts" began with mentioning the biggest selling album of the decade:

Michael Jackson was both the hottest and most immediately influential artist of the 80's. The Gloved One was far and away the top artist of 1983 in pop, black, and dance music, and also had the top album in all three formats, **Thriller**.

Thriller *was such a monster that it was also the no. 1 pop album of 1984. The Grammy winning collection was the first album to top the year-end chart two years running since the* **West Side Story** *soundtrack in the early 60's.*

The scope of Jackson's crossover potential was first suggested in 1980 when he was rated the year's top singles artist in both pop and black music. He was also that year's top black album artist, but was nosed out by Pink Floyd on the tally of top pop album acts.

Jackson's success confirmed once and for all the sales

potential of black music and opened the door for other black artists. And many follow his lead...

The recap of pop music in the 80's began:

Michael Jackson was the hottest pop artist of the 80's, though, Prince, Madonna, Whitney Houston, and George Michael gave him a run for his money in the second half of the decade...

Jackson was far and away the top pop artist of 1983 for both albums and singles. The only year-end pop title which eluded him in 1983 was the top single citation, which went to the Police's `Every Breath You Take'.

The publication's review of black music in the 80's also focused on Michael Jackson:

In addition to his dominance on the pop charts, Michael Jackson was the top star in black music in the 80's. Jackson was the no. 1 black music act for combined albums\singles three times, in 1980, 1983, and 1988. No other artist took that title more than once...

...Michael Jackson swept the 1980 recaps, emerging as the year's top black music artist in both albums and singles. His blockbuster **Off the Wall** *was an easy winner for top black music album. Jackson yielded just one award, top black music single, and that was to his brother, Jermaine, for `Let's Get Serious'.*

Jackson was a repeat winner in those same categories in 1983 with his mega hit, **Thriller***. Again he yielded just one award, top black music single, which went to Marvin Gaye for his landmark hit, `Sexual Healing'.*

Jackson also registered strongly in 1988, when in addition to

"Remember the Time"

his overall title he was named top singles artist...

Billboard polled its readers to find their favorite artists and recordings of the eighties, the results of which were published in the May 26, 1990, issue. Michael Jackson dominated the poll, placing eleven times in eight categories.

Rolling Stone likewise named *Thriller* the number one album of the 80's. The year-end issue of *Musician* magazine, dedicated to a review of the eighties, included a look at Michael Jackson's *Thriller* album, crediting *Thriller* for releasing "enough energy of one sort or another to create the rings around Triton". *People* magazine was not about to be left out in publishing an issue devoted to a look back on the decade. Their publication included Michael Jackson as one of the twenty people who helped define the decade.

Media stars of the decade were the focus of *Vanity Fair's* year end issue. Michael Jackson was chosen as the issue's cover photo. It was the first time Michael posed for a magazine since 1984. The striking picture, by Annie Leibovitz, has him perched up on his toes, in jeans and a white shirt, unbuttoned with his shirttails and long hair blowing back in an unseen wind. Tina Brown, then editor-in-chief of *Vanity Fair,* appeared on ABC's *Good Morning America* program to promote the issue and spoke with program host Charlie Gibson. Gibson questioned Brown's choice for the cover, describing Michael Jackson merely as "a guy who made one big album and a Pepsi commercial." Brown defended her choice replying that Gibson's remark was "a very slim claim for the biggest entertainer all time. We chose Michael Jackson because he is the premier entertainer of our time. He's the biggest. He's also in a funny way emblematic of the whole era of synergy because he does ads, a book, an album, MTV, all these things seem to us systematic of the 80's and as such he really does stand for the media explosion." Gibson then questioned her judgment, "You characterize him as the biggest entertainer of all time?" Brown again defended her point, "I think he is. In terms of the money he's made and the audiences he has commanded, absolutely yes. Number one."

In October, 1989, *Friday Night Videos* counted down their picks for the greatest artists of the decade. After showing videos by Prince, Whitney Houston, Madonna, Bruce Springsteen, George Michael, Phil Collins and Genesis, they announced their choice for the Number One Artist of the Decade: Michael Jackson. Clips of all of Michael's videos were shown. Another *Friday Night Videos* special edition aired in January, 1990, featuring the viewers' choices of their favorite videos of the decade. "Thriller" was voted as one of the viewers' favorites.

Entertainment Tonight named Michael Jackson as the Most Important Entertainer of the Decade and presented a short tribute to him including a montage of video clips and concert footage. The entertainment program had devoted a great deal of time following his Bad tour.

MTV's *Rate The 80's* revealed how viewers had voted in several phone in categories, including their choices for Best Movie, Video, and TV show of the 80's. Viewers phoned in their choices for one month. Michael Jackson had the most nominations with three.

"Remember the Time"

Michael placed fourth in the race for Mega Artist with 15% of the vote. *Thriller*, with 14% of the vote, placed third for Really Big Album. "Thriller" was chosen as the Greatest Video in the History of the World with 35% of the vote.

This award was presented to Michael when he made a surprise appearance on the *Arsenio Hall Show*. This was a dream come true for Hall who had earlier told an interviewer he hoped Michael Jackson would make an appearance on his show, even if it was a very brief appearance, just to say, "I don't do TV!" Hall's guest was Eddie Murphy. Murphy had been chosen by MTV viewers as the Humor God of the 80's. Michael made a special appearance on the show to surprise Murphy and present him with the award. Murphy then reciprocated by presenting Michael with the video award.

After the audience's deafening applause to Michael's unannounced appearance subsided, Michael spoke only briefly from behind his dark glasses: "Presented to the King of Comedy, of all time, the King." Eddie then presented Michael with his video award: "Viewers Award for Michael Jackson for the Greatest Video in the History of all Videos, `Thriller'". Michael smiled big and waved to the crowd before walking off the set.

USA Today's music critics chose "Leave Me Alone" as the number one Best Video of 1989. "Leave Me Alone" was further honored with a Teddy, an international and Canadian music award. Jim Blashfield won a Golden Lion Award at the Cannes film festival for his work on the special effects in "Leave Me Alone". The Golden Lion is the highest honor given in the category of commercials, short films, and videos.

American Top Forty with Casey Kassem counted down the Top 40 Dance Hits of the 80's as compiled by *Billboard* magazine. Michael dominated the countdown with four entries. "Wanna Be Startin' Somethin'" started the countdown, at number forty. Michael's remaining three entries were all in the top ten. "Bad" was ranked at number seven. The top three entries all belonged to Jacksons. "Beat It" placed at number three, just behind Janet's "Miss You Much". Sitting on the top of the heap as the decade's top dance hit was "Billie Jean".

MTV was busy at year end compiling video countdowns for the year and for the decade of nearly every imaginable configuration. Countdowns reflecting the Top 100 Videos of the Year, of the 80's, the Most Requested Videos Ever, Classic Videos, and Top Dance Videos to name just a few. The number one video of the 80's according to MTV was "Thriller". "Thriller" was ranked as the number one Classic Video too. Later MTV named "Thriller" as the number one Greatest Video of all Time, a list that would be revamped from time to time but would be consistently topped by Michael Jackson's "Thriller". A short time later "Thriller" was inducted into the Music Video Producers Hall of Fame.

In January, 1990, MTV announced its choice for MTV's Video Vanguard Artist of the Decade Award, Michael Jackson. The award was presented to Michael by VJ Adam Curry and MTV Network CEO, Tom Freston. Michael stood quietly during the presentation then of course made very brief remarks, "It's very beautiful. Thank you very

very much, MTV. It's wonderful. And to all the fans, thank you very much". The award presentation was followed by an evening of Michael Jackson specials and videos.

One thousand Artist of the Decade awards were produced by Platinum Limited Editions declaring Michael Jackson as the artist of the decade. The award includes a platinum album, a listing of Michael's record breaking achievements and a small metallic figure of Michael in a pose from "Smooth Criminal". Each is numbered and autographed by Michael. I have number 148.

On January 27, 1990, at the Beverly Hilton Hotel, The American Cinema Foundation awarded special honors to three entertainers. Elizabeth Taylor and Gregory Peck were honored for their career achievements in film. The Entertainer of the Decade honor was awarded to Michael Jackson. The award ceremony was a little late getting started, as Michael showed up two hours late. When he finally showed up, Sophia Loren presented Michael with his award, and he gave an incredibly long three minute speech. "I'm giving a long speech because I'm not on television." In fact, no cameras were allowed to film him. In his speech, Michael spoke of his deep affection for fellow honoree Elizabeth Taylor. Taylor had had similar praise for Michael in her own speech saying she was happy to be honored with "my beloved Michael, whom I would have loved and admired if I had never seen him dance or heard him sing."

The day before receiving this honor, Michael was again at the Beverly Hilton Hotel to help unveil a portrait that had been painted of himself. Brett Livingstone Strong painted the portrait, titled "The

Book", of Michael sitting in a chair holding a book on his lap. In the background is a statue of Peter Pan and another painting of Michael. The painting was sold to a Japanese businessman for $2.1 million, the largest sum ever paid for a portrait of a living person. It was subsequently acquired by Marty Abrams, as payment of a debt. Abrams listed the painting on eBay in 2010 for $2.75 million.

In February, Michael was honored at a breakfast press conference held at the Regent Beverly Wilshire Hotel by CBS Records. Michael received an award for being the label's biggest selling artist of the 80's, selling in excess of 110 million records. CBS Records' Tommy Mottola presented Michael with the award, a figure of Michael in a pose from the "Smooth Criminal" video against a large disk reading "100 Million". Mottola read a list of Michael's accomplishments and stated, "If I stood here ten years ago and told you any artist would accomplish what Michael Jackson accomplished, you would have probably laughed me off the stage." Michael attended the press conference dressed in his usual red and black:

Thank you Tommy, and thank you ladies and gentlemen. I'm sure it won't surprise you that I'm gonna make this one short again, but I have to say however, that no album sells itself. It's up to the people out there to buy it, and so I not only want to thank CBS Records and Epic Records, but I especially want to thank everyone everywhere who helped make this award what it is, first a possibility, and now a reality. Thank you Quincy Jones, thank you Dave Glew, thank you Bruce Swedien, John Branca, Mother and Joseph, Walter Yetnikoff and Hank Caldwell. And all of the children of the world. I love you. Goodbye.

On April 5, 1990 Michael was presented with the Entertainer of the Decade Award on behalf of the Capital Children's Museum. The award was presented by President Bush at the White House. Michael was dressed in red and black, black gloves and sunglasses. Mrs. Bush, who complimented him on his silver tipped boots, gave him a tour of the White House. He spoke with Vice President Quayle, autographed some Easter eggs for the annual White House Easter egg roll, and presented President Bush with a collection his compact discs. That evening, Michael was guest of honor at a museum fund raising reception.

The day before receiving the award, Michael visited the Children's Museum. He played with many of the exhibits and was uncharacteristically comfortable with the crowd around him, primarily because most were children. One year earlier, the Capital Children's Museum honored Michael with the Best of Washington Humanitarian Award for his fund raising efforts for the hands on educational museum.

Michael Jackson owned the 80's. He dominated any arena he chose to pursue. He topped *Billboard* charts for the decade and continued to do so for the next couple of decades; he commanded audiences for his live performances in numbers never seen before; he won more awards than any other artist in history and he single handedly transformed the music video industry. When deciding to do commercial endorsements, he commanded the highest fee ever paid and produced the most popular and successful ads.

For the 1990 Grammy Awards, Michael had two nominations.

"Leave Me Alone" won the Grammy for Best Short Form Video and *Janet Jackson's Rhythm Nation 1814* edged out *Moonwalker* for the Grammy for Best Long Form Video. Neither Janet nor Michael attended the award ceremony.

To celebrate their fiftieth anniversary BMI, Broadcast Music, Inc., an organization for songwriters, composers and music publishers, instituted a new award for career excellence, The BMI Michael Jackson Award. The award was presented to its first recipient on May 8, 1990, to appropriately enough, Michael Jackson. Michael accepted the award at the Regent Beverly Wilshire Hotel. Dressed in his customary red and black he was, as usual, brief in his remarks: "It is a pleasure to be associated with such a fine organization and I only hope to be celebrating BMI's widespread accomplishments five decades from now." He added, "I'm honored and happy to be in the room with so many people I admire. I love you very much."

A black and gold two page congratulatory ad was placed in *Billboard* and other publications to mark the special occasion. Over three hundred artists, songwriters and industry executives attended the award presentation.

On June 3, despite not having felt well for the past few days, Michael was home in Encino doing his regular Sunday dance exercises when he began suffering pains in his chest. He called his doctor, Steve Hoefflin, who drove him to the hospital. They arrived at St. John's Hospital and Health Center at 9:00 pm. His mother arrived shortly thereafter as did Jermaine who stayed the night with him. He was listed in stable condition and was confined to bed while tests were administered to determine the cause of the pains. Among the well wishers calling the hospital was President Bush.

It wasn't until three days later that the findings of the tests were announced. Michael was suffering from costochondritis, inflammation of the cartilage at the front of the rib cage, suspected to be caused from over exertion and stress. The inflammation takes weeks to heal and if treated early leaves no lasting effects. The battery of tests performed showed no problems with his heart or lungs. The stress he was suffering was thought to stem from big changes he was contemplating in the management of his career.

Eighteen months after he fired Frank Dileo, on August 21, 1990, it was announced Michael Jackson had hired a new manager, Sandy Gallin. At the time Gallin signed on as his new manager, Michael was in the process of, or at least rumored to be in the process of, making two other abrupt changes affecting his career. He was rumored to be organizing a new legal staff to replace John Branca. It was further rumored that Michael may be considering leaving CBS Records for David Geffen's Geffen Records.

Hiring Gallin fueled both rumors. David Geffen was said to be aiding Michael in organizing his new legal staff, made up Bert Fields, Lee Phillips, and Allen Grubman. Gallin also had ties with Geffen, making a possible switch from Epic to Geffen plausible. It was speculated that Geffen could have easily swayed Michael from CBS to Geffen Records but he still owed CBS four more albums, and the cost to buy his remaining contract from CBS would "have been greater than the gross national product of Uganda."

David Geffen's new association with Michael Jackson and his advising Michael in building a new managerial and legal staff was reported to help trigger the departure of Walter Yetnikoff from CBS Records. Geffen advised Michael that he could negotiate better deals with other lawyers than John Branca because Branca was close friends with Yetnikoff. Yetnikoff and Geffen clashed when Yetnikoff refused to allow Michael to contribute a song to the soundtrack album for *Days of Thunder,* which was released on Geffen Records. Later Yetnikoff revealed that Michael actually promised to lend a song to the soundtrack then regretted it. He asked Yetnikoff to play the bad guy and block Geffen from using any of Michael's songs. Yetnikoff further soured his relationship with Michael when he initially blocked Michael from contributing to *Listen Up! The Lives of Quincy Jones,* a documentary on, well, the life of Quincy Jones, because of a rivalry with Steve Ross, chairman of Time Warner. Ross' wife, Courtney, served as producer of the film. Michael later did contribute to the film, doing an off camera interview. The film was released in September, 1990.

On September 4, 1990, Walter Yetnikoff stepped down as CEO and president of CBS Records. His decision was said to be due to allegations against him mentioned in Fredric Dannen's book, *Hit Men*, and to his deteriorating relationship with the label's biggest selling artist, Michael Jackson.

Aside from managerial concerns, Michael was still busy picking up awards. The Los Angeles council of Boy Scouts of America was the next organization to create an award named for Michael. The Michael Jackson Good Scout Humanitarian Award was presented to Michael, in recognition of his humanitarian efforts for all mankind through his fund raising efforts for the Make-A-Wish Foundation, The Prince's Trust, the United Negro College Fund and Childhelp USA. Walt Disney Chairman Michael Eisner presented the award to Michael. Dressed in a gold and black military style jacket and sunglasses, Michael said only, "On behalf of the millions of past, present, and future Boy Scouts, I will try to abide by your motto of being prepared and always extending a hand to others."

My Family, The Jacksons, by Katherine Jackson and Robert Wiseman, was published in the United States in the fall of 1990. The book was previously only available in Japan. In the book Katherine reveals Joe's many infidelities including one, an affair with Cheryl Terrell, that produced his tenth child, Joh'Vonnie, born August 30, 1974. She also discusses filing, then later withdrawing, a request for divorce from Joseph. He was served with the papers, but refused to move out of the house. Besides her relationship with Joseph, there is very little insight in her book concerning her children, especially Michael.

Due out soon was a Moonwalker video game by Genesis/Sega. Michael aided in the game's design which is based on the Smooth Criminal story and he contributed three songs; "Beat It", "Bad", and "Smooth Criminal". The video game was introduced to video arcades and on game cartridges for use in home game systems.

Meanwhile, Michael had some long awaited projects due for release. Originally scheduled for release in November, 1989, his greatest hits package, *Decade* was now a year late. *Decade* was to be a double album of Michael's greatest hits with three to five new songs included, among them his cover of the Beatles' "Come Together". Slated for release simultaneously was a *Decade* video cassette. This project was later scrapped in favor of releasing a whole new album. Of course, before its release, there would be the usual delays. He was also renegotiating contract with Sony. This was gonna be big.

During 1991 Michael Jackson and Sony, the new owner of CBS Records, were involved in contract renegotiations. Some speculated that Sony's negotiating power was significantly reduced due to the souring relationship between Michael and Walter Yetnikoff. Yetnikoff's replacement, Tommy Mottola had little room for negotiating; Sony was eager to please Michael and keep him from leaving for another record company. Besides Sony's seemingly reduced negotiating power, Michael Jackson was considered one of the most powerful people in the entertainment industry.

Among the items Michael wanted included in the contract was to split expenses and profits 50/50 with Sony, and his own record label. CBS was one of the top bidders for the Motown Records Jobete Music catalog and some noted the company may have used its position as a possible buyer to entice Michael to re-sign.

Meanwhile, Janet Jackson left A&M Records in March and signed a new recording contract with Virgin Records. Her new deal was worth an estimated $40 to $50 million. It was the largest recording contract in history. At least it was for a couple of days. Then it was reported that Michael had finally resigned with Sony's Epic Records.

17

*If you're thinkin' 'bout my baby,
It doesn't matter if you're black or white*

"Black or White"
- Michael Jackson

Michael's new contract with Sony eclipsed Janet's by a country mile with some estimating the potential value at $1 billion. It was the first time a contract had been signed for record, TV and movie projects. The fifteen year contract provided for Michael to establish his own record label, deliver six albums to Epic, star in feature films, TV programs and produce a series of short films for his upcoming album, with Michael owning 70% of all video rights. Under the new contract, he received a $5 to $10 million advance on each album and a 25% royalty rate based on the album's sales. His record label would sign new and established acts and he received a salary of $1 million per year as its CEO. He was scheduled to begin work on his first movie project with Columbia Pictures, *Midknight* by the end of 1991. The movie never materialized. His new contract earned Michael another entry in the *Guinness Book of World Records.* The 1992 edition lists his deal with Sony as the largest contract ever at a more conservative estimate of $890 million.

In March, Michael accompanied Madonna to the 63rd Annual Academy Awards. They had been spotted dining out together earlier. Michael could be spotted seated next to Madonna in the front row. She was dressed in a strapless white sequined gown and boa, looking very Marilyn Monroe-ish. Michael coordinated with his date wearing a beautiful white jacket adorned with pearls, and two black gloves. Madonna was a scheduled performer, singing "Sooner or Later" from *Dick Tracy* the Oscar winner for Best Song. They were seen dining together again a couple of weeks later at another Los Angeles restaurant. They were rumored to be working together on a duet for Michael's upcoming album and possibly other projects as well.

When David Ruffin of the Temptations died of a drug overdose in June, it was revealed the former Motown singer was broke. Michael Jackson contacted Swanson Funeral Home in Detroit and made arrangements to pay the costs of his idol's funeral. He also sent a heart shaped floral arrangement to the New Bethel Baptist Church in Detroit with a note, "With Love, from Michael Jackson". He did not attend the funeral services for fear his presence would turn the proceedings into a circus.

"Black or White"

The Simpsons premiered its first episode of the fall season in September titled "Stark Raving Dad", featuring a huge white mental patient who was convinced he was Michael Jackson. Michael provided the voice for the character but it was credited to John Jay Smith. In the episode, Homer is institutionalized for wearing a pink shirt to work. His roommate is Leon Kompowsky, who thinks he's Michael Jackson. He was institutionalized for being upset that his *Off the Wall* album earned "only one lousy Grammy nomination." Michael sings a new version of "Ben", with the name Homer substituted for Ben. Michael later goes home with Homer where he helps Bart compose a birthday song for his sister Lisa. Michael reportedly wrote "Happy Birthday Lisa" and co-wrote "Do the Bartman" without any songwriting credit. Michael's speaking voice in the episode was his but a sound-a-like, Kipp Lennon, hand-picked by Michael, was used for the singing.

In October, 1991, a Michael Jackson fan visiting the Motown Museum in Detroit pried open the glass showcase in the Michael Jackson room and stole the sequined glove from the display. Museum officials asked that the glove be returned, and that no questions would be asked. They also attempted to contact Michael to try to get a replacement.

The glove was found two days later. Anonymous callers told police where the fan lived that stole the glove. Police went to the Flint home of Bruce Hayes who then took them to a friend's house in Grand Blanc where the glove was being kept in a video cassette box. It was returned to the museum and put back on display with a new security system to protect it. Hayes was charged with larceny inside a building and sentenced to two years probation and twenty hours of community service. I actually lived in Flint, Michigan at the time and was deluged by people asking if I was the one who took the glove! I did not know Mr. Hayes and unfortunately never got a chance to see the glove outside its museum glass showcase.

A similar glove was auctioned off by Christies in December. It was purchased by Robert Earl of the Hard Rock Café restaurants for $27,000. This set a record as the highest price ever paid for a piece of memorabilia. The record was short lived however. Six months later John Lennon's leather jacket sold for $43,100 at an auction in London. Later auctions of Jackson memorabilia would shatter these records.

Taking time out from finally finishing the new album, Michael played host to the eighth wedding ceremony of Elizabeth Taylor. Michael gave away the bride to Larry Fortensky on October 5, 1991 on the grounds of his Neverland Valley Ranch. A photo of the new couple and their host was featured on the next issue of *People* magazine. Michael's date for the event was once again Brooke Shields. Later Michael was one of the organizers of Elizabeth Taylor's sixtieth birthday party. Disneyland closed for the evening to host the bash. Michael loved to buy Elizabeth lavish jewelry as gifts and she once gave him an African elephant for a birthday gift. (I usually just sent him card, though I often thought of sending him a watch!)

The first week of November, only two years late, the first single from the new album began to be aired on radio stations in New York and Los Angeles. "Black or White" was officially released one week later. The new single set a record when it was initially released, being added to 96% of 237 of the nation's top forty radio stations the first day of release. The previous record, of 94%, was held by Madonna's "Like a Prayer". Like the recording of "Billie Jean", Michael mastered the vocals on "Black or White" on the very first take.

The single debuted on *Billboard's* Hot 100 at number thirty-five. It was estimated by the publication that the single would have debuted much higher had the new automated system of ranking singles, Soundscan, due to begin the following week, had been in effect. The second week on the charts, it shot up to number three. The following week, December 7, 1991, the number one single in the country was Michael Jackson's "Black or White". It is the fastest rising single since the Beatles' "Let It Be" rose to number two in two weeks in 1970. It was the first single to reach number one in just three weeks since the Beatles' "Get Back" in 1969. It ended the year at number one and stayed at the top of the singles chart into 1992, for a total of seven weeks, making Michael Jackson the first artist to earn number one pop hits in the 70's, 80's, and 90's. It was also a number one hit on the black chart, now dubbed the R&B chart. "Black or White" reached number one in the U.S., Great Britain., Australia, Italy, Spain, Mexico, Sweden, Denmark, Norway, Switzerland, Finland, Israel, New Zealand, and the Euro Chart Hot 100. The single went platinum in the U.S., selling over one million copies.

Michael had made a deal with Fox giving the network exclusive right to premier each video, or short film as Michael preferred to call them, released from *Dangerous*. On November 14, 1991, the video for "Black or White" premiered simultaneously on Fox,

BET, and MTV. Coinciding with this television debut, *TV Guide* featured Michael on its cover the week of November 2 and *Rolling Stone* featured Michael Jackson on its January 9, 1992 cover. BET, The Black Entertainment Network, aired a Michael Jackson special, *Armed and Dangerous*, featuring the video's premiere. MTV declared it "Michael Jackson Week" and aired Jackson videos and specials the entire week leading to the video's planetary debut, which they played twice, back to back. The next weekend was Michael Jackson Weekend on MTV.

  The music network began referring to Michael as "The King of Pop" in their ads for the video premiere. Some reports said this was due to Michael's request and was one of the stipulations for being allowed to air the video. Elizabeth Taylor was often credited for crowning him as the King of Pop, though Bob Jones claimed he came up with the title and urged Taylor to use it in her remarks. References to him as the "self-proclaimed" King of Pop are bothersome. Though he did enjoy it and encouraged its use in reference to him, he always maintained he had not dubbed himself with the title. Regardless, it fits perfectly. In my own dealings with Jackson, I was encouraged to use the title in my second book. Use of the new pop royalty title in my first book was completely my choosing. In publication of the second volume, I was encouraged by Bob Jones to also use the moniker in its title, *Michael Jackson: His Darkest Hour* then became *Michael Jackson: The King of Pop's Darkest Hour*. I was in no way forced to use the title and their support of the book was not contingent upon its use. This book also denotes his pop music title as he will forever be known as The King of Pop.

The video was seen in twenty-seven countries by an estimated 500 million people, the largest audience ever for a music video. Approximately 14 million people watched the video in the United States. It was the first video to be shown on German national TV news. To say the video caused a stir would be an understatement. Michael sings and dances with different races from around the world. Using what was then a relatively new technology, people of different races and sexes morphed into each other. Using the same process, a black panther is transformed into Michael who then dances without musical accompaniment, reportedly doing his interpretation of the animalistic behavior of the panther. Michael smashes the windows out of a parked car and throws the steering wheel through a store window. Dancing on the roof of the car he not merely grabs at, but caresses, himself and zips up his fly, lighting up switchboards at Fox like a Christmas tree. Due to the many complaints that the second half of the video was too sexually explicit and too violent, Michael decided to edit out the last four minutes of the video from further broadcasts and issued a statement:

It upsets me to think that `Black or White' could influence any child or adult to destructive behavior, either sexual or violent. I've always tried to be a good role model and therefore have made these changes to avoid any possibility of adversely affecting any individual's behavior. I deeply regret any pain or hurt that the final segment of `Black or White' has caused children, their parents or other viewers.

It was the edited version of "Black or White" that was

broadcast the following Sunday on MTV and Fox in the Michael Jackson special, *Dangerous*. The thirty minute special featured clips covering Michael's career then concluded with the new edited video which features Macaulay Culkin. In the rap segment of the video Michael is surrounded by a group of children made up of Culkin, and Dave Shelton and Mark Pugh, members of Another Bad Creation, and Wade Robson, a friend of Michael's. The little girl on the steps looks like Brandi Jackson is working with Uncle Mike again.

Controversy over the video hit virtually every newspaper, news program and morning radio show. Speculation rose over if Michael had lost his mind or if it was all carefully orchestrated. The controversy certainly didn't seem to hurt promotion of the album. People who otherwise wouldn't have known that Michael Jackson had a new album and video, couldn't take their eyes off of it. Michael Jackson or Sony couldn't have bought better, or more widespread, advertising. This coverage topped the thirty second commercials for the album directed by David Lynch that began airing in November. None of this hurt sales of the single either, in fact it probably spurred sales. The single debuted at number ten on the Top 40 Radio Monitor chart, the highest debut ever for this chart compiled by monitoring a national sample of 125 top forty radio stations twenty-four hours a day. The video also received the heaviest airplay of any other video to date on MTV. Because of the overwhelming response to the video, the "Black or White" video was chosen by *TV Guide* at the end of the year as one of the 12 Most Mesmerizing TV Moments from the last twelve months. Promotion of the *Dangerous* album had gotten off with a bang.

18

It ain't too much stuff
It ain't too much
It ain't too much for me to
Jam

"Jam"
-Michael Jackson

Michael Jackson's long anticipated album was finally released on November 26, 1991. Record store owners and record industry executives hoped Michael Jackson's new release would revitalize the slumping record sales of the music industry. While this is a lot to place on one pair of shoulders, Michael had done it before in 1983 and 1984 with *Thriller*.

Jermaine also had high hopes for *Dangerous*. He hoped

Michael Jackson: The Complete Story of the King of Pop

Michael's new release would boost sales of his own new album, *You Said*, anticipating fans of Michael's would pick up his album as well. This was not very likely. Jermaine's new single wasn't going to convince hard core Michael fans to buy his new album. Jermaine's single, "Word to the Badd", was a put down of Michael, criticizing him for losing touch with reality because of his superstar status:

> *Once you were made*
> *You changed your shade*
> *Was your color wrong?*
> *Could not turn back*
> *It's a known fact*
> *You were too far gone*
>
> *Reconstructed*
> *Been abducted*
> *Don't know who you are*
> *Think they love you*
> *They don't know you*
> *Lonely superstar*

While this version was released as a single, a cleaned up version appears on the album:

> *Once you were made*
> *You changed your ways ...*

Jermaine's hopes that his album sales would be helped by the release of *Dangerous* were soon dashed. *You Said* quickly peaked at number sixty on the R&B album chart, and it never made a showing on the pop chart. Jermaine tied to defend the song in his book *You Are Not Alone* explaining that the offensive version of the song was never supposed to be released and he was mortified when it was. He was venting his anger that his calls to his brother were going unanswered. Michael was hurt and angry. The song was actually written by L.A Reid and Babyface, producers Jermaine was intending to work with on his new album. That is, according to Jermaine, until they were hijacked by Michael. Michael retained the famed producers to record tracks for his album, but then never included any of their songs on the finished product. The upset culminated in a showdown at Hayvenhurst. Both Michael and Jermaine were summoned by Katherine to meet and settle their differences. Jermaine apologized for the release of the song and expressed his anger that he hadn't been able to reach Michael. Michael explained he never received any messages that Jermaine had called and promised to be more accessible to his family.

Reviews of *Dangerous* were generally favorable. *Us* and *People* each gave the album a favorable review and *Rolling Stone* gave the album four and one half stars, a rating between excellent and a classic. *Billboard* also gave *Dangerous* a glowing review, "...artistically, it's one of Jackson's finest efforts."

A few reviewers slammed *Dangerous* for being too commercial, containing material that was in their opinion shallow and bland but what would probably be successful commercially. Michael was blamed repeatedly for catering to mass appeal, putting his true artistic feelings on the back burner to ensure a commercially successful album. Others claimed if it didn't sell like *Thriller*, Michael's career would be considered as being in decline. So, as far as a few critics were concerned, Michael was doomed in their eyes regardless of how well the album sold, if *Dangerous* sold like *Thriller* and *Bad*, he was purposely being too commercial, if *Dangerous* sold "only" a few million, his career would be considered to be in trouble.

Actually the tracks on *Dangerous* cover a variety of different styles, all of which Michael has no problem mastering. Catchy tunes like "Black or White", "Remember the Time", "In the Closet", "She Drives Me Wild" and "Who Is It" show he is indeed the King of Pop. "Jam" and "Give in to Me" have a more hard rock sound with "Jam" featuring a rap segment. Rap is also incorporated into "Black or White", "She Drives Me Wild" and "Dangerous". A "Man in the Mirror" type gospel influenced sound delivers "Will You Be There" and the even better "Keep the Faith". The lyrics of "Gone Too Soon", dedicated to Ryan White, are a bit sappy but the song is a perfect showcase for Michael's smooth, beautiful voice. "Why You Wanna Trip On Me" is a sequel to "Leave Me Alone", sharing the same sentiment, why are people so concerned with his face, skin color, or supposed eccentricities? Interestingly, "Trip" was not written by Michael, but was penned by Teddy Riley and Bernard Bell.

One tradition Michael did keep was in featuring a well known rock guitarist on the album. Eddie Van Halen was featured on "Beat It" from the *Thriller* album and Steve Stevens played on "Dirty Diana" from the *Bad* album. Playing on "Black or White" and "Give in to Me" on *Dangerous* is Guns and Roses guitarist, Slash.

It was the first album with Sony not to be produced by Quincy

Jones. Teddy Riley co-wrote and co-produced seven of the fourteen tracks on *Dangerous* with Michael. Bill Boutrell who wrote and performed the rap lyrics on "Black or White", co-wrote and co-produced three songs. Glen Ballard and Siedah Garrett, writers of "Man in the Mirror" wrote "Keep the Faith" with Michael. Michael's own compositions include "Will You Be There" and "Heal the World", a continuation of the "We are the World" theme. Quincy Jones was not left out though. Riley and Boutrell were recommended to Michael by Quincy Jones. Also, according to Joseph Vogel's *Man in the Music- the Creative Life and Work of Michael Jackson*, before releasing the finished product Michael asked for Q's opinion. Jones declared it "a masterpiece".

The album was released on the usual formats with a special collectors CD which opens with 3-D diorama of figures from the album cover. The cover art for *Dangerous* was done by Mark Ryden with some obvious input from Michael. It features only Michael's eyes with the rest of the cover containing many images of animals, skeletons and statues with many references to Michael.

CBS Records initially shipped out four million copies of *Dangerous,* a new record. *Dangerous* is the first album to achieve advance orders of 50,000 units in the formerly Communist part of Germany. A spokesman for France's Virgin megastore said *Dangerous* was the quickest selling album the store has ever handled. It actually became his fastest selling album ever, topping 4 million copies in its first two months.

The cost to produce *Dangerous* probably also set new records, with an estimated cost of over $10 million. The expense seemed to all pay off when *Dangerous* debuted on *Billboard's* top album chart at number one. *Dangerous* also debuted at number one on the British album charts, the first album to do so on the strength of just three days of sales; it surpassed U2's new release, *Achtung Baby*.

The day following the release of *Dangerous*, Michael performed his new single on a TV special celebrating the tenth anniversary of MTV. The hour long special featured some of the biggest names in pop and rock music; Aerosmith, George Michael, REM, and a spoken tribute, of sorts, by Madonna. Each artist performed one song, except one. The special concluded with Michael Jackson performing two songs from his brand new album. Slash joined Michael for "Black or White". Michael's performance was energetic and fun, and he noticeably keep his hands off his crotch in the wake of the turmoil over the video. At the end of the song Slash tossed his guitar through the front windshield of a car that was parked on stage which then exploded. When the pyrotechnics were being tested Michael was careful to stand back saying, "I'm gonna get back, I was burned before by this kind of stuff."

A gospel choir joined Michael for "Will You Be There", with an angel, performed by Angela Ice, flying down to Michael and putting her arms, or wings, around him symbolizing hope. Vincent Patterson choreographed the performance which was filmed in an airplane hanger in Los Angeles, with Michael Jackson fan club members being invited to attend the filming and make up the audience.

When "Black or White" finally gave up the top spot on the

singles chart, the second single from *Dangerous*, "Remember the Time", was released, dedicated to an important lady in his life, Diana Ross. "Remember the Time" peaked at number three on the Hot 100 and spent two weeks at number one on the R&B singles chart. The short film for the second single debuted, just as "Black or White" had, simultaneously on Fox, BET and MTV on February 2nd.

The video had an Egyptian theme with Eddie Murphy as Pharaoh Ramses and model Iman as Queen Nefertiti and an appearance by Magic Johnson and it included an on screen kiss between Michael and Iman. The "Remember the Time" short film was directed by John Singleton, director of *Boyz 'N the Hood.* Singleton's next project was another movie, *Poetic Justice*, starring Janet Jackson.

To return the favor of appearing in his video, Michael sang on Eddie Murphy's then upcoming album, *Love's Alright.* He contributed background vocals on "Whatzupwitu" and joined many others providing backing vocals on "Yeah".

The album went on to sell 40 million copies worldwide and claimed the title of the best selling new jack swing album ever. Both *Bad* and *Dangerous* were remarkably successful. Had they not been released under the foreboding shadow cast by *Thriller*, they would have been celebrated more for their success. Sadly their success was somewhat overlooked when inevitable comparisons were made to their impossible to match predecessor.

Confirming rumors that had been circulating since before the release of *Dangerous,* Michael held a press conference on February 3 in New York's Radio City Music Hall to announce his plans for a new world tour. Michael Jackson and Pepsi would be teaming up for the third time for sponsorship of the tour and a new set of Pepsi ads. The tour, to start in June, was announced to cover four continents, with no U.S. dates scheduled. Michael announced at the press conference that he was touring to raise money for his Heal the World Foundation, a charity he created for children:

The only reason I am going on tour is to raise funds for the newly formed Heal the World, an international children's charity that I am spearheading to assist children and the ecology. My goal is to gross $100 million by Christmas, 1993.

Heal the World contributed to the Pediatric AIDS Foundation, "in honor of my friend Ryan White", Camp Ronald McDonald, the Make-A-Wish Foundation, Juvenile Diabetes and the Minority AIDS Foundation. The St. Thomas Boys Choir sang Michael's song, "Heal the World" and it touched Michael much the same way as the children's version of "We are the World"; "When I composed the song, it was my dream to hear it performed the way they just performed it, with such innocence and beauty. It took everything to keep me from crying".

The Heal the World Foundation stepped up during the LA riots to provide a mentorship program, immunizations and drug treatment programs for children. His foundation was also responsible for tons of relief supplies being airlifted to war torn Sarajevo.

Pepsi's new deal with Michael was the largest sponsorship deal ever between a corporation and a music entertainer. The first of the new ads, titled "Dreams" debuted in over 150 countries throughout the world, excluding the United States, in late July coinciding with the opening of the summer Olympic games in Barcelona, Spain.

In February, 1992, Michael left for a two week visit to Africa. The trip had been postponed from a year earlier due to the start of Operation Desert Storm. He was in Africa to visit Gabon, the Ivory Coast, Tanzania, Kenya and Libreville and was reportedly interested in making a film, "Return to Africa" for his own video library. The Ivory Coast crowned Michael King of the Sanwi in an elaborate ceremony and in Gabon, he received the Medal of Honor from Gabon's President Omar Bongo. Michael Jackson is the first entertainer to receive this honor, it is usually reserved for heads of state and dignitaries.

One of the members of Michael's twenty-six person entourage that traveled with him was *Ebony* and *Jet* magazine publisher Robert E. Johnson. Michael gave *Ebony* an interview for their May, 1992 issue and which focused on his trip to Africa and the *Dangerous* album. The issue's cover photo was of Michael wearing his crown he received when he was crowned King of the Sanwi. At the conclusion of the interview, which took only one page to print, Michael said, "You know, that's the most I've said in eight years...You know I don't give interviews. That's because I know you, and I trust you. You're the only one I trust to give interviews to."

Premiering once again simultaneously on Fox, BET, and MTV, was the third short film from *Dangerous* on April 23. Herb Ritts directed the short film, he had also directed Madonna's "Cherish" video and Janet Jackson's "Love Will Never Do Without You." The song was initially intended as a duet with Madonna, but reportedly there was a disagreement about the lyrics and Madonna dropped out. The female voice on the record was credited to "mystery girl" but was later revealed to be Princess Stephanie of Monaco. Michael's co-star in the short film is model Naomi Campbell. The song concerns a relationship in which the woman wants to stop hiding their love while the man wants to keep the relationship a secret, keeping it "in the closet". The gold band Michael sports might explain why he wished to keep this love "in the closet", but it is on the wrong hand.

Naomi Campbell admitted to being a little nervous when she first met Michael. Things obviously became much more comfortable on the set for her quickly. Knowing Michael is a prankster, she hid a squirt gun under her very short skirt and planned a surprise attack. On the last day of shooting on the video, a whipped cream fight broke out.

"In the Closet" was certainly Michael's most sensuous video to date, with a courtship dance that has Naomi and Michael caressing themselves and each other while Michael sings, "There's something about you baby that makes me want to give it to you." It proved to be too sexy for some. A Fox affiliated television station in Syracuse, New York refused to air the film feeling it did not fit in with the family viewing time. The video was later banned by the government in South Africa because it was "of a very sensual nature which could offend viewers."

"In the Closet" premiered the next day on *Friday Night Videos* during yet another show devoted entirely to Michael Jackson. A TV special *Live and Dangerous* featured several songs performed live from the Bad tour along with footage of his trip to Africa and a look behind the scenes of "In the Closet". The sexy single peaked at number six on

Billboard's top pop singles chart and was the third consecutive number one hit from *Dangerous* on the R&B singles chart.

Coinciding with the filming of the "In the Closet" video was the culmination of a MTV contest where winners of a "Dinner with Michael" contest got to bring a guest to a dinner party with Michael Jackson on the set of his latest video. The winners of the contest were chosen over several weeks from 4.1 million callers to MTV during the network's *Most Wanted* program. "Dinner with Michael" had the largest response ever of any MTV contest.

On May 1, 1992, President Bush presented Michael Jackson with an award acknowledging him as "a point of light ambassador". The award was in recognition of Michael's efforts in inviting disadvantaged children to his ranch. Michael Jackson, the only entertainer of the twenty-one recipients, said, "I wanted to come to lunch because I believe each person can make a difference in the life of someone in need. That is what a point of light is. I'm very, very happy to be here. I love you all. Thank you very much." Michael received two honors in February from the Pro-Set LA Music Awards. Michael was named Best Male Pop Vocalist and "Black or White" was named Video of the Year.

The fourth single from *Dangerous* was released in June with a remix of "Rock with You" as the B-side. The short film debuted on Fox, BET and MTV on June 19, and like all the videos before it, featured special appearances by some famous faces. For "Jam" Michael Jackson squares off against Chicago Bull champion Michael Jordan on the basketball court, and then on the dance floor. After a quick game of one on one with Jordan on the court, it is Jordan's turn to be humiliated as Jackson shows him a few of his own tricky moves, including how to moonwalk. The video also has cameo appearances by rap duo Kris Kross and Heavy D, who performs the rap portion of the song as he does on the album.

"Jam" stalled at number twenty-six on the pop charts, giving Michael his lowest charting single since "Walk Right Now" from the Jackson's *Triumph* album more than ten years earlier. "Jam" did seem to find a bigger audience on the R&B charts, becoming his fourth consecutive top ten hit from the *Dangerous* album, peaking at number three.

At the time "Jam" was released in the United States, "Who Is It" was released in Europe. "Who Is It" was also featured in his Pepsi commercials that were shown only in Europe. "Who Is It" is included on the *Dangerous Short Films* collection with a dapper MJ not doing a bit of dancing, or even singing. He is depicted as in great despair over the realization that his girl is deceiving him.

Operation One to One honored Michael Jackson in June with an award in recognition of his efforts in support of economically disadvantaged youth. The award was presented to Michael by the *Cosby Show's* Raven Symone in New York. Much of Michael's focus at this time was on his desire to make a difference and heal the world.

19

Heal the world, make it a better place
For you and for me and the entire human race

"Heal the World"
- Michael Jackson

The next project due for Michael was a new book, *Dancing the Dream,* which hit book stores in June, 1992. It was published by Doubleday, who also published *Moonwalk.* The introduction was written by Elizabeth Taylor. It is dedicated to Katherine Jackson, "Dedicated to Mother with love." Again, there is no mention of his father.

Dancing the Dream was said to be filled with one hundred previously unpublished photographs with twenty poems and essays penned by Michael. Actually some of the photographs and poems had been published before. The poems and reflections included in the volume concentrate mostly on, not surprisingly, children, animals and the environment. Poems dealing with finding a sea gull feather coated with oil, seals wondering if they will be clubbed by hunters, and elephants refusing to lie down and die giving up their tusks for man's trinkets illustrate the extent to which Michael was concerned with how man has treated animals. In "Mother Earth" he reflects on how man has mistreated the earth, "We've been treating Mother Earth the way some people treat a rental apartment. Just trash it and move on."

In "Ryan White" Michael writes of missing his friend and of how he suffered because of people's ignorance about his disease:

Ryan White, symbol of agony and pain

Of ignorant fear gone insane...

"Mother" is written for his own mother, to whom he has always been deeply devoted:

No matter where I go from here

You're in my heart, my mother dear

Children and the environment were also the main focus of Michael's new Heal the World Foundation which received all of the proceeds from the Dangerous tour. Heal the World focused on aiding children suffering from hunger, disease and abuse. Michael's goal was to raise $100 million from the tour for the foundation. This made the second time a tour was undertaken with all proceeds being donated to charity. Although he loved performing, his real passion may have been far away from the stage – helping the sick and suffering of the world and the Earth itself. He held a genuine compassion for others. He

"Heal the World"

consistently used his recordings and concerts and even award acceptance speeches to bring awareness to the need to heal the planet.

Just a few days before the kickoff of the tour, Slash joined Michael Jackson in Germany to film a video for an upcoming single, "Give in to Me". It is a performance video similar to "Dirty Diana". The songs share an aggressive sexual flavor except Diana is the aggressor in "Dirty Diana", and if taken literally, Michael is the aggressor in "Give in to Me":

> *Don't try to understand me*
> *Just simply do the things I say*
> *Love is a feeling*
> *Give it when I want it*
> *'Cause I'm on fire*
> *Quench my desire*

In July, it was announced in *Billboard* that the Second Annual Music Video Producers Association added "Beat It" and "Billie Jean" to their Hall of Fame. Later, Sony presented Michael with yet another special award in September, this one commemorating his four albums with sales of over ten million copies each.

Michael received an honor of a different nature from psychologist Dr. Wayne Dyer. Dr. Dyer dedicated his book, *Real Magic* to Michael Jackson. Dr. Dyer, who had spent several days at Michael's ranch, felt Michael deserved the honor because of his commitment to world peace and helping children. He said he admired Michael Jackson for standing up to a lifetime of pressure from the tabloid press.

Premiering during the MTV Video Music Award telecast was a public service announcement made by Michael Jackson as part of the network's Choose or Lose campaign designed to encourage young adults to register to vote. Dressed in his gold and black concert costume, with large mirrored sunglasses, he encouraged others to help make a difference. "We live in a country where we have a chance to make a difference. To create a better way of life for ourselves and for our children. The future is now. Let's come together and express our freedom of choice. Choose or lose."

Though Michael's performance of "Black or White" shown on the MTV Music Video Awards was a treat for fans to see a bit of his Dangerous concerts, the whole tamale was later broadcast on HBO on October 10, 1992. Hyped as the only chance for U.S. fans to see Michael in concert, the show was heavily promoted. The broadcast of the concert earned the highest audience on any cable network and won a Cable Ace Award. The concert was aired in sixty-one countries around the world.

Every detail of the show was nothing short of mesmerizing. His stage entrance was no exception. Smoke machines hid the stage behind a curtain of smoke and as fireworks suddenly exploded, Michael was shot up in the air from beneath the stage amid the sparks and smoke. He landed on stage dressed in black pants and silver beaded military jacket with gold bands criss-crossing his chest. He had an arm brace on his right wrist and three fingertips taped up on his right hand. He struck a pose with his fists clenched at his sides. There he stood, absolutely motionless for almost two minutes, as the crowd went wild. The crowd was whipped into a frenzy and he literally hadn't moved a muscle yet. He slowly removed his mirrored aviator sunglasses, tossed them aside and began to "Jam", and he didn't stop jamming for two hours.

"Wanna Be Startin' Somethin'" followed "Jam" with "Human Nature" coming next. "Human Nature" is best appreciated when seeing Michael perform the song live. A costume change into a white pinstripe jacket and white fedora signaled "Smooth Criminal" was up next. Michael and his four back up dancers perform the choreography now associated with the song from its video, including the gravity defying lean. The dancers each fell to their death from imaginary machine gun fire and Michael slowly walked off stage, stepping over their bodies which were then dragged off stage.

Siedah Garrett toured with the Dangerous tour and she and Michael performed their duet, "I Just Can't Stop Loving You", also better when seeing a live performance than listening to the recording. Siedah's sudden disappearance at the end of the song sets up the always great "She's Out of My Life" with a lucky girl being plucked from the audience for a much envied embrace.

"Now we're going to give you the old stuff the old fashioned way" introduced the Jackson 5 medley of hits, "I Want You Back", "The Love You Save" and ending with "I'll Be There". The old hits are presented "the old fashioned way" with the memorable choreography from his early days of performing with his brothers on Ed Sullivan Show and other TV appearances. Vocalist Darryl

Phillinessee sang Jermaine's lines in "I'll Be There". At the end Michael mentioned each of his brothers, "Jackie, Marlon, Tito, Jermaine and Randy and I love you all."

The dancers, now in zombie makeup and wardrobe, joined him for perhaps the best known dance routine ever for "Thriller". At the close of "Thriller", Michael is put in a coffin, it is covered with a cloth and when the cloth is whipped away, the casket and Michael disappeared. He reappeared seconds later on another part of the stage now dressed in what can only be described as his "Billie Jean" outfit. He worked his magic with that black hat and white glove. Plenty of moonwalking, spinning and freezing up on his toes, it was the awe inspiring spectacle it always was.

"Working Day and Night" came with another costume change to blue pants and a gold military jacket and concluded with another illusion. He disappeared only to reappear seconds later on the opposite side of the stage. A cherry picker on the opposite side of the stage begins rising out of the stage with Michael in full view, now dressed in black pants and red zippered jacket to the familiar beats of "Beat It". A fan blows his hair and what looks like a shredded Hefty bag around his shoulders. Both "Beat It" and later, "Earth Song" are typically started out with Michael taking a ride in the cherry picker over the heads of the audience members.

He exchanges the "Beat It' jacket for an oversized white shirt for "Will You Be There". An angel appears overhead, is lowered to the stage and embraces Michael in her wings at the songs' end. For just a few of the shows on the tour, "The Way You Make Me Feel" is next.

"Heal the World"

This number was for some reason eliminated from the set list after the first eight shows then was added back for the Japan concerts. "Bad" was also only performed for the first eight performances of the tour.

"Dangerous" is next with Michael and his dancers in black suits, white shirts and black ties, looking very gangster/Smooth Criminal-esque. A few lines and moves from "Smooth Criminal" are even thrown into the routine that will be performed on various TV shows in the U.S.

He literally lets his hair down for "Black or White'. Something about this number dictated that his hair not be pulled back in his customary ponytail. Groups of young children join him on stage for "Heal the World" surrounding an inflatable globe rising from the center of the stage.

The shows ended with a rousing rendition of "Man in the Mirror". His gospel influenced delivery, reminiscent of his 1988 Grammy performance, has him crashing to his knees at several points. For the grand finale, he dons a white space suit and helmet, a jet pack and takes off from the stage flying over the heads of the audience. This stunt involved a clever switch-a-roo, where Michael, after donning the space suit and helmet, changes places with a stunt man. The substitute Michael Jackson then jet packs off from the stage over the audience.

The Dangerous tour never did come to the U.S., playing dates in Europe, Asia, South America and Mexico. In total the tour played to 3.5 million people with sixty-seven shows. The show was created by Michael Jackson and Kenny Ortega, and was staged and directed by

Kenny Ortega. The musical director for the Dangerous tour was Greg Phillinganes. The rest of the band was made up of Ricky Lawson on drums, Don Boyette on bass, Jennifer Batten on guitar; rhythm guitar with David Williams and Brad Buxer on keyboards. Background vocals were handled by Kevin Dorsey, Siedah Garrett, Dorian Holley, and Daryl Phinnesse. Dancers for the Dangerous tour were Randy Allaire, Michelle Berube, Eddie Garcia, Jamie King, LaVelle Smith, Taco Falcon and Yoko Sumida. Jamie King would later be chosen as director of the Michael Jackson IMMORTAL World Tour. David Copperfield created the illusions. A huge fan of magic, Michael often incorporated illusions in his live shows.

"The Jacksons: An American Dream" aired in November, 1992. The five-hour long mini-series follows their lives through the Victory tour and superstardom for Michael with Pittsburg being substituted for Gary, Indiana. In early 1992, a nationwide search began for twenty-six youngsters to portray the Jacksons at three different ages. There were reports at this time that Michael suggested one actor to portray him in the movie; he could sing and dance, and was white. This story was later said to be false. Jermaine Jr. portrays his father as a young teen, and three actors, Jason Weaver, Alex Burrall and Wylie Draper portray Michael at various ages with each actor being approved by Michael. Lawrence Hilton Jacobs, Sweathog Freddie Washington of *Welcome Back Kotter,* was cast as Joseph Jackson, and Katherine Jackson was played by Angela Bassett. Holly Robinson was cast as Diana Ross and Berry Gordy was played by Billie Dee Williams. Vanessa Williams, who bears some resemblance to Motown executive

"Heal the World"

Suzanne de Passe, plays de Passe in the movie.

While it wasn't the total whitewash of the Jackson family story that one might have expected, it did gloss over some areas and completely ignore others. It did depict Joe's strictness with the children though statements made by certain family members indicate he was actually much more abusive. Very little mention was made of Joe's infidelity, showing Katherine discovering just one instance. The legal action that ensued after the Jacksons left Motown and signed with CBS Records was never mentioned. Also omitted is the controversy caused by the Victory tour planning and how vehemently Michael did not want to be a part of it.

Despite the conspicuous omissions, (Michael's *Off the Wall* album is never mentioned), "The Jacksons: An American Dream" was a surprisingly frank re-telling of the Jackson family story. Jackson 5 talent shows and later TV appearances were nearly perfectly re-created, duplicating the costumes, and especially Michael's moves and gestures. Wylie Draper did an exceptional job in re-creating Michael's unforgettable moves from the *Motown 25* performance of "Billie Jean", though the lip syncing needed work.

"The Jacksons: An American Dream" was the top rated show of the week and helped ABC win the all important November sweeps rating period for the first time in eleven years. The miniseries was watched by one third of all TV viewers, approximately 22 million households tuned in for the conclusion of the two-part movie.

A soundtrack album was released by Motown to coincide with the mini-series, *The Jacksons: An American Dream*. The soundtrack wasn't as successful as the movie, peaking at number 137 on the pop album chart and never showing up on the R&B album chart. A re-mix of Smokey Robinson's "Who's Lovin' You" was chosen as the first single. The live version of "Who's Lovin' You" never debuted on the pop singles chart and peaked at number forty-eight on the R&B singles charts. It was decided to include the single in the movie at the last minute, giving the cast only twenty-four hours to learn the song and new choreography. The choreographer for the Jackson Five mini-series was often time Michael Jackson associate, Michael Peters.

Michael's Heal the World Foundation and AmeriCares joined together to fund a project sending relief supplies to Sarajevo, the capital city of Bosnia, where millions of civilians were suffering from starvation. Michael attended a press conference held at John F. Kennedy International Airport on November 24, 1992:

The mission of Heal the World, my mission, is healing. Pure and simple. To heal the world we must start by healing our children. Today we have come bearing gifts for the children of war torn Sarajevo. In 1992, Sarajevo has become a symbol of so much that is tragic, but avoidable in our world: prejudice and ethnic hatred, the destruction of the environment, the shattering of family and future of the whole community...

An AmeriCares cargo jet was then loaded with 93,700 pounds of medical supplies, blankets, heavy clothing and shoes.

The fifth single from *Dangerous* was "Heal the World", one of Michael's favorite songs. Unlike the previous singles, there was no highly publicized Fox television debut for the song's video, which delivers the song's message with a compilation of footage of sick and needy children, including those Michael had visited and helped.

Although Michael performed the single on several TV specials and in concert, it had disappointing performance on the pop and R&B charts, never making it to the top forty. "Heal the World" peaked at number twenty-seven on the pop chart and number sixty- two on the R&B chart. The single did much better on the adult contemporary chart, where it went to number nine. The single had greater success in Europe where it quickly became a top five hit, peaking at number two in many countries. "Heal the World" delivers a positive message, but it is not the strongest song on the album, or Michael's strongest inspirational anthem. "Earth Song", "Man in the Mirror" and "Cry" are all better.

On December 9, *Billboard* handed out its music awards for 1992. Michael Jackson was among the artists nominated for Top Pop Singles Artist, which ended up going to Boyz II Men, and for the Number One R&B Artist, which Jodeci took home. Michael didn't go home empty handed however. In 1992 the Billboard World Artist Award for the Number One World Single and Album belonged to the same artist. The Number One World Single was "Black or White" and the Number One World Album was *Dangerous*.

Before handing over the award, there was a short video tribute to Michael Jackson recognizing the worldwide success of "Black or White" and *Dangerous* and also celebrating the tenth anniversary of the release of the largest selling album in history, *Thriller*. The award was presented to Michael, who was still on the road, by Phil Collins in a taped presentation. Michael, dressed in a red shirt and a black fedora, accepted the award graciously as always:

> *I am honored to be recognized by* Billboard *which is considered to be the bible of the industry. Nothing would have prevented me from sharing this special occasion other than Heal the World and my commitment to tour on its behalf. My heartfelt thanks to* **Billboard,** *to the children, and to my fans in general. Your support over the years has been an inspiration. Thank you so much.*

Phil Collins then presented Michael with a second award:

> *To commemorate the tenth anniversary of* **Thriller** *and to recognize that in the past ten years you have basically outsold us all as the number one best selling artist in the world, we're very happy to present to you this special Billboard Award.*

Michael, now with his arms full of awards, accepted the honor and introduced his own performance:

> *I am very touched by you saluting my efforts and more importantly that* **Thriller** *is remembered after a decade. I love you all. And now in my absence, here is a special performance of `Black or White'.*

A performance of "Black or White" from a tour stop in London was broadcast.

The new year would begin with Michael riding high on the charts and making an attempt to shed his media shy image. The year would end with him embroiled in a scandal that he could have never imagined.

20

Dangerous
The girl is so dangerous
Take away my money
Throw away my time
You can call me honey
But you're no damn good for me

"Dangerous"
- Michael Jackson, Bill Boutrell, Teddy Riley

Nineteen hundred ninety three was shaping up to be an impressive year for Michael Jackson. His latest release, *Dangerous,* was still selling steadily around the world, well over a year after its release. "Heal the World", the sixth single released from *Dangerous*, was just entering the pop and R&B singles charts. The Dangerous tour was scheduled to begin a set of Asian dates in late summer with money raised at each stop going to his Heal the World Foundation. Of course, there were lots and lots of awards to be accepted, records to set, and "firsts" to achieve. In other words, it was business as usual for Michael Jackson. More significantly, he would finally begin an attempt to shed his media shy image, becoming more accessible to the media and the public. No one could have guessed the year would take such a startling twist and end on such a disturbing, painful, note.

Michael participated in two festivities celebrating the inauguration of President Bill Clinton. First he joined several other celebrities, including Diana Ross, on the steps of the Lincoln Memorial the afternoon of January 18 to sing "We are the World" for a pre-inaugural celebration.

The next day, Michael was among the performers taking part in *An American Reunion: The 52nd Presidential Inaugural Gala*. Of the many performers taking part in the show, only two performed more than one quick number; Clinton friend and supporter Barbra Streisand, and the King of Pop. He walked through the crowd to the stage dressed in black pants and a red military style shirt, with his hair pulled back in a ponytail. He first addressed the new President on the need for continued and increased funding for AIDS research:

Thank you Mr. President elect for inviting me to your Inaugural gala. I would like to take a moment from this very public ceremony to speak of something very personal. It concerns a dear friend of mine who is no longer with us. His name is Ryan White. He was a hemophiliac who was diagnosed with the AIDS virus when he was eleven. He died shortly after turning eighteen, the very time most young people are beginning to explore life's wonderful possibilities. My friend Ryan was a very bright, very brave, and very normal young man who never wanted to be a symbol or a spokesperson for a deadly disease. Over the years I've shared many silly, happy, and painful moments with Ryan and I was with him at the end of his brief but eventful journey.

Ryan is gone and just as anyone who has lost a loved one to AIDS, I miss him deeply and constantly. He is gone but I want his life to have meaning beyond his passing. It is my hope President elect Clinton that you and your administration will commit the resources needed to eliminate this awful disease that took my friend and ended so many promising lives before their time. This song's for you Ryan."

Michael performed his anthem to his friend Ryan White, "Gone Too Soon", his voice cracking with emotion at the last lines. Despite a slight bobble with the lyrics, it was a moving tribute to his lost friend. A group of children joined Michael on stage for "Heal the World", which he dedicated to "all the children of the world". Michael later joined a specially reunited Fleetwood Mac and several other celebrities to sing "Don't Stop (Thinking About Tomorrow)".

The same day Michael showed up at the Lincoln Memorial to perform "We are the World", he was honored at the NAACP Image Awards. Michael's video for "Black or White" was honored as the Best Music Video. The announcement of his win and the following standing ovation was a surprise:

I really wasn't expecting to win this. I love you all very, very much. Thank you to the NAACP, and all of you, you're very dear, sweet, loving people. Thank you so much.

Later Wesley Snipes presented the NAACP Image Award for Entertainer of the Year to Michael Jackson. Snipes, who appeared in the "Bad" video, narrated a tribute to Michael showcasing video clips and live performances. Then Patti Labelle, with the Voices of Faith Choir, sang Michael's "Will You Be There". Michael rose from his front row seat with his mother, Bill Bray and Bob Jones. In accepting the honor, Michael seemed very touched and gave an usually long and thoughtful speech:

First I'd like to say thank you to my mother who is here tonight, she's the one in blue. Thank you for giving me life. I really mean that, I love you. There are two things the NAACP stands for which are the most important things in my life, freedom and equality. In every person there is a secret song in their heart. It says I am free, it sings I am one. This is the natural feeling of every child, to be free as the wind, to be one with every other child. All the troubles in the world are caused by forgetting this feeling and when I perform my connection is with people. It's just to remind me of that, to be free and to be one. In this spirit the NAACP has done its cherished work. Thank you for having the faith to see that I share your work, for I deeply feel I do. I accept this award on behalf of the world's healing when all our brothers and sisters will be as free and equal as we are today. I love you so much and I am very honored. Thank you for this award. Thank you so much.

Patti Labelle then coaxed Michael into singing a couple lines of "Will You Be There" before leaving the stage.

Michael didn't win anymore awards until six days later at the American Music Awards. For the 20th annual American Music Awards Michael Jackson had five nominations. But the audience got to see him before any winners were announced as he opened the award presentation performing "Dangerous". In accepting an offer from the show's executive producer, Dick Clark, to perform, Michael asked if he could open the show, to which Clark responded, "Michael, you can do whatever you want." Clark added, "I couldn't think of anyone more appropriate to kick off our 20th anniversary show. Not only is Michael one of the most exciting stage performers in the business, but one of the most honored as well."

A dancer dropped to the floor from machine gun fire, revealing Michael standing directly behind him. Dressed in a black suit with spats and a fedora, Michael joined several dancers in a "Smooth Criminal" flavored performance of "Dangerous" featuring his usual captivating choreography with plenty of crotch grabbing and carefully timed sound effects.

Elizabeth Taylor took the stage during the show to announce the recipient of the first ever International Artist Award. She narrated a video tribute to Michael Jackson then introduced a taped message from another of Michael's friends and fans, Eddie Murphy:

Hi, Michael. Knowing how uncomfortable you feel when someone says something nice to you right up in your face, I went 3,000 miles away to do this. Now, the inscription on your award says, `In recognition of his record-breaking international concert tours, and his album sales, and his heartfelt efforts to make this world a better place, *the American Music Awards presents its first International Artist Award to Michael Jackson January 25, 1993.' In addition the American Music Awards are proud to announce that when the award is given in the future, it will be known as `The Michael Jackson International Artist Award.' So, congratulations Michael, I know you better be smiling from ear to ear. I know you better smile bigger than that, I want to see gums! Congratulations.*

Elizabeth Taylor then called Michael to the stage from his front row seat at the Shrine Auditorium. He had now changed into a black leather jacket and removed his sunglasses before going on stage. The crowd was on their feet and cheering as Michael began to speak:

I love you very much, Elizabeth Taylor. Teddy Riley, you are a genius. Thank you Eddie, thank you all my friends. Traveling the world has been a great education for me and if there is one insight I've had it is this, wherever you go, in every country, on every continent, people yearn and hunger for only one thing, to love and be loved. Love transcends international boundaries and it heals the wounds of hatred, racial prejudice, bigotry, and ignorance. It is the ultimate truth at the heart of all creation. I would also like to thank God, and my mother and father, Katherine and Joseph Jackson. Thank you once again, I love you all.

The Soul Train Awards followed suit and also named an award after Michael Jackson with the Michael Jackson Award for Best R&B/Soul or Rap Music Video.

Favorite Soul/R&B Single went to "Remember the Time" and *Dangerous* was the winner for Favorite Pop/Rock Album. Michael was brief in his acceptance, "I really wasn't expecting to win. Thank you again Teddy Riley, the public, I love you very much. Thank you." Having won in two of the five categories in which he was nominated and being named the International Artist of the Year, Michael Jackson was the night's big winner.

Michael's recent appearances at the Inaugural festivities, the NAACP Image Awards, and the American Music Awards made him a big winner on the music charts too. The week following these events, *Dangerous* rose eighteen places on the R&B album charts, from fifty-seven to thirty-nine. The effect on the pop album charts was more pronounced, with a move up of forty three places to eighty-eight. "Black or White" and "Remember the Time" were honored with a BMI Award as two of the most performed songs of the year.

Michael's next high profile gig had been announced six month in advance. It would be providing the halftime entertainment at a little ol' football game called the Super Bowl. The show's producer and director, Don Mischer, must have known to expect something spectacular. He had worked with Michael before on *Motown 25*.

The day following the American Music Awards, Michael was in Los Angeles at a press conference to accept donations to his Heal the World Foundation. The National Football League (NFL) and Super Bowl XXVII halftime sponsor Frito Lay each donated $100,000 to Michael's charity. Michael's agreement to perform at halftime was contingent on it being a benefit for his charity. Michael spoke briefly, "I can't think of a better way to spread the message of world peace than by working with Radio City and the NFL and by being a part of Super

Bowl XXVII."

He also used the opportunity to announce Heal LA, a project he co-chaired with former President Jimmy Carter. Heal LA helped disadvantaged children focusing on drug education, immunization, and mentor programs. Michael was presented with a custom made Super Bowl jacket that read on the back, "Super Bowl XXVII Radio City Halftime Show Michael Jackson." Michael accepted the donations, the jacket and made this thank yous all in fifteen minutes.

January 31, 1993 was Super Bowl Sunday. The Dallas Cowboys faced the Buffalo Bills for Super Bowl XXVII in Pasadena, California, but more important was halftime. The press had been barred from rehearsals, so no preview of the spectacular was included in any of the pre-game coverage. Expectations were high, and in fact the other networks didn't counter with any real competition for the Super Bowl audience. Michael didn't disappoint.

When the time finally came, a giant video screen counted down the last ten seconds and it was announced, "Ladies and gentlemen, Radio City Music Hall Productions and the National Football League are proud to present an unprecedented Super Bowl spectacular starring Michael Jackson."

Crowds of people gathered around the stage now set up on the middle of the field. The performance opened with a grand illusion with Michael seeming to dance above two giant video screen, several stories in the air. Following this, fireworks went off at center stage and Michael jumped from beneath the stage and stood motionless amid the fireworks, smoke, and cheers from the 102,000 fans packed into the stadium. The illusions worked brilliantly. Dressed in black with gold bands across his chest, his right arm in a brace, and wearing sunglasses, he stood virtually motionless for over one minute before turning his head and slowly removing the glasses, replicating the opening of the Dangerous tour performances. More fireworks went off and dancers joined Michael on stage for a very short version of "Jam".

He removed his jacket, he now wore a flowing white shirt. He reached down for a black fedora that had been sitting on the edge of the stage, placed it on his head and began pumping his hips to "Billie Jean". He did a short performance of "Billie Jean" adding a crotch grab or two to his choreography from *Motown 25,* complete with the requisite moonwalk.

"Black or White" was up next in the mini concert with more fireworks set off at the song's conclusion. Then Michael addressed the crowd, his voice sounding unusually deep:

Today we stand together all around the world joined in a common purpose, to remake the planet into a planet of joy and understanding and goodness. No one should have to suffer, especially the children. This time we must succeed. This is for the children of the world."

Thousands of young people lined the stage as Michael sang "Heal the World" and a huge inflatable globe rose from the center of the stage.

More fireworks ended the truly spectacular and certainly unforgettable halftime extravaganza. An ad for Michael's Heal the World Foundation and the newly created Heal LA followed the performance, the airtime for which was also donated by the NFL.

Normally, during the halftime show of the Super Bowl, approximately 20% of the viewing audience is lost. This year, for the first time ever, the number of viewers tuning in increased by five million, attracting the largest TV audience in history, and earning Michael Jackson another mention in the *Guinness Book of World Records*. Approximately 133.4 million people in the U.S. tuned in to see the King of Pop, and an estimated one billion worldwide, and he didn't disappoint.

Reviews of the game the next day regularly mentioned halftime as being the most exciting part of the Super Bowl where Dallas beat the Bulls 52 to 17. NBC recognized that Jackson was pivotal in making the game the biggest TV attraction in Super Bowl history. Dick Ebersol, NBC Sports President, said of Michael's performance, "He was better than our wildest dreams... He's an enormous name with crossover appeal from kids to grandparents, an enormous curiosity even for those for whom he is not a star." That last part is certainly true. I had a friend who was a cool rock 'n roll band loving– muscle car driving –type who comfortably used words like "dude" and "babe". He was not part of the typical Michael Jackson fan base. He watched the game with his equally cool friends. During the game the halftime show was hyped and they each chipped in their wisecracks about Jackson. But, when halftime started everyone quieted down and all eyes were glued to the TV. His charisma and commanding stage presence insisted you pay attention. You couldn't take your off of him. He was mesmerizing. He was Michael Jackson.

Michael's spellbinding halftime extravaganza was not lost on record buyers. The pop album chart placed *Dangerous* at number forty-one, up thirty-seven places from the week before. The R&B album chart had *Dangerous* moving up sixteen places to number twenty-three. The following week *Dangerous* moved up another fifteen places to number twenty-six on the pop album chart. Just like his performance on *Motown 25*, his performance at the Super Bowl seemed to bring his music to a whole new audience. Michael Jackson is credited with raising the bar for Super Bowl halftime performances and is the reason why they are now expected to be and are regarded as such spectaculars.

Continuing his media blitz, it was announced that Michael Jackson had agreed to a live ninety minute prime time interview with Oprah Winfrey. The interview was said to be Michael's idea, and he agreed to discuss anything, though he didn't want it to be a "look at how many cars he has" kind of thing.

The special interview, broadcast live around the world from Neverland Valley Ranch, was heavily advertised with commercials counting down the number of days and even minutes until the special was broadcast. All major news telecasts carried coverage of the special interview both before and after the special aired.

Oprah reportedly had lots of footage of Michael's career handy to help fill time in case Michael turned out not to be too talkative. It wasn't necessary though as Michael was surprisingly candid and eager to dispel the many falsehoods about him that have been circulated, and believed, for many years. He refused to answer only two questions. One asking for a response to some of the allegations made by LaToya in her book, to which Michael said he couldn't answer because he honestly hadn't read the book. The only other question he refused to answer was whether or not he was still a virgin, at which he became quite embarrassed, "How could you ask me that?", and said only "I'm a gentleman". He allowed that he had been in love twice, with Brooke Shields and "one other girl". He added he was currently dating Brooke Shields.

Winfrey began the interview with questions about Michael's childhood and his feeling that he missed out on a lot of normal childhood activities, and he attributed the inspiration he drew from children as his way of recapturing what he had missed. Michael again confirmed that his father did in fact beat him as a child. He went on to explain that he did love his father, but didn't really know him. There had been times when, both as a child and as an adult, Michael had become physically ill when having to face his father.

Probably the most anticipated portion of the interview had Michael answering all of the rumors and gossip that had been told about him over and over again, in some cases for many years. He said the areas on his face that he had surgically altered could be counted on two fingers, denying he had his cheekbones, eyes, or lips surgically altered in any way. He added that he was by far not the only person to ever have plastic surgery, "If all the people in Hollywood who have had plastic surgery took a vacation, there wouldn't be a person left in town."

Among the many rumors he finally responded to were his reported efforts to buy the elephant man's bones, "Where am I going to put some bones?"; his desire to sleep in a hyperbaric chamber, calling it "one of those tabloid things, it's completely made up", not mentioning he started that story himself; and his proposal to Elizabeth Taylor. Taylor, who was with Michael at the time of the interview, came on camera to also deny that Michael had ever proposed to her and added that she never proposed to him either.

Answering the claims he had his skin bleached, Michael replied emphatically, "As far as I know of, there is no such thing as skin bleaching. I have never seen it, I don't know what it is." He went on to disclose, "I have a skin disorder that destroys the pigmentation of the skin. It's something I cannot help. When people make up stories that I don't want to be who I am, it hurts me. It's a problem for me. I can't control it." He added that the disorder runs in his family, on his father's side, and that he uses makeup to even out his skin tone. He then asked, "Why is that so important?"

Michael's dermatologist, Dr. Arnold Klein, later confirmed that he had diagnosed Michael as suffering from vitiligo, a disorder that causes discoloration of the skin. He prescribed a cream that blocked pigment production in the skin, to make it look more uniform. At the first signs of the disease, his makeup artist, Karen Faye, worked to cover the light patches on his skin to make them blend with his own darker skin tone. As the disease progressed and the majority of his body lost its pigmentation, it became necessary to reverse this action and work to blend the darker patches in with the lighter areas. Michael was also diagnosed with lupus, also an auto-immune disease, which commonly accompanies vitiligo.

Michael also responded to the more recent rumors being

spread about him. Regarding his demands to be called "The King of Pop", he said he never proclaimed himself to be anything. Oprah added at this point that she did not contractually agree to call Michael "The King of Pop".

The story that he chose a white boy to play him as a child in a Pepsi commercial, and claims that he is ashamed of his race, were answered vehemently, "Why would I want a white child to play me? I am a black American. I am proud to be a black American. I am proud of my race. I am proud of who I am. I have a lot of pride and dignity in who I am."

Viewers weren't given a look at his cars, but he did offer a brief look at his amusement park, all lit up beautifully with thousands of tiny white lights, and his private movie theater, complete with built in hospital beds for visiting children who are too ill to sit up. Michael's house and the rest of the grounds of the ranch, including his private zoo, were off limits.

Michael gave Oprah a quick moonwalking lesson on the stage in front of the movie screen, but not too much because, "I'm a little rusty." He sang a few lines of "Who Is It" a cappella, even singing the sounds of the instruments. Michael's latest video for "Give in to Me" was then premiered on worldwide television from his own movie theater.

Michael Jackson Talks To... Oprah attracted 90 million viewers in the U.S., making it the fourth most watched, non sports, program in history. Approximately half of all television sets were tuned in to see the King of Pop. The interview was heavily hyped beforehand, and afterward was treated as a major news story, with every news program, newspaper and talk show now offering expert information on vitiligo, the skin disorder that Michael had described.

The public's reaction to Michael's candid responses during the interview only continued the drive up the charts for *Dangerous*. Within three weeks of the interview *Dangerous* rose another thirty- one points on the album charts and was now at number ten, well over a year after its release. *Billboard* magazine officials said they had never seen such a rebound on the charts. Sales and airplay of his current single "Heal the World" also did a quick turn-a-round. The single, which had stalled at number fifty- two and had begun dropping, went back up the pop singles chart to number twenty-seven. Michael was riding high on a renewed wave of Michaelmania.

The Michael media blitz continued with his appearance at the 35th Annual Grammy Awards in February where Janet Jackson presented the Grammy Legend Award to her big brother. After narrating a tribute, "How To Become A Legend", Janet brought Michael on stage from his front row seat at the Shrine Auditorium, with his date, Brooke Shields, "Now I'm very happy to present the Grammy Legend Award for 1993 to my big brother, Michael Jackson." Looking dashing in black jeans and boots, and a beautiful white beaded jacket, Michael embraced Janet. Instead of performing on the show, as had been previously announced, Michael chose instead to speak. In his acceptance speech, which lasted an incredible four minutes, Michael poked fun at himself and showed his sense of humor that many hadn't had an opportunity to see. Approaching the microphone, standing next to Janet and putting his arm around her, Michael remarked, "I hope this finally puts to rest another rumor that has been in the press for too many years...me and Janet really are two different people!" He brought more laughs from the crowd when he began, "In the past month I've gone from `Where is he?' to `Here he is again!'". His comments prompted host Garry Shandling to ask, "When did he get so damn funny?" The rest of Michael's comments centered on his feeling that it was "nice to be thought of as a person and not as a personality,...:

Because I don't read all the things written about me, I wasn't aware the world thought I was so weird and bizarre. But when you grow up as I did in front of 100 million people since the age of five, you're automatically different. The last few weeks I have been cleansing myself and it has been a rebirth for myself, it's like a cleansing spirit. My childhood was completely taken away from me. There was no Christmas, no birthdays. It was not a normal childhood, no normal pleasures of childhood. Those were exchanged for hard work, struggle and pain, and eventual material and professional success. But as an awful price, I cannot recreate that part of my life. Nor would I change any part of my life. However, today when I create my music I feel like an instrument of nature. I wonder what delight nature feels when we open our hearts and express our God given talents. The sound of approval rolls across the universe and the whole world abounds in magic. Wonder fills our hearts for we have glimpsed for an instant the playfulness of life.

And that's why I love children and learn so much from being around them. I realize that many of the world's problems today, from inner city crime to large scale wars and terrorism and over crowded prisons are a result of the fact that children have had their childhoods stolen from them. The magic, the wonder, the mystery and the innocence of a child's heart are the seeds of creativity that will heal the world. I really believe that.

What we need to learn from children isn't childish. Being with them connects us to the deeper wisdom of life which is ever present and asks only to be lived. They know the way to solutions that lie trying to be recognized in our own hearts.

Today I would like to thank all the children of the world including the sick and deprived, I am so sensitive to your pain. I also want to thank all those who have helped me to channel my talents here on Earth. From the beginning, my parents, all my brothers and sisters, especially Janet. I am so proud of her, it's incredible. I remember when we were little I used to ask her to be Ginger Rogers while I was Fred Astaire. The Motown family, my teacher, Berry Gordy, Diana Ross, I love you. Suzanne de Passe, the wonderful, great Quincy Jones, Teddy Riley, my new godson Michael Gibb, my new Sony family Akio Morita, Mickey Schulhof, Tommy Mottola, Dave Glew, Polly Anthony, thanks for making one of my most creative efforts, the album Dangerous such an incredible success. I love you all so much. Sandy Gallin, Jim Morey, all the fantastic fans around the world, I love you very much.

Besides his honor as the Grammy Legend, Michael had two Grammy nominations. He was nominated for Best Pop Male Vocal for "Black or White" and for Best R&B Male Vocal for "Jam". He didn't take either Grammy home. The Grammy for Best Engineered Recording went to Bruce Swedien for *Dangerous*.

The video released in the U.S. for "Who Is It" is a composite of earlier videos and performances. The song was released by Epic as Michael's next single as a last minute replacement for "Give in to Me", in reaction to the overwhelming public response to Michael's brief a cappella performance of the song during his interview with Oprah Winfrey. In fact, a bit of Michael's performance of the song from the interview was included on the cassette single. "Who Is It" peaked at number fourteen on the pop singles chart and at number six on the R&B chart. Another version of a video for "Who Is It" is included on the video collection, *Dangerous: The Short Films."*

Michael had three nominations and received the Humanitarian of the Year award at the Seventh Annual Soul Train Awards that were handed out in March. Despite having sprained his ankle the day before during dance rehearsals, he attended the awards presentation and he performed as scheduled. His first nomination was for Best R&B/Soul Music Video for "Remember the Time" which went to Boyz II Men for "End of the Road". Michael's first appearance during the telecast came when he was named the Humanitarian of the Year. The award was presented by Michael's friend, Eddie Murphy:

I address these remarks to a very good friend of mine, Michael Jackson. Now, Michael, everyone knows you have broken every sales record known to man and that you have the number one and number two best selling albums of all time and the number one selling single of all time and he's the biggest selling artist ever, but tonight we're not

"Dangerous"

here to talk about that, we're here to talk about your achievements as a humanitarian and your concern about the well-being of children and brothers and sisters everywhere and Mother Earth herself.

As the cheers from the crowd threatened to drown Murphy out, he cut his remarks short and said, "Hey, just show the film, huh!" A short film tribute to Michael outlined a few of Michael's countless efforts to help others and make the world a better place. Michael, who was on crutches, was helped to the stage from his front row seat by Bill Bray. He was dressed in a black jacket with a red armband, and one shoe. After blowing kisses to the crowd, he apologized for his injury, and Murphy insisted he tell how it happened, "You can't just come out like that and not tell us what happened." Michael replied, "You really want to know? I was dancing and I went into a spin and I twisted my ankle very badly. But I wanted to come here to thank everyone." After poking fun at Murphy, "Eddie, I heard you have a new album out, that you're the one whose `dangerous'", Michael continued:

Ever since I was a child, I realized I had a lot of love to share from my soul. The black tradition is a tradition of soul which is a gift of love and joy. Soul is the most precious thing you can share because you're sharing yourself and the world needs that gift now more than ever. The child with AIDS, in the ghetto, is waiting for you along with the starving people in Africa and everyone else who needs healing. Make the world more beautiful by sharing with me the wonderful feeling you get when your soul is lifted up to become pure love. I accept this award on behalf of all the children of the world who are my inspiration and my hope...

He also picked up two other awards. "Remember the Time" was named the Best R&B/Soul Single-Male, and Best R&B/Soul Album, Male, went to Michael Jackson for *Dangerous*.

For the presentation of the Heritage Award, Michael Jackson Eddie Murphy traded places. This time Michael was the presenter and Eddie Murphy was the recipient. Michael had rarely, and never in more than ten years, appeared as a presenter on any award show. As Michael began the tribute to his friend, the cheers from the crowd grew deafening and Michael had to remind them that "this is Eddie's moment"

After a short collection of clips from Murphy's many films, Michael introduced his friend, "Ladies and gentlemen, please welcome the recipient of the 1993 Soul Train Music Award's Heritage Award, Mr. Eddie Murphy." Eddie Murphy then said to the crowd, "Isn't it nice seeing him getting out and giving people awards and stuff?" He also thanked Michael, "for hobblin' out here and giving me this award."

Later in the broadcast Michael changed into the gold Egyptian costume he wears in the video for "Remember the Time" and he performed the song sitting in an elaborate gold chair placed in the center of the stage, with his dancers behind him. Seated, he gyrated from the waist up and belted out the song like nobody's business, bringing himself up to stand, balancing himself on one foot a couple of times during the performance.

In mid March, Michael won a legal victory, something he would need to savor considering what was in store for him. Hugo Zucarelli sued Michael Jackson claiming he was never paid for

Michael's use of recording technology Zucarelli invented that was used in recording *Bad.* A judge dismissed the suit and Zucarelli ended up being booked on battery charges for attacking Michael's attorneys.

In April 1993, a music video debuted on the Fox network and BET. This was not a Michael Jackson video, however, he did appear in it. Eddie Murphy's video for "Whatzupwitu" from his album, *Love's Alright*, featured Michael Jackson and the Boys Choir of Harlem. The video is a light hearted look at Eddie and Michael singing and dancing against a backdrop of clouds, birds, and flowers. The single did surprisingly poorly on the charts, going only to seventy-four on the R&B singles chart and never making a showing on the pop chart.

Michael next joined former President Jimmy Carter in Atlanta on May 5 for Heal Atlanta, part of Michael's Heal the World Foundation. The Immunization/Children's Health Initiative was open to children under six who lived in Atlanta projects and had current immunization certificates.

Michael picked up an honor in May from the Guinness World of Records Museum, who presented him with the first ever Lifetime Achievement Award. The award was in recognition of his many world records: the best selling album in history (*Thriller*), winning the most Grammys in a single year (Eight in 1984), the biggest concert (500,000 people in four shows at London's Wembley Stadium), the biggest contract in the history of show business, (signed with Sony in 1991), and performing before the largest ever television audience (133.4 million during his halftime performance at the 1993 Super Bowl).

The master of ceremonies for the event was Casey Kasem and

the founding editor of the *Guinness Book of World Records*, Norris McWhirter. Michael, dressed in black with large mirrored sunglasses and a fedora, accepted the honor and spoke to the crowd of fans that had brought Hollywood Boulevard to a standstill, "I love you all and thank you very much for coming." Lori Byler, president of the Michael Jackson Observer Fan Club, then presented Michael with a second award in recognition of his work with children.

Airing on June 1, 1993 were the World Music Awards that were actually held on May 12 at the Sporting Club in Monte Carlo. The World Music Awards were established by Prince Albert of Monaco to recognize the top selling artists in major international markets and genres. This year the awards were being telecast in the U.S. for the first time. Helping to increase their stature and credibility was the presence of the King of Pop who would be attending, not to sing and dance, but to pick up three of their biggest honors.

He received his first award of the evening for Best Selling American Artist. The crowd rose to its feet as Michael ascended the stairs to the stage. He was seated in the front row of the Sporting Club with a little girl, and a young boy who was dressed as Michael in a black jacket and a black fedora. He spoke from behind large mirrored sunglasses:

Thanks to all my fans and friends in America for your continued support of my music. Thanks to Mickey Schulhof, Tommy Mottola, Dave Glew, and my entire Sony family, you made it happen. Thanks to Sandy Gallin and Jim Morey. I love you all. Thank you very much.

"Dangerous"

For Michael's second honor Princess Stephanie of Monaco introduced Michael:

The name of this year's Best Selling Pop Artist I'm sure will come as no surprise to anyone. He has been ruling the charts for some time now with a musical style that blends Pop, Rock, R&B, Gospel, Rap, and Motown. It is a combination that has captivated the world and garnered him with this year's World Music Award as Best Selling Pop Artist and his name is Michael Jackson.

Prince Albert of Monaco presented the final award of the evening for World's Best Selling Artist of the Era:

...Congratulations to all the artists whose work has been recognized here tonight. Only one recording artist is receiving three World Music Awards this year. As you have recently seen the accolades are justified. He not only set standards for all artists in sales and use of recording and video media but he demonstrates how the power of celebrity can be used to positive effect in helping to ease the problems of our world. It is with great pleasure that I present him with this award which names him World's Best Selling Artist of the Era. Once again, ladies and gentlemen, the King of Pop, Mr. Michael Jackson!

Michael walked out from backstage carrying his two awards he had won earlier then collected his third honor from Prince Albert. In the middle of this acceptance remarks, he asked Prince Albert to hold one of his trophies:

Thank you, your Serene Highness. I am honored to accept this World Music Award. It means a lot to me, for I sincerely believe that thorough music... could you hold this for me? Would you mind? Sorry, it's kind of heavy.

Then he continued:

> *I believe that through music we can help heal the world. It's through such charities as the Princess Grace Foundation of Monaco that this will be accomplished. Again, thanks to my fans around the world, I love you, and you wonderful people of Monaco for these honors. Merci, merci, encore!"*

An ad in the June 5, 1993 issue of *Billboard* magazine congratulated the winners at the World Music Awards. In the center of the page was the biggest winner, a photo of Michael holding his three heavy awards.

After months of persistence by *Life* magazine's director of photography, David Friend, the first ever photos of Michael Jackson's Neverland Valley Ranch were featured in the June 1993 issue of *Life* magazine. The photographs were taken by Harry Benson. The "Michael in Wonderland" photo spread featured photos of the beautiful meticulously manicured grounds of Michael's ranch, and the amusement park. There were also pictures of Michael surrounded by the children of his staff members and several of his pets including a first look at his twelve foot albino python, named Madonna, named so, according to Michael, "because she's blond, but *I* didn't name her that."

The series of photographs showed the splendor of Neverland and David Friend's accompanying text explains its owner's vision while visiting the movie theater with the hospital beds built in for young visitors too ill to sit up:

It is here, standing next to the hospital beds, that one understands the essence of Neverland to its owner, amusement is hardly the point of the place. This is actually the world Jackson would fashion were it left in his charge: safe and clean and timeless as a fable.

Sadly, these words and this ideal would be quickly forgotten in a couple of months.

As usual, Michael's other activities revolved around entertaining and helping children. A rally was held at a middle school in Los Angeles in June to launch a new D.A.R.E. program for the school aimed at helping to keep kids off of drugs and out of gangs. The new program, D.A.R.E. P.L.U.S. (Play and Learn Under Supervision), was supported by a number of celebrities, many of whom attended the rally. The celebrity who reportedly caused the biggest stir was the King of Pop. Michael was presented with a t-shirt, and said, "Thank you very much. I love you all. Thank you." Michael served as a member of the Board of Directors of D.A.R.E. (Drug Abuse Resistance Education.)

Michael hosted a group of one hundred children at his ranch in June from the Challengers Boys and Girls Club in Los Angeles. The Big Brothers of Los Angeles, who also benefited from his generosity, gave Michael a rocking chair made by the woman who made them for President Kennedy and the Pope.

Sotheby's held its semi-annual auction of Rock & Roll memorabilia on June 23. Michael Jackson's "Beat It" jacket was purchased by the Hard Rock Café for $7,762. Today the jacket is ranked by the Hard Rock Café as "the single most significant piece of pop culture in our collection".

Free Willy, a movie of a young boy's efforts to free a whale from captivity in a theme park, began airing in theaters in July. The soundtrack for the film, the first release on Michael's MJJ Records label, featured "Will You Be There" as the movie's theme song. Also included on the soundtrack was "Right Here" by SWV (Sisters With Voices), that included a sampling of Michael's "Human Nature". T3, made up of Taj, Tito Jackson Jr., contributed "Didn't Mean To Hurt You" to Uncle Mike's first release on his record label MJJ Music. T3's album, *Brotherhood* was released on MJJ Music and Uncle Mike served as co-executive producer and he joined his nephews on "Why". "Will You Be There" won the MTV Movie Award for Best Song in a Movie.

Jack the Rapper Awards, handed out in August in Atlanta, honored Motown founder Berry Gordy with the Original 13 Award for his legendary work in the music industry. The Our Children, Our Hope of Tomorrow Award, which was named after Michael Jackson, was awarded to, well, Michael Jackson. In a videotaped message Michael said, "I am honored and humbled."

The Rock & Roll Cookbook, by Dick and Sandy St. John, featured recipes from various rock stars. Included in the book is a recipe for Maple Pecan Butter Cookies from Michael Jackson. It does not reveal however how often he made these cookies, or if he wore just one oven mitt.

As the opening dates of the Asian leg of the Dangerous tour

grew nearer, the dates kept changing. Shows were scheduled, then cancelled, with dates and cities being changed frequently. U.S. Embassy officials in Seoul, Korea, tried to change a decision made by the Ministry of Culture denying Michael Jackson an opportunity to have a concert there. The South Korean officials were concerned about protecting any threats to their traditional Confucian values such as loud pop music and suggestive choreography. Finally, August 24, 1993 was announced as the opening date of the Dangerous tour in Bangkok, Thailand. As usual, this was to be no small production. Michael would be performing on a stage wider than any stage in America. It measured 270 feet across and took four days to set up and three days to take down. The equipment necessary to stage the show filled twenty semi trailers.

However the excitement of the opening of the tour would be buried by shock and disbelief at reports that Michael Jackson was under criminal investigation by the Los Angeles Police Department and the Santa Barbara County Sheriffs Department, creating the biggest scandal in Michael Jackson's career and quite possibly, all of show business. At least it seemed like the biggest scandal imaginable at the time. The investigation, which actually began on August 17, 1993, was brought on by the thirteen year old boy who, with his mother and stepsister, had accompanied Michael to Monte Carlo in May for the World Music Awards. The boy had made claims of child molestation against Michael Jackson.

21

In our darkest hour
In my deepest despair
Will you still care?
Will you be there?

"Will You Be There"
- Michael Jackson

The boy's claims were unsubstantiated, however, they were enough to prompt officials to open an investigation on August 17, 1993, and to serve search warrants on Michael's Neverland Valley Ranch, his condo in Century City and later a separate search warrant was issued for Hayvenhurst. The Los Angeles District Attorney, Gil Garcetti, headed up the investigation by Los Angeles officials and Tom Sneddon, the Santa Barbara County District Attorney headed up the investigation for Santa Barbara County. Michael was not home at the time of the search, having already flown to Bangkok for the kick off of the *Dangerous* tour. Jackson's camp cooperated with the search. Several boxes of photographs and videotapes were removed from the premises, none of which showed anything out of the ordinary and didn't incriminate Michael at all. A source from the police department told *The Los Angeles Times*, "There's no medical evidence, no taped evidence... The search warrant didn't result in anything that would support a criminal filing."

Michael's investigator, Anthony Pellicano, explained at a press conference that the allegations were the result of a plot by the boy's father to extort $20 million from Michael Jackson, "A demand for $20 million was made and presented. It was flatly and consistently refused. The refusals have in our opinion caused what has transpired in the last few days .. When we would not pay, a phone call was made to Child and Family Services, which started this investigation." Michael released the following statement to the press:

My representatives have continuously kept me aware of what is taking place in California. I appreciate the remarks of Chief Willie Williams and our Los Angeles police department. I am confident the department will conduct a fair and thorough investigation and its results will demonstrate that there was no wrongdoing on my part. I intend to continue with my world tour, and look forward to seeing all of you in the scheduled cities. I am grateful for the overwhelming support of my fans throughout the world. I love you all. Thank you. Michael.

A separate investigation was then begun by the Los Angeles

police department to investigate the boy's father and the more plausible extortion claims. This of course wasn't as juicy as the investigation against Michael, so it received comparatively little attention in the media. But it too would last for several months.

Coverage of the abuse allegations was top story news on virtually all news casts, all entertainment news programs, and front page news on newspapers for weeks. Scandal hungry tabloid TV shows wouldn't let go of the story for months. With a few exceptions, the identities of the boy and his father were initially concealed by the media. Photos of Michael with the young boy had the boy's face blocked out or blurred, and their names in documents were blackened out. God forbid if their lives would become disrupted due to the media's unrelenting and intense scrutiny into their personal lives prompted merely by accusations of extortion that were as of yet, unproven.

Meanwhile, the kick off of the Dangerous tour in Bangkok went on as planned. Michael dazzled and thrilled the sold out crowd starting with "Jam" and did not letting up for two hours. The crowd was unconcerned with the allegations being made against Michael and the media eruption, and continued to cheer him and held up banners supporting him.

Experts in various areas of the entertainment field, not necessarily directly connected with Michael Jackson, stated in numerous interviews that someone of Michael Jackson's status is an easy target for extortion. Michael Jackson was seen as an especially easy target for child abuse allegations because his deep affection for children was so well known and he spent so much time with children. Michael Jackson biographer J. Randy Taraborrelli consistently supported Michael and the claims of extortion, "I've seen so many extortion attempts against the Jackson camp and they never turnout to be worth anything." Taraborrelli told *Time* magazine that in researching his book on Jackson, "every damn butler, housekeeper, chauffeur and chef wanted $100,000 for their insights into his private life. I've written about Diana Ross, Cher, Carol Burnett, and Roseanne Arnold, but I never had that experience with any of my other books. And that was just me, a biographer. You can imagine what it's like for him with his millions."

Within just a few days, two tabloid TV shows had paid over $10,000 for copies of confidential documents in the case from the Los Angeles County Department of Children's Services. And this wouldn't be the end of the tabloid magazines' and TV shows' efforts to buy any information in the Michael Jackson case. As long as it was something negative, they were interested. It did not have to be true, just scandalous. And they would soon be bombarded with offers. The more money that was being offered, the more juicy the stories became.

It was learned that the boy's father, let's call him Evan Chandler, was a Beverly Hills dentist who wished he was a screenwriter. He had had one screenplay made into a movie that was based on an idea of his son's. The boy's parents, married in 1974, divorced in 1985 and were both now remarried and were involved in a bitter custody battle for the boy. It was also learned that Chandler was delinquent in his child support payments.

Michael first met the young boy one day in May, 1992, when his car stalled near a Rent-A-Wreck car rental company. Michael went to the car rental company to rent a car while his was repaired. The owner of the company, David Schwartz, quickly phoned his family and told them to come to the office to meet Michael Jackson. Michael and the owner's stepson, Jordie, quickly became friends with Michael calling the boy frequently.

Michael then began inviting Jordie, with his stepsister and his mother, to visits to Neverland. They would spend weekends at Neverland, or take trips together to Las Vegas and Florida. In May of 1993, they accompanied Michael to Monte Carlo for the World Music Awards. When these weekend trips to Neverland began to interfere with the boy's scheduled visits with his father, Chandler became furious. As part of the ongoing custody battle, Chandler filed a court document requesting the mother "not to allow the minor child to have any contact or communication with a third party adult male known as Michael Jackson." On August 17th, the judge refused Chandler's request.

The boy's mother, June Chandler, who was with the boy on the visits with Michael, first learned of the allegations from police, not from her son or his father, and was completely shocked. She said she had no indication anything untoward was going on.

According to the boy's testimony in court documents, his relationship with Michael heated up while they were in Monaco, and ended in July. Why then did the boy seem very comfortable and happy at Neverland with Michael when Ryan White's mother, Jeanne, met him there in July? Mrs. White-Ginder stated the boy was not uncomfortable, "I saw nothing out of the ordinary. Believe me, that young man was not afraid of Michael at all. He behaved just like a normal thirteen year old."

It was reported that Chandler asked Michael Jackson to set him up with film projects in the amount of $5 million per year for four years, for a total of $20 million, or he would go public with child abuse allegations. When his offer was refused, he became furious. On July 12, 1993, a meeting was held with the boy's mother, June Chandler, stepfather, David Schwartz, Michael's attorney, Bert Fields and investigator Anthony Pellicano. There the stepfather played tapes of phone conversations between himself and Chandler in which Chandler accuses Michael of molesting his son. Pellicano then drove to Michael's Century City condo where Jordie and his stepsister were staying. He talked with Jordie for forty-five minutes, asking very direct, specific questions about his relationship with Michael Jackson. Pellicano asked Jordie if Michael had ever touched him, if Michael had ever masturbated in front of him, or if Michael ever masturbated him. The boy answered "no" to each and every question. Pellicano asked if he had ever seen Michael's body, and the boy said no, but he did lift his shirt once to show him the blotches on his skin caused by his vitiligo. Jordie then complained that his father always wanted him to sit in the house and write screenplays, and that his father just wanted money. Pellicano then asked Michael the same questions, he also said nothing happened.

The very morning of the court ruling against him, denying his request that Jordie have no contact with Michael Jackson, Chandler took his son to a therapist, where he preceded to describe in detail his alleged relationship with Michael Jackson. The therapist then reported the allegations to Child and Family Services, as is required by California law. That, not a complaint by the father, instigated the criminal investigation against Michael Jackson.

Prior to the visit to the therapist, Evan Chandler went to the fantastic extreme of administering Sodium amytal to his son in his dental office. Sodium amytal is sometimes described as a truth serum. This is a misnomer. The drug is known to cause people to distort memories or manufacture them completely. They can also hold onto these "memories", convinced they are accurate. One crucial element in this case is that Jordie Chandler did not make any accusations against Michael Jackson until AFTER he was administered Sodium amytal. Scott Lilienfeld, a psychology professor at Emory University in Atlanta, noted, "And of particular relevance to the Jackson case, scientific evidence reminds us to be especially dubious of claims that emerge only after the administration of suggestive memory procedures." Under the influence of the drug, Jordie said Michael had touched his penis. During his visit with the therapist his account graduated to Michael performing oral sex on him.

Anthony Pellicano produced audio tapes of phone conversations between Chandler and the boy's stepfather, which Pellicano said proved the extortion plot. The phone conversations, taped by Schwartz, had Chandler threatening to destroy Michael Jackson, "It's going to be a massacre if I don't get what I want ... This man is going to be humiliated beyond belief. He will not believe what is going to happen to him - beyond his worst nightmares ... He won't sell one more record. If I go through with this, I win big time. I will get everything I want. They will be destroyed forever." Another telling remark in this taped conversation is Chandler's response when asked how this caper of his will help his son, "That's irrelevant to me." Throughout the whole ugly media massacre, there had been no indication from Chandler that he wanted Michael Jackson criminally punished for his supposed crime.

In these recordings there are many indications that Chandler was very interested in profiting from the situation he created. Instead of making any report to the police for what he alleged happened to his son, he arranged a meeting with Michael and his attorneys to discuss movie deals. The father initially asked for funding for four movies, at $5 million each, a total of $20 million. This was refused by the Jackson camp and a counter offer of $350,000 for one movie was made. After considering it, Chandler refused.

Michael's concert scheduled for Wednesday, August 25, was postponed until the next day as Michael was suffering from acute dehydration and was under a doctor's care. He was receiving liquids intravenously. The dehydration was said to be brought on by the heat and high humidity in Bangkok, and not from the stress of the investigation, but that seems doubtful at best. Tour sponsor Pepsi chief competitor immediately began running ads in newspapers, and put up billboards in Bangkok reading, "Dehydrated? There's Always Coke". The ads were immediately pulled after several complaints were received that they were in poor taste.

It was soon being reported in the news that the investigation had widened to include four more boys, "Pop star inquiry expands to 4 boys" misled readers into believing there were more allegations being made against Michael Jackson by additional boys. This was absolutely not the case. The investigators from the police departments Sexually Exploited Child Unit had *interviewed* four more boys, all friends of Michael's, about their relationship with him in an attempt to find corroboration for the thirteen year old's story. Jordie had given names to authorities of other boys he said were also abused by Michael Jackson, including Macaulay Culkin. The police found nothing to support the abuse claims. All of the boys interviewed told police their relationship with Michael was purely brotherly, that they were friends, and there was never any inappropriate behavior on Michael's part whatsoever. This eventually grew to a list of thirty boys to over one hundred who were interviewed by police and included Emmanuel Lewis and Jimmy Safechuck. Every one of these boys told police nothing inappropriate ever happened to them with Michael Jackson and they never witnessed any inappropriate behavior.

The police were questioning every person listed in an address book that was seized in the search. The police questioned all young friends of Michael's, and their siblings and their friends in hopes someone would have confided in them. They found nothing. The police reportedly even resorted to lying to the young boys in an effort to get them to admit to something. Michael's attorney Bert Fields learned of this and fired off a letter to Los Angeles Police Chief Willie

Williams:

> *I am advised that your officers have told frightened youngsters outrageous lies, such as, `We have nude photos of you', to push them into making accusations against Mr. Jackson. There are, of course, no such photos of these youngsters, and they have no truthful allegations to make. But your officers appear ready to employ any device to generate potential evidence against Mr. Jackson.*

Chief Williams' only response was that he was satisfied with the investigation by his officers.

In broadcasting the story, *Hard Copy* correspondent Diane Dimond reported, "And one more shocker, *Hard Copy* has obtained new documents in the criminal investigation of Michael Jackson and they are chilling, they contain the name of child movie actor Macaulay Culkin." Delicately tip toeing around the facts, this teaser certainly suggests Culkin was another "victim" of abuse by Michael Jackson. What was conveniently ignored is that Culkin told police there was never any improper conduct by Michael. Only the fact that four more boys were being questioned seemed to make the evening news insinuating that the investigation was widening to include more victims. The fact that each one of these boys said there was never any improper conduct by Michael Jackson was generally not reported or was tagged on quickly at the end of a report. Dimond built her career riding on scandalous stories – starting with Michael Jackson – and returning at every opportunity to lead the media crusade against him.

One of the young boys interviewed was eleven year old Brett

Barnes from Melbourne, Australia. Brett was a pen pal of Michael's who Michael had flown to California, with his mother and sister. Brett and his family were at Michael's ranch when the police conducted their search. The boy vehemently defended his friend telling a Los Angeles TV station, KNBC, "He's like a best friend, except he's big". He admitted that he had shared a bed with Michael, that both were fully clothed and on opposite sides of a big bed, "He slept on one side and I slept on the other. It was a big bed." He stated further that there was no inappropriate behavior. He said Michael was affectionate, but "like a big brother". Barnes added that he did know the boy making the allegations against Michael and that he had never mentioned anything unusual happening with Michael and Barnes never saw any improper behavior.

Wade Robson, a ten year old friend of Michael's, also said he had shared a bed with Michael but they were both wearing pajamas and they "just went to sleep." He stated further that, "Michael Jackson would never do anything like this." Joy Robson, Wade's mother, was not concerned with her son's relationship with Michael Jackson, "There's nothing unusual there at all. They're good friends. They're buddies." Today, Robson is a well known choreographer and was part of the tribute to Michael Jackson on the MTV Video Music Awards in 2009. He would continue to staunchly defend his friend.

In a show of unity, the Jackson family issued a statement to the press expressing their support of Michael:

We wish to state our collective, unequivocal belief that Michael has been made the victim of a cruel and obvious attempt to take advantage of his fame and success. We know, as does the whole world, that he has dedicated his life to providing happiness for young people everywhere. His compassion for the problems of all people is legendary. Accordingly, we are confident that his dignity and humanity will prevail at this most difficult time. Our entire family stands firmly at this side.

The outpouring of support for Michael was truly overwhelming. Many went public with vehement support of Michael. People who have worked with Michael for many years made public statements of their knowledge that Michael was incapable of ever hurting a child. Jerry Kramer, who worked with Michael on *The Making of Michael Jackson's Thriller* and *Moonwalker*, told the *Today Show* he didn't believe this was something Michael Jackson would do. He said further that he has only ever seen very normal behavior with Michael Jackson and children.

Alfonso Ribeiro, who first met Michael when he was twelve during the making of the Jackson Pepsi Ads, also expressed his support for Michael. Mothers of young children who have spent time with Michael, including Ryan White's mother Jeanne, spoke out that they implicitly trusted Michael with their children.

Michael Jackson biographer J. Randy Taraborrelli and Jackson researcher Lisa Campbell each appeared on news programs and each stated their beliefs, that he wasn't capable of committing the acts of which he was accused. Taraborrelli said in researching Jackson's life he found that "there have been many, many accusations made against Michael Jackson and none of them *ever* panned out, never found one instance that came to be even remotely true."

Michael's second concert in Bangkok had to be rescheduled for the second time when he was still suffering from dehydration. He released an audio taped message which was played for the press apologizing to his fans:

To all my fans in Bangkok, Thailand, I am sorry for not performing yesterday as I am really sick and still under medical treatment. I have been instructed by my doctor not to perform before Friday, August 27, 1993. I promise all my fans to perform at the National Stadium in Bangkok on August 27. I will see you all on Friday. I love you all. Goodbye.

The second concert in Bangkok did go on as planned on Friday. The crowd of 70,000 fans chanted, "Michael, Michael" and held banners reading, "We Love You".

The Dangerous tour's sponsor, Pepsi International, was also in support of Michael. Their sponsorship of the tour continued, and they continued to air two Pepsi commercials in Asia featuring Michael Jackson. Pepsi spokesmen initially stated they supported Michael one hundred percent, this was later downgraded to a more wait and see attitude, but they maintained there was no proof of any wrongdoing on behalf of Michael Jackson and unless the investigation took a sudden downturn, they would continue to support him. It later turned out they needed no such proof, but for now they still sponsored the Dangerous tour and said publicly that they supported Michael Jackson.

Perhaps the most fervent support for Michael Jackson came from his millions of fans across the globe. His accusers assumed the public allegations would destroy the King of Pop but they grossly underestimated his legions of fans. They continued to see him as more than an entertainer, he is an inspiration to all of his fans, young and old, and they love him. Radio stations reported that Michael Jackson's fans were jamming the phone lines in support of him. Record sales were reported to be increased since the allegations become public. The tens of thousands of fans jamming into stadiums in Bangkok and later Singapore and Taiwan certainly didn't seem to be swayed by any of the allegations. Fans surrounded his hotel, sang "Heal the World" and cheered wildly when Michael would wave to them from the window.

The next set of concerts were in Singapore at the National Stadium. The first of the two shows was on August 29, 1993, Michael's thirty-fifth birthday. Fans fought monsoon rains and traffic jams to attend the show. Many held banners reading, "We Love You" and "Happy Birthday" as they chanted, "We Love Michael!" During the third song of the set, the band began playing "Happy Birthday" and the capacity crowd of 47,000 sang along. Michael paced the stage, smiling, and seemed genuinely touched by the sentiment.

The second show in Singapore, on Monday, was postponed shortly before Michael was to go on stage, disappointing the capacity crowd. Michael had become ill. He had fainted backstage, was complaining of dizziness and he was vomiting. The show was rescheduled for Wednesday. The next day Michael was given several tests, including an MRI scan, and was declared by his doctor to be fit and ready to perform on Wednesday. Michael had suffered from a severe migraine headache. He often presented physical symptoms when stress levels in his life were off the charts. To apologize to his fans in Singapore, he released a second audio taped message that was played for the press by MJJ Productions' Vice President, Bob Jones:

I was suddenly taken ill last night and I am sorry for the cancellation of my performance and I apologize for any inconvenience it might have caused my fans in Singapore. I look forward to seeing you at the stadium tomorrow. Thank you for your continued support and understanding. I love you all. Thank you.

While in Singapore, Michael was honored with a special orchid bearing his name. The orchid accolade is usually awarded only to visiting royalty and dignitaries. It was presented to Michael by Sony Music Entertainment Singapore managing director Terence Phung, marketing manager Ian Ng and international A&R manager Joseph Loo.

On Monday, August 30, the Jackson family held a press conference, one that had been planned well before the allegations against Michael were made. Joseph, Katherine, Rebbie, Tito, and Jermaine met with reporters to announce their plans for the *Jackson Family Honors*, a reunion special and award show. They did however address the allegations surrounding Michael. Jermaine read a statement that the entire Jackson family supported Michael. Katherine also told reporters:

First of all, I'd like to let the world know that I'm behind my son. I don't believe any of the stuff that's being written about him, because I raised him and I know that's just a statement people are making. I love him. I've talked with him several times since this had come out and I plan to go and visit him and he knows when I'm coming.

Gloria Allred, an attorney hired to represent Jordie Chandler, held a press conference two days after being hired declaring that, "my client wants to have his day in court." Within a few days of her assertion about her client that, "he is ready, he is willing, he is able to testify", she withdrew from the case and refused to disclose why. Michael Freeman, the attorney representing the boy's mother, also withdrew from the case. Freeman said at one point that he felt Michael was innocent and was the victim of an extortion plot by Evan Chandler and his attorney Barry Rothman. Larry Feldman was now representing the boy. It seemed as though the boy may not have been so willing to testify after all.

Immediately after Gloria Allred was replaced, the boy's new lawyer, Larry Feldman, filed a civil suit in Los Angeles Superior Court accusing Michael Jackson of battery, infliction of emotional distress and fraud. The suit asked for unspecified monetary damages. This action certainly seemed suspect. Following an emotional statement by their attorney that the boy was ready to go to court, that attorney was fired and replaced with a civil suit being filed immediately. Some attorneys, not connected with this case, speculated that the filing of the civil case would kill the criminal case once the jury became aware that the plaintiffs are only interested in money. It would take much more than this however for the police investigators to give up on their investigation. Despite having no physical evidence and no corroboration for the boy's allegations, the criminal investigation would continue for several months.

On Friday, September 3, several Jackson family members, including his parents, arrived in Taipei, Taiwan, the Dangerous tour's next stop. Michael arrived in Taipei on the same day with Elizabeth Taylor, who wasted no time flying to join and support her friend, and was greeted by hordes of cheering fans who followed him to his hotel.

Michael by this time was emotionally and physically drained by the ongoing investigation and nonstop media frenzy. He was also in no mood for a family visit. He had previously refused to participate in the upcoming Jackson Family Honors program, but being under tremendous stress, Jermaine was able to wear him down and get his consent to be a part of it.

He was not sleeping and was not eating. According to Taraborrelli, Elizabeth Taylor had to at times feed him herself. She even threatened at one point to bring his parents up to his room if he refused to eat something. He immediately crammed some food in his mouth to appease her.

Continuing the tour under the intolerable amount of stress, he reached out to his second family, the Cascios. He asked Dominic Cascio if he would allow the kids to join him on tour. Knowing and trusting Michael implicitly, he agreed. Frank Cascio then flew to be at Michael's side in this hour of need. In his book, *My Friend Michael, An Ordinary Friendship with an Extraordinary Man,* he wrote: "I want to be precise and clear, on the record, so that everyone can read and understand: Michael's love for children was innocent, and is profoundly misunderstood."

The tour's next stop was Fukoka, Japan where he thrilled

"Will You Be There"

30,000 fans at his September 10th concert. Fans held banners reading, "We Believe You" and "We Believe You Always." There was also one special fan who got to see Michael perform in Japan. Michael had flown a terminally ill Dutch boy, fifteen year old Martijn Hendricsen, and his two brothers to Japan. They were driven in a gold limousine to Amsterdam airport to meet Michael Jackson and see the concert. Michael had responded to a request from the Make-A-Wish Foundation. Martijn, undergoing chemotherapy for cancer, had wished to meet his idol, Michael Jackson.

The September 10, 1993 issue of *Entertainment Weekly* magazine featured Michael Jackson on its cover with the caption, "How Bad?" Inside was a reader's poll that indicated Michael's popularity had actually risen since the allegations first become public. *Billboard* magazine reported similar findings. Michael's sales and airplay showed no adverse effect due to the unsubstantiated allegations being made against him. His current single, "Will You Be There" was ranked at number seven with a bullet on the Hot 100 singles chart and it was in the top ten, or at number one, on the airplay lists of many stations. Airplay of the song's video remained constant on MTV and Vh-1.

Over the weekend of September 11 and 12, fans marched in support of Michael Jackson in Hollywood. Flowers and cards were left at his freshly polished star on Hollywood's Walk of Fame. At a time when his latest single was reflecting his real life, asking, "In my darkest hour, In my deepest despair, Will you still care?, Will you be there?", the answer from his fans was a resounding "yes".

While his career was not yet directly affected, the scandal attached to Michael Jackson did take a toll in different ways. It was later announced that Michael Jackson would not be receiving the Scopus Award from the Friends of Hebrew University. He had been previously announced as the recipient in July, 1993. The award, from the American Friends of Hebrew University, was in recognition of his international humanitarian efforts. While the media liked to print that Michael had been dumped, Michael's publicist announced that he had asked to be withdrawn from consideration. A phone call to the West Coast Friends of Hebrew University confirmed the publicist's statement.

The next tour stop was Moscow, at the Lyzhniki Olympic Stadium. Michael left Moscow for Israel where 80,000 screaming fans jammed into the stadium to see him at the first of two shows in Tel Aviv. Besides sightseeing, Michael visited child cancer victims in Israel and he visited Tsirn Army Base.

Meanwhile, the tabloids and talk shows couldn't get enough of the "Michael Jackson Scandal". Soon former employees of Michael's would begin crawling out of the woodwork with inside information on Michael's personal life. This "information" was for sale to the highest bidder, and the tabloid magazines and tabloid TV shows were climbing over each other at the chance to land "the exclusive interview". Whether or not the information was true was not an issue. First up was Mark and Faye Quindoy, a Filipino husband and wife who had worked as a housekeeper and cook at Neverland from 1989 to 1991. The Quindoys had filed a lawsuit against Michael Jackson for overdue pay.

Later, they claimed they quit because they couldn't stand what they were observing at the ranch. They weren't concerned enough to mention any of it to the authorities though.

Mark and Faye Quindoy had now suddenly obtained a diary which they held at a press conference which they claimed they had kept while working at the ranch in which they described various questionable acts by "MJ". A very important thing to point out here is that, like so many others in this media fiasco, the Quindoys first told, and sold, their story to the media and did not take anything to the police. And then the police went to them, they did not take their "information" to any authorities. In response to the Quindoy's media blitz with their "diary" two detectives flew to Manila to question them. It would later be learned that FBI agents accompanied the detectives to question the Quindoys, marking the beginnings of a file the FBI would maintain on Michael Jackson. The Quindoys were found to be worthless as witnesses.

J. Randy Taraborrelli, author of *Michael Jackson: The Magic and the Madness*, also made one of numerous television appearances to express his belief that the allegations were "bogus" and that Michael will surely be cleared of the allegations. He also expressed his surprise by the lack of support from his celebrity friends, Diana Ross, Liza Minnelli, Sophia Loren, Oprah Winfrey, Eddie Murphy, Brooke Shields and Donald Trump. While the silence from some of his friends was deafening, it was also true that the media was not interested in interviews or stories that held a positive stance for Michael Jackson. I personally experienced this. Just a few months earlier my first book chronicling Michael's life and career was published. There was initially a high level of interest in my work by print and television media. After the story of the allegations became public interest in a book touting his greatness evaporated. Scheduled appearances on talk shows were cancelled and interviews that had yet to air never did.

Phillipe and Stella Lemarque, who worked for less than a year at Neverland were also working feverishly to sell their story. The Lemarques were also not above tailoring their story to fit their needs. They initially asked for $100,000 for a story claiming they saw Michael Jackson sexually caress young visitors, including Macaulay Culkin. As their asking price rose, the story changed. When their price increased to $500,000, Michael's hand moved to inside Culkin's pants.

Despite appearances in the media, there were still some who were firmly in Michael's corner. Sony issued a statement in October reinforcing their support for Michael:

Sony Music's support for Michael Jackson remains unwavering and unconditional. We are heartened by the overwhelming public support for Michael Jackson and widespread skepticism of the allegations brought against him. We are confident the allegations against him are without merit and believe the investigation will exonerate Michael.

Frank Dileo, in his first public statement since being fired as Michael's manager in 1990, supported Michael telling *Rolling Stone*, "I would trust my own children with him, and have...He lived in my house in Encino for seven months. There is no way that he did that. It's not in his nature." Dileo also told *Entertainment Weekly,* "Michael never really had a childhood and I think he is trying to experience it in later life. I would tell him to keep the knowledge that he is innocent and hold his head up." Bruce Swedien, a recording engineer and producer who had worked with Michael for years, told *Rolling Stone*, "I am mortified and disgusted by what has been reported with no evidence of anything untoward. Michael is one of the most decent people I've ever met in my life. These allegations are preposterous." Attorney John Branca told the same issue of *Rolling Stone*, "If the sense is that Michael was unfairly accused, I think people will empathize with him as a victim to such a degree that is will be a major positive in his career... I think people will be so disgusted, that they'll say, `Look at this guy. He did nothing wrong and look what the press did to him'. I think he will be a hero." Frank and Eddie Cascio traveled with Michael Jackson and stayed with him at Neverland while many other visitors were also there, including Jordie Chandler. They were there. They themselves spent time with Michael and knew his relationships with young people were all innocent.

Samuel Jackson, Michael's grandfather, died on October 31, 1993 in a Phoenix nursing home. Michael did not leave his tour to attend the funeral. Earlier in the month, Michael's thirty-five year old cousin, Tony Jackson, died in a car accident. Michael was very close to his cousin and while he wasn't able to return home for the funeral, he did pay all of the funeral expenses.

Michael was greeted by hundreds of cheering fans in Argentina and in Buenos Aires where thousands of tickets were given out to disadvantaged children. Another illness forced the cancellation of a show scheduled for October 21 in Chile. Some reports said he was suffering from throat problems, others blamed the illness on drinking tap water. The performance was rescheduled. A pulled back muscle was blamed for the cancellation of a show in Lima, Peru.

Seventy thousand fans packed into Aztec Stadium in Mexico City on October 29th were unconcerned about the investigation and shouted, "Michael!, Michael!" Michael kept the hysterical crowd on their feet for more than two hours.

A show scheduled for November 2nd in Mexico City was postponed due to Michael suffering from a toothache. Shows scheduled for November 4th and 6th were postponed as he recovered from oral surgery. He had been hospitalized overnight following the extraction of an abscessed tooth. All three shows were rescheduled.

During his stay in Mexico, Sony Music Mexico executives Aloysio Reis and Raul Vasquez presented Michael with a double platinum award for sales of *Dangerous* in excess of 500,000 copies in Mexico. Despite his continued legal problems, sales of *Dangerous* increased five hundred percent during his stay there and fans flocked to his concerts. In five shows, the Dangerous tour played to over 500,000 fans in Mexico. His previous three shows in Buenos Aires, Argentina, attracted 240,000 fans, two shows in Sao Paulo, Brazil played to 160,000 fans, and 85,000 fans attended a single show in Santiago, Chile.

It was being reported in the press at this time that the police had obtained a search warrant for Michael Jackson's body. His accuser had given police a description of Michael Jackson's body, including his genitals, describing blotches on Michael's skin caused from his vitiligo. Authorities wanted to inspect Michael's body to see if the boy's description was a match.

Elizabeth Taylor and Larry Fortensky flew to Mexico on November 9th to again be by Michael's side. Michael reportedly called Taylor and was feeling very distressed. After Michael's performance in Mexico on Thursday, November 11, Michael, Elizabeth and Larry never returned to the El Presidente Hotel. They boarded Elizabeth's charted plane and left Mexico. The plane refueled in Toronto, stopped briefly in Iceland, then landed Saturday morning at London's Luton Airport. The plane then left for Switzerland. Michael was seen clearing customs in England but it could not be confirmed where he went from there. Elizabeth Taylor was seen in Switzerland, but Michael was not with her. Then a startling announcement was made.

22

*I'll never betray or deceive you my friend
But if you show me the cash, then I will take it
If you tell me to cry, then I will fake it
If you give me a hand, then I will shake it
You'll do anything for money*

"Money"
- Michael Jackson

It was shocking to learn that the remaining dates of the Dangerous tour were being cancelled and even more shocking was the news that Michael Jackson was seeking treatment for a dependency on painkillers. An audio taped message was released to the press in which Michael explained the cancellation of the tour and his need for treatment:

As I left on this tour, I had been the target of an extortion attempt, and shortly thereafter was accused of horrifying and outrageous conduct.

I was humiliated, embarrassed, hurt and suffering great pain in my heart. The pressure resulting from these false allegations coupled with the incredible energy necessary for me to perform caused so much distress that it left me physically and emotionally exhausted. I became increasingly more dependent on the painkillers to get me through the days of the tour. My friends and doctors advised me to seek professional guidance immediately in order to eliminate what has become an addiction. It is time for me to acknowledge my need for treatment in order to regain my health. I realize that completing the tour is no longer possible and I must cancel the remaining dates. I know I can overcome the problem and will be stronger from the experience."

Michael's virtual disappearance pushed the already frenzied media into overdrive. Rumors of every sort imaginable came from literally all over the world. Speculation on his whereabouts included Elton John's house in London, Elizabeth Taylor's chalet in Gstaad, Switzerland, a resort in the French Alps, a hospital in Canada, a hospital in Connecticut, a facility in Kansas, and his own ranch in Los Olivos. One British tabloid, the *Daily Mirror,* held a "Spot the Jacko" contest offering readers a vacation to Disney World if they could correctly predict where Michael Jackson would appear next. The most widely believed location was the Charter Nightingale Clinic in London. Many sources reported Michael and five bodyguards were occupying the hospital's entire fourth floor. He was said to be receiving treatment by Dr. Beauchamp Colclough, who had been recommended by Elton John. Dr. Colclough had treated Elton John for dependency problems. The hospital refused to confirm whether or not Michael was there.

Elton John responded to the rumors that Michael Jackson was staying at his house when he was in London to accept a music award. Elton told the crowd, "Michael says, `hi', I would have brought him with me but he's busy hoovering (vacuuming) his fucking room!" Actually Michael had spent a short time, about two days, at Elton's house before moving to the Charter Clinic. Michael later described Elton John as "one of the sweetest people you could meet on this planet."

Wherever he was, Michael seemed intent on staying out of sight. His attorneys would not comment on his location, neither would Elizabeth Taylor, who had been instrumental in helping Michael get out of Mexico to receive treatment. Michael Jackson impersonators, presumably hired by the Jackson camp, began popping up in London and throughout Europe throwing photographers and reporters off track. Reporters in London staked out hotels, hospitals, Toys R Us stores and zoos hoping to be the one to finally find Michael Jackson. They found nothing.

Regardless if they didn't know where he was, the tabloids continued churning out stories claiming they knew not only where he was, put what his plans were. The *Sunday Express* headline read, "Drug Treatment Star Faces Life on the Run". The ever accurate and ethical *News of the World* ran the headline, "Hunt for Jacko the Fugitive". Many stories claimed Michael Jackson would never return to the United States, living the rest of his life in hiding somewhere in Europe. Others said Michael left Mexico and skipped the tour's next stop, Puerto Rico, which is a U.S. territory, fearing he would be arrested. Michael actually confided in Frank Cascio that this was actually the case. Other rumors being treated by some media outlets as fact included Michael preparing to come back to the U.S. to turn himself in, others had him on the verge of suicide. The most outrageous stories had Michael hiding out in Europe to undergo cosmetic surgery on his genitals so his appearance would no longer match the description the boy had given to police. Virtually all the tabloid stories and some of the more legitimate news sources cast doubt on Michael's painkiller dependency. But the dependency problem was all too real.

The Monday following the cancellation of the tour, attorney Bert Fields held a press conference and explained that Michael Jackson was indeed receiving treatment for a painkiller dependency and they expected the treatment to take six to eight weeks. Fields did concede that Michael Jackson was "barely able to function on an intellectual level." He would not disclose Michael's location but he did emphasize, "He has no intention of avoiding coming to the U.S."

More doubt was cast on Michael's painkiller dependency by Howard Manning Jr. who had deposed Michael in Mexico just before the cancellation of the tour. Howard Manning flew to Mexico City to take Michael's deposition for a copyright infringement case. Michael, along with Lionel Richie, Quincy Jones, Rod Temperton and Joe Jackson were being sued for stealing "The Girl is Mine", "Thriller", and

"We are the World". Manning spent seven hours deposing Michael for the case on November 8 and November 10. Michael's testimony was videotaped for use in the court case. Manning had deposed Michael in connection with another copyright case in 1989. He told the media that Michael was articulate, could remember details of writing songs with no problem, and he described him as a "coherent, sharp witness", "We became familiar with his brightness. This man knows pretty much about the business. He knows and can recall a good deal about songs he's written, or not written, that goes back years. There was no difference in that performance last week, no difference between that and 1989."

Manning added, "We were not informed of any addiction problem. We did not see any evidence of an addiction problem. The witness was alert, he didn't slur. He answered questions just as he had in 1989." Actually, Bert Fields felt Michael was in no condition to be deposed, but a motion to delay the proceedings had been denied and they had no choice but to continue with the deposition.

The case went to court in December. During the proceeding's, Michael's testimony was finally played giving the public their first sense of his condition upon canceling the Dangerous tour. After weeks of skepticism surrounding his statement of his painkiller dependency the public could finally see for themselves. Michael was obviously under the influence of some type of medication. He appeared very drowsy, barely able to concentrate. He had difficulty at times understanding the questions put before him, often asking that the questions be repeated. At one point he even struggles to name all the members of the Jackson 5, counting on his fingers to make sure he included everyone. (Actually, he got it wrong, he included Randy who wasn't a member of the Jackson 5, only the Jacksons.) The questioning is even stopped at one point so Michael can take a break as he is suffering pain in his mouth due to his recent oral surgery. When the questioning resumes, he admits he did take a painkiller during the break.

When the allegations against Michael first became public, Pepsi continued sponsorship of the Dangerous tour and said they supported Michael. Their support weakened dramatically and quickly and they soon developed a wait and see attitude. In what is quite possibly the worst cola decision since New Coke, Pepsi announced on November 14, 1993 that their relationship with Michael Jackson was over. Pepsico spokesman Gary Hemphill said Pepsi's sponsorship was to end when the tour did, so the ending of the tour means, "we no longer have a relationship." Pepsi's haste to put some distance between themselves and Michael Jackson over *unproven* allegations left a bad taste in the mouth of Jackson fans. Fans made bumper stickers declaring, "Pepsi dumped Michael, we're dumping Pepsi." A call to a company spokesperson did little to support their statement that they were just ending sponsorship of a now cancelled tour. When on the upswing again a few years later with the HIStory tour, fair weather friend Pepsi would once again serve as the tour's sponsor.

While Pepsi deserted Michael, Sony did not. On November 17, Sony issued a statement to the press expressing their support for Michael during his legal battles and his health problems, "Michael

Michael Jackson: The Complete Story of the King of Pop

Jackson's unique position as a world class artist and humanitarian is as important to Sony as it is to the tens of millions around the globe who have been touched by his art and his faith." Sony further commended Michael and his "... personal courage in facing up to the pain of addiction and the difficult path to full recovery that lies ahead. We will stand behind him every step of the way with all the unconditional support and encouragement we can provide." Granted, Sony had a large stake in not seeing the Michael Jackson money machine grind to a halt, and his record sales thus far had actually increased, but the public show of support was still welcomed.

Michael Jackson's millions of devoted fans around the world were standing solidly behind Michael too. They were not about to allow the media's bashing of Michael Jackson go unchecked and they were very eager to let Pepsi, Sony, and Michael Jackson himself know exactly how they felt. Michael Jackson fan clubs and fan magazines, such as Lori Byler's Michael Jackson Observer Fan Club, Carol Armstrong's Magic World of Michael Jackson and Adrian Grant's *Off The Wall* magazine, encouraged members to actively show their support for Michael. Fans wrote Sony expressing their support for Michael, and they wrote Pepsi condemning their decision to drop him. Pepsi, and all Pepsi products, were vigorously boycotted. Fans were encouraged to write newspapers and TV networks demanding fair coverage of the story. Michael Jackson albums were re-purchased by fans to show their support for him, and of course, Michael himself received a flood of cards, letters and flowers, white roses, as a symbol of innocence.

As skepticism about Michael's painkiller dependency ran rampant for days on end, there was finally, on November 22, a statement released by the doctor who was treating Michael. Dr. Beauchamp Colclough sent a letter to the press to "refute any suggestion that Mr. Jackson is `hiding out' or seeking any other care other than the program for analgesia abuse."

Mr. Jackson was presented to me on Friday evening, 12th November 1993 by Dr. David Forecast and Miss Elizabeth Taylor, after their trip from Mexico City... An initial assessment of Mr. Jackson's condition was made. A detoxification program was completed today. After an initial 36 hours, Mr. Jackson's started an intensive program of group therapy and one-to-one therapy with myself.

I confirm that no other medical, surgical, or psychological condition exits. I present this statement to strongly refute any suggestion that Mr. Jackson is `hiding out' or seeking any other care.

Superior Court Judge David M. Rothman, on November 23, denied a request filed by Michael's attorneys to postpone the civil suit until the criminal proceedings were completed. The judge ruled that the boy's right to a speedy trial prevailed over Michael Jackson's request to delay the proceedings and set a court date for March 21, 1994. Bert Fields stated that Michael wanted to testify and clear his name in the criminal proceedings before the civil trial. That would of course hurt the prosecution's case in the civil suit.

On the music front, the November release of Michael Jackson's *Greatest Hits* album was postponed because Michael had not yet finished recording the new songs to be included on the album. The album was now scheduled for release in mid 1994. But that didn't mean there wouldn't be new Michael Jackson products on the market for Christmas. In November, *Dangerous: The Short Films*, a collection of videos from the *Dangerous* album was released. Included was the complete version of "Black or White" which had been enhanced to now include racial slurs and a swastika painted on the car windows and store front window that Michael smashes out. Footage was included of the uproar caused by the video's premiere. Jewels included never before seen behind the scenes of "Black or White", making of "In the Closet" and "Jam". The short film for "Who Is It" that was only released in Europe was finally seen by his U.S. fans.

Epic released the video package betting Michaelmania was still alive and well. They were right. *Dangerous: The Short Films* was reported to be selling strongly, with some outlets reporting they couldn't keep it on the shelves. *Dangerous: The Short Films* debuted on *Billboard's* Top Music Video chart at number four, where it spent several months in the top five.

Also out in time for Christmas was *Pigtails and Frog Legs*, a holiday cookbook produced by the Neiman Marcus stores. The Foreword was provided by Michael Jackson titled "Nourish This Child", in which he expressed his feelings of how a mother shows her love in preparing food for her child. According to Neiman Marcus spokeswoman Liz Barrett, sales of the book were unaffected by Michael's legal situation.

The business side of Michael's life was also flourishing. On

November 24, it was announced that he had just closed the biggest music publishing deal in history. He had agreed to let EMI Music manage his music publishing company, ATV Music. The total value of the deal was reported to be $200 million, with Michael getting $100 million in advance. As part of the five year deal, EMI agreed to provide funds with which to acquire other music catalogs and then share ownership with Michael Jackson.

Just when it seemed Michael's legal problems had peaked, five former security guards that had worked at Hayvenhurst filed a lawsuit against Michael Jackson, Anthony Pellicano, MJJ Productions executive Norma Staikos and others, in November claiming they were fired because they "knew too much." The suit asked for unspecified monetary damages and charged Michael and the others with conspiracy, harassment, wiretapping, and surveillance.

As would be the case with other former employees of Michael's, suddenly appearing on TV claiming they had some critical information about Michael Jackson, their stories seemed to raise more questions about their own credibility than cast any doubt on Michael's innocence. This didn't prevent *Hard Copy* or *A Current Affair* from exploiting the stories of course. *Hard Copy* paid the guards $150,000 for their story. In fact, the most serious damage to Michael Jackson didn't come from what these former employees had to say, but the attention they were given by the tabloid media.

A few weeks later another former employee came forward with supposedly more damaging "inside" information on Michael. Branca Francia worked as a maid at Neverland Valley from 1988 to

1991. She claimed she quit in disgust in 1991. In December, 1993, she couldn't hold this "information" in any longer and just had to tell it to Diane Dimond of *Hard Copy*. She was paid $20,000 for her story. *Hard Copy* built her up as trusted confident of Michael Jackson's when actually the maid, who had been fired two years earlier, hardly knew Michael Jackson. Only after her exclusive interview with the tabloid TV show, and she cashed her check, did she give a deposition for the civil suit.

    Francia's story has more holes in it than that of the five guards. Among her claims were instances of her entering Michael's bedroom to find him in the shower with a young boy. And, according to the interview that was aired on TV, she suspected there was possible molestation of her own son, Jason. Again the question is raised of why, upon witnessing these things, did she not go directly to the police? Why would she wait two years to speak out, especially if she suspected abuse of *her own son?*

    The claims made by Francia simply do not fit. It was said that the floor outside Michael's bedroom was wired, so sounds or footsteps in the hallway were amplified, letting him be aware when someone was coming. Why would he then allow anyone to enter his room if he were in the shower, whether alone or with another person? Michael's shyness and self consciousness were so intense, he wore sunglasses and sometimes a surgical mask in public so people couldn't see his face. As a teenager he had acne on his face that caused so much distress for him that he stopped looking at people in the eye, and he would wash his face in the dark so he wouldn't have to look at his own reflection in the mirror. Sufferers of vitiligo tend to become very self conscious of the blotching. That hardly sounds like someone who would allow his household staff to parade around his bathroom while he was naked. Francia's claims were refuted by several other former employees. Eventually a settlement of $2 million was paid to Francia in connection to a "tickling incident' with her son, Jason.

    As the tabloid media never missed an opportunity to exploit the Michael Jackson story, the mainstream media took several poundings by people outraged at their unfair handling of the story and their apparent assumption that Michael was guilty. One of those who stepped up to publicly denounce the media was Oscar winning actor Maximilian Schell. Schell paid to have a one page hand written letter to Michael published on the back page of the *Hollywood Reporter:*

    To Michael Jackson (Somewhere on this planet)
Dear Michael,

    I am deeply ashamed - for the press, for the media, for the world. I don't know you - we met only once on one of those award dinners (Entertainer of the Decade). We shook hands - you were kind and polite. I don't think you knew who I was. How should you? Our world's are too far apart - (I am more "classical" minded -) but I looked into your eyes - they were kind.

    You are a great artist and I admire you. My little daughter (she is 4 1/2) loves you! Deeply - she even wants to marry you! ("But he never calls me!") She imitates you all the time - and quite well.

    We all love you. I would like her more to listen to Mozart but she loves YOU! AND I RESPECT HER TASTE! - That you survive this avalanche of dirt thrown at you - I admire tremendously. Thank you for what you are! God bless you.

Maximilian Schell

P.S. *"One can only see good with the heart. The essential is invisible to the eyes." ("The Little Prince").*

Shannon Reeves, the West Coast Region Director of the NAACP called a news conference for Monday, December 20, to discuss, "the media bashing of entertainer Michael Jackson and to address how other economically powerful African Americans have been victimized by the press:"

The coverage of the allegations facing Michael Jackson is excessive. You have made the point. There have been no charges filed. If there are charges filed in the Jackson case, those charges will be filed in the courtroom, not the newsroom. If there is to be someone to judge the case it will not be the evening news anchor, it will be someone who is elected or party to the bench. If there is someone to hear the facts in the case and make a decision, it will not be the news pool or editorial room or editorial board, it will be a jury of his peers.

Janet was offering support for Michael at each of her concerts asking her audiences to say a prayer for her brother. Janet kicked off her janet. world tour in November. Following her medley of hits after first hitting the stage, she spoke to her audience, "to ask something of you. Would you please bow your heads and say a silent prayer for my brother, Michael". She continued to ask the audiences in each city on the tour to pray for Michael.

The December 11, 1993, issue of *Billboard* magazine

celebrated twenty-five years of music and entertainment for concert promoter Marcel Avram. A special section devoted to Avram was comprised of the usual congratulatory ads placed by friends and associates. A completely dark page with only a picture of Michael's eyes read, "Marcel, Congratulations on 25 years. Love, Michael Jackson." One ad was different from the rest. Instead of congratulating the person being recognized in the issue, it was placed by Marcel Avram. The ad featured a color photo of Michael Jackson in concert that spanned two pages and read:

Dangerous World Tour 1993/94

Michael Jackson Produced by Marcel Avram Mama Concerts & Rau

It was accompanied by a listing of sold out concert dates and a note to Michael:

Michael, get well soon and hopefully we'll see you back on stage in the near future!

Thanks to S. Gallin, J. Morey, B. Fields, S. Chabre, B. Bray, B. Grey, H. Sinclare, N. Dugdale and everyone involved for making the biggest and most successful world tour that has ever been staged.

On November 26, the Los Angeles Police Department raided the offices of Michael Jackson's dermatologist, Dr. Arnold Klein, and his plastic surgeon, Dr. Steve Hoefflin. They hoped to compare information, or photos, contained in the files with the description of Michael's body Jordie had given to police. They confiscated Michael's medical records but did not reveal what they contained. A warrant for a body search was soon obtained for Michael Jackson.

Thus far, Pepsi had turned on Michael but Sony's support seemed genuine and unwavering. In late November, a spokesman for Walt Disney World in Orlando, Florida, said Michael Jackson's 3-D movie, *Captain EO* "continues to be one of our most popular attractions." There was said to be no plans to replace the attraction. Sadly, Disney's commitment turned out to be every bit as strong as Pepsi's.

Finally getting fed up with the media assassination of her son's character, Katherine Jackson, with Jermaine, appeared on CNN's *Showbiz Today* and even *Hard Copy* on December 2, to defend Michael. The family had apparently been advised by Michael's representatives to remain quiet about the allegations publicly. Katherine couldn't watch her son be treated so unfairly any longer. "They were telling us not to say anything, but I'm sorry, I'm his mother, I can't sit still and watch them crucify my son and not say anything." Katherine went on to discredit the former security guards refuting each of their claims one by one.

Jermaine added, "They found the one thing that he loves to try to bring him down with and that's being around children." He added that his brother is not the weakling many think he is and he will fight, "He's very strong and he's ready to kick some butt." In his book, *You Are Not Alone*, Jermaine adds, "The core fact is that my brother looked at life through a child's eyes. Age, status, persona and other people's expectations of him had nothing to do with it. He had a child's heart and he never outgrew a childlike enthusiasm for fun – and *this* is why he had a natural affinity with children."

"Money"

While some of his supposedly closest friends were being conspicuously silent, Michael was getting renewed support from friends Paul McCartney and Stevie Wonder. Even though McCartney and Michael had often disagreed on how best to administer the copyrights in the Beatle catalog, McCartney defended Michael in an interview with an Argentine newspaper, *Clarin*, "Linda and I are parents, and it's clear to us that Michael is not that kind of person." Stevie Wonder told *USA Today*, "I don't believe the allegations It's very sad. I'm there for him and I always will be."

Diana Ross talked to Michael on the phone and offered him advice, to come home and face the allegations being made against him, "He must come home and make a stand... Anybody who's accused of wrongdoing needs to." While she may have been offering him advice privately, publicly her silence on the matter was deafening. One of the most asked questions throughout this ordeal was "Where's Diana?"

LaToya, in another sudden change of heart, held a press conference at midnight on December 8 in Tel Aviv, Israel, to announce, "Michael is my brother and I love him a great deal. But, I cannot and will not be a silent collaborator of his crimes against small innocent children... I love my brother but it's wrong. I don't want to see these kids hurt." She claimed further that her mother had shown her checks Michael had written made payable to the parents of children "for large sums", and that the rest of the family defended Michael because he supports them financially and they feared he would cut off the money if they didn't. LaToya added that her mother would refer to Michael as "that damn faggot". LaToya revealed years later that she was forced to make these comments against her brother by her husband/manager Jack Gordon. According to LaToya, Gordon often threatened her life and Michael's if she refused to follow his instructions. Gordon died in April 2005.

The Jackson family, including Katherine, Joseph, Jackie, Tito, Jermaine, and Randy, immediately held a live press conference in front of Hayvenhurst to refute LaToya's most unbelievable, yet most inflammatory, claims to date. The impromptu interview was carried live by CNN. During the interview by CNN reporter Jim Moret, Katherine denied ever showing any checks to LaToya and ever making the remarks about Michael that LaToya said she did. In fact, Katherine had long fought any accusations about Michael's sexuality. Katherine angrily charged that LaToya was making these claims so she too could profit from selling her story to tabloids and talk shows. Joseph said, "We hope Michael's fans all over the world won't believe this." Jermaine answered LaToya's remarks saying, "There is no validity to what she is saying. It is absolutely not true. My brother is not a child molester."

Michael Jackson had been vastly underestimated by the media, something that they would continue to do over and over again. And Michael would show them to be wrong over and over again.

The Jackson family home in Gary, Indiana at 2300 Jackson Street. The house, the size of a two car garage, was home to Joe, Katherine and their nine children.

The gates of the Jackson family home in Encino, California, known as Hayvenhurst.

Ben, was initially issued with a cover featuring a horde of rats. The cover was later changed when the rat cover was viewed as too graphic for children. The "rat cover" version is now a collector's item among fans.

Studio A at Motown's Hitsville USA in Detroit, Michigan.

During the 80's and 90's Michael Jackson appeared on the covers of hundreds of magazines.

In October, 1988, Michael Jackson returned home to Motown. The former Hitsville USA building was now a museum. Michael made the biggest donation of cash and memorabilia to the museum to honor his friend and mentor, Berry Gordy. The presentation was held on the front steps of the museum.

Berry Gordy and Michael Jackson touring the Michael Jackson Room of the Motown Historical Museum.

Michael donated a black fedora and beaded glove, among other items, to the Motown Museum that were showcased in the "Michael Jackson Room", the only room in the museum dedicated to one artist.

Inducted into the Rock and Roll Hall of Fame as a solo artist in March 2001, the special Jackson memorabilia display included the black textured shirt from the "Scream" video, the white pinstripe "Smooth Criminal" suit, Grammy Awards, a blue and gold beaded military jacket, a white beaded glove, sunglasses, and worn black loafers.

Michael was renting this home at 100 N. Carolwood Drive in the Holmby Hills area of Beverly Hills in the spring of 2009. He and his children relocated there as he began work on his return to the stage with This Is It.

Photo courtesy of Misty R. Jones.

Fans flocked to Jackson's star on the Hollywood Walk of Fame to pay their respects and leave mementos.

Photo courtesy of Misty R. Jones.

News of the death of the King of Pop was front page news across the U.S. and throughout the world.

On July 13 2009, the scheduled start date of This Is It, t-shirts began being sold identifying each of the 50 planned shows.

Left to right: Memorial programs for the public memorial service and the private memorial held on July 7, 2009 and an invitation to the private burial on September 3, 2009.

Michael Jackson is interned in the Holly Terrace Mausoleum at Forest Lawn in Glendale, California.

The Grammy Museum in Los Angeles featured a special Michael Jackson exhibit.

In the summer of 2012 the four remaining members of the Jackson 5 set out on the Unity tour. From left; Tito, Jackie, Marlon and Jermaine.

Michael Jackson impersonators enjoyed renewed popularity following Michael's death. Frederick Henry headlined the "American Superstars" show at the Stratosphere in Las Vegas.

Taalib York is one of two lead singers fronting tribute band, Who's Bad. York copies the look and moves of the King of Pop while counterpart Joseph Bell comes closest to duplicating his voice and handles most of the ballads in their performances.

Photo courtesy of Michael Firestone
A wig, two hours in makeup and replicas of his costumes turn Michael Firestone into a very convincing substitute for the original.

Jackson??.... Or Firestone??
Firestone has mastered Jackson's look and moves down to his facial expressions and hand positions.

MJ Fan Fest featured the actual gates of Neverland Valley Ranch and a recreation of his private library.

The costumes he never got a chance to wear for This Is It were featured in the grand display at MJ Fan Fest in Las Vegas in December, 2011.

Some of the merchandise released and projects completed by the estate of Michael Jackson. Some of these projects were in the works at the time of Jackson's death.

23

With such confusions
don't it make you wanna scream
your bash abusin' victimize within the scheme
You try to cope with every lie they scrutinize
Somebody please have mercy
'Cause I just can't take it

"Scream"
- James Harris III, Terry Lewis, Michael Jackson, Janet Jackson

Friday, December 10, Michael Jackson once again proved all the rumormongers and skeptics wrong when he did in fact return home to the United States. He arrived at Santa Barbara airport in a private jet accompanied by the two young brothers from New Jersey, Eddie and Frank Cascio. Camera crews, photographers and reporters immediately staked out the ranch waiting for a glimpse of Michael, or any tidbit of information.

After returning home, Michael took more control over his defense and made some changes in his defense team. Pellicano and Fields were now off the case. Pellicano told *USA Today* that he had done all he could do and that he firmly believed in Michael's innocence. Fields was reported to have been replaced because of a blunder in court in November when he told a judge, and therefore the media and the whole world, that they expected an indictment very soon.

Behind the scenes, the situation was very unorganized. The attorneys, each representing a different firm, weren't really a team. Each was fighting for control, being aware that there was a lot of money and prestige at stake along with possible control of the legal matters in connection with his musical empire. Michael's manager, Sandy Gallin, told *The Wall Street Journal* that "When Michael was away and unreachable, there really wasn't anybody in control."

John Branca, the attorney who represented Michael throughout the eighties, was also exercising some influence in the decision to replace Fields. Attorney Johnnie Cochran Jr. then joined Michael's defense team with Howard Weitzman. Bob Jones had known Cochran since they went to high school together.

With his health much improved, Michael took control, took to his own defense and launched an offensive. "Demonstrating media power normally reserved for world leaders", Michael Jackson issued a long awaited statement which was carried live on CNN, E!, MTV and several other outlets on December 22, 1993 at 3:00 P.M. EST:

"Good afternoon. To all my friends and fans, I wish to convey my deepest gratitude for your love and support. I am doing well and I am strong.

As you may already know, after my tour ended I remained out of the country undergoing treatment for a dependency on pain medication. This medication was initially prescribed to soothe the excruciating pain that I was suffering after recent reconstructive surgery on my scalp.

There have been many disgusting statements made recently concerning allegations of improper conduct on my part. These statements about me are totally false. As I have maintained from the very beginning, I am hoping for a speedy end to this horrifying, horrifying experience to which I have been subjected.

I shall not in this statement respond to all the false allegations being made against me, since my lawyers have advised me that this is not the proper forum in which to do that. I will say I am particularly upset by the handling of this mass matter by the incredible, terrible mass media. At every opportunity, the media has dissected and manipulated these allegations to reach their own conclusions. I ask all of you to wait to hear the truth before you label or condemn me. Don't treat me like a criminal, because I am innocent.

I have been forced to submit to a dehumanizing and humiliating examination by the Santa Barbara County Sheriff's Department and the Los Angeles Police Department earlier this week. They served a search warrant on me which allowed them to view and photograph my body, including my penis, my buttocks, my lower torso, *thighs, and any other areas that they wanted. They were supposedly looking for any discoloration, spotting, blotches or other evidence of a skin color disorder called vitiligo which I have previously spoken about.*

The warrant also directed me to cooperate in any examination of my body by their physician to determine the condition of my skin, including whether I have vitiligo or any other skin disorder. The warrant further stated that I had no right to refuse the examination or photographs and if I failed to cooperate with them they would introduce that refusal at any trial as an indication of my guilt.

It was the most humiliating ordeal of my life - one that no person should ever have to suffer. And even after experiencing the indignity of this search, the parties involved were still not satisfied and wanted to take even more pictures. It was a nightmare, a horrifying nightmare. But if this is what I have to endure to prove my innocence, my complete innocence, so be it.

Throughout my life, I have only tried to help thousands upon thousands of children to live happy lives. It brings tears to my eyes when I see any child who suffers.

If I am guilty of anything, it is of believing what God said about children: `Suffer little children to come unto me and forbid them not, for such is the kingdom of heaven.' In no way do I think that I am God, but I do try to be God-like in my heart.

I am totally innocent of any wrongdoing and I know these terrible allegations will all be proven false. Again, to my friends and fans, thank you very much for all of your support. Together we will see this through to the very end. I love you very much and may God bless you all. I love you. Goodbye.

Those shows and newscasts that didn't air the entire statement, aired clip after clip of Michael declaring his innocence, "Don't treat me like a criminal because I am innocent."

With these few remarks, he sent his public support soaring. Polls conducted by various TV shows and publications showed a dramatic increase in the number of people who believed Michael Jackson was innocent. It was exactly what the public was waiting for, for Michael Jackson to publicly declare his innocence. The Jackson family issued a statement to the media following Michael's live address, "The Jackson family has always and will continue to stand by Michael. We believe in his innocence and are confident that his dignity and humanity will prevail."

Support for Michael continued on many fronts. Quincy Jones publicly denounced the media in their handling of the story, "The media is dealing with a feeding frenzy. They have overstepped their bounds by 200 miles to indict somebody before he's even tried, or even accused. It's amazing. But, I saw Michael over the holidays and he's holding up, he's strong. He looks good. We've got all our prayers with him."

Michael's manager, Sandy Gallin, who had been criticized by some for being conspicuously silent throughout this ordeal, staunchly defended Michael in an interview with the *Los Angeles Times* predicting Michael would be exonerated.

Fans in Washington, D.C. brightened Michael's holidays by

sending him a seven foot card wishing him the best for the holidays and a joyous new year. The goal, according to Fred Outten, the organizer of the project, was to recognize Michael Jackson, "not only as the world's greatest entertainer, but also for his lifetime humanitarian contributions to society."

On Martin Luther King Day, January 17, Michael hosted one hundred children at his ranch from the Community Youth Sports and Arts Foundation. The media was barred with the exception of Los Angeles TV station KCAL and BET, the Black Entertainment Network. All of the children interviewed said Michael was very kind and lots of fun to be with. None of them believed he was guilty of harming any child.

People magazine's year end issue listed their choices for "The 25 Most Intriguing People of the Year", which included Michael Jackson. The review of the "Best of Tube" for the year included *Michael Jackson Talks to...Oprah*, which was described as the TV mega-event of the year.

Billboard's year end issue counted down the top artists, singles and albums in several categories with Michael making a strong showing considering his album was released more than two years earlier and he spent the latter part of the year buried by scandal:

Top Pop Artists: #34 Michael Jackson

Top Billboard 200 Album Artists: #41 Michael Jackson

Top Billboard 200 Album: #38 *Dangerous*

Top Billboard 200 Album Artists - Male: #16 Michael Jackson

Top Pop Catalog Albums: #31 *Thriller*

Hot 100 Singles Artists: #17 Michael Jackson

Hot 100 Singles: #47 "Will You Be There"

Hot 100 Singles Artists - Male: #4 Michael Jackson

Hot 100 Singles Sales: #60 "Will You Be There"

Hot 100 Singles Airplay: #35 "Will You Be There"

Top R&B Album Artists: #30 Michael Jackson

Top R&B Albums: #28 *Dangerous*

Hot R&B Singles: #88 "Who Is It"

Top R&B Artists: #34 Michael Jackson

Hot R&B Singles Airplay: #69 "Who Is It"

Hot Adult Contemporary Artists: #12 Michael Jackson

Hot Adult Contemporary Singles and Tracks: #26 "Will You Be There", #35 "Heal the World"

Hot Dance Music Club Play Singles: #50 "Who Is It"

Hot Dance Music Maxi Singles Sales: #40 "Who Is It"

In a review of the year in music, the publication focused solely on Michael's music, "given that virtually no nugget of information has gone unexamined, we don't feel any real need to explore it here. On a business front, sales of Jackson's albums haven't diminished ..."

Michael's previous albums continued to sell strong. Eleven years after its release, *Thriller* had sold another one million copies in the U.S. during the year, bringing the U.S. sales to 22 million copies, remaining the best selling album in the United States. Worldwide sales of *Thriller* now topped 50 million, with it remaining the world's biggest selling album in history. For several years *Thriller* would play a game of leapfrog with the Eagles' *Greatest Hits* for the title of number one best selling album in the U.S. On a global scale, *Thriller* has no such competition. Michael Jackson's Dangerous tour was reported to be the number one grossing concert tour of North America of 1993.

Meanwhile, legal problems continued to mount for Michael. In December, concert promoter Marcel Avram filed a breach of contract complaint in Los Angeles Superior Court against Michael Jackson, TTC Touring Corp., and MJJ Enterprises. The suit, asking for $20 million in damages plus punitive damages, charged fraud, negligent misrepresentation and breach of fiduciary duty regarding Michael's contract with Avram's Mama Concerts to finance and promote the 1993 Dangerous world tour. Avram and Pebbles Music Inc., co-plaintiffs in the case, alleged Michael Jackson concealed the true facts regarding his condition and actions upon signing the contract. The concert promoter claimed Michael's performances on the tour "...were not first class as guaranteed by the contract but, instead, were mediocre, abbreviated, and mechanical as compared with his prior performances." Nineteen of the forty three scheduled dates were cancelled when the tour was ended in November.

The NAACP Image Awards were held on January 22 and broadcast in February. Making a surprise appearance was their 1993 Entertainer of the Year, Michael Jackson, in his first professional appearance since returning home from Europe. He was greeted by deafening cheers and a standing ovation. Dressed in a black military style jacket with red accents and a silver sequined armband, and no sunglasses, he seemed very upbeat, confident and comfortable. He presented the award for Outstanding Choreography but first took the opportunity to say a few words on his own behalf, pausing now and then to tell the cheering fans, "I love you too" and "I love you more":

Thank you for your warm and generous support. I love you very much.

For decades, the NAACP has stood at the forefront of the struggle for equal justice under the law for all people in our land. They have fought in the lunch rooms of the South, in the hallowed halls of the Supreme Court and the board rooms of corporate America for justice, equality and the very dignity of all mankind. Members of the NAACP have been jailed and even killed in noble pursuit of those ideals upon which our country was founded. None of these goals is more meaningful to me at this time in my life than the notion that everyone is presumed to be innocent and totally innocent until they are charged with a crime and then convicted by a jury of their peers. I never, I never really took the time to understand the importance of that ideal until now, until I became the victim of false allegations and the willingness of others to believe the worst before they have a chance to hear the truth. Because not only am I presumed innocent, I am innocent! And I know the truth will be my salvation. You have been there to support me when others weren't around and I thank you for that. I have been strengthened in my fight to prove my innocence by my faith in God and by my knowledge that I am not fighting this battle alone. Together, we will see this thing through and I'm very proud to be here...

The Los Angeles prosecutors office announced on January 24th that they were declining to file charges of extortion against Evan

Chandler. This fueled speculation that a settlement of the case against Michael Jackson was in the works.

Chandler had agreed to drop the civil suit in return in for an undisclosed sum of money. The amount of this settlement would be speculated upon by virtually everyone with a typewriter and the amounts would range from $5 million to $100 million, with each being reported with certainty, having come from "an inside source." Basically the amount of the settlement was not to be disclosed and the vast majority of the press were reporting various figures as fast as they could think them up. LaToya, predictably, even had her two cents to chip in, telling the tabloids that the amount of the settlement was actually $50 million to be paid over ten years. For someone who had been estranged from her family for a number of years, she sure did manage to get a hold of a lot of confidential information.

But like everything else connected with this case, there were the consistent "leaks" of information. The most credible and reliable sources claimed the actual amount of the settlement was $22 million, with a couple million going directly to Evan Chandler and to June Chandler, the remaining millions being put in a trust fund for Jordie. The settlement was paid in installments over several years and it was actually covered by a personal liability insurance policy with TransAmerica Insurance Company. The last installment was paid in 1999.

Attorneys for both sides made statements and each side reiterated that the settlement was in no way an admission of any guilt by Michael Jackson. Feldman addressed the assembled masses stating

"Scream"

it was time for his client to start the healing process. Johnnie Cochran also addressed the media stating again that the settlement was no admission of guilt on behalf of Michael Jackson.

Both sides insisted that the settling of the civil action would have no impact on the continuing criminal investigation, that "no one's silence was bought". However, having gotten the cash they were after in the first place, there was no motivation for the boy to testify in any criminal action. From the very start they were only interested in getting paid, not justice for the alleged harm done to the boy, no punishment for Michael, or the well being of the boy, only cash. With no reason for the "victim" to testify, there was no evidence, only hearsay testimony, not enough to justify filing criminal charges.

Los Angeles District Attorney Gil Garcetti maintained however that the settlement of the civil suit did not affect the criminal investigation. He refused to give up on the now five month investigation that so far had yielded no evidence to justify filing criminal charges against Michael Jackson. The case seemed further impeded by the fact that California law did not allow the state to compel testimony from juveniles in sex crime cases. One week after the settlement was announced, Garcetti announced that he would sponsor legislation to force sexual assault victims to testify in criminal cases even if they sue their alleged assailants for money. Obviously without the testimony of the boy, their case against Michael was non-existent. Now that he had a few million bucks lining his pockets there was no motivation to testify in any criminal proceeding. They had already gotten what they wanted, money. So, Garcetti had to try to change the law of California to force the testimony of victims in these types of cases.

DeWayne Wickham, a columnist for Gannett News Service and *USA Today*, consistently offered insight into the investigation and questioned the motives of the media as well as the investigators. Wickham questioned the media's willingness to convict Michael without any evidence against him while ignoring the more plausible claims of extortion against the dentist. One article, "Officials desperate to nail Michael Jackson", focused on the extreme measures being taken by investigators to find something incriminating against Michael. Wickham asked, assuming Garcetti was successful in amending the laws of California forcing the boy to testify and he still refused, what would he do, put the boy in jail?

The immediate reaction to the announcement of the settlement by some of the media and general public, was that it indicated guilt on the behalf of Michael Jackson. Immediately many felt Michael must be guilty if he was willing to pay the kid off, buying his silence. No thought was given to the boy and his father's willingness to accept a stack of cash to forget that the boy had been sexually abused. Will that make everything all better? There had been no indication from Chandler that he was ever interested in Michael Jackson being punished for what he had supposedly done to his boy, no indication that Chandler was interested in getting his boy's life back on track, no indication in justice at all, only money. The civil suit, asking for monetary damages, was filed against Michael as soon as the allegations became public and Chandler lost his leverage against Michael Jackson and all hope of getting his proposed private settlement offer.

At the time the allegations first came up Chandler arranged meetings with attorneys and representatives of Michael Jackson and Michael himself to discuss a settlement. He did not go to the police. He did not file any criminal complaint. He asked for money.

The settlement amount of $22 million was, to Michael Jackson, a relatively small amount of money considering his income at the time, his net worth, and the amount of future earnings he was capable of if he was able to get on with his career. A prolonged battle would only hurt his earning potential and to a much larger degree than paying the $22 million settlement.

In his book, *You Are Not Alone*, Jermaine defended the decision to settle the case, "This payment – said to be in the region of $15 million – was not hush money and it was not about cheating justice because justice was cheating Michael. It was, if anything, about saving him from a travesty of justice. People forget that the insurers governing his personal liability were also involved in this decision. Remember, Michael's intention was to fight this case. In the ever changing circumstances, and amid all sorts of other legal motions, a team decision was taken to settle but that settlement stated in writing that payment was not an admission of guilt."

Frank Cascio also said Michael was against settling the case. He wanted to fight and clear his name. The decision however was governed by the insurance company – who opted to pay the settlement over a long and costly legal battle.

It is also important to consider how closely the actions of

Michael's accuser followed the statements made by the Jackson camp when the whole thing hit the fan. Jackson investigator Pellicano stated the allegations were brought as the result of a failed extortion attempt by the father. Chandler did indeed engage in negotiations for film deals in return for not making the allegations public. Pellicano, Michael's attorneys and Michael Jackson himself consistently maintained the allegations were brought as an attempt to get money, nothing else. As soon as the civil suit was settled, Jordie refused to cooperate with prosecutors. Nothing in the settlement prevented the boy from testifying in any criminal proceeding. Chandler could have had the money *and* cooperated with efforts to prosecute Michael. But he didn't. He just took the money. It was learned through Pellicano that Chandler, from the very beginning, wanted to secure several film deals so he could then dissolve his dental practice and work on his screenplays full time. Shortly after the settlement in the civil suit was reached, Chandler left his dental practice.

A source told Reuters News Service that the photos taken of Michael Jackson's genitals did not match the description Jordie had given to police. Others claimed the photos did match. J. Randy Taraborrelli recounted however that Jordie Chandler was unable to correctly tell investigators whether or not Michael Jackson was circumcised.

Evan Chandler was found dead from a self inflicted gunshot wound to the head in November, 2009. It was reported that over the years since the 1993 allegations, he had been stalked and at least one time badly beaten in a parking garage in California, it was suspected to

"Scream"

be by loyal Jackson fans. He was said to have had several cosmetic surgeries over the years so Jackson fans would not be able to recognize him and he relocated to New Jersey. In his last years, he had become estranged from his son, even attacked him with a dumbbell in 2006 after which Jordie got a restraining order against his father. At the end of his life, he was critically ill and battling depression.

With all of the media bashing of Michael Jackson during this time, some speculated that the settlement of the civil suit would do irreparable damage to Michael's career. What wasn't considered was the unique connection Michael maintained with his fans. He always had a strong bond with his fans and always loved and appreciated them. Michael Jackson's fan base is more loyal than any dog and larger than some countries. His capacity to reverse damage or change people's opinion of him was also underestimated. Michael had in the past repaired damage to his image and had done so with relative ease. After months of unrelenting media bashing, Michael sent the public's support of him skyrocketing, all in four minutes on CNN. After literally years of people believing he actually bought the elephant man's bones, slept in a hyperbaric chamber, and bleached his skin, Michael changed lots of people's perspective of him after talking with Oprah Winfrey for ninety minutes. Many people who had thought of him as a weirdo now saw him as a person. Michael Jackson was in no way washed up. Jackson biographer J. Randy Taraborrelli agreed, saying, "The Michael Jackson redemption of 1995 will be something to behold."

24

Lift up your head
And show the world you got pride
Go for what you want
Don't let 'em get in your way
You can be a winner
If you keep the faith

"Keep The Faith"
- Glen Ballard, Siedah Garrett, Michael Jackson

Following the settlement of the case, Michael Jackson was focusing on continuing his career, fighting more legal battles and most important, concentrating on his personal life. In February, Michael attended a concert of the Fifth Dimension and the Temptations at the Sheraton Desert Inn in Las Vegas with Lisa Marie Presley who he had begun dating. The King of Pop and the daughter of the King of Rock and Roll were seated in a VIP section known, appropriately enough, as "King's Row".

He also continued to receive support on many fronts. The February 5, 1994 issue of *Billboard* outlined the overwhelming support Michael was receiving from the music industry. Sony was standing by their earlier statements of support. His *Greatest Hits* album had now been postponed for the umpteenth time in favor of a whole new album. Record chain owners reported sales of Michael Jackson's albums had actually *increased*. Most radio station DJ's, record store owners, and industry insiders felt Michael Jackson's career would continue to flourish.

Following his victory in the recent copyright suit for "Thriller", "The Girl is Mine" and "We are the World", a similar suit began in U.S. District Court in Denver, Colorado, in February. Crystal Cartier was suing Michael for $40 million claiming he pirated the song "Dangerous" from her. Cartier said she wrote her song in 1985 and recorded it in October, 1990. She held that she had sent out twenty-five copies of her version of the song to record companies and charged Michael Jackson, MJJ Productions, Sony Music Entertainment and Epic Records with violating copyright and trademark laws.

On Monday, February 14, fans waited in line outside a Denver courtroom to see Michael Jackson who had gone to Denver to testify in the copyright case to defend his work. In his testimony, Michael described his songwriting techniques and told of how long he has been composing songs. He testified that he began composing music at the age of seven and had his first song published at the age of fifteen. To date he said he has written "in general, a couple of hundred" songs.

Michael testified that the chords added to the base lick of "Street Walker" inspired him to write the melody of "Dangerous". He demonstrated how the base sounded on "Street Walker" and how he then wrote the vocal melody, singing parts of the music of Dangerous". He described how he created a vocal melody by using another song he wrote as an example, "When creating the song `Billie Jean', I was riding in my car and it started with the base lick again, which goes (he sings the base sounds of "Billie Jean")  and on top of that I hear the chords (he sings the chords of "Billie Jean") and then the melody, `She was more like a beauty queen from a movie scene, I said don't mind, but do you mean I am the one...' And the lyrics, the strings, the chords come together at that moment like a gift that is put right into your head and that's how I hear it."

Michael testified he had never before heard Cartier's version of the song and that he had a strict policy of not accepting unsolicited tapes, "I do not take unsolicited tapes. What happens when you do something like that is this situation." He said he only accepts songs from well known songwriters with a track record of success, citing Rod Temperton and Stevie Wonder as examples. After 3 1/2 hours of deliberation, the jury found in favor of Michael Jackson, that he was the creator of Dangerous.

Just after the completion of this copyright case, the public was ordering copies of Michael's latest release, his testimony from the case! The U.S. District Court in Denver was flooded with orders for a fifty minute audio cassette of Michael's testimony in which he sings portions

"Keep the Faith"

of "Billie Jean" and "Dangerous". The cassettes, priced at $15, were reported to be selling very well and some reports joked it was climbing the charts. Funds raised from the sale of the tape were put in a general fund of the U.S. Treasury.

Meanwhile the criminal investigation struggled on. Determined to not let the settlement of the civil suit hinder the criminal investigation, a grand jury was called in Santa Barbara County to hear testimony from over twelve people. Of the nineteen jurors, twelve of them had to be convinced there was probable cause that Michael had behaved improperly to justify filing criminal charges. Among those called to testify before the grand jury Miko Brando, who had worked for MJJ Productions and was close friends with Michael; MJJ Productions executive Norma Staikos; James DeBarge, Janet's former husband who lived at Hayvenhurst during their four month marriage; Dr. Arnold Klein's personal trainer, who had accompanied Klein to Mexico City in November; chauffeur Gary Hearne; Joy Robson, the mother of Michael's young friend Wade Robson and Anthony Pellicano. He answered questions for three hours in an effort by the grand jury to determine if he had obstructed justice, altered evidence, or influenced witnesses.

The big bombshell in the case was when prosecutors called Katherine Jackson to testify. She was accompanied by Randy. She was reportedly questioned about Michael's appearance in an attempt to determine if Michael had altered his appearance so it wouldn't match the description his accuser had given to police. When finished with her testimony, which took just over an hour, she refused questions from reporters but did issue one statement, "I'd just like to say that before I went I was sure of my son's innocence, now that I have finished my testimony, I still feel the same." Katherine's being subpoenaed to testify against her own son was highly unusual and it infuriated Katherine's attorney, Richard Steingard, Michael's attorneys, and most of all, Michael himself. Steingard told the press:

> *A prosecutor attempting or trying to use a mother against a son, a parent against a child is just wholly inappropriate and even more so inappropriate in this case because Mrs. Jackson has repeatedly and publicly denounced the allegations and insisted that her son was innocent.*
>
> *...I think there has to be a question whether there's an element of harassment, of the Jackson family, of attempting to divide them, to persecute them for a case that they can't make.*

Howard Weitzman was equally angered and frustrated:

> *...And now to try to humiliate Michael Jackson and harass him or his family by subpoenaing his mother seems to be to us the height of the indignity that the prosecutors could try to heap upon Michael.*
>
> *...if it was anybody but Michael Jackson, they wouldn't be spending our money, taxpayers money running around trying to create something that doesn't exist.*
>
> *...   In all the years of my experience, I've never before seen the mother of the target of an investigation called before the grand jury. It's just done in real poor taste. It borders on harassment.*

The order for his mother to testify before the grand jury seemed to infuriate and hurt Michael more than anyone. He immediately issued a public statement condemning the Los Angeles District Attorney's office:

For the purposes of headline grabbing, the L.A. District Attorney's office continues to persecute me and this has now expanded to include the harassment of my beloved mother.

If Michael Jackson happened not to be a superstar, it is very doubtful that the investigation would have lasted for so many months, if it was brought about at all. If he were Joe Average, steelworker in Gary, Indiana, it is very unlikely he would have been subjected to such scrutiny, spending untold amounts of taxpayers money questioning his friends, friends of friends, employees, or his mother, confiscating his medical records and conducting searches of each of his homes, and his body. Some felt Michael Jackson bought himself out of trouble with his millions. It could very well be argued he was only in the situation because of his millions, and his fame and wealth bought him undue scrutiny.

The American Music Awards were held in February, where Michael Jackson had two nominations. He was nominated for Favorite Pop/Rock Male Artist and Favorite R&B/Soul Male Artist. The Pop Male Artist went to Eric Clapton and the R&B award went to Luther Vandross. Michael did not attend.

The days leading up to the taping of the *Jackson Family Honors* were filled with conflicting reports on just who was and was not going to attend, who was going to perform, where the proceeds would be donated and just what the whole thing was for. The show was designed to be an annual event at which awards would be given to individuals in recognition of their humanitarian efforts. Those being honored at the first annual *Jackson Family Honors* were no doubt chosen in part to help ensure Michael's participation. Elizabeth Taylor was quite possibly Michael's closet friend and biggest supporter. Berry Gordy had been acknowledged by Michael as being his teacher, friend, and father figure.

Speculation over whether or not LaToya would show up only helped to fill pages in newspapers and fill airtime on TV talk shows. The big, and most important, questions were "Is Michael going to be there?" and "Is he going to perform?" The answers had a dramatic impact on ticket sales and sales of advertising time. Ticket prices ranged from $150 to $1,000. As the date of the show grew nearer, the extent of Michael's participation varied from one day to the next. At first, it was reported that Michael would appear at the show, but it wasn't certain if he would perform or not. Then Jermaine, the show's co-producer, said Michael would perform with the brothers and do a solo performance. It turned out this was wishful thinking.

The uncertainty over whether or not Michael would perform hurt ticket sales. While the $150 to $250 tickets sold out quickly, sales of the higher priced tickets lagged. In the month before the show, the MGM Grand Hotel received over 180,000 phone calls asking if Michael would sing. When they learned he may not, ticket sales tapered off. Two days before the show, the ticket prices were cut by as much as half as Michael's contribution, or even attendance, grew unclear. It left no doubt who people were paying to see.

Finally, after two postponements and all the controversy, the

"Keep the Faith"

taping of the *Jackson Family Honors* did take place on February 19, 1994 at the MGM Grand Garden in Las Vegas before a sold out crowd of 15,000. It was telecast live in twenty-eight countries. It was taped for broadcast in the U.S. on February 22. The show opened strongly with a performance of "Alright" from Janet. From there the show dimmed in excitement, as the audience was clearly only waiting it out for the first appearance of the King of Pop.

Other performers on the show included Celine Dion, Smokey Robinson, Dionne Warwick, Gladys Knight, Bruce Hornsby, Another Bad Creation, and comedian Paul Rodriquez. Quincy Jones and Louis Gossett Jr. also appeared. But it wasn't until Smokey Robinson took the stage to introduce Michael that the crowd finally got what they came to see:

It's now my great pleasure to introduce an extraordinarily talented human being. As much as I admire him as a writer and as a performer, I admire him even more as a caring and spiritual person. I've known him since the early days of Motown, and if I knew he was going to become the world's greatest entertainer, I would have treated him a little nicer. I want you all to please welcome `The King of Pop', Mr. Michael Jackson.

The crowd cheered loudly as Michael walked out on stage to present an award to Berry Gordy. The entire audience rose to their feet. Then they cheered some more. And then some more. It grew louder as Michael acknowledged his fans, waving, blowing kisses, and saying, "I love you!" Michael seemed relaxed and confident, dressed in black jeans, boots, and a black military jacket with a gold leaf pattern down the front. He looked healthy and happy, genuinely touched by the love of his fans cheering him. The cheers continued as Michael began to speak, and thanked his fans. "I love you. Thank you. Thank you to the fans. Thank you for your prayers. Thank you for your loyalty. Thank you for your love and your friendship." He then spoke of Gordy's influence on all of their lives and brought his mentor to the stage, "Ladies and gentlemen, a great and incredible human being, Mr. Berry Gordy!". Gordy approached the stage to accept his award but first expressed his love and support for Michael:

How time flies. Just the other day you were a nine year old kid auditioning for me and now here you are, the greatest entertainer in the world, presenting me with an award. How wonderful. Thank you, Michael. Michael, I believed in you when you were nine, I believe in you now, and I will never stop believing in you... I am so thrilled to be standing next to not only the greatest entertainer in the world, but one of the most sensitive human beings that ever was and I count him as my most wonderful accomplishment...

Michael later took the stage again to present the night's second honor to Elizabeth Taylor and again the crowd cheered at his presence as he began to speak. He spoke highly of his friend and her tireless efforts humanitarian efforts. In her acceptance speech, Elizabeth Taylor directed her comments not toward her humanitarian efforts, but toward her unending support for her friend in his time of suffering.

At the show's finale, Michael joined the rest of the family, on stage for "If Only You Believe". The family members took turns singing a few lines of the song. Michael's first few words were nearly

› "Keep the Faith"

drowned out by the screams from the audience as he sang his allotted four lines of the song. Actually, Michael would have much preferred to skip the show completely. He was coerced by Jermaine and other family members, asked to take part while under intense distress from the allegations and felt pressured to say yes. It ended up being a disaster.

Gary Smith, of Smith-Hemion, co-producer of the *Jackson Family Honors* filed a lawsuit for $2.2 million against the Jackson family for nonpayment of the cast and crew of the show. Instead of the projected profits of $6 million, the special was estimated to have lost $1.7 million. Jermaine, the show's co-producer, said, "While the final amount of the loss is not completely known, it is our intention that all creditors will eventually be fully paid."

Specifically, the lawsuit named Jackson Communications, Inc., Jackson Jubilee Inc., Transworld International, Ticketmaster - Las Vegas Inc., Ticketmaster of Delaware Valley, Michael Jackson and each member of the Jackson family with the exception of LaToya. Despite the long list of defendants, the complaint put a good deal of the blame on only one person, Michael Jackson, saying they had relied on Michael Jackson performing on the show to make it a success, "Smith-Hemion relied upon that commitment in determining to enter into the production agreement."

Disney officials for Epcot Center at Walt Disney World, reversing their statement made in November, announced in February that they were replacing *Captain EO* at the Orlando, Florida theme park. They claimed it was not due to Michael's troubles and that plans had been in the works to replace the movie for eighteen months to keep everything fresh and new. They had no comment for why this planned replacement was not mentioned in November when they specifically stated they had no plans to replace *Captain EO*. Disneyland in California, and in Tokyo, stated *Captain EO* continued as one of their most popular attractions and there were no plans to replace it at those locations.

In March, the Heroes, Legends, Superstars of Hollywood and Rock auction was staged by Beverly Hills' Superior Auction Gallery and Startifacts. The most talked about of the items going up for auction were a handful of handwritten notes from Michael Jackson, one of which contained a depressing poem:

> *I start to givin' up.*
> *Life is an agrivator* [sic].
> *The bills are pillin' up...*
> *This stuff ain't good for me.*

These notes were now given a second look for some renewed significance in light of his recent troubles. The first two lines however appear as lyrics in "Cheater".

Leading up to the Oscar telecast on March 21, Barbara Walters held her annual interview special. One of her three interviewees this year was Elton John, who spoke candidly about his dependency problems and his efforts to help someone else with their dependency problems. He confirmed once again that Michael was indeed having problems with addiction, that he helped put Michael in touch with a therapist:

> "Keep the Faith"

> *He was fragile. I know for a fact that he'd been mum about the amount of painkillers people had been giving him and stuff like that. And I know it wasn't a case of running out of the country for an excuse, he had a real problem.*

Elton also described Michael's condition when he first arrived in Britain:

> *He was like a zombie. And that's how he arrived in this country, a zombie. It takes a while to get over that and he's gone right back into that mayhem situation over there. I fear for him.*

Elton offered Michael encouragement, and was glad the press wasn't able to track Michael to his house during his stay there.

In the spring of 1994, after spending more than three months hearing the case, it was announced that the grand jury in Santa Barbara County had disbanded, never coming to a decision to formally charge Michael Jackson. The D.A. claimed the grand jury was held for information gathering purposes only. Michael's attorneys said the jury was disbanded because there was no evidence for them to consider. While the grand jury was disbanded, technically, the investigation still remained open in both counties.

In an outstanding show of support for Michael Jackson, and as an indication of how much his fans and the public believed in him, Michael Jackson was honored for his outstanding contribution to children. The Caring for Kids Award was awarded to Michael Jackson at New York's City Center in April. In a survey of 100,000 children, ages eight to sixteen, from New York, New Jersey and Connecticut, over 750,000 voted Michael Jackson as the person who cares most about children. The award is sponsored by Body Sculpt, a non-profit group that uses physical fitness to discourage kids from using drugs. Body Sculpt president, Vincent Ferguson, said the allegations against Michael Jackson didn't bother him one bit, "And it doesn't bother the children." Michael seemed very proud and happy in accepting the award. Surrounded by children on the stage, he read from a prepared statement thanking the children for the honor.

For the second time in 1994, Michael Jackson was featured on the cover of another premiere issue of a magazine. *People Today*, in its July, 1994 issue, offered a review of Michael's life and addressed the allegations he faced. The issue presented responses from a random sampling of interviews done with people on the streets of New York. Nineteen of these responses were printed in the issue, not one of which felt Michael Jackson was guilty of any wrongdoing. There were plenty of people however who expressed their belief that Michael was the true victim and that money was at the root of the allegations being made and the longevity of the allegations in the media. Person after person expressed their faith in Michael and their continued admiration.

The *People Today* issue explored the allegations against Michael and their most probable cause:

Mr. Jackson has shown us time and time again... he actually cares! That factor alone, leads loyal fans and Jackson Watchers to doubt allegations. Especially allegations that could be so very financially profitable for the accusing parties.

...`If Michael Jackson WAS guilty, this whole matter would have never come up in the media and press,' said a New York City P.I.

"Keep the Faith"

in response to our request for an opinion. `A suitcase full of cash would have quietly changed hands in some airport lavatory, and the matter would have dissolved. The very fact that you and I are hearing about it, means to me, that Mr. Jackson is outraged and has decided to confront the allegations directly. Only an innocent man would chose such a direction. Especially with so many eyes looking in his direction. For that matter, only an innocent man would be outraged!'

Certainly Michael couldn't have come out of this situation without being strongly affected by it. Learning that people will, without hesitation, turn on him for profit had to have deepened his distrust of others. He consistently appeared disgusted at the very thought of which he was being accused. He displayed dignity and strength of moral character and integrity that should be an inspiration to all. While his distrust of others may have been deepened, he resolved not to have this horrifying experience change him. He saw Evan Chandler as the catalyst behind the allegations, not Jordie. His love of children, the inspiration he drew from them and his trust in them remained unchanged. This was unfortunate for his incredible kindness and giving nature would eventually land him in an even more serious and just as ugly a situation again. For now he focused on getting his life and career back on track.

25

I am right back where
I want to be
I'm standing tall
Though you're kicking me

"2 Bad"
- Michael Jackson

While his world was crumbling around him, Michael did find some comfort. He had begun dating Lisa Marie Presley. She was ending her marriage to musician Danny Keough when she became involved with Michael Jackson. Michael reportedly proposed to her before her divorce was even final. The two had met many years earlier when Lisa was a young girl and her father took her to see the Jackson Five perform in Las Vegas and she met the group back stage. Michael remained enamored with her and was crushed when he learned she had married. Soon after her divorce was final, Michael and Lisa were married in the Dominican Republic on May 26, 1994. Civil judge Hugo Francisco Avarez Perez presided over the ceremony in La Vega, in the Dominican province of La Romana. Lisa wore a black strapless dress and the groom was also dressed in black. The marriage was miraculously not discovered by the media until a couple of months later. Initially his office denied the story to me, but eventually it was revealed to in fact be true. Lisa Marie Presley was now Mrs. Michael Jackson. On August 1st, Lisa issued a statement confirming "My name is Mrs. Lisa Marie Presley-Jackson. My marriage to Michael Jackson took place in a private ceremony outside the United States weeks ago. I'm very much in love with Michael, I dedicate my life to being his wife. I understand and support him. We both look forward to raising a family."

Pictures of the newlyweds were provided to the *National Enquirer*. Beautiful shots by Dick Zimmerman, filled eight pages in the issue that proclaimed, "They're madly in love… It's a real marriage, not a hoax."

The union of the King of Pop with the daughter of the King of Rock and Roll was scrutinized and treated with as much skepticism as everything else with Michael Jackson at that time. Speculation ran rampant as to *why* Lisa Marie Presley would marry Michael Jackson. Mutual attraction and love for each other was never considered a possibility. Michael's presumed agenda was obvious, he needed a wife to show he was normal, heterosexual and most importantly, not a pedophile. Her possible motives included having Michael help with her budding musical career, money and/or attention. Each of these is more absurd than the next. It is doubtful that the daughter of one of the most beloved icons in music history would have encountered any roadblocks in getting her foot in the door of a record company. She had lived most of her life relatively outside the spotlight, it is not something she seemed drawn to or welcomed. As the sole heir to the estate of the King of Rock and Roll, and considering Elvis's estate is one of the most profitable of any deceased celebrity, money could not be considered a real motivator for her either. It undoubtedly helped that Michael could be sure she accepted his proposal not for his money or fame. While they each insisted their marriage was genuine, it continued to be looked upon with skepticism.

Speculation also abounded about the possibility of Lisa encouraging Michael to become a member of the Church of Scientology. Lisa, a high profile and long time member of the controversial religious organization, did arrange for Michael to meet with leaders of the organization, but he never really considering joining.

One person who continued to assert that they were a real couple was Michael's friend, Donald Trump. Trump hosted the cozy couple at his estate in Florida and in New York when they lived in Trump Tower. In Florida, they rarely left their bedroom and when they did, they walked hand in hand around the grounds. They were genuinely crazy for each other. Other accounts of their relationship, by friends of Lisa's and people close to Michael all agreed they were a real couple.

An appearance at the MTV Video Music Awards only fueled the fire of skepticism. The program was introduced by the new Mr. and Mrs. Michael Jackson. Michael had the bright idea of planting a kiss on his bride on stage in front of the audience and the TV viewers. He didn't let Lisa in on his plan until the last minute. She hated it, thought it was stupid and said no. He did it anyway. After showing his sense of humor with the line, "Just think, nobody thought this would last", he kissed Lisa. Not expecting it and finding the idea distasteful, the kiss and embrace came off as extremely awkward. This display gave further "proof" for some that the marriage was one of convenience to help repair Michael's image.

Airing just before the release of *HIStory* was a high profile television interview with Michael and Lisa Marie on "Primetime Live" with Diane Sawyer which attracted sixty million viewers. Lisa and Michael sat boldly awaiting the deeply personal questions they surely were anticipating. Lisa pounced on questions prying into their intimacy. "Yes, we have sex!' seemingly annoyed by the thought that this was a marriage to help prop up Michael's image.

Michael came off as more than a little dense when Diane Sawyer asked if the days of having sleepovers with young boys were over, "Are there going to be more of those sleepovers in which people have to wonder?"

"Nobody wonders when kids sleep over at my house,

nobody wonders" was his unbelievable response.

When Diane pursued the question, he became more defiant. "But are they over?" she asked, "Are you going to watch out for it?"

"No" he responded, then paused and added "Watch out for what?"

"Just for the sake of the children and all you have been through?"

"No, because it is all moral and it's all pure. I don't even think that way. It's not what's in my heart."

He continued to be dense, or naïve, as Sawyer continued, "So, you will do it again?"

"Do what again?" Oh come on, Michael.

Sawyer filled in the obvious blank, "Have a child sleep over?"

"Of course, if they want. It's on the level of purity and love and just innocence, complete innocence. If you're talking about sex, then that's a nut. It's not me. Go to the guy down the street cause it's not Michael Jackson. It's not what I am interested in."

These comments earned him another lawsuit by Evan Chandler, claiming Michael violated the terms of the settlement by talking about the case. Michael issued a statement in response to the lawsuit:

The allegations made in the lawsuit are false, and I will vigorously challenge them. I am especially hurt that Mr. Chandler chose to involve my dear Lisa Marie in this meritless dispute. I also regret that Diana Sawyer and ABC, as well as my close friends and business associates at Sony and Warner-Tamerlane are also being sued. I am confident that we will ALL prevail in court, the proper place to put this matter to rest."

June 1995 saw the release of *HIStory, Past Present and Future Book 1,* a 2 CD set, one of re-mastered greatest hits, the other of all new material. The booklet that accompanies the CD set is especially interesting, containing song credits, dedications, thank yous and some great photos of the King of Pop over the past several years. Go ahead and get your copy, I will wait.... The booklet begins with words from his dearest friend, Elizabeth Taylor, a reprint of the Foreword from "Moonwalk" by Jacqueline Kennedy Onassis. Then there are two pages of thank yous from Michael beginning with Lisa Marie Presley and including, among others, his parents, Elizabeth Taylor, Berry Gordy, his fans, Paul and Linda McCartney and Deepak Chopra. The final thank you on the list is to Lisa Campbell, "Thanks, Lisa Campbell, for your support and love". That's right, yours truly. A few months earlier my second book detailing the life and career of Michael Jackson with a focus on the false allegations against him, had been published. Having Michael Jackson acknowledge my work in such a tremendous way was truly overwhelming.

The *HIStory* album marked an interesting first. It was the first album on which he is credited with playing an instrument. He is credited as playing keyboard and synthesizer, guitar, drums and percussion. Though it is not noted on which tracks he plays, other sources indicate it was for the first single, "Scream".

The disc from *HIStory* containing the new songs was characterized by many as a set of very angry songs. The tone of such reviews gave the impression that the source of the anger or frustration on Michael's part was mysterious. What could Michael Jackson of all people have in his life at this time to vent such anger about? Had no attention been paid to the absolute living hell that he had just endured? Was he just supposed to quickly and easily get over it, write some catchy dance tunes and move on? He surely felt betrayed by many and had experienced a level of humiliation that he could have never imagined. Joe Vogel noted that Michael used his recent experience and addressed his own frustrations as well as larger social issues of discrimination, greed, injustice and the far reaching invasion of the media.

Michael's feeling of being betrayed by those around him is front and center in "This Time Around" and "Money". "This Time Around" has some of his strongest lyrics:

> *This time around Ill never get bit*
> *Though you really wanna get me*
> *This time around I'm taking no shit*
> *Though you really wanna fix me*
> *Somebody's out*
> *Somebody's out to use me*
> *They really want to use me*
> *And then falsely accuse me*

In "Money" he addresses the willingness of people to "do anything for money":

I'll never betray or deceive you my friend but...
If you show me the cash
Then I will take it
If you tell me to cry
Then I will fake it
If you give me a hand
Then I will shake it
You'll do anything for money

The first single from *HIStory* was "Scream", his first and only duet with his sister Janet. "Scream" allowed both of them to vent some of their frustration at the media:

With such confusion, don't it make you want to Scream,
You've bashed, abused and victimized within the scheme,
You try to cope with every lie they scrutinize
Somebody please have mercy, 'cause I just can't take it

"Scream" debuted on the *Billboard* Hot 100 at number five becoming the highest debuting single ever on the Billboard singles chart. At least for now. It broke the record previously held by the Beatles' "Let It Be". A video was produced for the single for a budget busting $7 million, the most expensive video to date. Featuring both Michael and Janet together for the first time, the video showcased them in a futuristic spaceship setting with Janet sporting very dramatic makeup and hair, and a first ever dance sequence with her brother that is all too short. One shot had Janet flipping a one-finger salute to the camera that perhaps may have been stronger and more fitting coming from Michael.

"Scream" received a record breaking eleven nominations in the MTV Video Music Awards. Janet joined Michael on stage to collect the tiny moonman for Best Dance Video. She wore a tiny white top showing off her toned midriff with "Pervert 2" printed on the back. She spoke first to thank MTV, the fans, the video's director, Mark Romanek, and "my wonderful brother, Mike". Her wonderful brother spoke next, keeping it brief as always,: "Thank you very much. My favorite thing about doing the 'Scream' video was, it was really an excuse to work with my sister Janet, because I truly adore her. She's one of the sweetest people in the world. Thank you Mark Romanek, all the choreographers, I love you all, and the public, MTV, Sony, everybody, bye." "Scream" also won for Best Choreography and Best Art Direction. Later, the "Scream" video was awarded the Grammy for Best Short Form Music Video.

Michael performed on the show giving a mini concert with a medley of several of his biggest hits complete with costume changes. No ponytail this time, his hair was cut short. His entrance was to the spoken introduction to "Don't Stop 'Til You Get Enough". He opened with "The Way You Make Me Feel", followed by "Scream", then "Beat It" and "Black or White" with Slash featured on guitar. "Dangerous" with a bit of "Smooth Criminal" thrown in followed with him mouthing Janet's voice on the lines, "You know you want me" from her *janet.* album and a bit later, "Get the point? Good. Let's Dance" from *Rhythm Nation*. His set concluded with "You Are Not Alone". He received a standing ovation from the crowd,

Janet was shown in the audience beaming with pride while Lisa Marie looked remarkably unimpressed.

Many shots are taken at the media on *HIStory*. With "Tabloid Junkie" he encourages people to not buy the tabloids and not to believe something just because it is in black and white:

> *With the words you use*
> *You're a parasite in black and white*
> *Do anything for news*
> *If you don't go and buy it*
> *Then they won't glorify it*
> *To read it sanctifies it*
> *Then why do we keep foolin' ourselves*
> *Just because you read it in a magazine*
> *Or see it on the TV screen*
> *Don't make it factual*
> *Everybody wants to read all about it*

A more direct shot is taken in "D.S.", a thinly veiled assault aimed at Santa Barbara County District Attorney Thomas Sneddon, who headed up the investigation against Michael during the Chandler accusations. Titled "D.S.", the song's lyrics in the album's accompanying booklet refer to a central character named "Dom Sheldon". In the recording, Michael is clearly singing the name Tom Sneddon and not Dom Sheldon who "is a cold man" who "wants to get my ass dead or alive…"

HIStory's second single was "You Are Not Alone", the

video for which featured Lisa Marie Presley and her husband in the buff. No black loafers and white socks, no high water black pants, no glove. No nothing, except a length of gauze draped across his lap. Scenes of Michael and Lisa were intercut with shots of Michael (dressed in an unbuttoned sheer shirt revealing that Michael Jackson had an outie belly button) on stage alone in an empty auditorium. These scenes were filmed at the Pantages Theater in Los Angeles. Another version of the video has scenes of Michael standing nude in hip deep water with angel wings. That's right, wings.

"You Are Not Alone" was a number one hit, but not just any number one hit. It became the first single to ever debut on the Hot 100 singles chart at the very top of the heap. It was Michael's thirteenth number one single on the pop charts, making him the male artist with the most number one hits in history. He is trailed by Stevie Wonder, with ten, and Elton John and Paul McCartney each with nine number one hit singles. Michael's vocals on the single are remarkable, with him holding one note towards the end of the song for about a week and a half. "You Are Not Alone" also earned Michael a Grammy nomination for Best Pop Vocal Performance.

"Earth Song" was released as the next single in Europe and for some reason was not released in the U.S. With tremendously moving lyrics and emotional delivery, it really packs a punch, but scenes of animal poaching featured in the song's video make it hard to watch. Michael Jackson was environmentally conscious and actively working to bring awareness to the plight of the planet long before it was fashionable to be "green". "Earth Song" spent six weeks on top of the singles charts in the UK, making it his biggest single ever in that country. In Vogel's *Man in the Music,* an assistant engineer describes "Earth Song" being recorded live with an orchestra. "They rehearsed a bit without vocals in, then during the first take Michael sang, [he] just knocked them out of their chairs." While another take was recorded, the first one ended up on the album.

The lyrics of "They Don't Care About Us" stirred up a controversy that Michael could ill afford at the time:

Beat me, Hate me
You can never break me
Will me, Thrill me
You can never kill me
Jew me, Sue me
Everybody do me
Kick me, Kike me
Don't you Black or White me

The Anti-Defamation League was riled up over Michael's use of the words, "Jew" and "Kike". No apparent attention was paid to the context in which the words were used, that Michael was actually speaking out *against* the use of these words and the attitudes that would promote them. No attention was paid either to the fact that Michael spoke out in the lyrics against hatred of several other groups, not just Jews. Rabbi Shmuley Boteach explained in "The Michael Jackson Tapes" that Michael was not an anti-Semite. "If anything, I believe Michael had an intuitive affinity with Jewish people." Michael responded to Boteach, "I would never teach hatred, ever. "That's not what I'm about." In compilation albums released later the offending lyrics were covered up with sound effects or changed to "do me" and "strike me".

Two different videos were produced for the single, both directed by Spike Lee. One was set in a prison with Michael as an inmate, the second was filmed on the streets of Rio de Janeiro. The song was a hit throughout Europe, but the controversy back home kept if off many radio station play lists. It peaked at number thirty on the pop singles chart.

Michael described "Childhood" as the most autobiographical song he had ever written, asking "Have you seen my childhood?" "Childhood" reflects his feelings of being misunderstood and asking "Before you judge me, try hard to love me." While his vocals are beautiful, it is not one of the album's strongest tracks. The song was also featured on the soundtrack for the film, *Free Willy 2"*.

"Stranger in Moscow" also takes a page from Michael's real life, referring to his "swift and sudden fall from grace". The accompanying video, shot in black and white, has Michael wandering the streets in the rain, suffering from "armageddon of the brains" passing others looking hopeless and "alone and cold inside".

HIStory sold 7.5 million copies in five weeks and became the biggest selling double album of all time with global sales to date of 22 million copies. Accompanying the album was a collection of the videos for both the greatest hits portion of the album and the new hits. *Michael Jackson Video Greatest Hits HIStory* and *Michael*

Jackson HIStory on Film Volume II. HIStory had earned a Grammy nomination for Album of the Year, but lost to Alanis Morrisette's *Jagged Little Pill.*

Promotion of the new album was of epic proportions. Nine oversized statues of Michael Jackson, like the one featured on the album's cover, were put on display around Europe, one being floated down the Thames River in England. The Tower Bridge was forced to open to allow the thirty foot likeness of Jackson to pass. The June 24, 1995 issue of *Billboard* magazine included an advertisement for HIStory in the form of a newspaper titled, "Remember the Times" with the slogan, "Black or White and Read All Over."

Michael Jackson and the *HIStory* album were featured on many magazine covers and some even garnered an interview with the increasingly reclusive King of Pop. *Vibe* magazine did not score an interview but he was featured on the magazine's June/July 1995 cover. He sported many new looks within the pages of the photo spread on "Action Jackson". Some pics are of Michael alone, others he poses with Quincy Jones and his daughter, and stylist for the photo shoot, Kidada Jones. Kidada dresses Michael in sneakers and a smoking jacket; a Tommy Hilfiger collegiate style sweater; and in one of the more hilarious shots, in oversized red sweatpants and blue hooded sweatshirt, all hip hop style, very UN-Michael like. While the issue did not have an interview with him it did include thoughts from many of his friends and associates. Most notable was the very first one:

Michael is a true artist in every facet of its nature –

extremely aesthetic and very, very romantic. This is who he truly is despite degrading comments made in the past by certain larva. Michael, as well as myself, have been severely underestimated and misunderstood as human beings. I can't wait for the day when all the snakes who have tried to take him out get to eat their own lunch and crawl back in the holes from which they came. We know who they are and their bluff is about to be called. – Lisa Marie Presley-Jackson.

Quincy Jones also shared his thoughts:

Michael can go out and perform before 90,000 people, but if I ask him to sing a song for me, I have to sit on the couch with my hands over my eyes and he goes behind the couch. He is amazingly shy. What people forget about him is that for the first time, probably in the history of music, a black artist is embraced on a global level by everyone from eight to eighty years old. People all over the world, especially young people, have a black man as an idol.

A long lost love, Tatum O'Neal, added:

… When I was 12, he asked me to go to the premiere of 'The Wiz' with him, and my agent at the time said it wasn't a good idea, maybe because they felt he wasn't a big enough star yet. He never talked to me after that. I think he thought I just cancelled, but it wasn't me at all. I was a child doing what I was told. I want you to print that, because I don't think he ever knew that. I lost touch with him because of it, so I don't really know him anymore. But I love him; he's one of the nicest, most innocent people I've ever met. I love "She's Out of My Life" because I think it describes our

friendship at that time.

For the 1996 World Music Awards, Michael performed "Earth Song". He had a microphone clipped to his shirt but appeared to be lip syncing. It was a relatively toned down performance, adding only a few of his signature moves, each of which drew screams of delight from the crowd. Groups of children filed in behind him to provide background vocals. At the end of his song, he addressed the crowd giving sobering statistics on the perils of the rainforest and world hunger.

Prince Albert introduced Michael as "the man the world has crowned the King of Pop, Michael Jackson." Picking up the honors for Best Selling Pop Male Artist and Best Selling R&B Male Artist, Michael gave a brief speech with a special message and as usual, responding to the screams of "I love you" from the crowd:

*"Thank you very much. (I love you more, much more). These awards from you, World Music Awards, are very special to me as a person who loves and adores and has concern for people of all nationalities and ethnic origins. My music serves as my way of making mankind aware of the inequities that exist against all people of the world and aren't intended to be offensive to any ethnic group. I am not and never have been anti Semantic. And, do me a favor, don't' read the tabloids. I love you all very much. This is our future right here (*pointing to children on stage*). I love you."*

Michael also picked up honors that night for having the best selling album of all time, he was named the Best Selling American Male Artist and Best Selling Male Artist. Another special honoree that night was Diana Ross who performed a medley of her hits. During "Ain't No Mountain High Enough" she left the stage and walked through the audience. Her first stop was the lap of her once young protégé. Michael was clearly embarrassed by the attention and hid his face as they hugged. Her performance was greeted with a standing ovation with Michael being the first one on his feet.

Michael wanted desperately to be a father and wanted to start a family with Lisa as soon as possible. She was focused on trying to save Michael from his demons. He resisted and she was not able to save him from himself. Tensions mounted between them and soon they were barely speaking to each other. While Lisa Marie did not want to start a family with Michael if their marriage was crumbling, someone else in Michael's life was offering to carry his child. A nurse at Dr. Arnold Klein's office, Debbie Rowe, had known and admired Michael for years. When he vented his frustration at Lisa's resistance to have a baby with him, Debbie offered to carry his child. This turmoil in his personal life is what most likely contributed to his collapse in December 1995. He was known to suffer anxiety attacks at times of great stress in his life.

While in New York rehearsing for a big concert special to be aired on HBO, *Michael Jackson: One Night Only,* Michael suddenly collapsed on stage. He was rushed to Beth Israel North Hospital with low blood pressure and an irregular heartbeat. Michael's staff called Lisa to ask her to fly to New York to be by his side. She resisted at first but did eventually concede to show up for appearances sake. Lisa and Michael ended up having a shouting match with Lisa storming off. Katherine Jackson, who also flew to New York to be by her son's side, and Michael's people would not allow Lisa to see Michael the next day. One person who was said to be by his side each day of his hospital stay was Karen Faye.

Michael was to have attended the Billboard Music Awards that same evening to pick up a Billboard Hot 100 Achievement Award to commemorate having the first single to ever debut at number one for "You Are Not Alone". The award was accepted on his behalf by Tina Turner. In January, he was named as the Favorite Male Pop Artist at the American Music Awards. He did not attend that award ceremony either.

Later, in February, he was honored by the Brits as Artist of a Generation. He appeared on the program and performed "Earth Song" in a performance that was marred by an interruption from a member of the band Pulp. Epic Records condemned his actions:

Michael Jackson respects Pulp as artists but is totally shocked by their behavior and utterly fails to understand their complete lack of respect for fellow artists and performers. His main concern is for the people that worked for him and the fact that children should be attacked. He feels sickened, saddened, shocked, upset, cheated, angry but is immensely proud that the cast remained professional and the show went on despite the disgusting and cowardly behavior of the two characters that tried to disrupt it. Even though the evening ended on a sad note, he wants to thank all his fans and the media for their understanding and support.

Michael started his performance of "Earth Song" dressed in

baggy, ragged clothes, children joined him on stage mid way through the song. He climbed into his cherry picker, continuing the song and hanging off the edge as usual. He continued the performance flawlessly even as it was being interrupted. The intruder was gone before the cherry picker returned Michael to the stage. He removed the dark ragged clothes and concluded his performance now dressed all in white.

Sir Bob Geldof presented the award for Artist of a Generation, describing the recipient as a "child prodigy to adult genius. When Michael Jackson sings, it is with the voice of angels and when his feet move, you can see God dancing." Michael accepted the honor saying,

"I love you. Thank you Brit Awards and Sir Bob. I am humbled by this award. This is especially important coming from my wonderful family in the United Kingdom. You have provided me with so much love and you have given me your loyalty and your support throughout my entire career. And special thanks to Paul Russell. I love you all and especially I love all my fans. Thank you."

When they were not able to reconcile, and she was forced to give up her efforts to save him from his demons, Lisa filed for divorce in January 1996. There was no drawn out fight over money. She asked only for her maiden name to be restored and that Michael pick up the tab for her legal fees. The ending of their twenty month marriage was used to support the media's view that the marriage was one of convenience from the beginning. Their brief union was frequently noted by the media with a tone dripping with incredulousness. Imagine a celebrity marriage, known for their longevity, ending after only a year and a half. Lisa's next marriage, to actor Nicholas Cage, lasted less than sixteen weeks. Lisa and Michael did remain close following their split. Some said Lisa tried to reconnect with Michael sometime later and still later, he reached out to her. They both still cared very deeply for each other.

To promote the new album, Michael hit the road with the HIStory tour, where he played to massive audiences throughout Asia, Europe, Australia, and which included his first live shows ever in South Africa. Sadly, there were only two U.S. dates on the tour, in Honolulu, Hawaii where he became the first artist to sell out the Aloha Stadium. Further hindering his U.S. fans' ability to see any of his concerts, no HIStory tour performance was ever commercially released, though there are some somewhat decent bootleg copies available. A commercial release was planned but Michael was unhappy with that night's performance and the intended release was cancelled.

One show scheduled for September 1, 1997 in Ostend, Belgium was postponed due to the sudden death of Princess Diana. For the make up concert on September 3rd, "Smile" was added to the show in honor of Michael's friend. His statement released in response to her death read;

The sudden loss of Diana, Princess of Wales, is one of the greatest tragedies of the millennium. She was a friend to the world. As one who has been under scrutiny the majority of my life, I speak with authority when I say that I am horrified that the paparazzi, supported by the tabloids' animalistic behavior, may be acceptable to the public. It is totally unwarranted in a civilized society. The world's acceptance of the practice if continued will accelerate tragedies of this magnitude.

Michael attended a memorial service for the princess at the St. James' Episcopal Church in Los Angeles in September. He also lent his song, "Gone Too Soon" to a tribute CD for the Princess.

There were many familiar names working with Michael on the HIStory tour that had been part of the Bad and Dangerous tours and would work with him again for the This Is It shows. Kenny Ortega worked to stage and design the shows, Michael choreographed the shows along with Travis Payne and LaVelle Smith. Singers Kevin Dorsey, Dorian Holley and Darryl Phinnesse were all returning to tour once again with Michael Jackson. Drummer Jonathan Moffett was again touring with Michael and Jennifer Batten returned on guitar. Behind the scenes, Dennis Tompkins and Michael Bush once again designed all of Michael's costumes and Karen Faye continued as Michael's personal hair and makeup artist. It would be learned later that an anesthesiologist traveled with Michael on the HIStory tour, "taking him down" at night and "bringing him back up" in the morning as he long suffered from bouts of insomnia.

The performances opened with Michael landing on stage in a space craft. A figure emerges all decked out in gold from head to foot, full face helmet, and knee and shin guards. The helmet and the chest piece of armor are removed to reveal it is in fact the star of the show. He stands motionless for several seconds before starting off with "Scream". Up next is "They Don't Care About Us" with a bit of "HIStory" tossed in the mix with choreography that will be seen again in This Is It.

The knee and shin guards are shed for "In the Closet" and "Wanna Be Startin' Somethin'". A comparatively subdued presentation is adopted for "Stranger in Moscow", in keeping with the song's mood. Pinstripe suits, fedoras and spats are brought out for "Smooth Criminal", and he performed the choreography from the song's video flawlessly including the trademark, or patented, "Smooth Criminal" lean.

For "You Are Not Alone", he dons a sheer black shirt and he hits the long note at the end with perfection. A lucky girl is plucked from the crowd to join Michael on stage where they share a slow dance with Michael getting down on one knee before her at the appropriate time in the song.

"The Way You Make Feel" has Michael donning the familiar blue shirt and white tie belt to dance around the hot young girl crossing the stage in front of him. The choreography from the song's video is as delightful as always. Just as with the Dangerous tour performances, Michael offers the "old songs, the old fashioned way" for the medley of Motown hits including "I Want You Back", "The Love You Save" and "I'll Be There".

"Billie Jean' is kicked off with a very cool and low tech effect that will be used again in his 30th anniversary performances and was planned for This Is It. Dressed in black tuxedo pants, white glittery socks and a white t-shirt, he slowly walks from side stage with a small brown suitcase. His steps are accentuated with drumbeats. Setting the case on a stool, he nonchalantly opens it and pulls out a black sequined jacket and puts it on. Next he pulls out a white glove, also covered in sequins and puts that on. Last out of the suitcase is a black fedora. The crowd goes crazy recognizing simply from his costume that "Billie Jean" is next. All of his performances seem to come off brilliantly, but somehow "Billie Jean" seems to shine even brighter.

Zombies join Michael on stage for "Thriller" with Michael wearing a black and white version of the popular "Thriller" jacket. At the song's conclusion, Michael is encased in a casket, which has a wall of nails that magically passes through it, it catches on fire and Michael disappears. He reappears seconds later in a cherry picker wearing a red "Beat It" jacket and rises up over the crowd. Four back up dancers join him when he returns to the stage to recreate the song's choreography from the video, ending with Michael tearing off his jacket and beating it on the ground like it is on fire. Lots of jumping and spinning serve as a high energy finale to the song.

He delivers gems never before heard live in the U.S., a shortened version of "Come Together" followed by "D.S.", where his backup dancers perform wearing gas masks. It doesn't sound like he is singing "Dom Sheldon" here either. Black suits and ties are donned by Michael and the dancers for "Dangerous" with a performance that will be seen on a few award shows and specials in the U.S. A few moments of "Smooth Criminal" are again thrown in for good measure.

    The gold shin guards are back on with a flowing white shirt for "Black or White". At the song's conclusion, Michael is cautioned by the stage manager about the speakers and amps being overheated. Michael disregards the made up, rehearsed warning and continues the song. The speakers do overheat, catch fire and collapse on stage in a wonderful effect. Sirens and search lights come on while the wreckage is cleared. This devastation serves as the backdrop for "Earth Song". Michael climbs in the cherry picker for another ride over the audience. For the performance in Seoul, South Korea, he picked up an unauthorized tag-a-long. A young fan jumped onto the cherry picker, outside the rails, for the ride with Michael. Never missing a single note, Michael continued with the song while holding the young man's arm and putting his arm around his waist to keep him safe. When the cherry picker returned to the stage, the young man had to be pulled away by security guards. Luckily no one was hurt.

    This was not the only time he faced potential danger during a performance. During a performance in 1999 in Germany while standing on a raised platform, it began to fall as cables were not hooked up properly. Michael continued the song, rode the platform as it fell and jumped off just before it crashed. He joked with crew members later that he was always taught that the show must go on! It was serious though. He suffered an injury to his back that would become a chronic problem and require more painkillers.

    A beautiful white beaded military style jacket is donned for the final song of the concert, "Heal the World" with groups of youngsters circling the stage with an inflatable globe at the center. With that Michael sends his love to his fans, "I love you all", and leaves the stage.

More than 4.5 million fans attended the shows in fifty-eight cities in thirty-five countries. HIStory is the most attended tour of all time. In its eighty-two performances it raked in over of $163 million. It all kicked off in Letna Park in Prague in front of 125,000 fans. On August 29, 1997 Michael celebrated his 39th birthday in front of 50,000 fans at Parken Stadium in Copenhagen, Demark. He was presented with a birthday cake and fireworks that spelled out "King of Pop".

As usual, some stops along the way were benefit concerts. Proceeds from a show in Tunisia in October went to The National Solidarity Fund, a charity dedicated to helping the poor. A stop at the Olympic Stadium in Munich, Germany was a benefit concert for the Nelson Mandela Children's Fund, the Red Cross, and UNESCO.

On November 16, 1996 while the HIStory tour was in Australia, Michael married Debbie Rowe. His divorce from Lisa Marie had become final the month before. Debbie was five months pregnant by this time with their first child. According to J. Randy Taraborrelli, they had not planned on adding marriage to their agreement, but due to Katherine's insistence that they not bring children into the world to unwed parents, they relented, and agreed to marry. Bob Jones however insisted Michael's decision to marry Debbie was in an effort to placate the Saudi Prince Bin Talal Bin

Abdulaziz Al Saud Alwaleed when they were working on a deal together for theme parks and other ventures. Frank Cascio echoed this notion, saying the marriage was an effort to preserve his working relationship with the Prince.

Debbie never lived with Michael at Neverland fueling the speculation that would forever linger as to just how the children were conceived or if Michael was actually their biological father, given their light skin and hair. This was the couple's second attempt to have a child together. Debbie had miscarried earlier in the year. Whatever agreement they had has not been revealed.

After performing before 40,000 fans at Sydney Cricket Ground and after attending an after party, Michael met up with Debbie in their Presidential Suite at the Sheraton on the Park Hotel. The groom sat at a grand piano and played the Wedding March as Debbie made her entrance and became the latest Mrs. Michael Jackson. A statement followed asking "Please respect our privacy and let us enjoy this wonderful and exciting time." This was also a second marriage for Debbie. She had married a teacher, Richard Edelman, in 1982. That marriage ended in 1988.

Just a few days earlier, a musical stage production of "Sisterella", which was co-produced by Michael Jackson, won eight NAACP Theatre Awards. The show, an African American version of Cinderella, was a big hit with New York shows scheduled following the run in Pasadena. In 2011 it was announced that Tito's son, TJ, would take over the role of Prince Jean Luc in the stage production, the role originally meant for his Uncle Mike.

Not all of the awards for which Michael was nominated were an honor. In 1996 he was nominated for the Sour Apple Award for being one of the "least cooperative entertainment figures of the year", by the Hollywood Women's Press Club, Michael's favorite group of folks, the media. Michael sent a note explaining why he could not attend the award ceremony in humorous style, "I am sorry I cannot be here in person as I am currently in Japan for my HIStory World Tour and am hosting a holiday party for the employees of Star magazine tonight. Thank you very much for this award, and I wish all of you a very happy holiday season. I love you."

The follow up to *HIStory* was released on May 20, 1997. *Blood on the Dance Floor: HIStory in the Mix* features remixes of hits from HIStory and five new songs. The album set another record for sales of a remix album, with an estimated 6 million copies sold. The short film for "Blood on the Dance Floor" has Michael sporting a new look and frequenting a dance club. He is dressed in dark red leather pants and blazer with some chunky gold jewelry and his hair is in a very long braid down his back. Moving around the table dancer, he sings of his distrust of women:

Susie got your number
And Susie ain't your friend
Look who took you under
With seven inches in
Blood is on the dance floor
Blood is on the knife
Susie's got your number

"2 Bad"

And Susie says its right

The song, if taken literally, about a "Dirty Diana" type woman plotting to seduce but then stab him, it is quite catchy. It was originally recorded during the sessions for "Dangerous" but didn't make the final cut. The single peaked at a non deserving number forty-two on the Hot 100 in the U.S. but became a number one hit in many countries around the world including Great Britain.

Another song on the album, "Morphine" raised some eyebrows considering its composer had supposedly successfully completed a stay in rehab. The lyrics, "Demoral, Demoral, oh God, he's taking Demoral" were revisited by some in the media following his death. Subject matter not withstanding, the song is a great piece with a much harder rock edge than most of his work. Also notable, Michael is credited with playing guitar on the track. His apparent fondness for Demoral combined with having an anesthesiologist traveling with him to "take him down" at night in an effort to get some sleep obviously point to someone for whom drug rehab was not successful.

"Superfly Sister" is a quirky tune that gets more fun with each listen and is filled with seemingly autobiographical references. LaToya's union with her manager, Jack Gordon, seems to be the inspiration for lines, "Sister's married to a hood, sayin' that she's got it good", while he also seems to comment on what he saw as the irresponsible lifestyles of his brothers, "Mother's preachin' Abraham, brothers they don't give a damn". "Ghosts" and "Is This

Scary" round out the new tracks on the album, the rest of the tracks being remixes of songs from *History*.

Coinciding with the release of *Blood on the Dance Floor* was *Ghosts*, a short film which premiered in very select movie theaters. With the screenplay by horror master Stephen King and Michael Jackson, it opens with a sign welcoming you to "Normal Valley". Towns people lead by a middle aged, overweight white guy, with actual torches in their hands, head towards a house in Normal Valley. Michael, as the Maestro, is the resident of the targeted home. The old white guy tells Michael that he is weird and tries to run him out of town. Michael challenges him to a game of whoever gets scared first has to leave. Great special effects and makeup add to a big dance number to "2 Bad" with some creepy backup dancers very reminiscent of another ghoulish music video. Michael turns into a skeleton (with white socks and black loafers) dancing to "Is This Scary". The zombies surround the old white guy and Michael inhabits his body and joins the others in dance to "Ghosts" in a quite comical scene. The closing credits roll over footage of Michael in the makeup chair being transformed into Joe Average fat white guy by Rick Baker who transformed Michael into a werewolf in "Thriller". The dance routines were choreographed by LaVelle Smith, Travis Payne, Michael Jackson and Barry Lather.

Michael attended the "Ghosts" premiere at the Cannes Film Festival on May 8th in 1997. The short film was awarded the Bob Fosse Award for best choreography. At forty minutes in length, "Ghosts" is listed by the *Guinness Book of World Records* as the longest running music video.

In February 1997, Michael performed at a birthday celebration for his dear friend, Elizabeth Taylor, singing "Elizabeth, I Love You" which he wrote for the special, "Happy Birthday Elizabeth: A Celebration of Life". Speaking of a celebration of life, this same month, Michael finally became a father.

26

Everyday create your history
Every path you take you're leaving your legacy

"HIStory"
- Michael Jackson, James Harris III, Terry Lewis

On February 13, 1997, Debbie Rowe gave birth to a baby boy. Michael Jackson was finally a father. He was named Prince Michael Joseph Jackson Jr. While Prince is a family name, Michael's maternal grandfather and great grandfather had the name, it is a certainty that the cuteness factor of the King of Pop having a Prince was not lost on him. Michael reportedly snatched Prince from the hospital and headed home with Debbie left behind. Michael issued a statement the next day, "Words can't describe how I feel. I have been blessed beyond comprehension and I will work tirelessly at being the best father that I can possibly be. I appreciate that my fans are elated, but I hope that everyone respects the privacy that Debbie and I want and need for our son. I grew up in a fish bowl and will not allow that to happen to my child. Please respect our wishes and give my son his privacy."

The world got its first peak at Prince in the pages of, believe it or not, the *National Enquirer*. In a shrewd move, Michael sold pictures of his new son for publication. By outwardly providing pics to the media he took away the incentive for the paparazzi to stalk and hunt him for pictures of Prince. And he got to have control over the images used. Some shots were of Prince and his very famous father, others with Debbie, and a couple with the whole family. It would be one of only a few shots of Prince that would ever be made available. Michael was determined to keep his children safe and usually hid their faces with scarves or masks when in public with him. Perhaps exhibiting more than a little paranoia, he was concerned his children would be pursued if people could recognize them and even feared the possibility of kidnapping.

Pictures of the new Prince were also featured in the December 1997 issue of *Life* magazine. The King of Pop, in a silver beaded jacket and fedora, cradled his young Prince in his arms. Inside is a shot of dad holding up his Prince wearing one white glittered mitten. In an accompanying interview it is noted that "there is one subject to which Michael repeatedly returns during four hours of conversation and picture taking – Lisa Marie Presley. Michael's voice quickens, even quavers when he speaks of Lisa

Marie. How she enjoys the baby. How they are still close after an amicable divorce. How they frolicked overseas the month before. He seems to pine for her…. Even Debbie has acknowledged that Michael is still smitten. 'He cares about her very much, but it didn't work out and he was devastated. He loved her very much. Still does.'"

Debbie gave birth again on April 3, 1998, this time to a baby girl. Paris Michael Katherine Jackson was so named as she was conceived in Paris, and of course Katherine is his mother's name. Prince and Paris lived with their father at Neverland and rarely had visits from their mother, Debbie being introduced to them as a family friend.

Michael told Rabbi Boteach that he wanted to have many more children. He wanted to have more than his father did, and he "had ten". He is either taking the unusual step of publicly acknowledging Joe's illegitimate daughter, Joh'Vonnie, or Marlon's twin brother Brandon, who lived only a few hours. He shared with biographer J. Randy Taraborrelli that each of his sons would be named Prince.

In 1999, Debbie and Michael divorced. Michael retained custody of the children and reportedly paid a multi-million dollar settlement to Debbie. Some arrangement for continuing payments were also part of the settlement. She gave up her parental rights, which ended up being restored later when it was determined this was illegal. She purchased a ranch in Palmdale, California and began raising horses.

The 12th Annual Rock and Roll Hall of Fame Induction Ceremony in 1997 included the Jackson 5 who were inducted by, appropriately enough, Diana Ross. All of the brothers were dressed in dark suits, Michael in a black and gold military jacket with lots of gold braid, sunglasses in hand. The statues were handed out one by one and each brother spoke briefly each incorporating lines from one of their biggest hits, "I'll Be There". Michael spoke last, turning director at one point asking that only the front camera shot be used and holding his arm out to the side to make the side shot that he disliked unusable. After a few moments the actual director realized Michael usually got his way, so only the camera covering the front angle was used and Michael was able to put his hand down. *I'd like to say to our family, our children, our friends and most of all our mother and father, they are here tonight, my mother and father, you were there for us to love and protect us with an unselfish love, because you were there, we are here.*

*Berry Gordy, I love you. Like Diana Ross you were there and now you are here. I'm crazy about you. Berry could you **please** join us up here right now. Berry Gordy I want you to know that in my heart and mind you are a genius and a king. Without you Berry Gordy, I don't think music would be the same today.* (Confusion followed as Bee Gee Barry Gibb appeared on stage in a mass of Berry vs. Barry confusion. Gibb's son Michael also joined his dad on stage and Michael J introduced him as his godson.) Then Michael continued,

Berry Gordy, you promised us four consecutive number one records

and you delivered them all. I'll never forget it. It was a first in music history. And now there's many more singles that went number one for the Jackson Five, single after single. He then explained why he continued to look down as his notes:

I'm not very good on the teleprompter, that's why I have to look down. Your faith makes it possible for us to be here today. We love you from the bottom of our hearts, sincerely. And I just want you to know that without you, my mother and father, I don't think we would be here and of course, God.

*And to the fans, I don't want to take too much time, you were there conditionally, **un**conditionally, and I say thank you very much. Now we are in the Rock and Roll Hall of Fame... so whenever you call our name – I don't like that angle, I like **this one**- Whenever you call our name, I promise, I love you all of you, and we'll be there.*

Berry Gordy then spoke reminiscing about the old days and thanking the Jackson Five.

To close out the decade of the 90's, *TV Guide* joined with MTV to pick the 100 Greatest Music Videos Ever. To mark the occasion, and the upcoming special counting down their choices on MTV, the magazine featured the artist at the top of the heap on the cover of their December 4th issue. Not surprisingly, it was Michael Jackson. They also scored an interview with the King of Pop. He started off by talking about his concepts for music videos, which he prefers to be called short films, "What I didn't like were the videos that were a collage of images; I thought that if I were to do one, I would do something with a little more entertainment value. My dream was to make something with a beginning, a middle and an ending, like a short film". He also spoke of his unrelenting perfectionism and how some of the songs on *Thriller* didn't even measure up to what he had envisioned, noting that "Wanna Be Startin' Somethin'" disappointed him, "Songwriting is a very frustrating art form. You have to get on tape exactly what's playing in your head. When I hear it up here (points to his head), it's wonderful. I have to transcribe that onto tape. "The Girl is Mine" wasn't completely what I wanted, but it's very nice. But "Billie Jean" is there. I worked so hard on that. I worked for three weeks on the bass lick alone."

One of the most interesting topics of the interview centered on his costume devices, the single glove and white socks. "The glove was just – I thought one was cooler than two. I love to accent movement. The eye goes to where the white is – you know, the glove. And the feet, if you're dancing, you can put an exclamation point on your movement if it has a bit of light on it. So I wore the white socks...

He addressed the questions of whether he and Debbie were in fact the biological parents of Prince and Paris, responding to stories that Debbie had been implanted with a donated egg and impregnated by artificial insemination. Michael responded, "That's total garbage. It's just trash and not true."

In closing out the millennium, the World Music Awards honored Michael Jackson with the Millennium Artist Award in May 2000. The award was presented by Prince Albert of Monoco.

Michael's next entry earned in the *Guinness Book of World Records* focused not on his groundbreaking career achievements, but on his unmatched humanitarian efforts. The publication's 2000 edition named him as the record holder for Most Charities Supported By a Pop Star. Michael was listed as supporting thirty-nine charities through monetary donations, sponsorships of their projects, and participation in silent auctions. One interesting note with the impressive list, which centers on disease awareness and research and children's charities, is the exception of any charities focused on the welfare of animals. Given his love of animals it is somewhat surprising that not one animal rescue or sanctuary charity is included. This is hardly a criticism, just an observation given his concern for their welfare.

Another entry in the *Guinness Book of World Records*, that is unrelated to his music career, is the $1.5 million auction bid for the Best Picture Oscar won by *Gone with the Wind* . It holds the record for the most ever paid for an Academy Award. It could be seen among the knick knacks in the cluttered living room at Neverland.

He began visiting many different spots around the globe and had a penchant for announcing grand schemes for various amusement parks and attractions none which ever materialized. One was announced for his old stomping ground, Detroit, Michigan. Plans for a pair of extravagant millennium concerts also never happened and earned him another lawsuit for $21.1 million from concert promoter Marcel Avrim. When Michael showed up for court with tape across his nose the image was bookmarked by the media for endless use in showcasing his "weirdness". Michael was ordered to pay Marcel Avrim a settlement of $5.3 million for failing to perform the concerts as agreed.

In late February 2001, Michael broke his right foot while dancing at Neverland. He ended up hobbling on crutches for a number of public appearances. One of his first stops was in London, where he delivered a high profile address to Oxford University to help launch Heal the Kids, a charity he founded with Rabbi Shmuley Boteach and psychic Uri Geller. His thirty minute address to the packed hall was aimed at encouraging parents to spend more time with their children. As part of an effort to mentor and serve as a spiritual advisor for Michael, Boteach encouraged Michael to make amends with his father. Michael ended up placing a phone call to Joseph from London and telling him he loved him and forgave him. Michael shared with Boteach at the time that Joseph had become a nicer person with age.

To promote his Heal the Kids charity, Michael joined Rabbi Shmuley Boteach to kick off the Michael Jackson International Book Club which gave away books to help encourage kids to read. In keeping with his desire to improve kids' childhoods, Michael wished there was a day of celebration for children, "There's a Mother's Day and there's a Fathers Day, but there's no Children's Day… It would mean a lot. It really would. World peace. I hope that our next generation will get to see a peaceful world, not the way things are now."

The day following the Oxford address Michael served as

best man as his friend Uri Geller and his wife Hannah renewed their marriage vows, with Rabbi Boteach officiating. Michael was two hours late for the ceremony, forcing the reception to be held prior to the ceremony.

In early 2001, MTV named its first mtvICON, Janet Jackson. A special celebrating the music and videos of Janet featured many artists performing Janet's songs. Janet capped off the evening with a performance of her newest single, "All For You". Michael did not attend but did send his little sister his best wishes via videotape:

Janet, I am so thrilled that you are being honored tonight. No one deserves this more than you. You have achieved so much and you will only keep climbing higher and higher. Your talent knows no boundaries. I am honored and proud to be your brother. I love you."

In mid March, an appeals court in Rome found Michael not guilty of plagiarism in a case brought by Al Bano, who claimed Michael stole "Will You Be There" from his song, "The Swans of Balaka". This ruling overturned a lower court's decision in 1999, the court then found him guilty because he did not show up for the proceedings.

This same month, the Rock and Roll Hall of Fame inducted its latest impressive list of honorees including Aerosmith, Paul Simon, Queen, Steely Dan, Ritchie Valens, and the King of Pop. Paul Simon and Michael Jackson were each being honored for the second time. Simon had been inducted as part of the duo Simon and Garfunkel and Michael was already a member of the Hall of Fame, the class of 1997, with the Jackson Five. At the announcement of the class of 2001, Michael responded, "I am thrilled and humbled to receive this great honor. I could not ask to be in better company than the list of fellow inductees. Each and every one is a master from whom I have learned. My sincere thanks to the rock and roll historians and experts who have chosen me."

With his foot still in a cast, Michael let the crowd know, "there's not going to be any moonwalking tonight", as he hobbled on stage to accept the honor. It was rather ironic that after much buzz about Michael being the youngest inductee into the hall, he ended up walking with a cane to accept the honor. Michael set a record as the youngest inductee in 1997 as part of the Jackson 5, this year he set a record as being the youngest solo inductee. 'NSync did the induction honors. Dressed in an ivory suit with a really long coat and his hair smoothed and long, Michael expressed his thanks and gratitude, his voice in a lower register than usual:

"Thank you so very much. Thank you 'NSync, I am so proud to call you my friends. You're all so wonderful. Thank you. This is a tremendous honor and I am so happy to be here. As you can see there's not going to be any moonwalking tonight because I broke my foot dancing. I fell down the stairs in California. I broke my foot in two places so – but I have like six more weeks with this cast. So, it is gonna come off soon.

I'm honored to be inducted twice in the Rock and Roll Hall of Fame. It's a great blessing. For me the gift of music has been a blessing from God, from the time I was a child. So, I'd first of all like to thank my parents who bequeathed to me that gift. To my mother, Katherine, and to my father, Joseph Jackson, I love you both. To my brothers and my sisters, thank you, you're so wonderful. Rabbi Shmuley, I love you and thank you for helping me launch Heal the Kids.

Berry Gordy, Berry Gordy, Berry Gordy, Berry Gordy! As it was in the beginning, so many of us, um... I just have to say thank you. He was so important in our lives and he is really my real inspiration and I owe him so much. Quincy Jones, thank you, you talk about a thriller. Quincy, you're incredible. I love you Quincy. He is the man. The glamorous and talented and beautiful Diana Ross, who is my second mother, I thank you. Tommy Mottola, Sony, I love you. Thank you fans. Thank you. Bye.

Unfortunately, Michael did not take part in the traditional all star jam session. Michael posed for pictures backstage but did not answer questions from the press. It was claimed later that this was one of the convenient injuries Michael suffered to avoid stressful or uncomfortable circumstances. He supposedly hated the idea of participating in the jam session, was ill prepared, or was just too high to perform so his ankle was bandaged up to give him an excuse to avoid it.

While working on finishing *Invincible,* Michael's advisors were working on negotiating a deal for him to purchase Marvel Comics. According to Frank Cascio, in *My Friend Michael: An Ordinary Friendship with an Extraordinary Man,* Michael predicted the value of Marvel before the Spiderman movies were made.

Unfortunately the deal fell through. Michael was furious, having been led to believe the deal was nearly complete.

At this same time, Michael was reported to be interested in moving his MJJ Records label from Sony to a new home. A storm was brewing between Sony Records and their biggest selling recording artist.

Vh-1's latest countdowns of the 100 Greatest whatevers always included many Michael entries, some good, some not so good. The music network's ranking of the 100 Most Shocking Moments in Rock 'n Roll included his marriage to Lisa Marie Presley in 1994 at number 47; his purchase of the Beatles song catalog in 1985 placed at number 38; the scalp burns he suffered at the filming of the Pepsi commercial in 1984 was named as the 19th most shocking Rock 'n Roll moment and the second most shocking moment in Rock 'n Roll was the accusation of child molestation made against Michael in 1993. This was second only to the tragic murder of John Lennon. A later incarnation of this list would have Michael's tragic and shocking ending taking over at number one, not a list you wish to top.

On August 30, 2001, Michael opened trading on the NASDAQ in New York. This was to honor Michael for his commitment to excellence in the entertainment industry and for his humanitarian work. The ceremony was broadcast on the JumboTrons on the streets of New York City. After officially opening the market, Michael was presented with a huge birthday cake and a vintage poster of Shirley Temple. Michael spoke briefly, as usual: "I'm deeply moved as this very special moment for me. Thank you, David Wicks and NASDAQ. Thank you so much. I love you and all the fans. Thank you."

"You Rock My World", the first single off his upcoming *Invincible* album was released to radio stations in September and immediately received heavy airplay. The single, named the Hot Shot Debut by *Billboard* magazine, debuted on the Hot 100 at number thirty-four and at number thirty on the R&B/Hip Hop singles chart. In its first week of release, it was estimated that 63 million radio listeners were exposed to the new single. Sean Ross, editor of radio trade publication *Airplay Monitor*, said "Any question about whether Top 40 radio wanted Michael Jackson back has been pretty well answered. Clearly, there's at least initial interest." Meanwhile Tommy Mottola's patience were wearing thin with costs of producing *Invincible* skyrocketing to $30 million due to Michael's insistence that songs be constantly remixed and re-recorded with the results being no different than the first takes.

The video for "You Rock My World" debuted on MTV's "Total Request Live" and on Vh-1 on September 26, 2001 and on the Jumbo Trons in Time Square in New York City and on Sunset Blvd in Los Angeles. The long version was nearly fourteen minutes long, a shortened version timed in at five minutes. The edited version aired on BET every hour on the hour on September 28th. The short film featured appearances by Marlon Brando and Chris Tucker. In the film, dressed in a dark suit and fedora, with a do-rag under his hat, Michael pursues the girlfriend of a gangster and ends up winning her over with his arsenal of dance moves. While entertaining, it is not of the level of earlier efforts and the exchange at the beginning between Michael and Chris Tucker seems forced and very unnatural, especially for Michael. An equally awkward exchange between them on the record has Jackson agreeing that a girl "is "bangin'", sounding very out of character and ill at ease.

"You Rock My World" peaked on the Hot 100 at number ten and at number thirteen on the R&B/Hip Hop singles chart. It was Michael Jackson's fortieth top ten hit on the pop charts. With the single reaching the top ten in 2001, Michael Jackson became the only solo artist to place a single in the top ten in each of the 70's, 80's, 90's and 2000's. Michael's work on "You Rock My World" earned him a Grammy nomination for Best Male Pop Vocal Performance.

When 'NSync performed their hit, "Pop" at the MTV Video Music Awards in September, a gigantic Etch-A-Sketch drew out the words: "King…Of….Pop". Michael stepped from the rear of the stage and performed all of fifteen seconds with the group in a surprise appearance that was a very poorly kept secret. It was the highlight of the whole show and he received a standing ovation. In picking up the award for Best Group Video, 'N Sync member Justin Timberlake said, "We want to thank Michael for coming on stage with us. That was huge. He just made five fans very happy." He would soon make a lot of fans very happy as he was gearing up to celebrate his 30th anniversary as an entertainer in grand style.

27

You can't believe it, you can't conceive it
And you can't touch me, 'cause I'm untouchable
And I know you hate it, and you can't take it
You'll never break me, 'cause I'm unbreakable

"Unbreakable"
-Michael Jackson, Rodney Jerkins, Fred Jerkins III, LaShawn Daniels, Nora Payne, Robert Smith

Michael celebrated his 30th anniversary with two performances on September 7th and 10th 2001 at Madison Square Garden in New York City. The multi hour performances that included a brief reunion with his brothers, were edited down to a TV friendly two hour special that aired on CBS in November.

Michael's band included noted musicians with whom he had a long history; Brad Buxer and Greg Phillinganes on keyboards, guitarist David Williams, drummer Jonathan Moffet and Alex Al on bass. Al would be back for This Is It.

Guest stars performed Michael Jackson songs, or songs in tribute to him, capped off by a performance from the guest of honor. The first night's performance lasted over five hours with many starts and stops, technical difficulties and disorganization creating many gaps between acts. At one point the crowd began to chant impatiently for the King of Pop to take the stage. When Michael finally did take the stage all of the organizational problems melted away and Michael reminded everyone why he wears the title "King of Pop" so fittingly. E! Online's Josh Grossberg, in his review, wrote, "And what seemed like impending disaster for the disorganized affair soon turned into HIStory as the King of Pop reclaimed his title as one of the greatest entertainers in the music biz."

Michael watched the performances in tribute to him seated with Elizabeth Taylor, Liza Minnelli and pal Macaulay Culkin. He was dressed in black leather pants and a white sequined jacket and often blew kisses to the performers. No ponytail, he was wearing his hair cropped short.

The TV Special opened with Usher, Mya and Whitney Houston performing "Wanna Be Startin' Somethin'". Whitney's skeletal appearance caused widespread concern over her health. Next, Billy Gillman did a great job of performing "Ben", no small feat. Shaggy, with Rip Rock, performed "It Wasn't Me", which was said to be one of Michael's favorite songs. A quartet of divas performed "Heal the World". Monica, Deborah Cox, Mya and Tamia were joined on stage with a choir while film clips of Michael were shown of him visiting children and at various benefits and functions with Presidents and Princess Diana. Marc Anthony did a surprisingly good job with "She's Out of My Life" but without the unavoidable emotion that Michael pumped into it twenty-two years earlier. Michael had specifically requested that he perform the number.

Destiny's Child performed their own hit, "Bootylicious" with each of them wearing one white glove and white glittery fedoras. Beyoncé once stated she wrote the song with Michael in mind.

Liza Minnelli next butchered, rather performed, "You Are Not Alone". The song was hardly recognizable. Mercifully, her rendition of "Over the Rainbow" from *The Wizard of Oz*, was not included in the TV Special. James Ingram and Gloria Estafan performed "I Just Can't Stop Loving You" without any feeling or flair. Scenes shown from videos with Michael and Tatiana from "The Way You Make Me Feel", with Ola Ray from "Thriller", with Iman from "Remember the Time", and with Naomi Campbell from "In the Closet" had much more heat.

Usher, 98 Degrees, and Luther Vandross performed "Man in the Mirror" the song that should have been in Michael's set. That's Michael's song, pure and simple. It would have been just as improper to have someone else perform "Billie Jean'. It just shouldn't be done.

> "Unbreakable"

Elizabeth Taylor introduced Michael Jackson and the Jacksons. Michael rose up from the bottom of the stage amid explosions dressed all in white with gold shin guards and gold and white jacket and a gold helmet. He immediately removed his gloves, helmet, and jacket as they all approached the mic stands at the front of the stage and went into "Can You Feel It". Michael, looking rather bootylicious, had apparently lent another pair of shin guards to Randy and a spare sequined glove to Jermaine. "The Love You Save" followed "ABC" then "I'll Be There" with the same choreography from thirty years earlier. At the finish of "I'll Be There", Michael added some vocal work showcasing his tremendous range. For "I Want You Back", they resurrected the staged argument from the Victory tour over what song to do next with Michael consenting to do the old single, "the old fashioned way as on *The Ed Sullivan Show* in 1970." They instantly stepped back to 1970, doing the exact same steps. It looked as though they never stopped performing that number that exact way for the past thirty years.

'NSync joined the Jacksons on stage for "Dancing Machine". "Shake Your Body" was a fun and enjoyable ending of the Jackson set. But now it was time for the King of Pop to remind the public why he so richly deserved the pop world title. And that is just exactly what came next.

Actor/Comedian Chris Tucker introduced Michael's solo performance. Tucker had done an impression of Michael's dancing with one small difference. In the introduction, Tucker jokes that Michael called him to complain that he had seen the impression of him and pointed out that Chris was "kicking with the wrong leg".

Michael's solo portion of the show started with "The Way You Make Feel". Dancing behind a scrim, then coming out dressed in a blue shirt, black fedora and white belt tied around his waist, it was reminiscent of his blockbuster 1988 Grammy performance. Slash joined Michael on guitar for "Black or White" getting a huge response from the crowd and for the famed guitar solo on "Beat It".

For the next number, Michael pulled out a show stopper used in the shows on the HIStory tour, so most U.S. fans had never seen it. A stool stood center stage. Michael casually walks out from side stage wearing black tuxedo pants, white sequined socks and black loafers and a white T shirt. He's carrying a small suitcase. He lays it on the stool and opens it. He pulls out a jacket. A black jacket, covered with sequins. He puts it on and meanders around very casually. The crowd goes nuts. The next thing pulled from the suitcase is a black fedora. He slips it on his head and pushes the front down, shading his eyes. The crowd cheers louder. The last item is now pulled out the suitcase. A white glove. Just one. Covered with rhinestones. He holds it very nonchalantly like it means nothing. Now the crowd is insane. The glove goes on and each finger is carefully fitted. He steps to the microphone, snaps his fingers and instantly the spotlight moves to where he just ordered it to go. With one thrust of that magic pelvis, "Billie Jean" begins much like his now legendary performance from the *Motown 25* special. This time there are new moves added toward the end after he retrieves the fedora and just before he tosses the now obligatory hat into the crowd.

Michael's performance is topped off with his newest single from *Invincible,* "You Rock My World". He is backed by a group of all female dancers. Towards the end of the performance, he is joined on stage by Usher and Chris Tucker. In a comical moment, Tucker does his impression of Michael's trademark kick, Michael does his, then Chris Tucker does his version. With the wrong leg. Completely exasperated, Michael collapses on the floor.

The anniversary concert was a definite success. "Entertainment Tonight" reported, "For anyone who had any doubts... the King of Pop is definitely back! Who would have thought that a single white glove and an aptitude for moonwalking could lead to so much! It was with those trademarks, among others, that Michael Jackson verified his title as music's head honcho - as he celebrated his reign of more than thirty years as such this weekend at New York's Madison Square Garden!" USA Today reported, "The highlight, though, was when Jackson sang and danced "Billie Jean" on his own, re-creating his legendary anniversary special. Though it would have been impossible to recapture completely the magic of that moment, Jackson proved that he still has the grace, vitality and effortless virtuosity that made him an icon. If he can now get people to focus on those attributes – rather than personal quirks and foibles- this self-styled king may yet maintain his throne."

"Michael Jackson: 30th Anniversary Celebration" proved to be a ratings bonanza for CBS. Neilson Media Research estimated that 45 million viewers saw part or all of the special with viewership increasing steadily throughout the show. It was CBS's highest rated music special ever. Senior Vice President for CBS Specials, Jack Sussman, said the special was "an opportunity to see a performer who has had a long and successful career but who has been out of the limelight for a while. He's still one of the greatest performers ever, and when he gets onstage and the music starts, it's magic." Years later Sussman described being invited to Neverland to watch the rough cut: "He watched it for an hour and a half and did not say a word. After he turned it off, we sat at a table and he proceeded to give ninety minutes worth of notes from his head that were totally right on and improved the show.... It blew my mind how smart he was about the power of TV".

The week the anniversary special aired, *TV Guide* featured Michael Jackson with two commemorative covers. One cover had a black and white photo of a twelve year old Michael from 1970. The second cover had a color photo of Michael sporting a new look. His hair was short and straight, parted on the side with long side burns. He was dressed in a black button down shirt with a small gold chain at the neck. In true MJ style, he showed up for the interview two hours late, with Prince and Paris in tow. He answered the usual expected questions regarding his start in music and his relationship with his father:

"What is your relationship with your father?"

"It's much better now. He's mellowed out a lot since he's had grandchildren, you know. He has thirtysomething grandkids now."

The interview concludes with Michael speaking of his own parental skills. Asked, "Are you a good father?" Michael responded,

"I try my hardest. I try to bring them a lot of fun. Once a year I dress up like a clown, with the whole gear – the nose, the paint. And I give them candy and cookies." Prince pipes in, "And ice cream", to which Dad agrees, "And ice cream!"

Michael talked about performing with his brothers again for the first time in seventeen years, "Being on stage with my brothers was a wonderful experience. Like a revelation. It was almost as if it was déjà vu, as if it happened yesterday. Because I felt as if Ed Sullivan was introducing us when we first premiered 'I Want You Back'. I love my brothers and it was just a great celebration. It was so much fun."

This may have been an exaggeration. As the concerts neared, they began to become bogged down in controversy. This time, it was Jermaine who kicked it off by providing a letter to the press stating that he was not going to be a part of the event, he cited "exorbitant ticket prices" which ranged up to $2500, and the fact that no charity had been named to benefit from the event. He did end up taking part in the shows.

Of course the day following the second concert at Madison Square Garden was filled with tragedy as the terrorists attacks on the U.S. unfolded. Michael, his children, their Nanny, Grace, and members of the Cascio family headed out of New York the morning of the disaster and headed for the Cascio's New Jersey home. He charted a bus for the long drive back home as the entire county was a no fly zone for several days following the attacks.

Following the terrorists attacks of September 11, 2001, Michael began working on an all star recording of a benefit recording. Michael wrote, produced and financed "What More Can I Give" that was to be recorded by himself, The Backstreet Boys, 'NSync, Santana, and nearly three dozen other acts. Michael hoped to match the $50 million that had been raised by the "We are the World" single, "I believe in my heart that the music community will come together as one and rally to the aid of thousands of innocent victims. There is a tremendous need for relief dollars right now and through this effort each one of us can play an immediate role in helping comfort so many people. We have demonstrated time and again that music can touch our souls, it is time we used that power to help us begin the process of helping immediately." Recording sessions at various locations with the wide range of contributors seemed to continue over long periods while the single never really materialized. Sony helped to make sure the single never saw the light of day, as they were then at odds with their once prized artist. Tommy Mottola was concerned the charity single would detract from the singles released from *Invincible*.

Michael did perform the song at the "United We Stand: What More Can We Give" marathon concert held on September 21, 2001 at RFK Stadium in Washington DC. Michael led an all star group in performing the benefit single. The concert raised more than $2.5 million for victims of the terrorist attacks. Michael told the families of the victims, "You are not alone. You are in our thoughts and in our prayers."

Anticipation for the release of *Invincible* while high, came with mixed expectations. Naysayers, always eager to take a jab at him, never missed an opportunity to predict his album would fail, that his best days were behind him. Many doubted it would be among the top sellers of the fall. However, others had quite different view. Tom Calderone, senior vice president for music programming for MTV, believed it could be a big hit, "I heard about nine tracks, and they're all solid, they are just home runs".

Alan Light, editor-in-chief of *Spin* magazine, felt Michael had his work cut out for him with the release of *Invincible*, "It's not that (young) people haven't heard of Michael Jackson, it's worse than that. They've had ten years of the freak show and the allegations and the court fight. How do you get them to cut through that and listen to anything? It's certainly going to be an uphill struggle." Light did feel the album's first single, "You Rock My World" had the makings of a hit, "It's a nice understated, easy groove. It's obviously not going for the big knockout. They put out *HIStory* saying, 'This is gonna be bigger than *Thriller,* and that doomed it. He needed to put a song out there that will put him back into the public consciousness as a singer and musician, and then to build to something bigger."

Pete Howard, publisher of CD magazine, *ICE*, speculated on the success of *Invincible,* "When you talk about built-in fan bases, his has to be one of the biggest in pop, but predicting first-week sales is impossible. He has a lot of credibility to re-establish. If he can normalize his image, keep the eccentric behavior to a minimum and do a lot of promotion, he could do well."

Invincible was finally released on October 30, 2001. The November 3rd issue of *Billboard* magazine featured a special fold out ad featuring the album cover art in the limited edition four colors. In true Jackson style, it debuted on the *Billboard* Hot 200 at number one. And that was just in the United States. *Invincible* also debuted at the top spot in Great Britain. And Germany and France. And Australia, Belgium, and Demark. And Holland, Hungary, Malaysia and Norway. Sweden, Switzerland and Turkey too.

Billboard magazine reported that *Invincible*, in its first week of release, was outperforming the expectations of U.S. retailers. The album was outselling high profile new releases by Lenny Kravitz, Enrique Iglesias, the Backstreet Boys and Barbara Streisand. Once again proving his skeptics wrong, Michael's *Invincible* album debuted in the number one spot on *Billboard's* Hot 200 album chart and the R&B/Hip Hop charts, his fifth number one album as a solo artist. MTV's Tom Calderone said, "For someone who has not been visible musically in a long time I think it's a very strong first week." Within two weeks, *Invincible* sold over 4.4 million copies worldwide. To date total sales of *Invincible* are 11 million copies. *Billboard* magazine named *Invincible* as one of the world's top 20 albums of 2001. Due to the lack of promotion and comparatively disappointing sales, *Invincible* is his most underrated and overlooked album.

Invincible's sales are more impressive when you consider he was at the time embroiled in a dispute with Sony over control of his master tapes which resulted in Sony refusing to promote the album or make short films to support the singles. Michael was looking to have the licenses to his master recordings returned to his control, giving him complete discretion in their use and 100% of the profits. He was angered to learn the rights to his masters would not revert to him until 2009. Michael ended up at one point going on a tirade against Sony head Tommy Mottola calling him 'mean, racist, and very very very devilish". He made a public appearance at the National Action Network headquarters in Harlem, New York, with Reverend Al Sharpton in which he made a statement that record companies take advantage of their artists, "especially black artists". Mottola shortly after left Sony, though it is not clear if his departure was related to the feud with Michael Jackson. According to Joe Vogel, Sony was thrilled with the *Invincible* album when finally finished. The planned singles and short films that never materialized due to the strained relationship between artist and record company included "Butterflies", "Unbreakable" and a Grammy performance of "Whatever Happens". An elaborate short film for "Threatened" was also excruciatingly cancelled.

    The other theory is that there was a conspiracy by Sony and his management team to gain full control over the ATV music catalog. Not promoting the *Invincible* album, and having it fail, it would force Michael into dire financial straits causing him to have to sell his half of the song catalog to Sony, who owned the other half.

    Michael's tirade against Sony baffled those around him who

also knew Mottola, notably Frank Dileo and Bob Jones. Some claimed Michael just wanted to blame Sony for the comparatively weak sales of *Invincible*. Sony was said to be furious that Michael Jackson could walk away from the record company while still holding a 50% stake in the company.

Critical reviews of *Invincible* were mixed. While some dismissed it as rather lame and claimed Michael has lost his touch with the current music trends, others lavished praise on his latest work. A reviewer from *USA Today* described the album as "forced, calculated and cautious, lacking the spry exuberance of the sure-footed song wizard on *Off the Wall* and *Thriller*". Another review of the album singled out "Whatever Happens" for the "tasteful Santana guitar playing...". A review in *Billboard* magazine read, "His undeniable creative genius has sadly become increasingly overshadowed by tales of his personal life. He later adds, "Maybe it's too demanding to expect an artist who has previously set the standard of excellence and innovation in pop music to be continually on point... When you know a man is capable of greatness, it's hard to accept anything less."

The second single, in the U.S., was "Butterflies", not one of the strongest tracks on the album, but the soulful ballad, while seeming a little juvenile, does grow on you. Michael's vocals are impressive. "Butterflies" peaked at number fourteen on the Hot 100 on the strength of airplay alone after Sony cancelled its release as a single. It just missed becoming a number one single on the R&B singles chart, spending five weeks in the runner up spot. "Cry" was

"Unbreakable"

released as the second single in Europe and is a much stronger song. The gospel flavored song is reminiscent of "Man in the Mirror" and works wonderfully. While in "Man in the Mirror" Michael is prepared to change the world by starting with himself, In "Cry" he admits it may be quite a challenge without a little help:

> *You can change the world (I can't do it by myself)*
> *You can touch the sky (Gonna take somebody's help)*
> *You're the chosen one (I'm gonna need some kind of sign)*
> *If we all cry at the same time tonight*

A video for "Cry" was released throughout the world, but not in the U.S. Michael was so angry with Sony around the time of the single's release, he refused to appear in the video. The video was directed by Nicholas Brandt who had also directed the videos for "Childhood", "Earth Song" and "Stranger in Moscow". A song dedicated to all of the missing children was included on the album, "The Lost Children" includes some spoken portions by Prince Michael Jackson Jr.

Other standouts on *Invincible* include "Unbreakable", "Heart Breaker", "Break of Dawn" where Michael wants only to spend the night hours making love to his girl, not wanting the sun to ever rise:

> *I don't want the sun to shine I wanna make love*
> *Just this magic in your eyes and in my heart*
> *I don't know what I'm gonna do I can't stop lovin' you*
> *I won't stop 'til break of dawn makin' love*

In "Heaven Can Wait", Michael would rather put off heaven than leave his girl. "Whatever Happens" featuring Carlos Santana on guitar should have been released as a single. "2000 Watts" is a fun song with a hard rock sound. "Threatened" is a continuation of the "Thriller" theme featuring an introduction using clips of *Twilight Zone's* Rod Serling that works every bit as well as Vincent Price's rap at the end of "Thriller" and centers around an ever present monster:

> *You're fearing me, 'cause you know I'm a beast*
> *Watching you when you sleep, when you're in bed,*
> *I'm underneath*
> *You're trapped in the halls, and my face is the walls*
> *I'm the floor when you fall, and when you scream it's 'cause*
> *Of me*
> *I'm the living dead, the dark thoughts in your head*
> *I know just what you said*
> *That's why you've got to be threatened by me*

Guns and Roses guitarist Slash teams up with Michael once again playing guitar on "Privacy". Slash had hoped to feature Michael on his first solo album, "When I was thinking about who I wanted to work with, Michael crossed my mind. I thought about doing something that would see him totally cross over into rock." As Michael was rehearsing at the time for This Is It, Slash never got the chance to make the offer. Slash called Michael "the embodiment of music."

After announcing and then postponing singles from *Invincible*, such as "Break of Dawn" and "Unbreakable", Sony

"Unbreakable"

Music decided to end its promotion of the album, probably due to their continuing feud with Michael. This prompted fan clubs to band together to attempt to change their minds.

Invincible's cover, a close up sketch of Michael's face, was issued in five different colors. In addition to the familiar white cover, it was also issued in blue, red, green and orange. Another portrait of Michael that had been considered for the album's cover art was a striking shot taken in 1999 by French photographer Arno Bani. Dressed in a black jacket covered small shiny circular beads, Michael's hair is pulled back and his face is made up beautifully with his left eye surrounded in a patch of blue glitter makeup. This "Blue Eye" portrait was among eleven other pics put up for auction in Paris in December 2010. The "Blue Eye" portrait was the most striking of the series of photos Bani took during his photo sessions with Michael. The photos raised more than $265,000 at auction.

Joining *Invincible* on the store shelves were deluxe special editions of *Off the Wall*, *Thriller*, *Bad* and *Dangerous*. Each CD had been re-mastered and now included demo versions of songs, interviews with Rod Temperton and Quincy Jones, and songs not included on the original albums like "Carousel", "Street Walker" and "Fly Away".

The release of *Invincible* and the availability of these new treasures had Michael's earlier efforts returning to the *Billboard* Pop Catalog Albums chart. Also released around this time were two DVD's, "Video Greatest Hits HIStory – Special DVD Edition" with a previously unreleased eighteen minute long version of the "Bad" video, and "Dangerous: The Short Films" which included extra footage from "Black or White".

On November 7, New York's Times Square was brought to a standstill as fans swarmed the area to catch a glimpse of the King of Pop. Police were forced to close off the area when Michael made an unprecedented appearance at New York's Virgin Megastore where he signed copies of *Invincible* and posed for pictures with fans. The event was aired live on MTV's "Total Request Live". Dressed in a rather unflattering blue silk track suit, Michael sat down for a short chat with host Carson Daly and talked about the success of his new album, "It's a great honor. I'm very happy about it. I'm blessed that the fans accepted it the way they did and I am very honored, I really am. I don't take anything for granted. Every time there's a number one album or song, it's as if it is the first one. So, I'm very happy about that." Daly mentions that virtually every performer on "TRL" listed Michael Jackson as one of their primary influences on their career and asked who influenced Michael at the start of his career, "Lots of artists, mostly entertainers. I would say Sammy Davis Jr, James Brown, Jackie Wilson. There's so many great singers from Aretha Franklin to Streisand, and I love Beatles music. I just love great, great music."

In October, it was announced that Michael had agreed to play a cameo role in *Men in Black II* starring Will Smith and Tommy Lee Jones. The sequel was scheduled for release in July, 2002. His brief appearance has him asking Jones and Smith's characters if he can join the Men in Black team as "Agent M". It was a much smaller role than one he sought years earlier. Director Joel Schumacher shared that Michael Jackson showed interest in and campaigned for the role of the Joker in *Batman Forever*. A proposed deal had Michael playing the role of the Joker and Schumacher directing the "Scream" video.

In December, Michael gave an interview to *USA Today*. Of course he showed up a couple of hours late. For somebody with an incredible sense of timing, he was habitually late. He brought Prince with him and the interactions with his son provided some of the most touching and amusing parts of the article. While the paper was promised "unfettered" access to Jackson, once the interview began, it was apparent his marriages, skin color, painkiller addition, and of course the molestation accusations were off limits. He did not hesitate to condemn the tabloid press, "The fans know the tabloid garbage is crap." He also talked of working with his brothers again, saying he would like to do an album with them again, but not a tour. Asked if he questioned his own relevance on the music scene after such a long absence, "Never. I have confidence in my abilities. I have real perseverance. Nothing can stop me when I put my mind to it." He also spoke of constantly having his work compared to *Thriller,* if that album casts too big a shadow, "Absolutely. It is tough because you're competing with yourself. *Invincible* is just as good or better than *Thriller*, in my true, humble opinion. It has more to offer. Music is what lives and lasts. *Invincible* has been a great success." He addressed how fatherhood had changed him and how his relationship with his own father had improved, "It's much better.

My father is a much nicer person now. I think he realizes his children are everything. Without your family, you have nothing. He's a nice human being. At one time, we'd be horrified if he just showed up. We were scared to death. He turned out really well. I wish it wasn't so late."

After a protracted battle between Dick Clark and his American Music Awards and Michael Greene of the Grammys, Michael eventually forfeited an opportunity to perform on the Grammys. He elected to appear on the AMA's, telling Clark, "Yes, I am going to attend to pick up my award, and I will not appear on the Grammys. I'm a man of my word." The Grammys had refused artists the opportunity to appear on the Grammys if they also appeared on the AMA's prompting legal action from Clark.

As *Invincible* was released too late in the year to be eligible for Grammy consideration, Michael had only one nomination for Best Male Pop Vocal Performance for "You Rock My World". Michael did not win, did not perform, and did not attend.

Michael did attend and was presented with the AMA Artist of the Century Award by friend Chris Tucker. Dressed in black leather pants and silver beaded military jacket the thanked a long list of people "who are very important in my life".

In 2002, Michael Jackson was inducted into the Songwriters Hall of Fame. Fellow inductees this same year included Sting, Randy Newman, Barry Manilow, Nickolas Ashford and Valerie Simpson.

Vibe magazine featured Michael on its cover for its February

2002 issue, a close up shot of him resting his chin on a gloved hand. Michael has also granted an interview. The interviewer, meeting Michael at Neverland, notes, "I discover that, in spite of all the flash and tumult of Michael's time in the spotlight, he's remarkably unchanged – still caring, inquisitive, and sensitive."

VIBE: Does it bother you to see people emulate you, such as Usher, Sisqo, Ginuwine, and even Destiny's Child?

MJ: I don't mind it at all. These are artists who grew up with my music. When you grow up listening to somebody you admire, you tend to become them. You want to look like them, to dress like them. When I was little, I was James Brown, I was Sammy Davis Jr., so I understand. It's a compliment.

VIBE: Is there anything that you would like to say to VIBE readers?

MJ: I love Quincy Jones. I really do. [Quincy Jones founded *Vibe* magazine] And also, I want to tell the readers not to judge a person by what they hear, or even what they read, unless they hear it from the person himself. There is so much tabloid sensationalism. Don't fall prey to it, it's ugly. I'd like to take all the tabloids and burn them. I want you to print that! Some of them try to disguise themselves, but they are still the tabloids.

Michael had six nominations for the NAACP Image Awards. He took home three. "Michael Jackson: 30th Anniversary Celebration" won for Outstanding Variety Special and Michael won for Outstanding Performance in a Variety Special, "You Rock My World" won for Outstanding Music Video, where he was competing against Janet's "All For You" video. Michael did not attend the ceremony. Perhaps he had his hands full with a new baby at home. Michael's third son, Prince Michael Joseph Jackson II was born only two days earlier.

28

You can change the world
You can touch the sky
You're the chosen one
If we all cry at the same time
Tonight

"Cry"
- R. Kelly

A surrogate was used for Michael's latest addition to his family. Michael claimed he was present at Blanket's birth and that he had an agreement with the mother not to reveal who she is. He later said that the surrogate used for Blanket was a woman he had never met. At another point he says it was a woman with whom he had had a relationship. He always maintained it was his own sperm cells used for all three of his children. It was later speculated that

Blanket's mother was a Norwegian woman who was also the mother of a young man, Omer Bhetti, who would for a short time, also be suspected of being Michael's son. Prince II was given the nickname "Blanket" and is usually referred to by this name. Michael explained he frequently used the term "Blanket" to mean providing love and good care, to blanket one with loving care. Frank Cascio offers a different version of the story. His mother, Connie, was holding the new baby and remarked he was as cuddly as the blanket he was wrapped in. And the nickname was born.

As his children grew, Michael maintained a level of strictness that would probably surprise most people. And he worked to maintain a high level of security around his children. They were home schooled, with about the best music teacher you could ask for, and he was serious about them keeping up their grades. Time spent in front of the TV and computer was kept at a minimum. On a class trip to a local museum, he carefully lead the kids to each exhibit, reading and explaining at each display, requiring Prince and Paris to pay attention.

In March, 2002, Liza Minnelli married David Gest. Gest had two best men, Michael and Tito Jackson. Gest and Minnelli first met at Michael's 30th anniversary concert six months earlier, where Gest was the show's producer. Liza's maid of honor was Elizabeth Taylor. Michael pulled double duty when he also gave the bride away.

The first annual Magical Life Award goes to....Michael Jackson! The newly founded award was voted on by children through the Celebrate the Magic Foundation. The foundation's press release read:

The humanitarian award is given to individuals who have demonstrated with true humanitarian service, the peace, love and happiness, characterized by the magic of children and in so doing, has helped make the world a kinder and gentler place. The Magical Life Award is being presented in honor of Celebrate the Magic Day, when 1 million children around the world, will sing an inspirational song, at the same time! An international event to promote world peace, love, and happiness through the Magic of children."

One of the songs the children would sing was "Heal the World".

The statement said further:

When given the opportunity to vote for the person that inspired them the most, to stay in touch with the Magic of their inner child, thousands of children from around the world, voted for Michael Jackson."

Ebony magazine, in its April 2002 issue featured a poll of readers of their favorite musical artists. Michael was named as one of the "10 Most Important Black Music Personalities of All Time In All Genres", and as Favorite Contemporary Male Singer. The Jackson 5 was named as Best Male Group Of All Time. "I'll Be There" was named as Favorite Song, and "Billie Jean" was chosen by the readers as the Greatest Pop/R&B Song Of All Time.

In April 2002, Michael taped a performance of "Dangerous" as part of the 50th Anniversary celebration of Dick Clark's *American Bandstand*. The crowd, while cheering for other performers like

Cher, Stevie Wonder and Kiss, went ballistic when the King of Pop took the stage, and, of course, brought the house down. He did his performance twice for the taping which aired on May 3rd. Fashioned after the History tour performances, imaginary machine gun fire shot out as a dancer dropped to his death revealing Michael Jackson standing behind him. Dressed in a black suit and tie, a shiny red shirt that looked like it was plastic, and a fedora, Michael performed "Dangerous" with a bit of "Smooth Criminal" moves thrown in.

Michael attended the MTV Video Music Awards on his 44th birthday where Brittany Spears presented a tribute to the King of Pop. But it was unclear what exactly it was for. It appeared to be to celebrate his birthday, but Michael believed he was being honored as the Artist of the Millennium. According to Frank Cascio, his manager at the time, Trudy Green, told Michael he was being honored as the Artist of the Millennium, but this turned out not to be the case. Spears presented a cake, and Michael gave his prepared award acceptance speech.

During a visit to Germany in November, to pick up a Pop Artist of the Millennium award, a real one this time, hordes of fans gathered outside his hotel room, as usual. They chanted and asked to see Michael's new baby, Prince Michael Jackson II. He obliged and held his infant son in his arms with his feet over the railing of the balcony. Unfortunately for Michael, this was all captured on tape. Footage of him 'dangling' his infant son over a balcony caused a furor worldwide with some going to the unfathomable extreme of

"Cry"

calling for his kids to be taken away from him claiming he was an unfit parent. Amid the unrelenting coverage of the incident now forever known as "the baby dangling" incident, Michael issued a statement calling it "a mistake... I got caught up in the excitement of the moment. I would never intentionally endanger the lives of my children." Michael did point out though that for broadcasts, the footage was deliberately slowed down to make it look as bad as possible, "I got caught up in the moment. I was holding on tight. And it happened for like, two seconds. But, when it gets on the news, they slow it down. They make me look like I'm this eccentric idiot, dangling this baby over a balcony, like a nut. They don't show you the whole story." The footage continued to air, always with narration calling him "bizarre" or "weird". The word "dangling" couldn't be used enough either, prompting images of Michael holding his young son by his fingertips as he flung him over the railing. While it was potentially dangerous, and certainly thoughtless, it also certainly garnered much more attention simply because it involved Michael Jackson.

The April 2003 issue of *Vanity Fair* featured an article by Maureen Orth on Michael Jackson that revealed explosive revelations like he had a prosthetic nose, bleached his skin, not due to his vitiligo disease, but because he no longer wanted to be black, and most outrageous of all was the story of him paying $150,000 to have a voodoo curse placed on a list of "enemies" that reportedly included Steven Spielberg and record industry mogul David Geffen. The placing of the curse involved having forty-two cows slaughtered so Michael could bathe in the blood. Apparently that ensures the curse will in fact be placed where directed and not end up as a total waste of time, money and sense, not to mention cows. The sole source of the story was Myung Ho Lee who claimed to be a former advisor of Michael Jackson's and was at the time embroiled in a multi-million dollar lawsuit against him. No other sources corroborated the story. It was also reported in the issue that Michael provided wine to a particular young boy when he was just twelve years old. The young man denied the story as soon as it was released and let it be known he was never contacted by Orth for the story, that no effort was made to confirm the "facts" in the article.

    This would not be the only time Michael would be accused of hating, or being ashamed of his own race. Bob Jones, in his bitter tirade against "the King" recounted Lee's accusations and claimed Michael did hate black people. Jones claimed Michael preferred whites over blacks, and lighter skinned blacks over those with darker skin. Among those who refuted these claims was Gotham Chopra, who had known Michael for decades, "It was very disturbing to him that people thought he always wanted to be white and he was bleaching his skin. He identified as a black person and so it was troubling to him that everyone thought that he was a hater of his own race. And the lupus, why he didn't just come out more clearly and say that was the problem, I'm not sure. But I know it was something that bothered him a lot." According to Jones, Michael also hated Jewish people. And women.

    Admittedly Michael Jackson was a bundle of contradictions;

enormously shy yet explosive on stage, an astute businessman yet over leveraged his assets endangering his Neverland Ranch and ownership of the ATV music catalog; at home with top musicians and top business people, but also very childlike. But a hater of black people? And Jewish people? Hard to accept given that, well, he was black and had worked with and had associated with countless black people throughout his life as well as Jewish people. One of his closest advisors at one point was Rabbi Shmuley Boteach. Elizabeth Taylor had converted to Judaism decades earlier. Many who knew and worked with Michael over the years state that he really lived the message he spread, of wanting all people of all races and creeds living in peace.

  E! Entertainment Television completed their edition of their series, *True Hollywood Stories* on Michael Jackson which first began airing in June 2003. I was fortunate enough to be asked by the network to take part in the interview program. When the film crew, who set up in my home, noticed my extensive Jackson album collection, they asked to photograph each of the covers for use in the special. The program was later updated and re-aired following his death.

  "Living with Michael Jackson", a TV special aired in 2003 in which Michael Jackson welcomed British documentary maker Martin Bashir to Neverland Ranch. Bashir spent about eight months with Michael, visiting him at Neverland and traveling with him and his children. Bashir was with Michael in Germany at the time of the infamous "baby dangling" incident. He traveled with Michael and his kids, with their faces covered with scarves or masks, to Las Vegas where they went on an extravagant shopping spree. Michael spent an estimated $6 million on some bric-a-brac, giant urns, paintings, etc. It was reported later than most of the items were later returned. He was clearly uncomfortable commenting on his financial affairs. He expressed his mistrust and hatred of tabloid journalism suggesting all the tabloids be gathered together to make mountains of them, and "just burn them all".

Bashir had packed up his equipment with all of the footage to put together the TV special and was out of Neverland when Michael had the bright idea of inviting him back to meet a young cancer patient friend who had spent time at Neverland with his family. Gavin Arvizo was thirteen years old when he, his sister, Davelin, and his brother, Star, first met Michael and became friends. Michael told Bashir how Gavin and Star would sleep in his bed and he would sleep on the floor. When they asked to sleep in Michael's room (Michael did NOT offer) he said only if it was okay with their parents. He explained that he felt it was the most loving thing you can do, share your bed with someone. Michael became agitated and visibly repulsed when Bashir suggested this was not proper, and Michael insisted there was nothing sexual about it, that Bashir was trying to turn it into something ugly. These statements would help create a nightmare for Michael he couldn't have possibly imagined and from which he would never fully recover. *Living with Michael Jackson* attracted 27.1 million viewers and earned ABC their highest ratings in twelve years and in this case, that was not such a good thing. The young cancer patient seen in the special would later make accusations of molestation against Michael Jackson.

It was infuriating to see that Michael had not learned his lesson from the Chandler debacle and was not cognizant of how his statements would be received by viewers, the media, Child and Family Services, the DA, all stars of the nightmare he lived ten years earlier. He understood his sharing of his home and bed with others to be out of a pure and moral place, but that is NOT how it played to others.

Years later Frank Dileo addressed Michael's penchant for getting himself into bad situations. He noted that Michael always looked for the good in people and at times trusted the wrong people. Beyond his not seeing that his spending time with young boys was not well received by most people, he would also begin to make poor decisions on who he picked for advisors in his career, who he put in control of his finances and who he had surrounding him from day to day. Jermaine added, "He had the biggest heart and he truly wanted to help children, nurse, nurture and make them happy, especially the unloved, the less fortunate, the sick, the infirm (sic) and the dying. This was not some trite, trendy mission statement on behalf of a pop star, it was a purpose that he lived and breathed, dedicated vast amounts of time to many causes and donating hundreds of millions of dollars to numerous charities."

In response to the purposely contrived and slanted view of Michael's life featured in the Bashir documentary, a program consisting of footage taken at the same time as the documentary by

Michael's videographers was produced. *Michael Jackson: The Footage You Were Never Meant To See* aired on Fox on February 20th. This program showed how the Bashir footage was edited and Bashir's own commentary was added to manipulate the final product.

While this second firestorm brewed, Michael did attend to other business. In June 2003 Michael visited Gary, Indiana for the first time in about twenty years. He was in town to tend to, what else, a lawsuit. This one brought by Gordon Keith, who had signed the Jackson 5 to Steeltown Records. The brothers were being accused of infringing on the name Ripples & Waves. Some sources say the brothers were known by the name Ripples & Waves Plus Michael very early in their careers, though Jermaine says this is not true. Another band in Gary at the time used the name Ripples & Waves. While in Gary, the mayor presented him with the key to the city and he visited his former home and Roosevelt High School. A judge later ruled that the Jackson brothers were not part of the dispute and removed their names from the lawsuit.

At the BET Awards in June, Michael made an extremely rare award show appearance, not to collect an honor, but as a presenter. This was special to him. He was presenting the Lifetime Achievement Award to his life long idol and inspiration, the Godfather of Soul, James Brown. Michael surprised Brown on stage, mimicking his idol's fancy footwork and was donned with Brown's trademark cape. Dressed in silver pants, white shirt, and one single black glove and smoothed straight hair, Michael deviated from his prepared remarks to express how much Brown had meant to him, his voice cracking with emotion:

What is a genius... One whose inspiration demands change. A genius... I couldn't refuse to give this award tonight because nobody has influenced me more than this man right here. From the bottom of my heart, since I was a child, at six years old, he was the one I looked up to more than any other entertainer. And I still do today.

Ladies and Gentlemen, I'm deeply honored to present to James Brown the Lifetime Achievement Award and no one deserves it more than this man."

Number Ones, a compilation of greatest hits was released in November 2003. The title is a bit curious as there are songs included that did not reach number one on the charts – at least in the U.S., but perhaps they did in one part of the world or another, or perhaps they were number one in his heart. No doubt to spur sales, the album was issued with four different covers, each featuring a different shot of Michael Jackson in a familiar dance pose. Promoting the release of the *Number Ones* album was a TV special, "Michael Jackson: Number Ones" on CBS on January 2, 2004. A review of his unparalleled career included concert clips and performance footage including a great clip of "Ben" from what looked to be the 1981 Jacksons tour. Dick Clark, Beyoncé, Quincy Jones, Slash, and others all offer their memories and thoughts on Michael Jackson, his amazing career and his influence on them. The special concluded with "One More Chance" from *Invincible* featuring career footage and video clips. The special was a production of Optimum Productions and was executive produced by Michael Jackson and John McClain and was later released on DVD.

John McClain is a music industry executive that has been friends with the Jackson family for many years. He played an integral role in kicking Janet's music career in high gear, signing her up with A&M Records and helping to introduce her to producers Jimmy Jam and Terry Lewis, her equivalent of Quincy Jones. He has worked with both Janet and Michael for decades.

The Radio Music Awards took place in October. For the event, a special Humanitarian Award was created and presented to… you guessed it, Michael Jackson. Michael accepted the award from Beyoncé, dressed in black with at least two wide silver belts and silver knee pads and shin guards. He accepted the honor in recognition of his humanitarian work, especially with "We are the World" and introduced a video of highlights for his latest benefit single, "What More Can I Give" in response to the September 11th terrorist attacks, 'I hope once again we can set out on a mission to lead the world on a path of harmony by asking ourselves everyday, 'What More Can I Give?'"

Michael received another humanitarian award in April, 2004, this time from the African Ambassador's Spouses Association. The award ceremony was held at the Ethiopian Embassy in Washington, D. C. Just before receiving this honor, Michael met with Congresswoman Sheila Jackson-Lee and some members of the African ambassadors to discuss another cause he cared deeply about, the status of the fight against HIV-Aids.

Another collection of Michael Jackson hits was released one year after *Number Ones*. *Michael Jackson: The Ultimate Collection*. But this collection was different. It was a 4 CD box set with a DVD of the Dangerous tour, *Live in Bucharest*. The four music CD's not only contain many of his biggest hits from the very start of his career with the Jackson 5 to the Jacksons through his solo hits from *Invincible* but also some previously unreleased songs and demo versions of hits. A demo of "Shake Your Body (Down to the Ground)" is titled "Shake A Body". Demos of "Sunset Driver" which was recorded during the time of the *Thriller* recording sessions is a treat as well as "Scared of the Moon" recorded in 1984. The demo of "Cheater", from the *Bad* recording sessions in 1987 is included with an early version of "Dangerous". One fun song never before heard is "Monkey Business" which, while not credited as such, might just be a duet of sorts with Michael Jackson and Bubbles. Another intriguing previously unissued track is "We've Had Enough". Many, many tracks were recorded for each album, and only so many could make the final cut. A wonderful book accompanies the set detailing the date each track was recorded and the song's lengthy credits. Biographer Nelson George contributes a brief overview of Michael Jackson: *The Singer; The Writer: The Arranger*. All of this is featured among many great photos throughout his career.

Shockingly, in 2004 Bob Jones, who had worked with Michael since his early days at Motown and with Michael on his own since the 80's, had received a letter from Michael dismissing him. No reason was given for the dismissal. To say it soured their relationship is an understatement. Jones went on to co-author a scathing book on Michael with Stacy Brown. And he testified for the prosecution in Michael's upcoming trial albeit his testimony was largely innocuous. Jones died in 2008 without ever mending fences with Michael.

Prior to start of the trial, Michael was paid a visit by former childhood rival and friend Donny Osmond. Osmond had been working on a cover of Steve Wonder's "I Wish" and he played it for Michael, at Stevie Wonder's request. Osmond later told *Rolling Stone*, "We have always been linked in a parallel universe, with us and our families, but we've never actually done anything together. And his face lit up and he said, 'What are you thinking?' And I played him 'I Wish'. And he loved the track with these two kids who are now adults talking about 'I wish those days would come back once more'. And he said, 'I love it, let's do it'. We were going to do a duet, and then he called me up as soon as that thing hit, and said, 'I've got to pull out'."

A court hearing held in April determined Michael Jackson would face trial. After entering a not guilty plea, his attorney, Thomas Mesereau told the media outside, "This case is about one thing only. It's about the dignity, the integrity, the decency, the honor, the charity, the innocence, and the complete vindication of a wonderful human being named Michael Jackson." Another hearing held in August had Michael showing up to court with his entire family, all dressed in white as a show of unity and innocence. Michael Jackson was headed for the most difficult and painful period of his life.

29

*I was wanderin' in the rain
Mask of life, feelin' insane
Swift and sudden fall from grace
Sunny days seem far away*

"Stranger in Moscow"
- Michael Jackson

The airing of the *Living with Michael Jackson* special and the accusations made by the young boy in the special gave rise to a new investigation of Michael Jackson by the Santa Barbara Sheriff's Department. On November 18, 2003, while Michael was in Las Vegas, seventy authorities from Santa Barbara county raided Neverland Valley Ranch. They spent fourteen hours searching the ranch, slashing his mattresses and paintings and inventorying everything. The sheriff's office was accused of overdoing it a bit with the large number of officers sent to conduct the raid. Michael was furious that Neverland was being raided, telling Frank Cascio that he couldn't believe they were trying "to fuck with me again". Much would be made of the fact that the Sheriffs department took this accusers word and pounced on Jackson without ever investigating the claims being made or the family making them. It is difficult to believe that District Attorney Thomas Sneddon was not drooling at the prospect of finally getting his man.

A statement released by Stuart Backerman, Michael's publicist, in response to the raid on the ranch read:

The outrageous allegations against Michael Jackson are false. Michael would never harm a child in any way. These scurrilous and totally unfounded allegations will be proven false in a courtroom. Naturally, the implications are distressing to everyone who hears them, which is precisely the point. Michael through his attorneys, led by Mark Geragos, has already made arrangements with the District Attorney to return to Santa Barbara to immediately confront and prove these charges unfounded.

Following the raid on Neverland, Santa Barbara County District Attorney Thomas Sneddon issued an arrest warrant for Michael Jackson. Michael Jackson and attorney Mark Geragos flew from Las Vegas to Santa Barbara, and Michael surrendered to authorities. Broadcast live on TV, a handcuffed Jackson was lead into the Sheriff's office. He was patted down, had a mug shot taken, and was booked. His arrest record shows Michael Jackson was 45 years old, 5' 11" tall, 120 lbs with brown eyes and black hair. Geragos gave a statement:

Michael is greatly outraged by the bringing of these charges. He considers this to be a big lie. He understands the people who are outraged, because if these charges were true, I assure you Michael would be the first to be outraged, but I'm here to tell you today – and Michael has given me the authority to say on his behalf – these charges are categorically untrue. He looks forward to getting into a courtroom, as opposed to any other forum, and confronting these accusations head on.

Following his release on $3 million bail, Michael returned to Las Vegas and took over the penthouse suite of the Regency Tower at the Las Vegas Country Club. It was soon discovered that there was secret videotaped footage of Jackson and Geragos on board the XtraJet private plane ride from Las Vegas to Santa Barbara. When an attempt was made to sell a copy of the tape, lawsuits and injunctions were filed preventing the tape from being sold. It was regarded by law professionals as the most egregious of all invasions of the attorney-client privilege. Geragos sued the owner of XtraJet, Jeffrey Borer, and was awarded a settlement of $20 million. This was overturned on appeal many years later and Borer was ordered to pay $2.5 million.

In an interview with *60 Minutes* Michael claimed he had been abused by the police, even providing photos of himself with large bruises on his arms. He described the area in which he was held as having feces on the walls. None of this story seemed to

"Stranger in Moscow"

match other accounts of his arrest and booking, which indicated he was treated fairly and even posed for pictures. Later that night of the airing of the *60 minutes* interview, Michael took a near fatal dose of morphine.

His arraignment was held in January, 2004. Following court proceedings for the day, making his way out of the court house, Michael was greeted by loud cheers from a huge crowd of supporters outside. Wishing to acknowledge their support, he climbed on top of his SUV and waived to his fans. He even pulled his videographer up on the vehicle with him to get a shot of the frenzied crowd. Michael waved and clapped. This was then, and has ever since, been portrayed in the media as him *dancing* on top of the SUV. Now, I have seen Michael Jackson dance. A lot. This was *not* Michael Jackson dancing. According to Mark Geragos, Judge Melville had a sense of humor in regard to Michael climbing on top of the SUV outside the court following his arraignment and did not take it as a sign of disrespect of the court. Court proceedings had been completed. Michael was acknowledging his fans like he always had, he was not performing and at no time thumbed his nose at the authority of the court.

Fans who hung around the courtroom to show their support for Michael certainly had their efforts pay off. Big time. Michael's aids distributed invitations for them to attend a party at Neverland Valley Ranch that afternoon, "In the spirit of love and togetherness, Michael Jackson would like to invite his fans and supporters to Neverland Valley Ranch. Please join us Friday, January 16, 2004 from 11am to 2pm. Refreshments will be served. We'll see you there."

Certainly by this point, if not for the past several years, Michael regretted ever settling the 1993 case. Given his income at the time, his incredible net worth, and mega future earning power, the price tag, relatively speaking, was not that much. Settling the case however did help convince some that he was guilty and made him out to be an easy target for even more allegations. In hindsight he wished he had gone to court with that case, which he would have certainly won, and finally and forever been vindicated.

Michael was infuriated to be facing such charges again. He sensed the possibility of a conspiracy against him by Sony. Exhibiting shrewdness, or perhaps growing paranoia, Michael knew if he was convicted he would be forced into default on his bank loans, allowing Sony to finally get their hands on the prized ATV song catalog.

Damaging information was leaked from the grand jury transcripts to the media. While the parties to the case were barred by the judge from speaking publicly about the case, he did allow Michael Jackson to address this leak in general terms. He appeared on Fox News with Geraldo Rivera to read a statement:

In the last two weeks a large amount of ugly malicious information has been leaked into the media about me. Apparently, this information was leaked through transcripts in a grand jury proceeding where neither my lawyers nor I ever appeared. The information is disgusting and false. Years ago I allowed a family to visit and spend time at Neverland. Neverland is my home. I allowed this family into my home because they told me their son was ill with cancer and needed my help.

Through the years I have helped thousands of children who were ill or in distress. These events have caused a nightmare for my family, my children and me. I never intend to place myself in so vulnerable position ever again.

I love my community and I have great faith in our justice system. Please keep an open mind and let me have my day in court. I deserve a fair trial like every other American citizen. I will be acquitted and vindicated when the truth is told.

After reading this statement, he asked for the public's prayers for his children and himself.

Jury selection began in early 2005. It would take weeks to finally seat the jury. The jury members finally empanelled to hear the case consisted of twelve jurors and eight alternates. Of the twelve, whose ages ranged from twenty to seventy-nine, eight were women, and they were white and Latino, no African Americans. Only one of the eight alternates was African American.

Feb 28, 2005 opening statements began in the case of the People of California v. Michael Joe Jackson. In his opening remarks, Thomas Mesereau stated Michael would take the stand in his own defense, something he very much intended to do. But, as the trial proceeded, it became apparent that he didn't need to. Michael arrived for court each day on time, with one glaring exception, dressed very sharply and surrounded by various combinations of family members. He rarely spoke to the press and never answered any of their questions, only remarking on one day that he found the day's testimony "frustrating" and another day he expressed that he felt "angry". All accounts of his courtroom demeanor have him sitting silently with his defense team paying rapt attention to every detail, every word spoken. On one occasion early on in the proceedings, he addressed the judge directly, remarking that he couldn't hear what he was saying. He was admonished by the judge.

He did make one public statement outside the courtroom one day early on in the proceedings to thank his fans and family for their support:

I'd like to thank the fans around the world for your love and your support from every corner of the earth; my family, who's been very supportive, my brother, Randy, who's been incredible; I want to thank the community of Santa Maria. I want you to know that I love the community of Santa Maria very much. It's my community. I love the people. I will always love the people. My children were born in this community. My home is in this community. I will always love the community from the bottom of my heart. It's why I moved here.

Aphrodite Jones, a journalist who covered the Jackson trial for Fox News admitted she readily bashed him and offered any damning insights possible to the case, as was the case with virtually every media outlet with a representative assigned to covering the trial. And this was no small group. Over 2200 members of the media from thirty-four countries covered the trial of Michael Jackson. Upon reflecting on her work and the outcome of the trial she had a change of heart and saw how the media turned toward tearing down the King of Pop once again. Her book, *Conspiracy*, offers a thorough review of the trial culled from trial transcripts and court documents pointing out how the actual court proceedings differed dramatically from the media's coverage of the trial. She drew the conclusion that Santa Barbara District Attorney Thomas Sneddon would stop at nothing to finally get a conviction of Michael Jackson, hanging his case on the accusations of what turned out to be a family of grifters with a history of making monetary demands of people, most often, celebrities. Sneddon even threw in conspiracy charges against Michael Jackson that when examined, and if a man's freedom weren't hanging in the balance, were laughable.

Jones even managed to get the Foreword for her book provided by Jackson's lead defense attorney, Thomas Mesereau. In the Foreword, he noted, "In the Michael Jackson case, most media conclusions were shallow, misinformed, and self-serving. I know in my heart of hearts that Michael Jackson was not guilty of any of these grisly charges." He also noted that "The prosecution spent more money and time trying to convict Michael Jackson than any prosecution in history." Media coverage was not skimped on either, "More accredited media from around the globe covered this trial than the total number of reporters who covered the O.J. Simpson and Scott Peterson trials combined." It was a widely held belief that a conviction in this case would spawn book and movie deals worth enormous amounts of money. "However, a conviction was necessary to successfully complete any of these projects. If Michael

Jackson had been sent to prison, it would have generated more media coverage than any event in history. Billions of dollars hung in the balance."

Jones noted that TV producers pushed for coverage that focused on the prosecution, anything that was "anti-Jackson". "The more negative the commentary, the more attention the story got. It was a vicious cycle that almost everyone in the media got caught up in."

As a further indication of the media's resistance at this time to report or publish *anything* positive about Michael Jackson, Jones, who has written many books on high profile trials, was repeatedly told by publishers that they would not publish anything that was pro-Jackson. She self published her book.

Michael was initially represented by well known attorney Mark Geragos. Both Michael and his brother Randy had contacted Johnnie Cochran early on for help. Cochran, who represented Michael at the conclusion of the 1993 allegations, was in the hospital at the time diagnosed with a brain tumor. Cochran recommended Thomas Mesereau Jr. for the job. When Cochran later lost his battle with cancer in April, Michael took time from his own distressful and turbulent trial to attend his funeral. He also had others in his thoughts. When Thomas Mesereau's sister was battling cancer, Michael sent her flowers and wrote her a poem. She would also lose her battle with the disease.

Unfortunately Mesereau was not available at the time. When Mesereau suddenly became available to represent Michael

Jackson he took over for Geragos. Jackson's defense team was then made up of associates, Susan Yu and Robert Sanger and headed by the incomparable Thomas A. Mesereau Jr.

Brian Oxman, an attorney for the family was also part of the defense team initially. He was later removed from the team by Tom Mesereau. Mesereau had filed a termination notice with the court in connection with Oxman and advised him not to show up at the court house. When Oxman showed up anyway, it resulted in a confrontation in the parking lot with Mesereau that was broadcast live on TV. Oxman continued to make television appearances purporting to be speaking on Michael's behalf. This was not the case. Michael ended up issuing a statement that Oxman did not represent or speak for him.

The prosecution was headed by Santa Barbara District Attorney Thomas Sneddon with Gordon Auchincloss and Ron Zonen. Sneddon was of course on the case in 1993 against Michael and was unable to get an indictment. He had waited a long ten years for the opportunity to go after him again and was not going to let this chance slip through his fingers. He was ever more aggressive and determined to finally get his man, frothing at the mouth at the thought of putting Michael Jackson behind bars. He desperately wanted to "throw the brotha in jail". He was cocky, self assured and terrible at hiding how much he wanted to nail Michael Jackson.
Michael Jackson was facing a total of fourteen counts:
One: Conspiracy involving child abduction, false imprisonment, and extortion.

Two through Five: Lewd act upon a child under the age of fourteen.

Six: Attempt to get a child under the age of fourteen to commit a lewd act upon Michael Jackson.

Seven through Ten: Administering an intoxicating agent – alcohol- to assist in the commission of lewd acts upon a child.

Eleven through Fourteen: misdemeanor counts of providing alcohol to minors.

The prosecution's case centered on the theory that Michael plied young kids with alcohol and showed them pornographic images in an effort to seduce them into sexual acts.

Unindicted co-conspirators were named who supposedly aided in the conspiracy against the Arvizo family. Ron Konitzer Deiter Weisner, Frank Cascio, Vinnie Amen, and Marc Shaffel were all named. Many witnesses recalled seeing Weisner and Konitzer around the ranch, meeting with Michael, but did not know exactly what their connection with Michael was. Janet Arvizo would refer to them as "the Germans". Frank Cascio is a long time friend and associate of Michael's having first met him as a young boy. When Frank later began working with Michael, he chose to go by the name Frank Tyson. Often times Frank's sister and brother would all be at the ranch when the Arvizo family and many other children were also visiting. Marc Shaffel is a film producer who had worked on a few Jackson projects, but had a bit of a questionable background, having produced gay pornographic films.

Frank Cascio told ABC News and Rabbi Shmuley Boteach

that pornography was pulled up on the computer in Michael's bedroom, but the boys had helped themselves to the computer and the porn site. Cascio was also a friend of Rabbi Boteach's. Boteach wrote in *The Michael Jackson Tapes*, "Later, Frank would become an unindicted co-conspirator in Michael's trial, accused of attempting to abduct Michael's accuser's family. But Frank was never violent or threatening in any way, and I found the idea of him harming, or threatening to harm, Michael's accuser's family utterly inconceivable." Biographer J. Randy Taraborrelli told of conversations with Michael regarding the accusations against him and the tone that Michael used, he found the sexual overtones applied toward his relationship with kids to be repulsive.

Being named an Unindicted co-conspirator showed there was not enough evidence against them to charge them. But if Michael was convicted of conspiracy, the prosecution would then have the grounds on which to base formal charges against them.

Michael's accuser this time was Gavin Arvizo, who viewers saw in the "Living with Michael Jackson" documentary. He was a young cancer patient, with a very rare form of the disease, who had been given a death sentence by his doctors. One of his last wishes was to meet Adam Sandler, Chris Tucker and Michael Jackson. Gavin's wish was granted in 2000 when he was able to meet Michael Jackson and visit Neverland with his family. When Gavin was diagnosed, Jamie Masuda, owner of the comedy club The Laugh Factory, worked to organize benefits to raise money for Gavin's treatment and helped get him in contact with his heroes, Chris

Tucker and Michael Jackson as well many other comedians and celebrities.

The Arvizo family, mother Janet, father David, Star, Gavin and their sister Davelin, ended up making several extended visits to Neverland as Gavin battled cancer and underwent chemotherapy treatments. They credited Michael with boosting Gavin's spirits, helping him feel better about losing his hair, and even contributing to his eventual recovery and remission. They grew very close to him and began to refer to him as "Daddy". The family stayed in the guest units on the ranch but soon the kids were asking to stay in Michael's room with him. Michael always responded that if it was alright with their parents, then it was okay. There seemed to be quite a crowd at times in his two level bedroom suite that actually sprawled out over two thousand square feet. Often times Frank Cascio and his brother and sister would be visiting as would other friends and kids of associates of Michael's. When Gavin and Star stayed the night, Michael insisted they take the bed and Michael and Frank slept on the floor.

It was soon learned that the Arvizo family had a history of fabricating allegations in the past in hopes of landing a settlement. It was shown that testimony for the kids was prepared and rehearsed. They had on several occasions boldly solicited money from others, mostly celebrities, for payment of Gavin's medical expenses even though his medical expenses were fully covered by insurance. Janet Arvizo continued to solicit cash donations and collected a handsome settlement from JC Penney, with a fabricated claim of sexual abuse, some years earlier all while collecting welfare checks and any other public assistance she could apply for.

Gavin, Davelin and Star and his mother Janet all talked positively about Michael and their perception of Michael's miraculous effect on Gavin's cancer. They each held him in high regard and thought of him as a father figure, views they expressed on more than one occasion, both on tape and in numerous notes and cards given to their famous friend.

It needs to be emphasized that NO mention of Michael Jackson providing alcohol to the boys, NO mention of pornography being shown to the boys, and NO mention of any molestation was ever made to police until AFTER they met with attorney Larry Feldman. That's right, the very same attorney who represented Jordie Chandler in his claims against Michael Jackson ten years earlier. What a coincidence that the Arvizos would get out the yellow pages for the greater Los Angeles metropolitan area and just so happen pick out the exact same attorney as Jordie Chandler. They were then referred to therapist, Stanley Katz. Katz was of course the very same therapist Jordie Chandler was sent to see. Another uncanny coincidence.

The E! network produced a series featuring re-enactments of the highlights of each day's testimony in court. Actors were hired to play each of the prosecuting attorneys, and the defense team, the actor playing Mesereau coincidentally having a long mane of white hair. The actor portraying Michael had little to say or do, staying seated quietly at the defense table. Edward Moss, who has parodied

Michael in several films, was hired by E! to portray Michael Jackson. The re-enactments proved to be quite silly, but the program also offered insightful commentary by a panel of three attorneys the members of which varied from time to time but usually included attorneys Howard Weitzman and Shawn Chapman Holley, daughter of Johnnie Cochran.

While E! was free to discuss the trial, *Tonight Show* host Jay Leno was not. As a potential witness, Leno was subject to the gag order issued by Judge Melville not to talk about the case. Leno's attorneys filed a motion with Judge Melville asking that Leno be permitted to make Jackson jokes but not share any of the information he may have regarding the case. The motion was eventually granted, but in the meantime, since he was barred from making Jackson jokes, he simply brought in other people during his monologue to make wisecracks at Michael's expense. While his testimony supported the defense's claim that the Arvizos repeatedly approached celebrities and asked for money he apparently felt no air of hypocrisy in making jokes at Michael Jackson's expense.

It is excruciating to think how simply this could all have been avoided. If Michael had not done the *Living with Michael Jackson* special, or had chosen a reputable interviewer for the project, or not had the idea to invite Gavin and his family *back* to Neverland, or if he had simply had the sense to know how it would be perceived if he spoke on camera about sharing his bed with young visitors, the furor would never have erupted.

The prosecution offered eighty witnesses in the case, former associates of Michael's, former Neverland employees, one ex-wife, some names from the 1993 allegation case, experts in one field or another, and several others, some of whom would prove not to be as helpful to the prosecution as they would have hoped. They also had the detriment of having found NO forensic evidence in their search of Neverland. It would be common in cases of this nature to have some type of DNA evidence; hair, fluids, something. In the search of Michael's home the sheriff's office found nothing to support the accusations being made. Prior to the start of the trial, Michael cooperated with police in providing a DNA sample. Officers met him at the ranch and swabbed the inside of his mouth. A filmmaker, Larry Nimmer, was hired by the defense to shoot footage of Neverland Ranch to create a tour of the grounds for the jury. From this footage, Nimmer created a documentary of the ranch, *The Untold Story of Neverland*.

During the course of the trial, the entire Jackson family stayed at Neverland Valley Ranch with Michael. Michael opted to stay in one of the guest houses, wanting to never live in the main house again following the sheriff's raid on his once beloved home. In the event things did not go his way he, according to LaToya, began giving instructions to family members in the event he faced conviction. He was also aware of the possibility of an assassination attempt on his life given the nature of the allegations against him. It has been learned since that he took the preventative measure of wearing a bulletproof vest under his suits to court each day.

The prosecution's case was kicked off with the man who

started it all, Martin Bashir. The entire documentary, *Living with Michael Jackson,* was shown to the jury. Outtake footage from the documentary was also shown to the jury showing quite pointedly how Bashir was effusive in praise for Michael, but for the narration for the documentary, his tone shifted and made his contact with Gavin look and sound sinister. Bashir refused to answer most of the defense's questions during cross examination by Mesereau, quoting the Shield Law that prevents journalists from revealing information received in connection with a story.

The atmosphere surrounding the trial grew even more tense as the day grew nearer that Michael Jackson would face his accuser in court. Gavin Arvizo was scheduled to take the stand following the testimony of his brother, Star, and his sister, Davelin. The morning that Gavin was to take the stand however there was no Michael showing up for court. Mesereau was informed that Michael Jackson had sought medical treatment and was at the hospital. Judge Melville ordered his appearance in court and threatened to revoke his $3 million bail and put him in jail. A caravan of dark SUV's soon began making their way to the court house in Santa Maria. Michael was ushered into court, shuffling his feet. He was disheveled; hair uncombed, and was wearing pajama pants and slippers with a dark blazer. He moved slowly and seemed to be in pain. He made his way into the court room and was seated behind the defense table before the jury was brought in, so they were unaware of his attire that day and only learned from Judge Melville that Mr. Jackson had sought medical treatment that morning accounting for his tardiness.

"Stranger in Moscow"

Whether the pain he was experiencing was physical or emotional, he did seem to be genuinely suffering. While he has been known to become stricken with convenient medical problems when facing incredibly stressful times, he appeared physically impaired as he was being helped into the court house. Michael later addressed it, "People said I was faking during the trial, but I fell coming out of the shower and bruised my lung very badly. There was a scan done and you can see the swelling. There's no faking with this. I was going to court every day in immense pain". The media was completely obsessed with the sight of Michael arriving for court that day. In pulling footage from the days of the trial, footage from "Jammie Day" is inevitably shown, despite the fact that the trial lasted four months, he was taped each of these days arriving and departing from court. He arrived each and every day on time, impeccably groomed and dressed in sharp suits, perfectly styled hair and wire framed glasses. How many times has the Jammie Day footage been chosen to air over any one of the other days during the course of the trial? And why couldn't one of the many people around him manage to round up a pair of pants? With some of the media coverage of Michael Jackson at the time you would get the distinct impression that the most significant things he ever did were to hold his infant son on a balcony and arrive for court one day in his jammies.

After arriving to court as ordered, Michael's accuser took the stand. Gavin's account of the specific acts of molestation differed quite dramatically from that of his brother Star, who claimed to have witnessed one act from a staircase in Michael's bedroom. Accounts of Gavin's demeanor on the stand brought about more questions about his credibility. He was described as too calm, too rehearsed when relaying disturbing details of molestation. He appeared composed and unemotional as he relived the times he was supposedly masturbated by Michael Jackson. Some remarks made by Gavin echoed those made by Jordie Chandler some ten years earlier. They were actually too similar, Jordie's account having been recently published online.

Part of the prosecution's case was to claim Michael had plied Gavin, Star and perhaps other youngsters as well, with alcohol as a ploy to wear them down and get them into sexual situations. To further entice them, Michael was said to have shown the kids pornographic images on his computer and in magazines. Stacks of adult pictures were shown to the jurors during the course of the trial. The images were exclusively heterosexual images. No gay porn and no kiddie porn was found at his home; and no gay or kiddie porn was found on his computer. It would be explained by multiple witnesses that the kids actually spent time alone at the ranch and accessed Michael's computer on their own and accessed the adult websites themselves. They also helped themselves to adult magazines that were stored away in a briefcase.

One magazine in particular was presented in court and shown to Star by Tom Mesereau. He testified that yes this was one of the adult magazines Michael had shown to them. He was sure of it. Then Mesereau pointed out the date on the magazine and that it was several months *after* the family's last visit to Neverland.

"Stranger in Moscow"

Neverland Valley staff also testified that the Arvizo kids broke into the wine cellar, when Michael Jackson was not at the ranch, helped themselves to alcohol and at times appeared intoxicated around the ranch. Both Star and Gavin denied ever breaking into the wine cellar or ever drinking any alcohol.

The boys testified that Michael had provided them with wine to drink, which he called "Jesus Juice". The media had fun with this too. It was learned from the testimony of a flight attendant that Michael requested to have wine served to him in Diet Coke cans on flights. He was a nervous flier and preferred not to have any children traveling with him see him drinking alcohol.

The Arvizo kids were said, by many witnesses, to have run wild on the ranch. They drove golf carts recklessly, were loud, disrespectful and rude to the staff and often made wild demands. Over time, their behavior grew more and more out of control.

Both Star and Gavin testified that they had each previously lied when speaking positively about Michael Jackson, claiming they had been forced to do so. This admission of earlier lies and the contradicting testimony did nothing to bolster the credibility of the Arvizo boys. They both also denied that Michael Jackson had ever given any help to their family, minimizing the positive influence Michael had had, the gifts he gave and the aid he provided to the family. Earlier, in interviews with social workers from the Los Angeles Department of Child and Family Services Gavin said, "He's never done anything to me sexually." He added he "never slept in bed with Michael."

Janet Arvizo would prove to be an absolute disaster for the prosecution. Her testimony over the three days she was on the stand seemed to grow more and more bizarre. She would only direct her testimony toward the jury box, not speaking directly to the attorney questioning her, and she would not make eye contact with any of the attorneys or especially Michael Jackson. Having remarried to a man named Jay Jackson, she demanded she be referred to as Janet Jackson. Judge Melville ruled she be referred to as Janet Arvizo to avoid any confusion. She refused to follow court room rules and, according to Aphrodite Jones, became a joke to court room observers. She tried to deny the notes and filmed expressions of gratitude they had paid to Michael Jackson for his help for the family and especially in helping in Gavin's miraculous recovery. Aphrodite Jones wrote in *Conspiracy:*

From the witness stand, Janet did her best to deny that Michael had helped cure her son of cancer. She questioned Michael's motives and denied that he acted out of love and goodwill. But the fact was – Jackson had devoted a lot of time and effort to Gavin Arvizo, and with prayers and help from Michael, Gavin's stage four cancer had gone into remission. There was no denying that Jackson had played a part in the child's miraculous recovery. No doubt in anyone's mind."

Janet's welfare fraud was brought up in cross examination, further eroding the jury's opinion of Janet Arvizo. Later, in 2006 Janet Arvizo plead guilty to welfare fraud.

Janet Arvizo was brought to the stand as a central part of the prosecution's conspiracy charge against Michael Jackson. The lunacy of the conspiracy charge probably helped to weaken the whole case by the prosecution and gave credence to the idea of a vendetta Sneddon had against Michael Jackson. The DA hoped to prove that Michael Jackson, in collaboration with his five unindicted co-conspirators, schemed to hold the Arvizo family at Neverland Valley against their will. It would be learned through testimony that while being held "captive" at Neverland, the Arvizo family actually repeatedly left and repeatedly returned to Neverland. Shopping sprees, dental appointments and beauty treatments were all charged to Neverland Entertainment. Never once while "free" from Neverland did any one member of the family attempt to get help or notify authorities. Another ludicrous aspect of this allegation is the fact that Neverland Valley is not fenced in nor does it have any walls surrounding it. Anyone being held "captive" could have simply walked off the property! Her testimony included the far fetched claim that at one point during her "captivity" at Neverland, she feared she and her family would be set adrift by Jackson's co-conspirators in a hot air balloon, never to be heard from again. The rest of the conspiracy charge had Michael and his cohorts attempting to ship off the Arvizos to Brazil, permanently. There was however no evidence that the Brazil trip was even known to be in the works by Michael or that it was intended as a one way trip.

Janet maintained that all of her comments, and all remarks made by her children, were scripted for the rebuttal video, "The Michael Jackson Interview: the Footage You Were Never Meant to

See". She went so far as to claim all of the outtake footage was scripted as well. Her testimony seemed to grow more and more outrageous and – unbelievable.

Judge Melville ruled testimony about alleged past acts would be permitted in this case. In a huge win for the prosecution and a devastating blow to the defense; testimony from other boys and past Neverland employees from the 1993 case were found to be permissible. However only the testimony of Jason Francia aided the prosecution. Jason Francia, the son of former Neverland maid, Branca Francia, had accepted a settlement from Jackson stemming from tickling incident. As for Jordie Chandler, some said he was no where to be found. Other sources indicated he was found by prosecutors and they pleaded with him to testify against Michael Jackson. He refused. In his stead, his mother, June Chandler was called to testify.

June Chandler's testimony was largely innocuous and not the bombshell testimony the prosecution had hoped for. What was learned was that the large settlement received from Michael Jackson in 1993 bought her and her son so much happiness, they no longer needed to even speak to each other. June Chandler had not spoken to her son in the eleven years since. In cross examination, Mesereau was able to make June Chandler look money hungry.

Bob Jones, fired by a note from Michael Jackson in 2004, had recently co-authored a scathing book about his former friend and employer. The book was written with Stacy Brown who still claims to be a friend of the Jackson family. In the book, not yet released at the time of the trial, Jones bashes Michael and speculates on the child molestation charges, describing Neverland as a lure for young children. Jones ended up being called as a witness for the prosecution. In his book, Jones described a time while on a flight with Michael that he witnessed Michael licking the head of Jordie Chandler. On the stand however, he could recall no head licking ever really occurring. Taraborrelli and Aphrodite Jones, who both closely covered the trial, recalled the "I don't recall no head lickin'" line becoming a joke among some of the media members covering the trial. Bob Jones' and Brown's book, released just prior to the verdict in the case, was not a big seller.

Bob Jones had fiercely defended Michael at the time of the Chandler allegations. In the Foreword for my second book, *Michael Jackson: The King of Pop's Darkest Hour*, he referred to the "false and cruel allegations" made against Michael. Following his sudden and cold dismal in 2004, there was a seismic shift in his perception and memory.

Another prosecution witness that caused the atmosphere to grow even more anxious was the appearance of Michael Jackson's ex-wife and mother of his two oldest children, Debbie Rowe. Debbie was called by the prosecution to testify that the positive remarks she made in the rebuttal video were also scripted, just as the Arvizo's had testified. But, contrary to what was expected, Debbie testified that her answers to the interviewer's questions were unrehearsed and unscripted. Though she was at the time of her appearance in court trying to regain her parental rights that she had signed away some time earlier, she described Michael as a great father and had nothing but praise for him. Debbie, who hadn't seen Prince or Paris in two years, had become nervous about the presence of the Nation of Islam in Michael's life and sought to regain visitation rights with her children.

One of the major problems with the prosecution's case concerned the time line of events offered by the Arvizo's, which was subject to change from time to time. The claims of molestation were said to have occurred *after* the airing of the Bashir documentary, *after* the recording of the rebuttal video and *after* the boys were interviewed by social workers from the Department of Children and Family Services. So, while Michael's world had been turned upside down from the fallout of the Bashir documentary that even lead to the kids being visited by social workers, and during the efforts at damage control, *that* is when Michael supposedly made his move towards sexual acts with Gavin. This timeline simply is not logical. According to Gavin, the acts of molestation in fact did not occur until AFTER their visit to Larry Feldman. Tom Mesereau suggested to Gavin, on the stand, that after he went into remission the family felt they were being faded out of Michael's life and the visits to Neverland were ending, that is when the accusations were made. Gavin denied it.

Comedian George Lopez was called to testify how he came to meet the Arvizo family, through Laugh Factory owner Jamie Masuda, and how he visited with Gavin after he was diagnosed with cancer. He also described being hit up for money repeatedly by the father, David Arvizo. Lopez admitted he eventually severed ties with the Arvizo's after realizing they were only interested in him for money.

A forensic accountant was brought in by the prosecution to attempt to recreate Michael Jackson's financial status in 2003. The prosecution claimed his deteriorating financial condition was what prompted him to "capture and hold" the Arvizos at Neverland and force them to make a rebuttal video in response to the Bashir documentary. He was, per the prosecution's theory, desperate to salvage his image and financial empire. However the state's expert had to admit to Mesereau that his information was incomplete and he had absolutely no idea of the future earning power of Michael Jackson.

Media coverage of the trial was fiercely slanted toward the prosecution. The public heard a great deal more about "Jesus Juice" than the insane ramblings of Janet Arvizo, a key prosecution witness, and the accounts of the acts of molestation acts by Gavin and Star that just didn't mesh.

Then it was time for the defense to present their case. It would include fifty witnesses and would also include some names familiar from the 1993 case.

30

*Lift your head up high
And scream out to the world
I know I am someone
And let the truth unfurl*

"Wanna Be Startin' Somethin'"
- Michael Jackson

Wade Robson met Michael Jackson some twenty years earlier as a young child. Mesereau called Robson to confirm for the jury that, despite allegations being made by the prosecution that he too had been molested by Jackson, that NO inappropriate behavior by Michael Jackson occurred during any of his visits to Neverland, that nothing untoward ever happened in the company of Michael Jackson. Robson maintained this stance against the prosecuting attorney's badgering on cross examination.

Brett Barnes was also called by the defense. He had told investigators back in 1993 that nothing inappropriate ever happened with Michael Jackson and he was back to testify for him again, quitting his job at a casino in Australia so he could make the trip to Santa Maria. He testified that he remained friends with Michael Jackson for many years, spent lots of time in his bedroom, always with a group of others and never did anything sexual or inappropriate happen. Barnes also stood solid against the cross examination by prosecutors.

Next up for the defense was Macaulay Culkin. Culkin, like Robson and Barnes, contradicted the prosecution's claim that he also was a victim of Michael Jackson. Culkin held that Michael never molested him, never touched him inappropriately, and never exhibited any inappropriate behavior in his still continuing friendship with him. Each of these young men also testified that they never witnessed any inappropriate behavior on behalf of Michael Jackson with any other visitors to Neverland.

Culkin was not the only famous face offering testimony in the case. Larry King ended up testifying outside the presence of the jury. He told of a conversation with Larry Feldman in which Feldman spoke of Janet Arvizo as a 'wacko" and thought she was only out for money. Judge Melville ended up ruling that King's testimony was disallowed as hearsay and the jury never heard it.

The defense calls, Jay Leno. Leno appeared in court to tell of repeated voice mail messages he received from Gavin Arvizo.

Leno returned the calls while Gavin was in the hospital, something he did on a regular basis with many kids and organizations. Leno described Gavin's messages as not sounding like they were coming from a child, and seeming "scripted", as he was lavish with praise for Leno. While Leno testified of his phone conversations with Gavin, Gavin had told the jury that he left voice mails for Leno, but had never spoken with him.

While at a benefit for Gavin, put on by the Laugh Factory, the Arvizos met Comedian Chris Tucker. They had become friends with the *Rush Hour* star and began to refer to him as a brother. Tucker had also provided the family with gifts, trips and money. He began to be hit up for money regularly, something many celebrity acquaintances had testified to. Celebrities testified that they contributed money for Gavin's health care, unaware his expenses were covered by insurance. Janet took to soliciting funds under the guise they were for Gavin's health care while still collecting government benefits besides. Tucker testified that he began to be wary of the Arvizos and tried to warn Michael to be careful because, "somethin' ain't right".

Following the defense resting, the prosecution was allowed to show the video of Gavin's police interview. Sneddon, nearing retirement, needed and looked forward to a conviction of Michael Jackson. He wanted to go out with a big win and he was convinced this was going to do it for him. A celebration party was even held before the verdicts came back from the jury. Good thing, it would have been a terrible waste of all that punch.

"Wanna Be Startin' Somethin'"

After fourteen weeks of testimony, the case of The People of the State of California v. Michael Jackson went to the jury on June 3, 2005. It took seven days for them to reach a verdict. They were very organized in reviewing the testimony, appointing a note taker for the group, a time keeper and one juror who became very well acquainted with their ninety-eight pages of jury instructions.

When it was announced on June 13, 2005 that the jury in the Michael Jackson case had reached a verdict, a string of dark SUV's began the long drive from Neverland Valley to the Santa Maria courthouse. The procession of vehicles was broadcast on live TV. It was approximately two hours after the announcement that a verdict had been reached that the procession of vehicles made their way outside the courthouse. Michael exited the vehicle dressed as elegantly as ever in a dark suit with the familiar gold crest, aviator glasses and looking more stressed than ever before but also somehow vacant and expressionless, almost non-comprehending the enormity of the moment. His parents and other family members surrounded him. Michael's family members were staunch supporters during the course of the entire trial. From day one through the time the case was sent to the jury, it was his mother, Katherine, though who never missed a single day in court. She was there for her son and her faith in him never wavered. Only on one occasion did she leave the courtroom, and that was during the presentation of the pornographic images found at Neverland, known by the media folks as "porn day". Katherine and Joe accompanied their son to the reading of the verdict as well as each of his brothers and sisters, Janet making just her second trial appearance.

Once the defendant and his team arrived and the jury was brought in, each verdict was read with an audio feed of the proceedings being provided to those media members and supporters waiting outside. Of course every network in the world was broadcasting the scene outside the courthouse live. One by one each count and its verdict were read,

Count One --Not Guilty of conspiracy as charged in count one of the indictment.

Count Two -- Not Guilty of a lewd act upon a minor child as charged in count two of the indictment.

Count Three -- Not Guilty of a lewd act upon a minor child as charged in count three of the indictment.

Count Four -- Not Guilty of a lewd act upon a minor child as charged in count four of the indictment.

Count Five --Not Guilty of a lewd act upon a minor child as charged in count five of the indictment.

Count Six --Not Guilty of attempting to commit a lewd act upon a minor child as charged in count six of the indictment.

Count Seven -- Not Guilty of administering an intoxicating agent to assist in the commission of a felony as charged in count seven of the indictment.

Lesser offense of count seven – Not Guilty of providing alcoholic beverages to persons under the age of 21.

Count Eight -- Not Guilty of administering an intoxicating agent to assist in the commission of a felony as charged in count eight of the indictment.

Lesser offense of count eight – Not Guilty of providing alcoholic beverages to persons under the age of 21.

Count Nine -- Not Guilty of administering an intoxicating agent to assist in the commission of a felony as charged in count nine of the indictment.

Lesser offense of count nine– Not Guilty of providing alcoholic beverages to persons under the age of 21.

Count Ten --Not Guilty of administering an intoxicating agent to assist in the commission of a felony as charged in count ten of the indictment.

Lesser offense of count ten– Not Guilty of providing alcoholic beverages to persons under the age of 21.

Upon hearing a verdict had been reached, I personally made a beeline for home to watch and record all of the coverage. It took me a much shorter amount of time to get home than it did for Jackson's motorcade to reach Santa Maria from Neverland Ranch. I was completely anxious and both eager and fearful to hear the verdicts. As the first verdict was *finally* read, "Not Guilty", I sprang out of my seat like I had just been shot in the butt with a dart, exclaimed "YES!!!", forced myself to sit back down and listen to the next verdict, count two... "Not Guilty"...repeated fourteen times. There were no more beautiful twenty-eight words in the whole world.

With the verdicts read, Judge Melville's only words to the defendant were, "Mr. Jackson, your bail is exonerated and you are released." Forty-five minutes after he arrived, Michael left the courtroom a free man. He looked like hell, but he was a free man. He walked out of the courtroom with his defense team and his family, appearing very fragile, his face looking pained yet vacant. He waved rather weakly to the fans that had gathered outside with the volume of their cheering increasing with his acknowledgement of them. He climbed in one of the string of black SUV's and made his way back to the ranch. The ordeal of the trial took an immeasurable toll on him, one that would take years to recover from, if ever. The defense table remained composed through the reading of the verdicts with the exception of co-counsel Susan Yu, who wept. When the last verdicts were read, Michael wiped his eyes. His only words to Mesereau inside the courtroom were, "Thank you, thank you, thank you". Mesereau met with Judge Melville immediately following the court proceedings and later made his way to join Michael at Neverland.

One woman outside the courtroom that day, standing with the MJ supporters, had a cage full of doves. After each not guilty verdict was read, another dove was released into the air. Screams of joy and relief rose after each verdict was read. And Thomas Sneddon failed to get his long fought conviction of Michael Jackson. Thomas Mesereau's only statement to the media was that "justice was done".

Judge Melville read a statement from the jury:

We the jury, feeling the weight of the world's eyes upon us , all thoroughly and meticulously studied the testimony, evidence, and

"Wanna Be Startin' Somethin'"

rules of procedure presented in this court since January 31, 2005. Following the jury instructions, we confidently came to our verdicts. It is our hope that this case is a testament to the belief in our justice system's integrity and truth.

Later two jurors did an about face and claimed they had been forced to vote not guilty. Of course they were also shopping book deals at the time.

The motorcade of black SUV's made its way back to Neverland Valley Ranch on live TV. The road leading to the gates of Neverland were lined people waiting to welcome Michael back home, cheering loudly as the SUV's approached.

Thomas Sneddon held a brief press conference immediately following the verdicts. With a much less cocky demeanor than in the past, he announced only that he was proud of his team and was disappointed in the verdict. In taking questions, he stated he had not spoken with the Arvizo family and denied he carried any vendetta against Michael Jackson.

The clean sweep for the defense must have taken the wind out of the sales of the multitude of media members counting on at least a few juicy guilty verdicts to fuel their ongoing assault on the King of Pop. Stories on the prison life of Michael Jackson, books documenting the final fall of the King of Pop, movie deals all disintegrated. Court TV and their star "reporter" Diane Dimond, who was also back from ten years earlier, would be taken to task time and time again by Jermaine Jackson, Thomas Mesereau and others in TV appearances they each made following the end of the trial. The unyielding efforts of the media to color the trial proceedings no doubt contributed greatly to the general public's surprise at the acquittal. One member of the media, a long time Jackson basher by trade, proclaimed that Michael Jackson was acquitted because of his wealth and because he had a brilliant attorney. While there is no question he did in fact have a brilliant attorney, there is no clear way in which his wealth aided in the result of fourteen not guilty verdicts. It seemed no credence was given to the fact that maybe, just maybe, the jury actually paid attention to the facts of the case, followed the rule of law and did their job.

Larry King wasted no time in getting Tom Mesereau on his show to discuss the case and the verdicts. Mesereau shared that he always remained confident throughout the trial and felt the prosecution was not objective in putting their case together. He pointed out again that they never investigated the accuser or his family, turning a blind eye to what was going on in the case. A team of seventy sheriff's officers stormed Neverland without any investigation of the accusers. More sheriffs, prosecutors and other personnel were involved in this case than would be put on a serial murder trial. He said with no uncertainty that "Michael Jackson is not a pedophile, he never molested any child and would never conceive of such a thing." The notion of a malicious prosecution case was approached as a possibility.

Mesereau took the opportunity to speak out against the media's slanted coverage of the trial, singling out Court TV in particular as being an "arm of the prosecution". He described their coverage as "amateurish, very unprofessional and very disturbing".

With the acquittal, some pointed to Michael Jackson's celebrity as playing a part in "getting him off" when actually a better argument can be made for the fact that his celebrity played a much larger role in getting him the courtroom in the first place. He was described by many, Jermaine and Tom Mesereau among them, as being too nice and too trusting of people. His good natured intentions, kindness and naiveté in concert with his fame worked to make him vulnerable to such allegations. Fortunately the jury avoided the media coverage and was not swayed by it.

Mesereau's advice to Michael post trial no doubt echoed that of many others around him, that he needed to be tougher on who he invited into his home and who he tried to heal. Even if his intentions were pure and innocent, he had to know that the perception of impropriety would be all it would take to land him in trouble again. Allegations of this nature disturb people and the simple case of being accused is enough for some to assume guilt.

Big brother Jermaine kept a promise to appear on *Larry King Live* regardless of the verdicts and maintained his belief that Michael was "1000 percent innocent" and that the prosecution held a vendetta against his brother. In speculating on Michael's future, Jermaine supported the notion of Michael leaving the county "to heal". He did believe that after getting that much needed rest, Michael would perform again, "it's in his blood".

Asked about the media coverage, Jermaine also singled out Court TV as being "ignorant" and stated they "did not report the news, but injected opinions." He also supported the idea of a malicious prosecution case saying if it were him, he would do it and "kick their butts". His advice for Michael mirrored that of Mesereau's, that he needed to be more choosy on who he lets in his life, "he's too nice. He gives too much and wants to help everyone." Both Jermaine and Mesereau expressed their belief that Tom Sneddon did hold a personal vendetta against Michael and was not objective in this case.

Michael's former spokesperson Raymone Bain told one interviewer how Michael shielded his children from the events of the trial, "It was almost as if he was living two lives. He didn't want his children to be affected by that. We went through a lot of stress - just the stress of getting up every morning to be in court at 8:30. Then when he would leave there every day, he left behind all of the baggage and all of the stress from the trial and he became Daddy; going over their homework, taking them to buy ice cream, taking them to the movies – just giving them quiet time. He would leave the stress and the strain and the worry and the problems at the front door. He would walk in and he would make it appear as if everything was okay when it really wasn't. His life was hanging in the balance. I still don't know how he was able to do that."

Any handling of business concerning the case would resume after the kids were in bed for the night. Then Michael would often times be on the phone with Tom Mesereau in the evenings. During the trial, Michael would call Mesereau and cry, he was so deeply concerned about what would happen to his children. He never mentioned himself, he was scared and concerned for his kids.

Dennis Tompkins and Michael Bush designed and made each of the suits Michael wore to court each day. They would meet with Michael in the very early morning hours each day to help him prepare for the day in court. Karen Faye was also on hand to help. According to Faye, they would start each day by getting on their knees in prayer.

While some have said Michael's dependency on painkillers was kicked into high gear during the trial, Mark Geragos, who represented Michael for eighteen months, said he never saw any signs of drug use and found Michael to be engaged in his defense. Mesereau echoed these thoughts, having never witnessed any dug use, never seeing Michael under the influence of drugs, and always finding him alert and completely engrossed and engaged in his defense. Whether he had turned to the use of painkillers during this time or not, the trial absolutely exacted a toll on Michael that it does appear he never really fully recovered from. He was not eating or sleeping and became even thinner and more gaunt during the duration of the trial.

Following the verdict, Michael was driven back to Neverland Valley Ranch. He was not in good shape. He was badly dehydrated and weak from not eating and completely exhausted from not sleeping. He was in dire need of medical attention. He was taken for help by Deepok Chopra, heading toward San Francisco to check into a hospital and hopefully be a little off the grid. They only drove about twenty minutes north of Los Olivos when they stopped at an emergency room at a small hospital. He received IV fluids for twelve hours. The doctor attending to him reportedly told Chopra that if he hadn't sought treatment, he could have died that day.

The day following his acquittal, Michael issued the following statement to those who stood by him, continually believed in him and supported him, his fans:

Without God, my children, my family and you, my fans, I could not have made it though. Your love, support and loyalty made it all possible. You were there when I really needed you, and I will never forget you. Your ever-present love held me, dried my tears, and carried me through. I will treasure your devotion and support forever. You are my inspiration. Love, Michael Jackson.

Fans further showed their love and support by snatching up Jackson albums. Sales of Michael Jackson albums skyrocketed the week following his acquittal.

Michael ended up staying for a week with Chopra at his home in San Diego. While there, he asked for a prescription for OxyCotin. Chopra denied his request and tried to help Michael deal with his emotional pain in other, less dangerous, ways.

A motion to take the children away from their father was filed by attention hungry attorney Gloria Allred. Someone once said you do not want to get between Gloria Allred and a TV camera. Arguing that a lower burden of proof was necessary to have the children removed from his custody, she felt strongly that he was an unfit father. Her attempt to take his kids away was not, of course, successful. Michael has been described by virtually everyone who had been in contact with him and with his children as a very involved, attentive, caring father.

Sometime after the trial, in a conversation with J. Randy Taraborrelli, Michael Jackson finally admitted, though he hated to say it and did not want his mother to know, but "I hate that kid". That is what it took for Michael Jackson to use the word "hate". He rarely ever spoke a negative word about anyone.

With the trial finally behind him and hoping to get some serious R&R, Michael and his children left the U.S. for the Middle Eastern country of Bahrain. He had told Frank Cascio that he wanted to get out of the country, "They don't deserve me. Every one of them can fuck themselves." Michael and his children lived for several months in Bahrain as guests of Abdullah bin Hamad Al Khalifa, a member of the royal family. Michael had become acquainted with the prince through Jermaine. Jermaine had become aware of the sheik when he converted to Islam. Abdullah reportedly paid at least a portion of Michael's outstanding legal fees to the tune of $2.2 million as they entered into a plan for Michael to begin work on a new album for the Sheikh's 2 Seas Records company. He recorded in Bahrain and later in Ireland, New Jersey and Las Vegas. One song, "You Are So Beautiful" is said to be in response to the love and support of his fans. The album never materialized and their relationship soured. Michael ended up being sued for $7 million in a breach of contract suit. Michael claimed the funds were a gift. In November 2008 a settlement was reached out of court.

From Bahrain, Michael and his family were off to Ireland

where they stayed at Castlehyde, Michael Flatley's place. Flatley, of *Lord of the Dance* fame, welcomed Michael and introduced him to Guinness beer. While in Ireland, he worked with will.i.am in the recording studio. It was an event for *Access Hollywood*, who was on hand for at least one session with the pair. During the taping, Michael hinted at his insomnia problem, asking that the lighting be adjusted to hide shadows on his face to "make me look like I've slept". It was one of his last recorded interviews.

31

Once all alone
I was lost in a world of strangers
No one to trust
On my own, I was lonely
You suddenly appeared
It was cloudy before but now it all clear
You took away the fear
And you brought me back to the light

"You Are My Life"
- Michael Jackson, Babyface, Carole Bayer Sager, John McClain

Following his acquittal, Michael and his children spent time in London. They went shopping at Harrods and took a trip to Madame Tussaud's, perhaps to check out the wax models of their famous father on display. Actually the museum would begin work on a tenth image of Michael with the announcement of his This Is It shows in London. He is the celebrity with the most wax likenesses from Madame Tussaud's, only the Queen of England has more.

Michael finally returned to the United States, taking up residence in Las Vegas. Part of the reason for his return was said to be that he missed his mother. It was not to show up in court again. Prior to his return, a summons for jury duty had been sent for Michael Jackson. His attorneys were able to get him out of it by letting the authorities know he was now living outside the United States. It may have been a novel experience however for him to observe a lawsuit that he was not a direct party to. It is surprising that he, over the years, did not earn another spot in the Guinness Book of World Records for "Most Sued Pop Star".

Following the trial, Michael's finances were in worse trouble than ever. He faced gigantic and growing debt estimated at $270 million and was being charged sky high interest rates on bank loans. Sony saved him from defaulting on crucial loan payments, stepping in and refinancing his debt at more reasonable interest rates. This was however not out of the goodness of their heart. As part of the deal with Sony, Michael agreed to give them an option to buy half of his holdings of the ATV song catalog for $250 million if he defaulted on the loan payments. It had long been rumored that Sony was extremely anxious to lay their hands on the entire ATV catalog, to the point of plotting to destroy their biggest recording star to get their hands on it.

Colony Capital worked with Michael in forming a joint venture to save Neverland from foreclosure. Michael was introduced to Colony Capital CEO Thomas Barrack by a Lebanese financer, Tohme Tohme, who was an acquaintance of Jermaine's. An agreement was reached whereby Jackson would co-own Neverland with Colony Capital, and its name was changed back to Sycamore Valley Ranch, its name prior to being dubbed Neverland. Michael sold an undisclosed portion of his rights in the property for $35 million. The ranch is currently owned by this joint venture, Sycamore Valley Ranch LLC. Michael never again returned to Neverland. The ranch, now tainted with betrayal, no longer held the charm or represented the private world he had created for himself. Neverland was eventually dismantled, with the animals being moved to zoos and animal sanctuaries. The amusement park rides were also removed and sold.

Michael was put in contact with Jack Wishna, a big wig with the gaming industry and began negotiating a plan to develop a multi year standing Vegas performance gig in the vein of Celine Dion and Elton John. It was a bitter disappointment when the deal never materialized. Given his condition at meetings, he had appeared incoherent and weak, the organizers could not feel confident Michael would show up for the performances.

There were signs however of Michael getting back on track. A three CD set of greatest hits was released in July, 2005. *The Essential Michael Jackson* is a great collection of hits from his days with Motown with the Jackson 5 and his solo hits with Sony. There were also the stray awards here and there to collect.

On the heels of his acquittal, a film, *Miss Cast Away and the*

Island Girls, with Michael Jackson appearing in a cameo role as Agent MJ was released on DVD. The parody film, written, directed and co-produced by Michael's pal, Bryan Michael Stoller had originally been scheduled for a theatrical release in the summer of 2004. Due to Michael's mounting legal issues, the theatrical release of the film was postponed and the DVD was released almost immediately following his acquittal. Michael's short scenes in the movie were filmed at Neverland Ranch.

A year after his acquittal, Michael Jackson was honored with the Legend Award at the MTV Video Music Awards Japan in Tokyo and he was on hand to accepted the honor. After a grand introduction featuring career highlights and fandemonium, Michael made his entrance, dressed in black with his sunglasses clipped to the front of his t-shirt. He looked healthier, not as skinny, and looked more relaxed, much less distressed than a year earlier. His voice cracked when he expressed his affection for the Japanese people:

First I'd like to say thank you MTV Japan. It's a great honor. But most of all I'd like to say to the Japanese people from the bottom of my heart, I love you very very much. I promised myself when I came up here that I wouldn't get emotional because I think you're very sweet, generous, kind people and -from the bottom of my heart – I thank you I thank the fans around the world and the fans in Japan.

He said "I love you more" in response to the crowds cheers and started gyrating behind the microphone stand, getting a little funky and riling up the crowd. Then he continued,

"You Are My Life"

> *But I thank my children, Prince, Paris and Blanket for being there for me and I love them very much. And I say thank you to all of the people that believe in me and I believe in you and I love you very much.*

He then ran to the front of the stage to greet the fans.

One of Michael's next public appearances was to pick up another honor. Actually he picked up an armload of awards. In November, 2006, he attended an award presentation held at the *Guinness Book of World Records* office in London. He was presented with eight awards:

Youngest vocalist to top the U.S. Singles Chart (age 11 with the Jackson 5's "I Want You Back"

First Vocalist to enter the U.S. Single chart at No. 1 ("You Are Not Alone")

Most weeks at the top of the U.S. Album Charts (non soundtrack) (37 weeks -"Thriller".)

Most Successful Music Video ("Thriller")

First Entertainer to earn more than $100 million in a year ($125 million in 1989)

Highest Paid Entertainer of All Time

Most Successful Entertainer of All Time

World's Best Selling Album of All Time (*Thriller*)

This last award was actually presented to Michael a few days later at the World Music Awards.

At the 2006 World Music Awards, Michael was named as the year's recipient of the prestigious Diamond Award, presented to

Michael Jackson: The Complete Story of the King of Pop

artists who have record sales in excess of 100 million copies. The final award of the evening was presented by Beyoncé. In her introduction for the King of Pop, she acknowledged the deep influence he had on her life and career, noting she would have never started performing if it weren't for Michael Jackson. Highlighted were Michael's dizzying sales figures, 104 million for Thriller alone, 750 million overall and his humanitarian efforts and extraordinary generosity were noted with a total of $300 million given to charities in his lifetime. In addition to the World Music Awards Diamond Award, Michael was also presented with a certificate from the *Guinness Book of World Records* commemorating his outstanding achievements with *Thriller* becoming the world's best selling album of all time. Michael accepted the awards dressed all in black, smoothed hair, no sunglasses:

"To the World Music Awards and all my fans around the world, Ladies and Gentlemen, I am greatly humbled by this award. I have to say that what Quincy Jones, Bruce Swedien, Rod Temperton and myself created the Thriller album, it was my dream that Thriller would become the biggest selling album ever. And (I love you!) God has answered my prayers, 25 years later Thriller becoming the biggest selling album of all time with 104 million sold. I thank God and you for the success. There have been so many who have loved me and stood by me throughout the 42 years I have been in the entertainment business. I cannot name all of them, I'd like to thank my wonderful children, Paris, Prince and Blanket for their unconditional love and support. My mother, my father, Joseph

Jackson and my brothers and my sisters – my entire family for their love and support. I love all my fans from the bottom of my heart. And, I love you, Beyoncé."

He may have meant that last remark more than anyone knew. A couple of years later, prior to her marriage, Michael showed up unannounced at a party hosted by P. Diddy. His first question for the host was "Where's Beyoncé?"

On Christmas Day, 2006, the world said goodbye to the Godfather of Soul and Michael lost his friend and childhood idol, James Brown. Michael expressed his grief, "I am extremely shocked and saddened by the death of my mentor and friend, James Brown. Words cannot adequately express the love and respect that I will always have for Mr. Brown. There has not been and will never be another like him. He is irreplaceable. I send my love and heartfelt condolences to his family."

Michael attended his funeral on December 30th and gave some remarks. After being introduced by the Reverend Al Sharpton he spoke about Brown's profound influence on him and sounded very much like today's artists' when they speak about Michael Jackson:

Hello. What I am going to say is brief – but to the point. James Brown is my greatest inspiration. Ever since I was a small child, no more than like six years old, my mother would wake me no matter what time it was, if I was sleeping, no matter what I was doing, to watch the television to see the master at work. And when I saw him move, I was mesmerized. I have never seen a performer perform like James Brown and right then and there I knew that that was exactly what I wanted to do for the rest of my life because of James Brown.

James Brown, I shall miss you and I love you so much and thank you for everything. God bless you. I love you.

Ebony magazine, in their December 2007 issue, featured a layout of brand new photographs of Michael Jackson accompanied by what would sadly become his last interview. The photos were striking. Michael looked healthy and sported many new, fresh looks. Kicking off the interview, the interviewer notes:

Sitting on the sofa next to Michael Jackson, you quickly look past the enigmatic icon's light, almost translucent skin and realize that this African-American legend is more than just skin deep. More than an entertainer, more than a singer or dancer, the grown-up father of three reveals a confident, controlled and mature man who has a lot of creativity left inside him.

During the course of their chat, Michael talks about his influence on MTV and his contribution to the evolution of the music video:

I used to look at MTV. My brother [Jackie], I'll never forget, he'd say, 'Michael, you gotta see this channel. Oh, my God, it's the best idea. They show music 24 hours a day... 24 Hours A Day!' So I said, 'Let me see this.' And I'm watching it, I'm seeing all this stuff going on and saying 'If only they could give this stuff some more entertainment value, more story, a little more dance, I'm sure people would love it more.' So I said, when I do something, it's gotta have a story—an opening, a middle and a closing—so you could follow a

"You Are My Life"

linear thread; there's got to be a thread through it. So while you are watching the entertainment value of it, you're wondering what is going to happen. So that's when I started to experiment with 'Thriller', 'The Way You Make Me Feel' and 'Bad' and 'Smooth Criminal' and directing and writing.

He also spoke of living on through his music:

I always want to do music that inspires or influences another generation. You want what you create to live, be it sculpture or painting or music. Like Michelangelo, he said, "I know the creator will go, but his work survives. That is why to escape death, I attempt to bind my soul to my work.' And that's how I feel. I give my all to my work. I want it to just live.

Thriller 25 was released in 2008 to mark the twenty-fifth anniversary of the release of *Thriller*. The album included remixes of *Thriller's* tunes with Akon, will.i.am and Fergie. A DVD of short films included in the package included "Beat It" "Billie Jean", "Thriller" and his *Motown 25* performance of "Billie Jean". The remix of "Wanna Be Startin' Somethin'" with Akon peaked at number eighty-one on the Hot 100. The album reached number two in the U.S. and number three in England. It reached number one in eight countries and was a top ten hit on over thirty national charts. The original *Thriller* was also sent back to the top of the Pop Catalog charts. This same year, *Thriller* was inducted into the Grammy Hall of Fame and later the Library of Congress included the album among twenty-five recordings in the National Recording Registry as being deemed culturally significant. *Off the Wall* has also been inducted into the Grammy Hall of Fame.

The Jacksons were honored by BMI with the Icon Award in 2008. Janet presented the award to her brothers with their parents in attendance. Michael did not attend. Rumors began spreading that the Jackson Five were mounting a reunion tour. Michael never consented to do the tour yet it was being bandied about as fact, fueled no doubt by Jermaine's comments that the group was in fact planning a Jacksons tour. Michael responded to the rumors: My brothers and sisters have my full love and support, and we've certainly shared many great experiences, but at this time I have no plans to record or tour with them. I am now in the studio developing new and exciting projects that I look forward to sharing with my fans in concert soon."

He was referring to a solo concert, not a Jackson reunion tour. Organizers for the never to be Jackson reunion tour, AllGood Entertainment issued a cease and desist order to AEG Live, promoters of This Is It, stating that Frank Dileo signed an agreement agreeing that Michael would participate in a Jacksons concert. Michael was supposedly going to be paid $24 million and was prohibited from agreeing to any other concert deals for 1 1/2 years.

With a spending habit approaching $15 to $30 million per year in excess of what he was bringing in at the time, his financial situation continued to deteriorate. To meet expenses, he took out a massive $270 million loan from Bank of America which was secured by Neverland and his portion of the Sony/ATV music catalog. The loan was eventually sold by Bank of America to Fortress

"You Are My Life"

Investments, a firm in New York that primarily deals with distressed debt, at an exorbitant interest rate of 20%.

It was time Michael Jackson went back to work. He had been working on new songs for a new Pop/R&B album with various artists including Akon, Ne-Yo, will.i.am and Lenny Kravitz. His goal with this album was to make happy dance songs with a message. He told Ne-Yo, "I am not trying to follow any trends. I'm not trying to go back in time. I'm just trying to do quality music with a melody that's infectious and has a message." One song, titled "Breathe" compared the human body to nature. He was working on the lyrics with his friend Deepok Chopra. Other new tracks in the works was a song paying tribute to perhaps Michael's greatest idol, James Brown, "Miss You", produced with will.i.am. Other songs included "The King" said to be an all star track featuring a variety of performers who cite Michael as their inspiration and a dance track called, "The Future". "Hold My Hand", a collaboration with Akon, had been leaked on the internet in 2008. Another song, "Don't Be Messin' Around" also surfaced with Michael on piano of which Bruce Swedien said "he does it very well". He was said to be in the process of picking the tracks to be included on the album while gearing up for This is It.

A separate album of classical compositions and a thirtieth[h] anniversary reissue of *Off the Wall* were also planned. Ed Hardy's Christian Audigier was said to be working with Michael on a clothing line. On top of these new projects, he started to hear the stage calling his name, calling him back home.

32

Another day has gone, I'm still all alone
How could this be you're not here with me
You never said goodbye, someone tell me why
Did you have to go and leave my world so cold?

"You Are Not Alone"
- R. Kelly

Facing mounting financial woes and wanting his children to see him perform, 2009 started out holding great promise for a triumphant return to the stage for the King of Pop. This could not be done on any small scale of course. It had to be bigger than big, it had to blow people away. It stood to be the greatest show on earth. But, he never made it back on stage in front of his fans. The year which was so promising early on crashed into a heart wrenching tragedy.

The year started with more people getting in line to sue Michael Jackson. On January 21, John Landis filed suit against Michael Jackson for non payment of royalties on "Thriller". In a couple of months he would be followed by Ola Ray. One day later another suit was filed against him by Raymone Bain for unpaid bills.

Randy Phillips, CEO of AEG Live, met with Michael in the summer of 2007 with the idea of having Michael perform a series of concerts at the new O2 arena AEG was opening in East London. These initial talks failed to bring about an agreement and eventually fell through. After facing possible foreclosure proceedings on Neverland, and other financial pressures, Michael was much more interested in discussing the string of London concerts. He met once again with Phillips in November 2008. Phillips told *Rolling Stone,* "Michael was a very smart marketing person. People say he was feeble and manipulated, but he was powerful and a manipulator. He was ready. He wanted to clean up his finances." Michael had confided to Phillips that he wanted to pay off his debts and that he had his eye on a house in Las Vegas that had belonged to the Sultan of Brunei. He was also keenly interested in making movies.

Michael had turned a corner and was regrouping advisors and professionals who he knew and trusted. Frank Dileo was back as manager and he re-teamed with attorney John Branca. Branca and Dileo helped close the deal for the London shows. In May, Michael sent a letter to Dr. Tohme Tohme firing him as his representative. Reportedly, Michael feared and mistrusted him. Dr. Tohme Tohme would end up being sued by the executors of Michael's estate for ripping him off in many of his business agreements with Michael where he was paid exorbitant fees and earnings.

He was also still intimidated by his father. *Rolling Stone* reported that Joseph Jackson had recently undergone efforts to gain back some amount of control of Michael's career management, now that the London shows had been announced. Michael vehemently fought his efforts and even complained to Randy Phillips that whenever he does anything, his family members "come out of the woodwork". Michael tried to avoid his father, refusing his calls and refusing to see him. One day in March, Joseph showed up at Michael's house with concert promoter Leonard Rowe. Joe urged Michael to have Rowe take over as business manager and even succeeded in getting Michael to sign documents to this effect. Michael shared with Dileo that he only signed to get Joseph off his back. Michael later reversed this decision sending Rowe a letter advising "you do not represent me" and "I do not wish to have any oral or written communications with you regarding the handling of my business and/or personal matters." Rowe later denied ever receiving this letter.

He now had many motivators to pursue the concert run in London; his children, his dream house, paying off his mounting debts and coming back for the sake of his beloved fans. As part of the deal, Michael requested an English estate with horses and room for his kids to play be rented for him during his stay in London. As more and more shows were added, he wanted to make sure he and his kids were not cooped up in a hotel room for months on end. Italian furniture maker Colombostile was hired to design lavish custom pieces that were very ornate and even gaudy, similar to some of the furnishings seen over the years at Neverland. Michael and the kids were practicing their British accents for their extended stay in Great Britain and Michael was anxious for them to experience traditional British fare Sheppard's pie and fish and chips.

For the shows, he reunited with Kenny Ortega, who he had worked with on the Dangerous and HIStory tours. Dancer Travis Payne, a veteran of his earlier tours, was back as choreographer. Dorian Holley was the vocal director, singer Darryl Phinnesse was back as a vocalist, both veterans of the Bad and Dangerous tours. Jonathan Moffett, who Michael called "Foot", had been the drummer for the Jacksons and Michael's solo tours going back decades and was back on duty for This Is It. He had chemistry with Michael, a kind of knowing how and when to punctuate his movements without even knowing the specific choreography.

Guitarist Orianthi Panagaris, a young guitarist from Adelaide, Australia, had begun playing guitar watching tapes of Carlos Santana. She was invited to play at a Santana concert when she was eighteen. When she played with Carrie Underwood on the Grammys she caught the eye of Michael Bearden, the musical director for This Is It and she was invited to audition. Before she knew it she was following Michael Jackson back and forth on stage jamming to "Beat It". The release of her own CD, *Believe* coincided with the premier of the *This Is It* film and spawned a hit single, "According to You".

515

Michael Jackson: The Complete Story of the King of Pop

The full This Is It cast included:
Band:
Percussion: Roger Bashiri Johnson
Drums: Jonathan "Sugarfoot" Moffet
Lead Guitar: Orianthi Panagaris
Rhythm Guitar: Tommy Organ
Bass: Alfred Dunbar
Keyboards: Morris "Mo" Pleasure
Keyboards/Musical Director: Michael Bearden
Singers for This Is It included Dorian Holley, Darryl Phinnesse, Ken Stacey and Judith Hill. The eleven dancers to make the cut were Mick Bass, Daniel Celebre, Mekia Cox, Misha Gabriel, Chris Grant, Shannon Holtzapffel, Devin Andrew Jammieson, Charles Klapow, Dres Reid, Tyne Stecklein, Timor Steffens.

Each of the dancers were new to the MJ experience. All were young, some barely being in their teens the last time Michael Jackson toured with *HIStory*. As always, he looked for dancers that loved what they did and were "full of heart". One dancer recalled Michael stating, "I don't want any fake flowers without the fragrance". The choreography for This Is It was described by the choreographers and the dancers as being very specific, particular and "hard". Rehearsals were held six days a week and could be grueling even for this young batch of dancers. Michael would watch all eleven dancers at rehearsals doing the classic choreography for his biggest hits and their own improvised moves. Afterward he would have notes for each of them on their movements, "Michael brought out the best in everyone".

Ortega later recounted the phone call he received from Michael asking to join him in creating the shows. Ortega's goddaughter answered the phone and called out, "Some guy says he's Michael Jackson". When Ortega picked up the line, Michael responded, "No one ever believes it's me."

Michael Bearden had grown up in the southern part of Chicago, not far from Gary, Indiana, and had actually seen the Jackson Five perform in area clubs before coming to the attention of Motown Records. He was now afforded the opportunity to share stories with Michael about seeing him perform with his brothers in the early days.

The grand announcement of the This Is It string of concerts took place on March 5, 2009 at London's O2 Arena. Fans, hungry to catch a glimpse of him, packed the arena for this brief announcement. They screamed with joy as he made his way toward the podium, an hour and a half late. Michael addressed the crowd briefly speaking in the lower tone rarely used in public appearances:

"These will be my final shows, performances in London. This will be it - when I say this is it, I really mean this is it because... I'll be performing the songs my fans want to hear. This is it, I mean this is really it, this is the final... this is the final curtain call, okay- And um, I will see you in July. And... (responding to cheers on the crowd) I love you, I really do. You have to know that. I love you so much, from the bottom of my heart. This is it. See you July!"

Following Michael's announcement of the shows, 1.6

million people from reportedly two hundred countries, signed up for tickets for the ten shows. They sold out in minutes. More shows were added, for a total of thirty-one shows. It was reported later that this number was not random. Prince had performed twenty-one shows at the same venue and Michael just wanted to beat his number by ten. Each of those performances sold like hotcakes too. So, even more shows were added. Michael Jackson was now scheduled to perform an incredible fifty shows at the O2 arena. A total of 750,000 tickets sold out in four hours. They are said to be the fastest selling tickets ever in London. He was uplifted by the record breaking ticket sales and it brought about a renewed energy in him and new enthusiasm for the shows. He was excited to perform for his fans once again and especially to show his children first hand what dear old dad did for a living. Michael had sold out more shows than any other artist in history and had earned yet another place in the *Guinness Book of World Records*. At Michael's request, a ceremony to mark his latest entry was scheduled to take place at the conclusion of the series of shows.

A sellout of fifty shows at the O2 was unprecedented, even more impressive for an artist who hadn't toured in thirteen years and had largely been seen since only entering court rooms. Chris Martin of Coldplay, who does a cover of "Billie Jean', told Joseph Vogel, "To sell out like that is a testament to talent. It is just amazing to sell out fifty shows in one city in a big arena. It's the biggest comeback since Lazarus."

Some would claim later that Michael was unaware or, even

furious that fifty shows had been scheduled, that he had only agreed to do ten performances. Articles suggested he was not healthy or fit enough to pull off the shows. Speculation and doubt mounted insisting Michael was incapable of performing like his old self, or at all. Those working most closely with him however all agreed Michael was excited about the shows. Certainly the details of the shows that would be learned over the next few months and the rehearsal footage that would soon be seen would support the idea that Michael was excited about the shows and in top form to pull them off. AEG Live CEO and President Tim Leiweke told *Billboard* magazine, "Despite everything you read about him, he was fine. The man took a physical for us to go do these concerts. The man is very sane, the man is very focused, the man is very focused." Frank Dileo prophetically told Frank Cascio, "It's amazing what he can still do at fifty years old. We've just got to keep those crazy doctors away and everything else will be great."

The tour was set to begin on July 8th with two performances per week, and would last until March 2010. The start date was then reset for July 13th. It was reported that the delay was due to Michael's frail health. This doesn't seem plausible. How was he going to turn his physical well being around in these four extra days? It seems that he could have made far more money hawking his new "Frail to Fit in Four Days" health program than he stood to make from the tour. A more reasonable explanation has the start date being pushed back to allow time to actually build the sets needed for the ever expanding production. Set to include illusions, floating lighted orbs, dancing fire, huge staging, videos and 3D special effects with the world's largest LED screen, more time was needed to put it all together.

Another reason for the postponement given was that the London rehearsals were booked in error at Wembley Stadium, rather than the O2 Arena. The extra days were added for the needed London rehearsal time. Still, the brief postponement seemed to fuel speculation that Michael Jackson was not physically fit enough to pull off this string of shows. Earlier in the year a story even circulated that he needed a heart and lung transplant as soon as possible, or he was going to die.

While the performances would be grueling they were scheduled with enough time in between for Michael to rest and rejuvenate for the next performances. The fifty shows were scheduled in two blocks, with a three month hiatus in the middle. The first set of shows were scheduled from July 13, 2009 to September 29. Then he would have three months off before starting up again on January 7, 2010 and winding up on March 6, 2010. The shows themselves were even paced to give Michael spots to catch his breath. Short films, twelve in all, were produced especially for the This Is It shows as part of the spectacular stage presentation but which also added to his opportunities to rest. The shows would be physically grueling, and he wanted to make sure he was back in full form for each show. He put his heart and soul into each and every performance. He wanted his band, dancers, and singers to give their all as well, to give the fans "talent they have never seen before."

"You Are Not Alone"

As part of the preparation for the shows, and to get the required insurance, Michael was given a through physical exam, which he passed "with flying colors". The exam was said to be comprehensive and took four or five hours. No serious health problems were found.

Dr. Conrad Murray had been chosen by Michael and was to be hired by AEG to serve as Michael's personal physician throughout the course of the London shows. AEG refused at first, and argued that there were doctors available in London if Michael should ever need one. Michael countered that his body was the engine that the whole show depended on and they needed to make sure he was well taken care of. Not able to argue with that, AEG obliged and agreed to hire Dr. Murray as his personal physician for $150,000 per month. No doubt eager to earn his big paycheck, it was learned later that Dr. Murray faced foreclosure on his Las Vegas home, was delinquent in child support payments and faced an approximate $400,000 in legal judgments against him, though it should be noted none of these judgments were in connection with malpractice suits. Closing his offices in Houston and Las Vegas, Dr. Murray sent letters out to his patients announcing he was leaving his practice for "the opportunity of a lifetime".

The shows in London were the first step in a multi-year plan for AEG and Michael Jackson. The long term plan included concerts in European and Asian cities with possible shows in the U.S. to follow, perhaps up to three years out. A possible concert film also figured in the plan.

Michael had an important message to deliver with these shows. He was very concerned about the environment and wanted to raise awareness of the effects global warming on our planet. Many of the numbers in the show, "Earth Song" in particular, were aimed at delivering this message. He also wanted to bring joy and excitement to his audiences, to remind people that "love is important". Of course the performances would also be the dazzling spectaculars he was noted for. Ortega told *Rolling Stone* that Michael said, "When the show opens, I don't want to hold anything back. I want this to be the most spectacular opening the audience has ever seen. They have to ask themselves, "How are they going to top that?' I don't even care if they're applauding. I want their jaws on the ground. I want them to not be able to sleep, because they are so amped up from what they saw."

To begin rehearsals, Michael moved back to Los Angeles, renting a mansion in the Holmby Hills area of Los Angeles at 100 N. Carolwood Drive. He rented the home from Roxanne Guez wife of the Ed Hardy Company CEO Hubert Guez. It was a short drive to the Staples Center, about 16 miles, where rehearsals would eventually be moved as the production of the show grew.

The home was surely grand enough for the King of Pop and his princes and princess. At 20,000 square feet and three levels, it had eight bedrooms, thirteen baths, and thirteen fireplaces. Michael's master bedroom suite measured 4,000 square feet. The house included a wine cellar, a fully equipped gym, a billiards room, and a theater. The grounds were as grand as the house with a huge swimming pool and elaborate gardens.

Auditions were held in spring to pick the dancers to join the This Is It tour. Over 5,600 dancers showed up from all over the world for a chance to be a part of Michael Jackson's show. Rehearsals began at CenterStaging Musical Productions, in Burbank before moving to the larger Staples Center in May. Reports at the time varied from Michael was too ill and frail to perform to he was back bigger and better than ever and showing the much younger dancers and band members how it's done.

To get in shape for the tour Michael began daily workouts with friend and former bodybuilder and *Incredible Hulk* star Lou Ferigno. Their workouts focused on core training with a balance ball and bands. One day Ferigno brought some three pound dumbbells to use and Michael protested that he did not want to build any big muscles! Following his morning workouts, he would dance. And dance. He would have lunch with his kids, then it was off to rehearsals in the evening. He made a point to enjoy meals with his three children, something he valued highly, like he promoted with his Heal the Kids Foundation efforts with Rabbi Shmuley Boteach.

Kai Chase, the chef who was hired to cook for Michael and his children (following an initial job interview with Prince, Paris and Blanket), had one night a week set aside to "splurge". Favorites like fried chicken and Mexican food were indulged in. When rehearsals began, these indulgences were benched and exchanged for only healthy foods.

The afternoon of Wednesday, June 24th, he headed to the

Staples Center as usual for rehearsals. He had a couple of meetings, one with Randy Phillips, Frank Dileo, Kenny Ortega and Ken Ehrlich to discuss a Halloween TV special, airing *Ghosts* with some footage of "Thriller" from the London shows. Following the meeting, Michael spent time reviewing some special effects to be used in the performances – reviewing the "Earth Song" mini movie for the very first time - and he ate dinner; grilled chicken and broccoli. Then rehearsals began and lasted until after midnight.

Kenny Ortega, as well as the musicians, choreographer, and Frank Dileo all described Michael as being completely back on his game, better than ever, out dancing the younger performers that surrounded him. Ortega said, "He was so brilliant onstage, I had goosebumps." Ortega described Michael this night as being "back" and "electric". Ken Ehrlich, also in the audience that night, echoed the sentiment, "I got chills, literally. The hairs on the back of my neck were raised. Those are the moments you hope for". Leaving the Staples Center that night, Michael hugged Dileo and said, "It's is our time again, Frank. It's time for us to take it back."

He reportedly went home following the rehearsal and, as usual, couldn't sleep and was desperate to get some rest. Following the administration of a series of drugs, Dr. Conrad Murray consented to Michael's pleas and administered a dose of propofol. According to Dr. Murray, following what he called a two minute bathroom break, he found Michael in bed, not breathing. There would be many problems surrounding the time line of events this morning and many questions for Dr. Murray to address.

He administered CPR but Michael did not respond. Murray ran downstairs and called for someone to call 9-1-1. It was 12:21 when the 9-1-1 call was made. Paramedics arrived three minutes seventeen seconds later. They tried for approximately forty-two minutes to resuscitate Michael with no response. He was then transported by ambulance to Ronald Reagan UCLA Medical Center at 1:07 pm. There emergency room doctors continued to work on Michael for over an hour. Still no response. They reportedly kept working on Michael until his mother, Katherine, was able to make it to the hospital. Soon, Katherine and some other family members, arrived. Prince, Paris and Blanket had followed behind the ambulance. Frank Dileo was there. Dr. Murray was also there. Jermaine made his way to the hospital and got to kiss his brother goodbye. Fans, hearing the news that the King of Pop had been taken to the hospital in cardiac arrest began gathering outside. At 2:26 PM on June 25th, 2009, Michael Jackson was pronounced dead. Shortly after a visibly shaken Jermaine Jackson made a brief announcement to the press:

This is hard…

My brother, the legendary King of Pop, Michael Jackson, passed away on Thursday, June 25th, 2009 at 2:26 pm. It is believed he suffered cardiac arrest in his home. However the cause of his death are unknown until the results of an autopsy are known.

His personal physician, who was with him at the time, attempted to resuscitate my brother as did the paramedics who transported him to Ronald Reagan UCLA Medical Center. Upon arriving at the hospital at approximately 1:14 PM, a team of doctors, including emergency room physicians and cardiologists attempted to resuscitate him for a period of more than one hour. They were unsuccessful.

My family requests that the media please respect our privacy during this tough time and may Allah be with you Michael always. Love you.

Frank Dileo was at the hospital, "I got to kiss him and tell him goodbye... I lost a very dear friend, someone who I admired, someone who was the greatest talent I ever met or worked with." He also delivered the unbearable news to Michael's three children, who then asked to see their father one last time. Katherine chose not to view his body, preferring to remember him in happier times. His body was later loaded in a helicopter to be transported to the coroner's office for an autopsy, all live on network and cable news channels.

As the news spread, people passed it on via Twitter and text message. The Twitter website, after receiving five thousand messages per minute, crashed. AT&T had a record number of text messages. Google encountered technical problems with a surge of Michael Jackson searches, initially thought to be a virus attack. They rated the story as "volcanic". TMZ encountered several outages. America Online's instant messaging shut down for forty minutes. They had never seen anything like this before, issuing a statement, "today was a seminal moment in internet history. We've never seen anything like it in terms of scope or depth." CNN had twenty million hits on their webpage in the hour the story broke, an increase of 500%. *The Los Angeles Times* website also experienced outages. Wikipedia became overloaded with five hundred edits made to Michael's entry within twenty-four hours. The following day most sites were working properly again with the exception of mjfanclub.net, which was still slow. This gave way to a new phenomenon known as e-mourning.

    After alerting friends and family of the shocking news, fans began buying Jackson CD's and downloading his music at levels literally never seen before. *Thriller* became the number one album on the iTunes music chart, eight other Jackson albums held spots on the iTunes top ten chart. Michael Jackson's songs occupied the Top 10 downloads by iTunes in twenty-one countries. Michael Jackson and Jackson albums dominated each of the various *Billboard* charts too. The Top 75 Hot Digital Downloads had twenty-one solo hits and four Jackson hits, a new record. Six Michael Jackson tracks landed in the Top 20 Hot Ringmasters, which equaled the mark for most simultaneous titles in the top twenty.

    Jackson albums dominated the *Billboard* Comprehensive Album charts and continued to do so week after week and month after month. N*umber Ones, The Essential Michael Jackson* and *Thriller* held the top three spots while the new release, and former number one album, *The E.N.D.* by the Black Eyed Peas had to settle for number four on the chart. Michael Jackson and Jackson titles made up a major chunk of the catalog charts, but was also outselling every new release album, occupying several spots in the top ten, and the chart overall. Michael Jackson is the only artist to accomplish the feat of having a catalog album outsell new releases. His albums made up the entire top ten on the Top Pop Catalog charts, another first.

In the first week of his death, Jackson record sales outpaced those of Elvis Presley and John Lennon. And it did not give up anytime soon. Nielson Soundscan showed a total of 422,000 Michael Jackson records were sold in the three days following his death. He had sold 297,000 copies up to this point in 2009. The following week sales soared to a total of 794,000 copies. Sony Music shipped about 2 million Jackson CD's in the U.S. as retailers were not able to keep up with demand. Many stores reported selling out of their supply of Michael Jackson CD's on Thursday. They replenished their supply and sold out again over the weekend.

In the minutes following his death, online music retailer Amazon.com ran out of Michael Jackson CD's with sales reaching levels at 700 times that of the day before. Michael Jackson albums occupied every single spot on the site's top selling albums the next day and sales of his CDs accounted for 60% of all CD's purchased on the site. Bill Carr, VP of music and video at Amazon.com announced, "This is simply unprecedented. We've seen the death of Johnny Cash and Frank Sinatra and many other artists but none of them compare to what we're witnessing today." The website carried a tribute to the King of Pop. In Great Britain, Michael Jackson albums held fourteen of the top twenty places on the Amazon.com sales chart with *Off the Wall* taking over the top spot.

"You Are Not Alone"

Memorials sprang up throughout the world. Every spot in the U.S. with a connection to Jackson attracted fans and the memorials grew. Fans held vigil outside the hospital and outside his rented home in Holmby Hills where someone painted on the curb at the corner, "Michael Jackson Died Today 6/25/2009". Mourners gathered outside the family home in Encino, the constant increased traffic prompted the issuance of a temporary ordinance making it a tow away zone. There was also increased traffic at Neverland Valley Ranch and at his star on the Hollywood Walk of Fame. Initially fans began leaving their remembrances at the wrong star. Michael's star had been covered up with the traditional red carpet for a movie premier. Fans then gravitated toward another star for another Michael Jackson, the radio broadcaster. The movie premiering reportedly had a scene that referenced Michael and in which LaToya appeared. Out of respect for Michael the scene was cut from the movie's premier. Michael Jackson's star on the Walk of Fame continues to be one of the most popular on the walkway for photo ops.

Fans gathered outside the family former home in Gary, Indiana and outside the Motown Museum in Detroit, Michigan where they left notes, flowers and candles. Outside the Apollo Theater in New York Michael's music rang out and people danced in celebration of his life. The marquee of The Apollo read:

"In Memory of MICHAEL JACKSON

A True Legend 1958 – 2009".

The sudden and shocking loss of the King of Pop

overshadowed the loss of another high profile celebrity that very same day. Just hours before losing a king, the world lost an angel when Farah Fawcett lost her ongoing battle with cancer. While her loss was tragic and sad, it was not unexpected. Fawcett had produced a documentary following her cancer treatment and her determination to beat it. In a sense there was a celebration of her life and a chance to say goodbye before her passing. Good thing, because her death was vastly overshadowed by the emotional wallop of suddenly losing the King of Pop.

The level of mourning following the death of the King of Pop was unsurpassed. It eclipsed that of Elvis Presley, John Lennon and Princess Diana. Not one corner of the world doesn't know Michael Jackson and all corners mourned his passing and celebrated his life, his music and his legacy. Fans gathered outside London's O2 arena the site were Michael was scheduled to perform in seventeen days. Outside the arena, a giant screen showed an image of Michael and read, "Michael Jackson 1958 – 2009 At this time our thoughts are with Michael's family, friends and fans." Fans gathered also outside the Lyric Theatre in London where a live show based on "Thriller" was being performed. In Baghdad, not only U.S. soldiers, but Iraqi citizens mourned his loss. Memorials popped up at the Eiffel Towel in France and a candle light vigil was held in Hong Kong. In the Philippines, prison inmates at the Cebu Provincial Detention and Rehabilitation Center staged an encore performance of "Thriller" that had been a YouTube hit a couple of months earlier.

Jackson fans in Japan staged an impromptu tribute in Yoyogi

Park in Tokyo. *Billboard* magazine reported that the news of Michael's death in Japan "caused such a stir in Japanese society that three cabinet ministers took the unusual step of commenting on his passing." The Defense Minister eulogized him. Many Japanese television stations began airing special Michael Jackson programs. In Mexico City a memorial sprang up at the Angel of Independence monument. Fans gathered and memorials were placed at the Notre Dame cathedral and a candlelight vigil was held by fans in Beijing.

Talk of "Wacko Jacko" subsided as his talent, artistry and showmanship once again took center stage. Magazines that readily bashed him when convenient rushed tribute editions to the newsstand. Tributes flooded the internet, radio airwaves and television. Radio stations immediately turned to an all Jackson format for the afternoon, with airplay for his songs skyrocketing a reported 1735%. A Phoenix DJ remarked "Heaven just got a great front man." *Rolling Stone* magazine's Anthony DeCurtis wrote in his Foreword for Joseph Vogel's *Man in the Music: The Creative Life and Work of Michael Jackson*, "He was among the greatest performers I have ever seen, and his music could light up a dance floor instantaneously. Every time I listen to his songs, I discover new thing to love about them, inventive touches that I had never noticed before. In this one specific sense his death was a blessing: It forced people to re-encounter his artistry and to realize once again how important he had been to them, how much his music had meant to their lives. For younger people who had not grown up with Michael Jackson, it provided perhaps their first opportunity to hear his music free of clichéd preconceptions about him."

The House of Representatives held a moment of silence on the floor of congress in honor of Michael Jackson. President Obama reportedly sent a note of condolence to the Jackson family and later spoke of Michael in an interview.

News networks covered the story nonstop. MTV actually returned to playing music videos and offered a review of Michael's video history in "Incredible MTV Moments". Vh-1 aired several Jackson video tributes, including "Michael Jackson: King of Videos", a wonderful review of his unrivaled contributions to music videos. E! Entertainment Television updated their "True Hollywood Story" of Michael to include coverage of his death. The episode of the series on Janet Jackson was also updated to include the devastating loss of her older brother. MTV, Vh-1, E!, BET, CNN and TV Guide channel and the major networks all produced special programming celebrating the life and career of Michael Jackson, tracking his last few days, and highlighting his vast influence on today's performers. The specials continued for months.

The Jackson family responded to the outpouring of love and support from Michael's many millions of fans the world over: "In one of the darkest moments of our lives we find it hard to find the words appropriate to this sudden tragedy we all had to encounter. Our beloved son, brother and father of three children has gone so unexpectedly, in such a tragic way and much too soon... We want to thank all of his faithful supporters and loyal fans worldwide, you who Michael loved so much. Please do not despair, because Michael will continue to live on in each and every one of you. Continue to spread his message, because that is what he would want you to do. Carry on, so his legacy will live forever."

The last time most of the family members saw Michael was at a family gathering on May 14th. He was described by Janet, Jermaine and his nephew Taj, Tito's son, as being happy and upbeat at the family function and was excited about his upcoming shows. He shared with Taj his plans to do a film following his fifty London shows and he had interest in directing. Janet recalled having a great time with Mike and sharing many laughs. They had several phone calls later to talk about the great time they had together.

Admirers and those closest to Michael flooded the media with statements of grief and condolences to his family including Elizabeth Taylor, Quincy Jones, Diana Ross, both of his ex-wives; Lisa Marie Presley poured her heart out on her MySpace page, describing herself as "gutted" and adding, "I am going to say now what I have never said before because I want the truth out there for once. Our relationship was not 'a sham' as is being reported in the press. It was an unusual relationship yes, where two unusual people who did not live or know a 'Normal life' found a connection, perhaps with some suspect timing on his part. Nonetheless, I do believe he loved me as much as he could love anyone and I loved him very much." Debbie Rowe's statement read, "...this world as lost a beautiful and loving soul."

Artists he had been working with recently were also devastated at the loss. Will.i.am noted, "He was a gift to the world, he is a bright light and I wouldn't be surprised if the world stopped spinning tomorrow." Akon said, "He set the standard for everyone to follow. Period." Lenny Kravitz stated "He was a beautiful human being". Slash noted "He was talent from on high".

Those who were inspired by Michael felt a tremendous loss, Justin Timberlake, Ne-Yo, and Usher among them. Deepok Chopra wrote a blog the day following Michael's death. His remembrances of his friend concluded, "But when the shock subsides and a thousand public voices recount Michael's brilliant, joyous, embattled, enigmatic, bizarre trajectory, I hope the word 'joyous' is the one that will rise from the ashes and shine as he once did."

The *Today* Show aired a special edition on June 26th, postponing their usual segments including their Friday summer concert, for a show focused exclusively on the death of Michael Jackson, stating it did not feel like a day for a concert. Frank Dileo appeared on the program describing how heartbroken he was to lose his friend of more than thirty years. Dileo described Michael as being very happy the past few days and feeling optimistic about the upcoming shows. Michael appeared to be healthy, was eating, and working out. Dileo would bring Michael food and make sure he was eating. *Today, The Early Show* and *Larry King Live* later each broadcast shows from Neverland Valley Ranch, talked with Jermaine Jackson and toured the grounds. The house had been cleared out of Michael belongings long ago, the spiral scratches in the finish on the dance studio floor, from practicing his lightening quick spins, being one of the few reminders of the home's former resident. Neverland

"You Are Not Alone"

was later featured in the November 2009 issue of *Architectural Digest*.

The BET Awards, already scheduled for Sunday, June 28th, were quickly revamped to become a tribute to Michael Jackson. More artists made arrangements to attend and more fans showed up. Program host Jamie Foxx did a great job of paying tribute to the King of Pop and encouraging a celebration of his life and countless contributions to the music world.

Moments of the show were definite tear jerkers. Ne-Yo did a beautiful rendition of "Lady in My Life" and near the end of the show Ne-Yo joined Foxx for a duet of "I'll Be There". Images of Michael appeared on a giant screen behind them. The audience was quiet and it is doubtful that there was a dry eye in the house.

Janet Jackson made a surprise appearance to express the family's gratitude for the outpouring of support:

"My entire family wanted to be here tonight, but it was just too painful. So they elected me to speak with all of you and I'm going to keep it very short but I'd just like to say that to you, Michael is an icon. To us, Michael is family. And he forever will live in all of our hearts. On behalf of my family, and myself, thank you for all of your love, thank you for all of your support. We miss him so much. Thank you so much".

The special BET Awards tribute to Michael Jackson brought the award show their highest ratings ever.

The only sour note of the evening was struck by Michael's own father. Joe Jackson attended the award show flanked by some business associates. A CNN reporter (when you do think CNN ever covered the BET Award arrivals before??) asked Joe how he and Katherine were doing. Joe responded grinning ear to ear, "We're great!". He then actually dodged further questions on how the rest of the family was coping and went on to plug his new record label and introduced his business partner. It really went a long way to make Joe appear to be cold and heartless. He mentions at one point that we have lost our greatest superstar, and made no mention of the fact this superstar just happened to also be his son.

    Joe raised eyebrows again the next day when he held a press conference and tried to cover his tracks claiming he spoke of the record company because he had been asked about it. This was not the case. The reporter consistently asked questions about Michael and how the family was doing. Joe blew those questions off and continued to talk about his new venture.

    The aftermath of Michael Jackson's death was centered on three major questions; first and foremost, "Why is this man dead?" What exactly caused him to lose his life? Second, "what about the money?" His financial condition at the time of his death raised many questions over the amount of his debt, values of his assets, etc. Lastly, the most salient question, "what will happen to his children?" Fortunately this last question would be the first answered and with much less contention than was first feared.

33

Smile though your heart is breaking
Smile even though it's aching
When there are clouds in the sky
You'll get by

"Smile"
- Charlie Chaplin, John Turner, Geoffrey Parsons

As the autopsy report was being anticipated, speculation abounded as to the cause of death. Most pointed to a drug dependency issue and the possible involvement of painkillers Demoral and/or OxyCotin. Michael's longtime friend and spiritual advisor, Deepok Chopra had tried to confront Michael in the past about his drug use, "I think his death is a drug overdose. It is the result of these terrible doctors who are drug peddlers, who put people on drugs and continue to enable them and perpetuate them. I confronted Michael many times about it. He would deny it. Then he wouldn't call me. Then he would get upset. And then he would apologize. I would tell Michael, 'You are going to die', all the time. And he would say, 'No, I've got pain. I only take them when I'm in pain and the doctors think it's okay'. Personally speaking – and I'm not a criminologist –this is a homicide." Chopra believed Michael's drug dependency problems grew upon the start of the criminal trial. He called for the investigation of doctors who introduce people to narcotics and create dependency. He pointed out that legally prescribed narcotics kill more people in the world, especially the U.S., than street drugs.

Gotham had known Michael for twenty years, since he was fifteen, and had spent a lot of time with him and had accompanied him on tour. He told he never experienced or witnessed any inappropriate behavior with other young boys, but he was aware of drug usage. When confronted with it, Michael would sometimes acknowledge it but would not own up to the amount being used.

Many pointed to Michael as having taken painkillers as well as anti-anxiety medications Xanax and Valium and possibly injections of Demoral. Reportedly members of the Jackson family attempted to reach out to Michael on a number of occasions and stage an intervention. He would grow angry or defensive, or just refuse to see them.

After weeks of withholding the coroner's report while the death investigation continued, it was revealed that the coroner had

"Smile"

ruled Michael Jackson's death a homicide. This ruling indicated that the death was at the hands of another, but does not necessarily indicate a crime had been committed. A manslaughter investigation was centering on Dr. Conrad Murray. Cause of death was ruled to be acute propofol intoxication with benzodiazepine effect. No illegal drugs were detected in his system, and no alcohol was detected in his system. It was noted that the standard of care for administering propofol, an anesthetic, was not provided and the equipment needed for patient monitoring and resuscitation was not on the site. Investigators believed Michael had used propofol as a sleep aid for up to two years. The investigation centered on the doctors who supplied him with the drug. Using propofol as a sleep aid is a gross miss use of the drug. The milky white drug is commonly referred to by the nickname, "milk of amnesia" due to its use in surgical procedures when patients wake up quickly with no memory of the procedure they just had. While the drug does put a patient out in a short time, it is not restorative sleep. Medical professionals repeatedly told various reporters that this drug is only to be used in a hospital setting as an anesthetic and always with an anesthesiologist on hand to constantly monitor the patient. Use inside a home is unheard of.

    Typically the administration of propofol is done with the patient being intubated and ventilated with an anesthesiologist monitoring the patient. The level of propofol found in his system was similar to that used for patients undergoing major surgery. Having lorazepam in his system contributed to the depression of the respiratory and cardiovascular systems.

When a copy of the autopsy report was released, it showed that Michael weighed 136 pounds, he had numerous needle marks on his arms and scarring on his face and neck. He had hair loss at the front of his scalp and the rest of his hair was cut short. He had tattooed lips, eyebrows and eyeliner. Among medical problems that were found was the fact that he had vitiligo, arthritis in his fingers and lower back, an enlarged prostate and some inflammation of his lungs that may have made him short of breath; "All organs present and no abnormalities noted for a 50 year old male, with some congestion of the lungs."

None of the health conditions noted were serious enough to be life-threatening thus eliminating one possible defense for Dr. Murray, that Michael may have hid some serious medical conditions from him that could have contributed to his death. Michael's heart and other major organs were healthy, there was no plaque build up around his heart. His body did show signs of the efforts to resuscitate him, bruising on his chest, fractured sternum and some cracked ribs. He had also had a balloon pump inserted into his heart in an effort to restart it.

The autopsy report stated:

The cause of death is acute propofol intoxication. A contributing factor in the death is benzodiazepine effect.

The cause of death is homicide, based on the following:

1.   Circumstances indicate that propofol and the benzodiazepines were administered by another.

2. *The propofol was administered in a non-hospital setting without any appropriate medical indication.*

3. *The standard of care for administering propofol was not met. Recommended equipment for patient monitoring, precision dosing, and resuscitation was not present.*

4. *The circumstances do not support self-administration of propofol.*

An auxiliary report, Anesthesiology Consultation, makes the following notes on "Relevant information on propofol and its administration:

Respiratory and cardiovascular depression is usually dose dependent and is accentuated if other sedatives, such as benzodiazepines, are present.

There are NO reports of its (propofol) use for insomnia, to my knowledge.

Full patient monitoring is required any time propofol is given. The most essential monitor is a person trained in anesthesia and in resuscitation who is continuously present and not involved in the on-going surgical/diagnostic procedure. Other monitors expected would be a continuous pulse oximeter, EKG and blood pressure cuff, preferably one that automatically inflates. ... Of course, airway devices and drugs for resuscitation must always be present. Supplemental O2 should always be delivered to patients receiving propofol, and they should always have a recovery period with monitoring and observation by trained recovery nurses.

The standard of care for administering propofol was not met.

The levels of propofol found on toxicology exam are similar to those found during general anesthesia for major surgery (intra-abdominal) with propofol infusions, after a bolus induction. During major surgery, a patient with these blood levels of propofol would be intubated and ventilated by an anesthesiologist, and any cardiovascular depression would be noted and treated. Anesthesiologist would also comment on the presence of other sedative drugs in the toxicology screen. Lorazepam, a long acting benzodiazepine, is present at a pharmacologically significant level and would have accentuated the respiratory and cardiovascular depression from propofol.

A nurse practioner, Cherilyn Lee, who had met Michael through a friend, soon came forward with information that he had a few months earlier begged her to obtain some Diprovan for him. Diprovan is the brand name for the drug propofol. She cautioned Michael on the dangers of the drug, that it has a very narrow margin for error and can cause breathing to stop. She refused to obtain it for him. He was only sleeping three hours at a time and was desperate to get some sleep. So he asked someone else. On the Sunday before his death, Father's Day, Michael contacted Cherilyn Lee again. An assistant was on the phone with her, but she could hear Michael in the background "tell her one side of my body is cold and the other side is hot". This was later described as possibly being a symptom of withdrawal.

"Smile"

Within days of his death, photos were released of Michael's last rehearsal performances. These still photos, along with the short video clip of Michael and his dancers performing "They Don't Care About Us" went a long way to silence those who insisted Michael was not in any shape to perform. It was confusing to see how this tireless performer could appear to be so unstoppable yet be described by so many others as "fragile" or "frail'. Among those who were in attendance at this last rehearsal, in addition to the cast and crew, were Frank Dileo, Miko Brando, Randy Phillips and Ken Ehrlich. Dileo noted that his stamina was good, his heart was strong and he was definitely interested in doing the fifty shows. Tour Director Kenny Ortega described Michael's performances as awesome. He was not like a fifty year old performer returning to the stage, he was timeless, ageless, involved in *every* aspect of the show.

Johnny Caswell, a co-owner of the studio where rehearsals began, CenterStaging, told USA Today, "He was energetic, passionate, diligent, prepared, excited and an effective leader...These folks followed him like he's the Pied Piper. He was a perfectionist. This guy was ready to go." Another observer of rehearsals, Ed Alonzo, a magician contributing to the illusions that were part of the show said, "It was an amazing show. The thing was days away from being perfected. It was incredible. Even though it was just a walk through with the dancers, his moves were dead-on – the same Michael Jackson we (saw) through the years in music videos." Tour musical director Michael Bearden said Michael's voice was "stronger than I ever heard it". He also said, "I'm hearing all these rumors about him being frail and in a wheelchair, but he was upright. And he sounded like the Michel Jackson from back in the day... all the power, all the ad-libs, all the inflection with no problem."

AEG Live CEO Randy Philips responded to stories claiming Michael was too weak to actually perform, "Since his death, Michael has been portrayed as weak, frail, manipulated. He was none of that. If anything, he was the manipulator. Healthy and in charge of everything, he knew just what he was doing. He was a clever business guy. He used to drive me crazy, but I loved him."

Long time friend Steve Manning said Michael was looking forward to the tour. "There was a new vitality and zest for life in him. That was his greatest love: performing." Long time associate Miko Brando echoed those remarks, "he wasn't nervous about his comeback. He was looking forward to it." Miko Brando described Michael as a best friend, loving and caring, always there for you. Michael was the Best Man at Miko's wedding, held at Neverland, and is the godfather for Miko's daughter. Deepok Chopra saw a similar attitude in Michael. He had left Chopra a voice mail message three days before this death, he was in good spirits and he said he had some good news to share. He was very upbeat and told Chopra, "for sure this time I am coming back, with a bang."

Lou Ferigno described Michael in several interviews the last time he had seen him as being in great shape. He was devastated by the loss of his good friend who he first met twenty years earlier. They shared a connection in that they both grew up with abusive fathers and both delved head first into their respective passions, music and body building. He introduced Ferigno to his kids telling them he was the original Incredible Hulk. When it came time to get in shape for the string of London concerts Michael turned to Ferigno to train him. He had known him for a long time and knew he could trust him. Ferigno noted Michael was thin, but he was always thin and seemed very healthy and did not appear frail. He also noted that he never saw any signs of drug use.

While the investigation continued, many shared their memories of Michael. Berry Gordy told CNN he was pleased with the outpouring of love for Michael Jackson. He felt he deserved it and wished he could be here to see it. Gordy felt strongly that the upcoming shows in London would have been a huge success given Michael's perfectionism and dedication. Echoing his sentiments was former CBS Records head Walter Yetnikoff who was confident Michael's upcoming performances would have been successful.

Attorney Howard Weitzman told Larry King that what he most remembers about Michael is that he was a "playful person who always looked at the good side of things." Weitzman stated he never believed or accepted the child molestation charges made against him. He described Michael as "truly was one of kind, literally he was creative, he was an icon in the literal sense of the word. I don't think there are any other Michael Jacksons out there."

Donald Trump echoed Weitzman's comments emphasizing that Michael Jackson was NOT a child molester and had great memories of Michael playing with Trump's kids. He described him as the greatest entertainer he had ever seen. Trump had had Michael and Lisa Marie as guests at his estate in Florida and witnessed them spending a lot of time together before they married. He described how loving they were with each other and that they spent many hours in their room without ever coming out. He was certain their relationship was genuine.

A long time friend of Michael's, and Blanket's godfather, Al Malnik appeared on TV to share his memories of his "loving and sensitive friend" and to share some fun and priceless videos of Michael playing with his kids. Hilarious footage of Michael being taken to a "surprise location" shows him going in a grocery store that stayed open just for him. Michael is seen enjoying the daylights out of filling his grocery cart, something the rest of us generally dread.

MTV aired the results of a vote of fans for their favorite Michael Jackson video with "Thriller" topping the list. *Entertainment Tonight,* in tribute to the King of Pop, presented their picks for the top 10 Most Memorable moments on TV for Michael Jackson with his performance on *Motown 25* topping the list.

Immediately following Michael's death, the three children were taken to Hayvenhurst in Encino with their grandmother, Katherine Jackson. Katherine then filed documents in court requesting custody of the kids. The court filings showed Katherine Jackson as filing for custody, not Joseph and Katherine Jackson. Joe and Katherine have been separated for years with Joe taking up residence in Las Vegas. Katherine also filed for control of the estate, believing there was not a will.

As with all things Jackson, speculation by the media was rampant with possible scenarios concerning the future of Prince, Paris and Blanket. Some thought Debbie Rowe, as the biological mother of Prince and Paris, would have a case for custody. Others contended their rightful place was with their grandmother, Katherine. A few even mentioned that long time nanny Grace Rwaramba should be the one to be granted custody as she has a long term bond with the children. Any plans or decisions on Debbie Rowe's part remained in question, as she was devastated by his loss and was trying to keep a low profile from the press. When the paparazzi tracked her down, followed her, and refused her requests that they keep their distance, she lashed out angrily at them which was of course caught on video and broadcast repeatedly, capturing, from accounts of friends and acquaintances of Debbie's, a very uncharacteristic picture of her. She is described by those who know her as a kind, strong person. And a HUGE Michael Jackson fan.

Grace Rwaramba was a part of Michael's life for seventeen years, first as his executive administrator then for the last twelve years as the nanny for his three children. She was introduced to Michael by his friend Deepok Chopra. Some reports also pointed to a very close personal relationship between Michael and Grace, some calling Grace the true love of Michael's life. Their romantic relationship was said to be a not very well kept secret among the household staff. They did have rough patches though, the last one culminating in Grace being dismissed in December 2008, after which she moved to London. She had actually been terminated by Michael at least twice, once for planning an intervention for him. Grace was reportedly the first person the kids wanted to see after suffering the loss of their father. Katherine did ask Grace to come to Hayvenhurst to be with the children. Grace described Michael as "an exceptional human being. He was gifted, deeply compassionate and loved his family dearly, above all his beautiful children." Michael's close friend Deepok Chopra described Grace's relationship with the kids as "one of their strongest nurturing influences".

It was clear from all accounts that the care and well being of his children was first and foremost in Michael's mind. After reuniting with Frank Dileo for preparations for the tour, Michael repeatedly asked Frank to make sure his kids were well taken care of. Frank made that his prime concern following Michael's death, just as he had asked. Before the will surfaced, Frank predicted Michael would want his mother, Katherine, to care for his children.

Within a few days, it was revealed that Michael did in fact leave a will, written in 2002 following the birth of Blanket, and that he very predictably named his mother as guardian for his children. His choice to take her place if she was unable to care for the kids was somewhat of a bombshell: Diana Ross. Those who knew Michael however and knew of his affection for Diana and his admiration for how she has raised her own five children were less surprised. What is surprising is that Michael apparently made this nomination without asking Diana. She was reportedly shocked to hear he had named her as successor guardian of his children.

Judge Beckloff, on August 3rd, awarded permanent custody of the children to their grandmother. Katherine Jackson and Debbie Rowe had reached an agreement that allows Debbie to re-enter the lives of her children. As part of the hearing, statements were introduced by Prince, Paris and Blanket stating they preferred to stay with their grandmother. Debbie and Katherine, while they had previously spoken on the phone, met for the first time following Michael's death. Katherine described the meeting as being very emotional, greeting each other with a hug and lots of tears. She added, "All the rumors about Debbie Rowe wanting to take the children away are completely false... Debbie's happy with the arrangement the way Michael left it and she sees nothing wrong with me in raising the children and I respect her and love her for that."

Other surprising mentions in the will included the deliberate omission of Debbie Rowe, "I have intentionally omitted to provide for my former wife, DEBORAH JEAN ROWE JACKSON." Michael's entire estate is left to his family trust, "I give my entire estate to the Trustee or Trustees then acting under that certain Amended and Restated Declaration of Trust executed March 22, 2002 by me as Trustee and Trustor which is called the MICHAEL JACKSON FAMILY TRUST." The trust then provides for the estate to be divided with 40% going to a trust for his mother, 40% to a trust for his children and 20% to unnamed children's charities. Michael's father, Joseph Jackson is conspicuously not mentioned. Only Tito's sons and a couple of cousins are singled out and mentioned in the trust document as contingent beneficiaries. A committee comprised of John Branca, John McClain and Katherine

Jackson are responsible for choosing the charities stipulating that they be "for the benefit of children or children's causes".

The trustees of the trust were Michael's long time friend and attorney, John Branca, long time friend and music industry executive John McClain and attorney Barry Siegel. Siegel resigned as successor trustee, so per the terms of the trust, Branca and McClain continued to represent the trust and estate of Michael Jackson. Michael did not indicate in the document where he wished to be buried. The trust was originally prepared on November 1, 1995, before he had any of the children. It was last amended and resigned on March 22, 2002, just a month following Blanket's birth. John Branca read the will to the Jackson family at Jermaine's house. Jackie and Tito's son Taj serve as consultants to the estate.

The terms of the trust dictate that 40% of the trust assets are to be given to the Katherine Jackson Trust. Upon Katherine's death, her portion of the estate will revert to his three children, The Michael Jackson Children's Trust. If any of his children are not living at the time, their share goes to their children, if any. If no grandchildren exist, the assets are then transferred to the Michael Jackson Relatives Trust with two cousins and each of Tito's three sons as named beneficiaries. Each of Michael's children are to receive income from the trust paid at the discretion of the trustees until they reach the age of twenty-one. At age thirty, each beneficiary receives one-third of their share. At age thirty-five, they receive half of the remaining share, with the balance being paid out upon reaching age forty. Some speculated that with the expected growth rate of the estate, it was possible that each of the three kid's share could reach $1 billion by the time they are able to gain full access to their shares.

Michael's estate was said to be in debt to the tune of $400 - $500million. He was sure good at spending. The Carolwood house was rented for the bargain basement price of $100,000 per month and he was estimated at one point to be spending an average of $15 to $30 million more per year than he was earning. His assets however were equal to, or indeed by most accounts, vastly outpaced this massive debt. The valuation of the Sony/ATV music catalog ranged from $1.5 to $2 billion. Mijac Music, Michael's music catalog of his own compositions, the song catalog of Sly and the Family Stone, songs from the producing team Kenny Gamble and Leon Huff, and songs by Ray Charles and Elvis Presley, is also a major publishing holding and was valued at approximately $75 million. Despite such massive assets, cash flow was definitely a concern, it was said he had cash on hand of $668,000.

The earning power of the estate of Michael Jackson looked to eclipse that of Elvis Presley, whose estate earned $52 million in 2008. His own music catalog, given the sales figures in response to this death, looked to become one of the most highly valued music catalogs in modern music history. It looks to eclipse the catalogs of Elvis Presley, Frank Sinatra and the Beatles.

Future earnings of the estate would be enhanced by the release of previously unreleased songs. Michael typically over recorded for each of his albums then many songs had to be omitted from the final cuts to make each album. New material recorded with

Akon, will.i.am and Ne-Yo also held great promise. Michael told Frank Dileo he was not ready to share some of these songs with him just yet. They were on computer hard drives in Michael's house and were reportedly cleaned out by LaToya with his other belongings and some of the furnishings in the house within a few days of his death, some of which was actually rented. Dileo expressed concern to *Rolling Stone* that "that's who's going to run his estate?"

In a hearing held in October, Judge Beckloff ruled that the trustees' powers would be expanded to allow them to begin handling legal claims being filed against the estate. Until now there was technically no party responsible for answering such issues. Among those getting in line to file claims against the estate were John Landis, for $1.3 million, for what he claimed were unpaid profits from "Thriller", and the video's producer, George Fosley Jr. who filed a claim against the estate for $1 million that he claimed he was owed. Leonard Rowe had his hand out for $300,000. The biggest claim came from AllGood Entertainment for $300 million, claiming Michael backed out of an agreement for a Jackson family reunion tour. According to the claim, Michael and Frank Dileo began planning the This Is It shows after agreeing to the plans for a Jacksons tour. The attorney representing the estate trustees, Howard Weitzman, replied that "AllGood's creditor's claim and its underlying lawsuit are frivolous and wholly without merit." The suit was later dismissed.

A motion was filed by Michael's father in which the trustees, Branca and McClain, were accused of fraud and conflict of interest.

Joe Jackson was looking to receive money from the estate. He was claiming Michael had been helping for years to cover his monthly expenses in excess of $15,000, while he received monthly social security benefits of $1700. Attorneys for the estate argued that Joseph Jackson had been purposely left out of his son's will, was not an heir to the estate and had no legal standing to bring the motion. A few months later Joe withdrew his petition.

    This did not however put an end to the infighting among the family members over Michael's will. A long hard fought battle would ensue with Randy and, surprisingly, Janet, leading an effort to have the trustees replaced claiming Michael's will was forged. They were said to be interested in having the estate release funds to Katherine Jackson in an effort to secure an inheritance for themselves. They would need to have the existing will and trust deemed invalid to pull this off as the trust states any funds in the Katherine Jackson Trust at the time of her death will revert to the Michael Jackson's Children's Trust – and NOT to his siblings.

    After much anticipation for funeral plans to be announced, reports surfaced that there would be a public memorial, including a public viewing, held at Neverland Valley Ranch on Friday, July 3rd, the day Michael and crew were to leave for London. Fans gathered outside the gates of the ranch and media trucks lined the two lane road leading to Neverland. Law enforcement officials worked feverishly on plans to stage the event and handle the onslaught of people upon the small town of Los Olivos. Neighbors of Neverland were against the idea, they did not want their tranquil surroundings interrupted. They were also very much against any plans to turn Neverland into a Graceland type of attraction. After attempts to work out the logistics failed, it was announced that no such service would be held at Neverland after all.

Plans for a memorial service to be held at the Staples Center in Los Angeles were announced for Tuesday, July 7th. The date remained in question for some time as the Staples Center was already booked for the circus to set up. An agreement was struck with the circus whereby they would delay their set up until after the memorial service if their elephants could be safely stored at the Staples Center. It seemed somewhat appropriate that the circus would be booked for the venue on this day, Michael, a big fan of the circus, would have certainly loved it.

A total of 17,500 tickets were being made available for the public, with 11,000 for the Staples Center and an additional 6,500 for the Nokia Theatre overflow area where it would be shown on a closed circuit TV. These 8,750 pairs of tickets were being disseminated to the public through a special website. Those wishing a chance at attending the memorial service needed to register for the random drawing. More than 1.6 million registrations were received, bogging down the website.

Four huge panels with Michael's image were placed outside the Staples Center. Fans plastered them with signatures and notes. Some waited hours in line for the chance to add their thoughts and wishes to the banners as images of Michael throughout his life lit up the JumboTrons around the outside of the center.

Law enforcement officials feared as many as one million people could show up and bring LA to a stand still. They began cautioning people that they would not be able to get close to the Staples Center without a ticket and wristband and urged those without tickets to stay home and watch the service on TV where they would get a much better view and would feel much more a part of the farewell. Fortunately people paid attention and the massive crowd scenes were largely averted.

They had plenty of alternatives available to watch the memorial service. It was being broadcast by most major networks, was streamed live on multiple websites and was shown in up to eighty movie theaters in thirty-one states. Viewing parties were hosted with the service shown on JumboTrons in malls, outdoor arenas, etc. The press corps in Russia, covering President Obama, was reported to be watching the memorial coverage. A website, Michaeljacksonfuneral.com, was set up to post and read tributes and to donate to his favorite charities. A skywriter created a heart shaped image overhead the Staples Center. A giant floral heart arrangement reading, "We love you Michael" was placed outside the Staples Center with a banner bearing a picture of Michael smiling which read, "Thank you for the memories, Michael. Love Always, Christian Audigier and Family." It was estimated that the audience could top one billion viewers, making the farewell to the King of Pop the most watched worldwide event ever.

34

Born to amuse, to inspire, to delight
Here one day
Gone one night

"Gone Too Soon"
- Buz Kohan

The day of the public memorial service, major arteries around Los Angeles were blocked off and traffic was re-routed. Up to one-third of the Los Angeles police force was on duty. An area around the arena from one to four blocks was blocked off and the exit from the highway was closed. Only those with wristbands would be allowed past the barricades. As many as 2,200 credentialed journalist descending upon Los Angeles and traffic into LA was reported to experience an increase in the several days

"Gone Too Soon"

leading up to the event. Gates were to open at 6:00 AM for ticket holders. Mounted police surrounded the perimeter of the arena.

The morning of the memorial, the family members and close friends met at Forest Lawn in Hollywood Hills for a private ceremony. Shortly after 8:00 AM, a motorcade left the family home in Encino and headed to Forest Lawn. Once inside the Hall of Liberty, the doors were closed and media was not allowed. Not many details of this private ceremony are known, though it was concluded with "Gone Too Soon", a request from Paris. Programs for this private service featured beautiful pictures of Michael from throughout his career with remembrances starting with:

He had it all... talent, grace, professionalism and dedication. He was the consummate entertainer and his contributions and legacy will be felt upon the world forever. Quincy Jones

He was magic. He was what we all strive to be. Beyoncé Knowles

Whitney Houston added:
He was my friend. He was one of the reasons I got into the music business. He inspired me. He taught me. He laughed with me. Whitney Houston.
(A couple of years later, in reaction to the death of Whitney Houston, the executors of Michael's estate paid tribute to her with a full page ad in the *Los Angeles Times*)

An essay titled "The World Will Never Be the Same", recalls the world's reaction to the news that the King of Pop had passed, the rush to check the headlines bringing the internet to a halt. "Leave it to the King of Pop to go out in such a way as to make the world recognize his passing." Following the private ceremony, the brothers each serving as pallbearers, loaded the casket into the hearse for transport to the Staples Center.

The program for the public memorial had a gold cover with a beautiful picture of Michael, said to be one of Katherine's favorites, with the words:

Michael Jackson

King of Pop

A Celebration

Of the Life of Michael Jackson

1958 – 2009

Inside were more beautiful pictures of Michael and notes from many family members, friends and colleagues. Each of Tito's three sons included touching notes for their Uncle Mike, as well as many other nieces and nephews. LaToya, Rebbie and Tito remembered their brother along with a quote from "Dunk". Personal assistant Evvy Tarasci, photographer Harrison Funk, who took the cover photograph, longtime hair and makeup assistant, Karen Faye and nanny Grace Rwaramba all included notes to their employer and friend with one signed "Uncle Tookie", aka Frank Dileo. Tom Mesereau Jr. also remembered his once client and friend fondly. Two of his closest personal friends, Frank Cascio and his family and the family of Miko Brando expressed their love. It was noted in the booklet all would not be possible without their mother, Katherine,

"Without the love and devotion of Michael Jackson's beloved mother, Mrs. Katherine Jackson, this program would not have been possible." Joe is not mentioned in the book. Not once. A sole photograph in the book includes Joe with his six sons.

The first person on stage at the Staples Center was Smokey Robinson. He read statements from two people who could not attend; former South Africa President Nelson Mandela and Diana Ross. In her statement, Ross said she would be there for his children if they should ever need her. Others who chose not to attend included both of his ex-wives, Lisa Marie Presley and Debbie Rowe, Elizabeth Taylor and Quincy Jones. All were said to be too overwrought with grief to attend.

There was a pause in the program following Smokey's remarks leading up to the Andre Crouch choir taking the stage and singing the line "We are going to see the king" from "Soon and Very Soon" as the five Jackson brothers and one other man, serving as pallbearers brought in Michael's coffin. All were dressed in dark suits, sunglasses and matching yellow ties. And one single white beaded glove. Some wore the glove on the right hand, some on left, arranged so each pallbearer would handle the casket with their gloved hand. The casket was shinny gold, topped with a huge spray of red roses. The sight of his brothers carrying Michael's casket into the Staples Center was heart wrenching. The brothers then joined the rest of the family in the front row of the Staples Center. Katherine was surrounded by Prince, Paris and Blanket. The boys also dressed in dark suits and yellow ties. Blanket was wearing white socks and black loafers, clutching a doll of his very famous father, a sad and emotional sight.

Pastor Lucious Smith, a longtime family friend, spoke first followed by a performance by Mariah Carey with Trey Lorenz of their cover of "I'll Be There". She was reportedly the only artist who did not have time to rehearse. It was beautiful. They were followed by Queen Latifah who recalled getting her first Jackson's album, *Dancing Machine* as a youngster. She then shared a poem written especially for the occasion by Maya Angelou. Lionel Richie sang "Jesus is Love" with Berry Gordy speaking next. He gave a heartfelt speech about his once young protégé, recalling how he studied the greats, then became greater, rose the bar, then broke the bar. He humorously recalled the weekly baseball games, the Gordys vs. the Jacksons and how Michael's catching skills were a little weak. Gordy went on to call Michael Jackson, "the greatest entertainer who ever lived", receiving a standing ovation from the crowd, and saying Michael "was like a son to me".

During the speeches and musical performances, a huge screen at the back of the stage projected images of Michael. "You Are Not Alone" was played against a backdrop of a beautiful video montage. Stevie Wonder's comments leading up to his performance of "Never Dreamed You'd Leave in Summer" included a hope that he would not live to see this day and the thought that as much as we all needed Michael here with us, God must have needed him more.

Kobe Bryant and Magic Johnson next took to the stage to pay tribute to the King of Pop. Bryant spoke of Michael's countless humanitarian efforts and noted his being listed in the Guinness Book of World Records for Most Charities Supported by a Pop Star. Magic Johnson recounted his visit to Neverland to discuss his part in the video for "Remember the Time". Johnson ordered grilled chicken for dinner and Michael was served Kentucky Fried Chicken. Knowing Michael Jackson enjoyed such a common thing made Johnson's day.

Jennifer Hudson delivered a performance of "Will You Be There" accompanied by the This Is It dancers, band and singers. The song closed to the background screens intended for use in the planned concerts showing lines recorded by Michael for the shows, "In my darkest hour, in my deepest despair, Will you be there?". She was followed by Al Sharpton's rousing eulogy with John Mayer's performance of "Human Nature" following Sharpton. Mayer played guitar but did not sing, feeling it fitting to let the conspicuous absence of Michael's voice stand for itself. Mayer was initially going to perform "Smile" but switched to "Human Nature" late in the game when he learned Jermaine wished to sing the same song.

Humor and heartfelt grief filled Brooke Shields' comments. She recalled teasing Michael, calling him a slacker for not starting in show business until the ripe old age of five, while she had started at eleven months of age. She concluded by quoting Michael's favorite song, "Smile", followed by Jermaine taking the stage and giving a beautiful and moving performance of that very song, despite a transposition of some lyrics. He ended the song, tossing his red rose boutonnière on to his little brother's casket.

Martin Luther King III and Bernice King, the children of Martin Luther King Jr., recalled a day when Michael Jackson telephoned their mother, Correta Scott King three months prior to her death. She had suffered a stroke and was unable to speak but she listened to Michael and Bernice saw her face glow. Congresswoman Sheila Jackson Lee from Texas introduced her intention to present to Congress Resolution 600 naming him as an American Legend, Music Icon and World Humanitarian. Martin Luther King Jr.'s children and Jackson Lee, along with Reverend Al Sharpton, were specifically requested to participate by the Jackson family.

Usher provided one of the most emotional moments of the memorial, stepping down to touch the casket and breaking down at the last lines of "Gone Too Soon". Smokey Robinson took the stage once again to share his memories of a young Michael Jackson singing his song, "Who's Lovin' You" and putting a level of passion and emotion into the song that the young boy could not have possibly known. Robinson referred to Michael as "my little brother". The song was then performed with almost equal emotion by twelve year old Shaheen Jafarghdi who had been a finalist in "Britain's Got Talent". Michael had heard of his performance and invited him to be a part of the London O2 shows.

The memorial concluded with Kenny Ortega introducing the This Is It band, singers and dancers who joined the other performers on stage for "We are the World". The Jackson family, minus Joe and Katherine, also joined in the finale. A couple of the family members then addressed the audience, Jermaine offering his thanks, Marlon recalling a humorous story about running into Michael in a record store in disguise, but still wearing his trademark black loafers, then he broke down. Paris, Michael's eleven year old daughter then wished to add her own impromptu remarks: "I just want to say that ever since I was born, my daddy has been the best father you could ever imagine. And I just want to say I love him so much". She turned, sobbing into Aunt Janet's arms. The brothers then carried Michael's casket out of the Staples Center to "Man in the Mirror", a heartbreaking sight. Following the public memorial, the family headed to the Beverly Wilshire Hotel for a private gathering.

The casket was made by Batesville Casket Company in Indiana. Batesville has made caskets for the funerals of several high profile people including those for Presidents Ronald Reagan, Gerald Ford, Richard Nixon, John Kennedy and Harry Truman. And entertainers Bob Hope, Farah Fawcett, and two of Michael's idols; Fred Astaire and James Brown.

The memorial service was a grand celebration of the life of an incredibly special, kind, gifted and generous person, a tribute certainly befitting the King of Pop, an ideal blend of thoughtful, heartbreaking tributes and humorous recollections. With all of the touching tributes during the memorial, a fitting headline would have been; "Jackson Tribute Touching, But Paris Steals Show". *People Magazine*, in their story on the tribute to the King of Pop, stated "for a man who wished to be thought of not as a personality but as a person, Paris' words would have surely pleased Jackson – and broken his heart."

Ken Ehrlich produced the event with Kenny Ortega. They did a brilliant job of orchestrating the high profile event in an excruciating short amount of time and struck the perfect balance of celebrating his life and grieving his loss. They contacted artists who knew and were inspired by Michael to perform.

An unidentified young man at the memorial service, sitting in the front row with the Jackson family caused widespread speculation in the days following the service. Twenty-five year old Omer Bhatti was said to possibly be Michael's son and his mother was speculated to be a Norwegian woman also suspected to be the mother of Blanket. Omer lived at Neverland from the early 90's to the early 2000's. Following Michael's death, he was staying at Hayvenhurst with Prince, Paris, Blanket and the rest of the family. It was later decided Omer was not Michael's son.

On July 10th, a memorial service was held in Gary, Indiana. Joseph Jackson was the only family member to attend, as did Jesse Jackson. Area performers sang Jackson classics including "Thriller" and "Man in the Mirror".

The July 13 – 26, 2009 edition of *TV Guide* paid tribute to Michael Jackson, "One critical fact often gets overlooked in all the statistics and hype and hoopla: Michael Jackson was amazingly talented.... And now that he's gone, once the gossip and the exploitation and the vultures pass by the music he made is what will remain." *TV Guide* joined the herd of publications rushing a special Michael Jackson issue to the newsstands. It was issued with two different covers, one of a young Michael from the Jackson Five era and one from the *Dangerous* era, sporting his "In the Closet" look.

TV Guide explored how Michael revolutionized music videos. Martin Scorsese, who directed Michael Jackson in "Bad", said "Michael Jackson was extraordinary when we worked on 'Bad'. I was in awe of his absolutely mastery of movement on the one hand and of the music on the other. Every step he took was absolutely precise and fluid at the same time. It was like watching quicksilver in motion. He was wonderful to work with, and absolutely professional at all times and it really goes without saying – a true artist. It will be a while before I can get used to the idea that he's no longer with us."

The week following the public memorial, Michael Jackson continued to dominate the music charts. *Billboard* magazine's Comprehensive Chart (based solely on sales regardless of release date) had Michael Jackson holding six of the top ten positions headed by *Number Ones*.

Official This Is It tour merchandise began to be sold online including items that had already been approved by Michael. Concert t-shirts bearing the tour logo were sold in honor of the opening night with a "1" on the back indicating it was for day one of the tour. Shirts for the tour's second night were sold with a "2" and so on, up to number 50. Ticket holders were offered full refunds or the option of a souvenir ticket in lieu of the cash refund. The souvenir tickets were designed by Michael and were printed with a special lenticular printing process, to produce a moving image. An approximate $6 million in ticket sales were not refunded when fans opted for one of the souvenir tickets.

On July 13th, the date that was to be opening night for This Is It, fans gathered outside the O2 arena in London bringing pictures, candles and flowers. They sang along with Jackson's music as it was played for the crowd and images of Michael were shown on the JumboTrons outside the arena in honor of the King of Pop.

35

Your love is magical, that's how I feel
But I have not the words here to explain
Gone is the grace for expressions of passion
But there are worlds and worlds of ways to explain
To tell you how I feel

"Speechless"
- Michael Jackson

In the days following his death, investigators searched Michael's Carolwood home and came away with a huge stash of prescription drugs and other medical equipment. Police found propofol and other prescription drugs in the home as well as oxygen tanks in his bedroom and in a security guard shack. Some of the prescription bottles had labels with the names of pseudonyms other bottles had no labels at all. It was learned that some prescriptions had been obtained using aliases including some familiar and famous names; Josephine Baker and Jack London, his own son, Prince Jackson, and members of his staff including chef Kai Chase. One unexplained item found at the house was a white shirt, still with its $3.99 price tag, with blood stains all over it, hanging in the closet.

LaToya told London newspaper, *News of the World,* that she believed Michael had been murdered. She believed this to be part of a conspiracy to get his money, though she refused to name who she knew to be part of this conspiracy.

The investigation centered on Dr. Murray but at least five other doctors were also being questioned. During the course of the investigation, search warrants were served on Dr. Murray's offices in Houston and Las Vegas, as well as his home in Las Vegas. The search warrant stated that investigators were looking for evidence of excessive prescribing and prescribing to an addict, evidence of manslaughter. A subpoena for information was served to Dr. Arnold Klein, Michael's long time dermatologist. Dr. Klein's office was said to be cooperating with the investigation.

Early January 2010 brought an announcement that the District Attorney in Los Angeles would seek an indictment of Dr. Conrad Murray for involuntary manslaughter, citing gross negligence and alleging that the treatment Dr. Murray administered to Michael Jackson was "an extreme departure from the standard of care normally followed by physicians." The announcement continued, "The coroner found the propofol was administered to Jackson without any medical need and that recommended resuscitation equipment was missing."

Dr. Murray told police he had been treating Jackson for insomnia with propofol, which Michael had called "his milk" for about six weeks, and was trying to wean him off of the drug, giving him smaller doses in combination with lorazepam and midazolam. After administering several doses of these other sedatives throughout the night, Michael was still awake the next morning. At 10:40, Dr. Murray administered 25 milligrams of propofol and Michael went to sleep. A short time later Dr. Murray found him not breathing. An affidavit from a search warrant detailed the times and dosages of the sedatives administered to Michael in the early morning hours of June 25th. The affidavit detailed the times and amounts each drug was administered:

1:30 am 10 mg Valium

2:00 am 2 mg lorazepam (Ativan)

3:00 am 2 mg midazolam (an anti-depressant)

5:00 am 2 mg lorazepam

7:30 am 2 mg midazolam

10:40 am 25 mg propofol

After administering the propofol, Dr. Murray told police, he remained with Michael for about ten minutes before leaving the room for two minutes to use the bathroom. There were serious questions however surrounding the timeline involved with Dr. Murray's recounting of the events of that morning. Cell phone records showed that three separate phone calls were made by Dr. Murray between 11:18 am and 12:05 pm. During his first interviews with police, he never told police he had administered propofol to Michael Jackson.

Another problem arose over the amount of propofol Dr. Murray admitted administering to Michael. The concentration of the drug found in Michael's blood was an amount normally used for major surgery. Other troubling issues centered on the fact that the necessary equipment to monitor and resuscitate the patient should breathing stop was not present, the patient was left alone when they require constant monitoring while under the influence of the "milk", and further, when CPR was administered, it was with the patient still on the bed. A hard surface is recommended for the administration of CPR, patients are to be placed on the floor. The efforts to tidy up the place before calling paramedics certainly smacks of someone trying to cover their tracks.

At this same time, California Attorney General Jerry Brown announced his office, the Bureau of Narcotic Enforcement, was beginning their own investigation into some of the doctors whose names had come up in the Michael Jackson case. No other doctors however would be charged in the case.

With the death investigation continuing, friends and associates of Michael's appeared on numerous television programs sharing their experiences and memories with Michael over the years and telling of any knowledge or suspicion they had of any drug use on his part. Miko Brando never saw any evidence of drug use around Michael. No IV poles, no prescription bottles, etc. Jermaine and Frank Dileo also had no knowledge of any drug use by Michael.

"Speechless"

Frank added that if Michael was using drugs, he would have surely hid it from him, as he was strongly against such things. It is odd that Jermaine told of no knowledge of any drug use by Michael when other family members had tried to hold interventions for him.

The defense repeatedly claimed Dr. Murray did not prescribe or administer anything to Michael Jackson that should have killed him. There were serious questions however regarding the setting in which the drugs were administered and the timeline of events that morning and Dr. Murray's response. He did not have the necessary medical equipment available for the resuscitation of his patient, or for monitoring his patient. He did not even seem properly trained in CPR, which according to some, is not even the preferred method of resuscitation. The timing of when Michael stopped breathing and when 9-1-1 was finally called raises additional serious and troubling questions.

Deepok Chopra offered some insights into Michael's health conditions and a possible link to childhood trauma. Michael had been diagnosed with vitiligo and lupus, which commonly go hand in hand. There might also be a connection between childhood trauma, the physical and emotional abuse he suffered at the hands of his father, stress and these autoimmune diseases in adulthood, according to Chopra. It may also include a penchant for plastic surgery- a form of self mutilation- as he felt self conscious about his appearance and had a compulsion with his body image. Chopra described Michael as being a victim of circumstances, his own body image, media frenzy and enablers, resulting in him distancing himself from his family and friends who cared for him and making himself available to enablers. The effects from the verbal and physical abuse he endured during his childhood would manifest itself in various destructive ways throughout his life. Perhaps it also fueled his unrelenting perfectionism and incessant need to constantly top himself, adding to his stress levels.

Many speculated that Michael's drug use intensified during the trial. Tom Mesereau however described Michael as being coherent and articulate with him. He was lucid, intelligent and cooperative throughout the trial. While Mesereau heard rumors of drug use on Michael's part, he was never witness to any of it.

Michael Jackson was finally laid to rest seventy days after his death, on September 3rd, at Forest Lawn Memorial Park in Glendale, California in a private ceremony. Well, at least semi-private. An eight page invitation was sent out to invited guests that included a stunning photo of Michael in the yellow shirt and wide gold belt, that he had worn in the performance of "Come Together" on *Moonwalker* and a quote from *Dancing the Dream,* "If you enter this world knowing you are loved and you leave this world knowing the same, then everything that happens in between can be dealt with." The invitation read,

We loved him,
We laughed with him,
We sang with him and
We danced with him
But on this day,

"Speechless"

We Celebrate Him

Please join us as we lay
Our beloved son,
Cherished brother &
Devoted father,
Michael Jackson,
In his final resting place.

Another quote from Michael accompanies a black and white head shot from his early childhood:

In a world filled with hate,
We must still dare to hope.
In a world filled with anger,
We must still dare to comfort.
In a world filled with despair,
We must still dare to dream.
And in a world filled with distrust,
We must still dare to believe."
Michael Jackson

The invitation to the service stated a firm start time of 7:00PM. It was delayed. Reportedly Katherine Jackson was too distraught by the thought of burying her son and could not bring herself to get ready and get out the door. Family members started arriving at 8:10 in a lengthy motorcade of black SUV's with the hearse at the end. The brothers, dressed in dark suits, black armbands, sunglasses and matching red ties this time, and single gloves, again served as pallbearers, bringing in their brother's casket for the ceremony. The red roses that were draped across the gold casket for the public memorial were now exchanged for white flowers. Rather fittingly, Michael was literary late for his own funeral, an observation also made by Gotham Chopra live on CNN while awaiting arrival of the family. Gotham noted that in the twenty years he knew Michael, he was never on time for anything.

Guests began arriving early and included Elizabeth Taylor, Berry Gordy and Suzanne de Passe, Quincy Jones, Macaulay Culkin, Thomas Mesereau, Corey Feldman, Chris Tucker and Lisa Marie Presley who shared a hug with Katherine. Other attendees included Stevie Wonder, Steve Manning, Leonard Rowe, Dave Dave, a burn victim Michael had befriended, Miko Brando, Kenny Ortega, Randy Phillips from AEG, Travis Payne and Al Sharpton. In all, about two hundred people attended the ceremony. Among those who were invited but declined to attend, were Diana Ross and Debbie Rowe.

Arrivals to the service were broadcast live with pool footage provided by the family. The footage ended abruptly when the hearse arrived and the casket was removed by the brothers. Footage, without sound, was then carried from an overhead camera.

Gladys Knight sang "His Eye is on the Sparrow". Rev. Al Sharpton gave a eulogy, and Joe Jackson spoke. Paris led Prince and Blanket to place a crown, designed by Dennis Tompkins, on top of their father's casket.

Following the ceremony, guests made their way inside the

mausoleum. Katherine was reportedly too overcome with grief to stay and had to make her way outside again. Paris was crying. Lisa Marie was also said to be very emotional. The service concluded at about 10PM.

Michael's private resting place is in the Holly Terrace in the Great Mausoleum, overlooking rolling green hills with plenty of trees. He is interned at the far end of the hall from the entrance to Holly Terrace, beneath a stained glass window. The Great Mausoleum features a stained glass replica of Leonardo da Vinci's the Last Supper and the surrounding Court of Honor features reproductions of the works of Michelangelo. Forest Lawn's majestic setting is a fitting resting place for the King of Pop.

Security was one of the major concerns of the family in choosing the most suitable resting place. Randy was charged with the grim task of checking out all locations and finding the most suitable spot. Forest Lawn is a three hundred acre hillside which has become the final resting place for many of Hollywood's biggest stars, and many of Michael's idols, Sammy Davis Jr. and Walt Disney among them. The grounds are exquisite and the area is filled with grand architecture and replicas of classic art and lots of trees all of which Michael loved.

LaToya shared in one interview that Michael's coffin is lined with blue velvet and he is dressed as if he were ready to go on stage. His outfit was designed by Michael Bush and Dennis Tompkins. They were reluctant to share what exactly they dressed him in, but allowed only that it includes favorite elements of his looks over the years. LaToya said that the jacket is draped with beautiful white pearls and he is wearing a wide gold belt like a prizefighter. LaToya stated that while he is not wearing one white glove, one was placed in the coffin with him. Michael Bush, who actually dressed him, refuted this saying Michael saw the glove as being very closely connected to the song and performance of "Billie Jean", and not connection of himself, so it was not included. He is also wearing a pendent put on him by Paris. Michael wears one half of the two-piece pendent and his daughter wears the other half. Bush spent nine hours picking out and preparing the outfit for Michael to be buried in. He dressed him and then was asked by a sole remaining staff member of Forest Lawn to help place him in the casket. Bush obliged, saying tearfully that he had to do it "he's my best friend". Karen Faye, like Tompkins and Bush, was asked by the family to do his hair and make up a final time. She agreed, considering it "an honor" to do so. He carries with him notes from his children.

36

You were there, before we came
You took the hurt, you took the shame
They built the walls, to block your way
You beat them down, you won the day

"You Were There"
-Michael Jackson, Alan "Buz" Kohan

The fall of 2009 had many Michael Jackson related projects lined up, the biggest of which was the release of the rehearsal footage for the This Is It concerts. The movie, also titled *This Is It,* was culled from approximately 130 hours of footage taken during months of rehearsals, behind the scenes preparations and short films made to air as part of the live performances. Much of the footage was for Michael's personal video library, for analysis of the performances and some footage was thought to be potential for a concert film. All footage used in the movie was approved by Jackson's estate. John Branca said of the film, "We had the feeling that when people saw the true side of Michael, they would fall in love with him all over again. The public would see Michael as an artist, a perfectionist; a man who insisted on getting his way, but who did it with great charm. And most of all with great talent."

AEG showed fifteen minutes of footage to the heads of four major studios and a bidding war broke out. Columbia pictures came out the winner paying $60 million for the rights to the film with Michael's estate set to receive 90% of the profits. AEG Live was set to recover all of its expenses and held a perpetual share of the profits from the video rights. Katherine was said to be very pleased with the film, though she could not bear to view it. In a public letter she wrote, "An event of this dimension not only keeps Michael's spirit alive, more than that: It gives millions of fans the opportunity to experience his music and celebrate the life of my son. I am sure Michael would love it."

Initial plans to have the movie released around the time of Michael's birthday were scrubbed as there was not sufficient time to get it finished. A release date was next chosen to coincide with Michael's favorite holiday, Halloween. The movie had a two week limited run with a global release on October 28th, but with tickets going on sale a month in advance. A global launch of the film was scheduled with twenty-five premieres worldwide, fifteen of which would be held simultaneously. Red carpet galas celebrating the

"You Were There"

film's release were planned in cities around the world.

Advance ticket sales for the film set records throughout the world. It was noted on the Michael Jackson website that, "It is believed no movie in history has generated so many ticket sales so far in advance of its release." Up to 80% of online ticket sales were for *This Is It* in the first twenty-four hours of going on sale. Unprecedented demand for tickets was seen in Great Britain, Australia, France, Germany, Holland, Sweden, Belgium, New Zealand, Australia, Thailand and Japan. In London, ticket sales for the movie in the first twenty-four hours exceeded those of *Harry Potter* and *Lord of the Rings*. In the U.S., it was reported that online searches for *This Is It* was 60% higher than any other film. Advance ticket sales on September 27th saw hundreds of shows around the United States and the world selling out within an hour. Showings in Los Angeles, San Francisco, Houston, Nashville and New York sold out as well as in London, Paris, Sydney, Bangkok and Tokyo.

The Regal Cinemas Stadium 14 in Los Angeles, for its grand opening, planned to show the film on every one of their screens. Fans lined up beginning three days earlier for tickets to an advance screening. The first five-hundred people in line received one of the commemorative lenticular tickets that were designed by Michael for the London O2 shows.

Coinciding with the film's release was a new song and album. "This Is It" was released a couple of weeks before the movie, on October 12th. The single included background vocals by the Jackson brothers, added after Michael's death, to complete the song which plays to the film's closing credits. The accompanying album contained songs that inspired the movie. The first disc contained the original versions of songs from the movie, in the order they appear in the movie. Concluding the first disc are two versions of the "This Is It" single, one being an orchestral version. The second disc is made up of demo versions of some of Michael's classic hits and includes a reading of a poem, "Planet Earth". The booklet included in the *This Is It* soundtrack set features photos of Michael from his last rehearsals.

Immediately following the release of the new single on the internet and for radio airplay, it was learned the song was not so new after all. Nor was it written entirely by Michael. It was co-written by Michael with Paul Anka back in 1983 with the title "I Never Heard" and was intended for inclusion on an Anka album. Other sources said the song was recorded during the *Dangerous* sessions. With the single's release, Anka threatened to sue the estate, but the administrators realized the mistake and cut Anka in for a share of the profits.

The estate also put together a touring exhibit of memorabilia. Michael Jackson: The Official LIFETIME Collection opened in Japan's Tokyo Tower in the spring of 2010. Certainly the most impressive collection of Michael Jackson memorabilia to be displayed, it even included the five ton, 24 karat gold engraved sign that welcomed visitors to Neverland Valley Ranch.

"Michael Jackson: A Musical Legacy", a special

memorabilia exhibit opened in October at the Grammy Museum in Los Angeles replacing an earlier exhibit, "Michael Jackson: HIStyle" which opened in February 2009. A temporary memorial exhibit had also been erected just following his death. Showcased in the exhibit were a black fedora, a couple of beaded gloves, an autographed USA for Africa sweatshirt, original handwritten lyrics to "Beat It", and the white suit he wore for the *Thriller* album cover shot. A pair of gold knee and shin guards, designed by Michael Bush and Dennis Tompkins, were also displayed in the exhibit. Some of these shin guards worn by Michael were made of 24 karat gold. Several bejeweled military style jackets, designed by Bill Whitten, were on display including the dark blue and gold number he wore for the presentation of his star on Hollywood's Walk of Fame. It was noted the jacket weighed close to fifteen pounds. Monitors played footage of each of Michael's appearances on the Grammys. An extra highlight was a lighted dance floor with tiles that light up at your step allowing you to pretend you are in the "Billie Jean" video. A separate listening room ran each of his videos nonstop. Many of the items were on loan to the museum courtesy of Michael Jackson while several others were courtesy of John Branca.

Michael Bush commemorated his time working with Jackson in his book, *King of Style: Dressing Michael Jackson* in which he gives a delightful sneak peak behind the seams of costuming Jackson for decades. Bush's partner, Dennis Tompkins, died in December 2011.

Another Jackson exhibit, "Michael Jackson: the Official Exhibition" was unveiled in London at the O2 bubble. The Rock and Roll Hall of Fame in Cleveland, Ohio paid special tribute to the King of Pop with a display as did Moscow and Hong Kong.

A project that was in the works prior to Michael's death was an elaborate coffee table book based on his life and including never before seen photographs. The book, the *Official Michael Jackson Opus,* was promoted as including groundbreaking technology that allowed the use of a computer to bring images of Michael to life on a page, though this feature was delayed and promised to be delivered later. And then it was delayed some more. Then not delivered at all. The project had already been approved by Michael and he had had a meeting on the project just three days before his death. He was said to look just fine, no signs of any problems. The original plan had the Opus including coverage of the London O2 shows. The amended plan had friends who knew and worked with Michael contributing a line, paragraph or essay to be included in the volume along with many photographs and samples of Michael's own artwork. The four hundred page book was released in December with copies available for pre-order months in advance.

The photographs were beautiful and the essays contributed were equally beautiful and touching. Those contributing essays for the special tribute book ranged from fellow artists and celebrities that he had worked with and befriended, Smokey Robinson, Lionel Richie, Arsenio Hall, the industry greats that he worked with and studied, Quincy Jones, Berry Gordy, Suzanne de Passe and Tony Jones (also from Motown), Teddy Riley, Jimmy Jam, Travis Payne, John Landis, John Singleton, Spike Lee, Ken Kragen and Frank Dileo. Others included artists Michael had commissioned artwork from and studied art with, photographers that worked with him at different periods of his career, and an especially touching note from a recipient of one of the Heal the World care packages airlifted to Sarajevo.

A deal to re-release Michael's autobiography was made that featured a new introduction by Berry Gordy and an afterword by his original editor, Shaye Areheart. Gordy echoed much of the same sentiment he so beautifully expressed at the memorial service, calling Michael, "simply, the Greatest Entertainer That Ever Lived". Areheart recounted her days of meeting with Michael to work on the project and concluded, "...He was an extraordinary man. I have never met anyone like him, and I doubt I ever will."

Another book in release at the time was from Michael's former spiritual advisor and friend, Rabbi Shmuley Boteach. Culled from over thirty hours of audio taped interviews with Michael made in 2001 and 2002, *The Michael Jackson Tapes* were made with the intention of publication. Michael was keenly interested in repairing his reputation, gaining the respect of authorities and using his celebrity to help heal families in an effort dubbed Heal the Kids. The aim was to encourage parents to have dinner with their children, read bedtime stories and promote healthy family life. With his subsequent arrest in 2003, the idea of publication was put on the back burner. Following his death, it was thought that people were willing to judge him more charitably and publication of the tapes seemed more viable.

Throughout his extended association and friendship with Michael Jackson, Boteach repeatedly notes that he did not believe Michael was gay, "I never saw anything that would lead me to that conclusion. Michael never hinted that there were any men around to whom he felt attracted and I never saw any man who could possibly have been Michael's lover." Michael always expressed an attraction to women, but did grow to distrust them, seeing them as using their sexuality to manipulate men. He believed most women would marry him for his money.

Boteach also notes that many hours of these tapes were made at Neverland, even at a period of time when Gavin Arvizo and his family were guests at the ranch. He never saw any improper conduct from Michael and never suspected such. "Much of the world came to regard Michael as a pedophile. I never saw anything that would even remotely have me accept that conclusion. I never believed the allegations against him brought by the family of Gavin Arvizo".

In speaking of his treatment by the press and all he has been subjected to, Michael sadly and prophetically notes, "And anybody else would be dead as a junkie right now, who'd been through what I've been through." Boteach expresses concern over whether Michael could have been saved and speculates that perhaps being found guilty in 2005 and serving a prison sentence would have been perhaps the only chance for Michael to be saved. That seems more than a little alarming, an unjustified prison sentence to clean someone up?

Michael speaks of his abusive relationship with his father and his ongoing efforts to try and win his approval. He sought love and affection that he did not get from his father by honing his craft and becoming enormously successful in his career, to get love from his millions of fans around the world. Sadly, it was not enough, he felt isolated by his fame. Someone once noted, he never sought worship, he longed for love.

Other tributes to Michael abounded for the next several months. The Soul Train awards honored Michael Jackson as the Entertainer of the Year. The MTV Video Music Awards were started off with a grand tribute to the King of Pop that included his kid sister, Janet. Her entourage of dancers included well known dancers and choreographers many of whom had worked with Michael, Janet or both for years. Travis Payne, who should have been in London with Michael at the time of the VMA's for the O2 shows took part in the tribute along with Dangerous and HIStory tour alumnus Cris Judd and choreographer and friend of Michael's since he was a child, Wade Robson.

The VMA telecast started off with remembrances of Michael Jackson by Madonna. She spoke for several minutes recounting the parallels in their lives but noted that Michael was robbed of his childhood and the tremendous impact that had on his life. She called him, "one of the greatest talents the world has ever known". She described his indelible style, "The way he moved had the elegance of Fred Astaire and packed the punch of Muhammad Ali. His music had an extra layer of inexplicable magic that just didn't make you want to dance, but actually made you believe you could fly, dare to dream, be anything that you wanted to be. Because that is what heroes do and Michael Jackson was a hero."   She also recalled the time in 1991 she tried to get to know Michael better and invited him out on a date. He accepted. Madonna tried to get him to do things he didn't seem to allow himself to do, "eat french fries, drink wine, have dessert and say bad words." When she heard of his death, she described that she felt she "had abandon him, that *we* had abandon him" being too busy passing judgment. She concluded that there "will never be anyone like him – he was a king."   She told of her sons, then ages four and nine being completely obsessed with Michael Jackson. "There's a whole lot of crotch grabbing and moonwalking going on in my house". That thought brought a smile to Jermaine's face, seated in the front row. "Michael Jackson was a human being, but dammit he was a king. Long live the King."

Scenes from the "Thriller" video appeared on screen as the dancers took the stage dressed in various well known Michael Jackson costumes recreating what can only now be called the "Thriller" dance. The last Michael Jackson song performed in the tribute was "Scream". On cue of her lines in the song, a glass partition shattered and Janet stepped on stage and sang her lines in the duet. The video footage of the dance sequence now had Janet erased, and she once again performed the steps along side her brother's video image. The performance ended with a picture on the screen of Michael looking down on his sister and undoubtedly very proudly.

In response to the resolution brought to congress by Representative Sheila Jackson Lee from Texas (presented by Jackson Lee at the public memorial service) House Speaker Nancy Pelosi put the kibosh on the idea noting that congressional members are able "to express their sympathy or their praise any time that they wish, I don't think it's necessary for us to have a resolution." Jackson Lee said she would try again.

On what would have been Michael's 51st birthday, Spike Lee threw a Michael Jackson Bash in Brooklyn's Prospect Park and the day was designated as Michael Jackson Day. Lee planned a similar bash to mark Michael's 52nd birthday a year later, looking to make it an annual event. Lee further planned to pay tribute to Michael Jackson with a movie titled *Brooklyn Loves Michael Jackson*. At this same time, Diana Ross' son, Evan, celebrated his 21st birthday with a Michael Jackson themed party in West Hollywood. Michael Jackson was Evan's godfather.

In another tribute effort, fans were invited to register to be a dot that would be used to create a portrait of Michael Jackson. Each dot, registered to a MJ fan, would be placed in the mosaic by artist David Ilan. On April 1, 2010, a Michael Jackson Tribute Event was held at the Debbie Reynolds dance studio in Hollywood, California.

Among those that had placed their dot on the portrait were Jermaine Jackson, Diana Ross and her son Evan, Gladys Knight, Tatiana Yvonne (Thumbtzen), Jesse Jackson, nurse Cherilyn Lee, biographer J. Randy Taraborrelli, researcher Lisa Campbell, impersonator Frederick Henry, Teddy Riley, Gotham Chopra, and This Is It collaborators Dorian Holley, Jonathan Moffett, Travis Payne, Judith Hill, Ken Stacey, Michael Bearden and Tommy Organ. "The Way You Make Me Feel" co-star Tatiana Yvonne called him "the love of my life." The very first dot placed on the portrait is registered to Michael. The second dot is assigned to Prince Michael Jackson Jr. Dots three and four are registered to Paris and Blanket.

As part of her fall premiere week, Oprah Winfrey dedicated a show to her memories of Michael Jackson and her reaction to his passing. Footage of the famed 1993 Oprah interview was interspersed with Oprah's comments on memories of that time. Michael's children appeared in a later edition of *Oprah* as part of an interview with Katherine and Joseph, in which we learned from Paris, that Michael made "the best french toast in the whole world."

Oprah later landed an interview with Lisa Marie Presley with Michael as the sole topic. Lisa shared that for years after their marriage ended, they remained close and their relationship continued to be on again, off again. She told Oprah she very much loved Michael when they divorced but she saw the drugs and the doctors moving in and it scared her, reminding her of the circumstances surrounding her father's downfall and eventual death when she was a young girl. Lisa spoke of a long conversation she had with Michael in 2005. He tried to get her back. She felt distant and "indifferent", something she now regretted. She wanted to save him. "I know that it's naïve to think that I could have, but I wanted to. Had I made a phone call, had I stopped being so shut off from him, had I just said, 'how are you?' I really regret that I didn't."

October 2009, the popular dance contest show, "Dancing with the Stars" aired a special tribute to Michael Jackson. Dancers performed familiar choreography to "Thriller", and danced to "I Want You Back" and "Man in the Mirror". Katherine, LaToya and Jermaine were seated in the audience to take in the tribute personally. Michael was also "gleed" when an episode of the popular musical show, *Glee* paid tribute to him.

To celebrate Halloween and pay tribute to the King of Pop, many groups around the country and the world performed the "Thriller" dance and participated in zombie walks. Thrill the World organized simultaneous "Thriller" dances around the globe. Other cities across the county were vying to break the world record for the largest zombie walk. Thrill the World creator Ines Markelle said, "Now that Michael is gone, there are a lot of people who have jumped on as a way to honor the great artist that he was." In excess of four hundred events were planned in cities around the world, twelve different locations in China were planning on performing the "Thriller" dance as well as locations in Russia, Mexico and England. By October, Yahoo listed Michael Jackson among the top ten most searched Halloween costumes on yahoo.com.

The World Awards Media Save the World Awards were held

in Vienna, Austria in July. Jermaine attended and accepted an award on Michael's behalf. Save the World Awards had already set out to honor Michael this year, they had honored him previously in 2003. Jermaine called the award "a special moment for Michael, a special moment for his legacy," and performed "Smile" at the award presentation.

More details of Michael's life and his physical condition were shared by Michael's longtime dermatologist, Dr. Arnold Klein, in an appearance on *Larry King Live*. Klein confirmed that he did in fact diagnose Michael with vitiligo. He had a severe case that resulted in speckled skin. He used creams to destroy the pigment in the rest of his skin. Dr. Klein told King that Michael did not wish to be white. He used the creams to even his skin tone only. The condition made his skin very sensitive to sunlight, so he wore hats and used umbrellas. Dr. Klein also confirmed that Michael did have lupus, which frequently goes along with vitiligo. The hair loss he experienced at the front of his scalp was a result of the lupus.

Michael had been seeing Dr. Klein regularly in the last weeks, had been in the office on the Monday before his death, was in a good mood and was dancing in the office. Dr. Klein said further that he had never seen any needle marks and that Michael was not emaciated. Dr. Klein called Michael the greatest entertainer and the most generous person he had ever known.

Dr. Klein then raised eyebrows when Larry King asked about reports that Klein is actually the biological father of Michael's oldest two children. Klein only responded that he didn't know for sure. Apparently Klein is another individual Michael had asked at one point to donate sperm.

Nearing his retirement, Larry King counted down the Top 25 Moments on his program with the top five spots voted on by viewers. The "Death of a Legend" came in at number three on the list. The only two stories ranking higher were the inauguration of President Obama and the tragedy of September 11, 2001.

Ebay became awash with Michael Jackson memorabilia, with all things Jackson suddenly in high demand. A California driver's license, which expired in 1989, with the Hayvenhurst address, was listed for $500,000. Fashions were also once again being influenced by the King of Pop. Many runway shows and department stores featured military styled jackets. Catalog companies highlighted "Pop Icon" jackets and the Franklin Mint offered a "Pop Icon" charm bracelet.

Along with various auctions of memorabilia, TV specials, booming record sales, and the upcoming movie, also enjoying renewed popularity were Michael Jackson impersonators. During the difficult times in Jackson's life, many impersonators were forced to find work overseas, where Michael Jackson maintained tremendous popularity, or they were forced to leave the business. Now they were suddenly in high demand in the U.S. as well. Frederick Henry, a Michael Jackson impersonator since 1988, and full time since 1995, had pursued work overseas during the difficult times, now headlined American Superstars, a lineup of impersonators at the Stratosphere in Las Vegas. As his popularity soared, the casino increased security to keep fans from mobbing him after the shows. Special "meet and greet" passes were sold for fans to meet Henry following the performances. Henry, who met Jackson on three occasions, definitely mastered Jackson's moves and encouraged his fellow "Michaels" on a blog, "now is the time to shine again...It's been a long time for some of us Michaels to survive." His counterparts committed to step up and practice more and sing better to pay the best possible tribute to the greatest entertainer of all time. Henry went on to headline a Michael Jackson tribute show in Spain.

Who's Bad, a tribute band started in 2003 by Vamsi Tadepali, features two lead singers that alternate during shows performing sets of MJ favorites. Taalib York copied the look as well as the moves of his idol who he started imitating at age six. York never got to meet his idol but did get to speak with him once, an experience he describes as "amazing". Joseph Bell concentrates more on the voice, handling most of the ballads in the show, including his favorite, "Human Nature". The group earned high praise from Frank Dileo, "The show was great... Michael would have been proud." An earlier incarnation of the group featured E'Casanova as the frontman. Casonova stills performs as Jackson.

The premier performer is unquestionably Michael Firestone, who began studying the moves of the King of Pop when he was six years old. He mastered his moves flawlessly, thanks to the pause button on his VCR, and was able to come incredibly close to duplicating his looks. His real name is Michael Joseph Firestone, named after his grandfather who they called coincidentally, Papa Joe. The parallels in their lives do not stop there. Also a devoted father of three, a talented musician and artist, Firestone's speaking voice and mannerisms are remarkably like Jackson's, conveying the much the same graciousness and sensitivity. Along with an affinity for video games and superheroes, they also share a love of animals. Firestone's own menagerie includes dogs, a Bengal cat, hamsters (which he is afraid of), rabbits, and a python named Slash, with plans to add a monkey, though not a chimp.

Sadly he never got to see Jackson perform live, he held fourth row tickets for This Is It. He did see him in person once in Las Vegas, and they had a brief exchange. He also had a long phone call from the King of Pop after coming in second in a songwriting contest. During their chat, Firestone said "you know I do a tribute show to you" to which Jackson replied a non-convincing "Sure, of course". Keystrokes could be heard letting Firestone know he was searching for him online. After viewing his performance of "Billie Jean" he offered Firestone a couple of notes; that he was kicking with the wrong leg and needed to face the audience at a particular point in the performance. Firestone also shares Jackson work ethic, "If you go home after a show and have the energy to go out and party afterward, you're not working hard enough."

Firestone loves what he does and finds inspiration from Jackson in "everything – his eyes, his hair, the highwater pants with the white socks, his overall style, and his heart." "Billie Jean" and "Thriller" he describes as "fun to do" with other favorites being

"Speed Demon" for its rock sound and "Stranger in Moscow", "I could sing that song all day long." The drill is described by Firestone (and some of the This Is It dancers) as some of the most challenging choreography with the whipping of the hand and walking with one foot in front of the other for "Beat It" - being "more difficult than it looks".

Firestone's incredible attention to *every* detail shows in his performances. He created and toured with his Moonwalker show, before going on to headline MJ Live in Las Vegas and building his own all new show, promising, "…you ain't seen nothin' yet!" I believe him. Seeing a Firestone show will give fans who were able to see Jackson live a chance to relive it and give those who never saw a Jackson concert a chance to experience the excitement of his live performances. Firestone does the King of Pop proud.

Special previews of *This Is It* were held at midnight on Oct 27th with the regular showings premiering on October 28th. The Los Angeles premier at the Nokia Theater was attended by family, friends and colleagues like Berry Gordy and including those who worked with Michael in creating the shows, Michael Bearden and Kenny Ortega. The Jackson brothers attended the premier, but Tito elected to only walk the red carpet with his brothers and avoided entering the theater and watching the last days of his younger brother's life, feeling he just wasn't ready yet. Katherine, none of his sisters, and Michael's children did not attend, but the kids did view the film in private. A memorial wall was set up outside for fans to sign. This was going to be big.

37

This is it, here I stand
I'm the light of the world
I feel grand

"This Is It"
- Michael Jackson, Paul Anka

Sony released fifteen thousand prints of *This Is It* in ninety-nine countries for the largest simultaneous global premier ever for a music film. Box office receipts from opening day and through the first weekend topped $101 million worldwide, setting motion picture history as the highest grossing concert film of all time. The overwhelming response prompted the limited two week run to be immediately extended throughout the busy movie-going Thanksgiving weekend. *This Is It* ended up grossing over $262 million worldwide, making it the biggest grossing documentary or concert movie of all time.

 Kenny Ortega did a brilliant job of piecing together the film to give a look at Michael's creative genius, his stunning performances and his attention to detail. When first approached by Randy Phillips to do the film Ortega felt he was not up to the task, he was devastated over Michael's loss and could not think of taking on this overwhelming project. But, he relented thinking it was his responsibility to put this together, who else should do it? Thank goodness he did. Without Ortega masterminding this project, we would not have had this last wonderful look at the King of Pop. Ortega and his team worked seven days a week from the end of July to early October when the film was turned over to Sony.

 New film footage shot especially for the concerts were showcased with Michael looking like he just stepped off the set of the "Smooth Criminal" short film, being placed in scenes of old movies with Rita Hayworth and Humphrey Bogart. New scenes for "Thriller" were shot, which while it seems like a horrible idea to try and re-do "Thriller" the new footage was amazing, with additional spoken spooky lyrics from Vincent Price. A short film introducing "Earth Song" was included in the movie with Michael's narration on his love of trees and the planet and his efforts to bring awareness to the urgent need for action. Other effects lined up for the show included illusions - Michael loved magic - pyrotechnics, aerialists, and a grand finale that looked to be truly grand. The rest of the film gives a sense of how much of a central role Michael played in

"This Is It"

directing *every* aspect of the show. It offers a look at another side of the performer few have seen before. Working behind the scenes with the musicians, dancers and singers giving direction for all aspects of the show. Michael chose the dancers, worked with them on the choreography, worked with the musicians on getting the exact sound he wanted, contributed to stage direction, and offered comments and insight on the lighting. The descriptions Michael offered on how he wanted the music were less technical than one might expect. The slower pace for the top of "The Way You Make Me Feel" is described as "like you're draggin' yourself outta bed".

The show was to open with a spectacular special effect. "Light man" a robot looking creature would appear holding a lighted ball, all reflecting various video images. The ball was to float out over the audience while pieces of the light man's outer shell broke away revealing the star of the show. Other effects lined up included a giant electronic spider that was to crawl onto stage for "Thriller", from which Michael would emerge. A bulldozer was going to be driven on stage for "Earth Song", fire effects and aerialists were planned for "Dirty Diana" which was going to be an especially grand production and somewhat risqué at least as far as Michael's performances typically were concerned.

At the show's opening, after light man is revealed to be Michael, he was going to stand still on stage and drink in the crowd's reaction, reminiscent of the jawdroppingly cool opening of the Dangerous tour performances. Music Director Michael Bearden started a pool to guess how many minutes he would stand there, motionless, the first night. He picked six minutes and the rest of the cast put in their bets on whether it would be longer or shorter than six minutes.

Technologies were being used, and in some cases especially developed, for his costumes. The costumes were designed by long time Michael associates, Michael Bush and Dennis Tompkins with Zaldy Goco. Some costumes would actually have lighted elements incorporated into them, and others would have video sewn into the fabric, allowing moving pictures to be shown on his costume. His costume for "Billie Jean" used technology developed with electronics company Philips. The costume followed the look usually associated for the song, black highwater tuxedo pants, black sequined jacket and white sequined socks and glove. This time, his socks would light up, either in a single color or in a rainbow of colors. The light would then travel up the tuxedo stripe on his pants, through his jacket to his glove. Designers worked with Kevlar to produce a "Beat It" jacket that would actually catch fire and burn after Michael took it off and threw it to the ground. "Let it burn, and lights out."

Thousands of sequins, beads and crystals were used on many of his costumes. The jacket designed for the anthem songs, "We are the World" and "Heal the World", was covered in beads, crystals and sequins sewn in patterns and techniques representing many different areas of the world. Designers took five days to direct where each stud was to be placed on the leather jacket for "Black or White", which ended up weighing ten pounds. Zaldy worked to create shoes for Michael that would mimic the fit of his lovable old loafers exactly. He said they were the only shoes he could dance in.

The show's ending, called "MJ Air" also promised to be phenomenal. On the 3D screen, a plane would taxi up, Michael was to walk up a flight of stairs from the stage to the door of the plane that actually opened out of the screen. With the door closed, the 3D plane would taxi and take off seemingly over the heads of the audience while Michael simply exited the stage from behind the giant movie screen. The 3D screen depicting the airplane landing had people ducking beneath its wings.

One of the coolest effects lined up for the shows was actually quite simple and borrowed from the HIStory tour. It consisted of the stool and small suitcase for the set up for "Billie Jean". After pulling from the case the familiar black beaded jacket, hat and single white glove, he would order the stool and case to disappear, with it being lowered on one of the elevators in the stage. Then he would order the spotlight to move at his command, glide with his impeccable style and grace into that spotlight and rip into "Billie Jean". For the rehearsal included in *This Is It* the stool and costume pieces were not used, but what looked like an impromptu run through of "Billie Jean" left his entourage of young dancers in awe. Michael's reaction was only, "Well you get a feel for it". It would have been nice if he'd had a hat available and if somebody would have thought to snatch his sunglasses away from him. Of all the expense and ingenuity poured into developing the technologies needed to bring the extravagant effects to reality, Ortega realized the most awe inspiring special effect of the whole show was Michael himself. Several songs in the show, "Human Nature" and "Billie Jean" among them were set up to be just Michael with his audience. Ortega added, "He was in charge like an old fashioned entertainer. Technology didn't run the show, Michael ran the show. And when he stopped-you watched. And you held your breath. And that's what made Michael Jackson, Michael Jackson on stage and why he was different from anybody else you ever went to see in concert." N This point is proven in the response to the film. Without the special effects in place, the specialized lighting and the 3D short films, audiences were awed by his sheer talent.

Even though he mentions in the film that he is saving his voice and is just warming up, his vocals are nothing less than perfect. He does not sing all parts of all the songs, focusing instead on staging, choreography or the musicians at times. He does cut lose and sings full out on "I Just Can't Stop Loving You" where he is egged on by the dancers and crew. He admonishes them afterward saying, "Don't make me sing out, now". His gestures to duet partner Judith Hill here are delightful. He issues a reminder at the end of "I'll Be There" that he is saving his throat then sounds incredible finishing the classic. Good thing he cautioned us that he was saving his voice or we might have never known. His vocal work on "Human Nature" is priceless, if you can get past the silly shoulders in the jacket he is wearing.

His moves are just as polished as they were twenty years earlier. Ortega mentioned that the dancers, who were literally half

Michael's age and younger, were struggling to keep up with him. "The dancers who were less than half his age, I mean we're talking 18-21 year old dancers, 22 year old dancers – Michael is 50 on that stage. These were 11 of 5,700 kids from all over the world that were the best dancers on the planet that we had picked to be on the show and they were brought to their knees watching Michael Jackson during the rehearsal."

Michael does look thin, even for him, but his voice, moves, and energy all seem to be at peak levels, proving "It ain't too hard for me to jam", quieting the naysayers that were convinced he no longer had what it took to perform. Michael was as magical as ever and would have certainly made, or surpassed, his goal to show his audience "talent they've never seen before." Ortega told *Entertainment Weekly* magazine that the last two nights he "kicked it up a notch and took our breath away."

Very few errors or missteps are included in the film which show Michael always being very gracious, "That is why we rehearse". It was part of the agreement to do the film that he not be depicted in a negative light, but he has always been described as being enormously professional, polite and gracious when working and this film certainly illustrates that. Suggestions or critiques he offers are "with love, l- o-v-e, love." The only thing close to a complaint comes when he is having difficulty adjusting to his ear piece, something he had never used early in his career. He complains it feels like "a fist is being shoved in your ear".

Some songs are performed in nearly finished form, while

others are just being "blocked" or being performed for a sound check. *This Is It* is a hybrid of a concert film and a documentary giving audiences a taste of the spectacular production in store for his fans and an awe inspiring look at the King of Pop creating his magic. The film reiterates how involved Michael was in *every* detail of the show. He was involved in the sound, the choreography, the short films shot especially for the shows, the staging, the effects, lighting, *everything*.

The final song showcased in the film is "Man in the Mirror" with Michael doing what is referred to as a sound check, but what comes off as a rousing rendition of the song that again blows away the younger performers lucky enough to be witness to it. The film ends abruptly with the end of this song.

Though footage does exist of the band, dancers, singers, crew learning on June 25th the awful news that Michael had been taken to the hospital, it is deliberately left out of the film, though a brief shot was included of the group gathering in prayer for Michael in the film's trailer. In remembering this awful day for *Entertainment Weekly,* Ortega fought back tears, "Every once in a while I still have a moment where it's difficult for me. People were falling to their knees, walking in circles, holding on to each other, wailing. It was like a bomb dropped."

Besides wanting his kids to see him perform live and coming back for the sake of his beloved fans, Michael had a higher purpose for doing these shows. He had positive messages to share about his concern for the planet. Kenny Ortega described Michael as "A new

Michael. He was 12 years a dad, a businessman, an entertainer's entertainer. That wonderful, innocent part of Michael was ever present, but there was another Michael there, with more worldly concerns. He had deeper reasons for wanting to do this than I've ever seen for him to want to do anything else before". Choreographer Travis Payne said, "This was to be the biggest platform possible for him to re-familiarize the messages that had been in his music and films for years... Michael was going to remind everyone of the job we have to complete with regard to reversing the damage to the planet."

His kids did play a large part in him wanting to put together the biggest and best show ever. Ortega remembered Michael telling him, 'Kenny, my kids are so fascinated with what I've been doing my whole life, they're like superfans. So I want to share with my children now that they're old enough to appreciate it and I'm still young enough to do it." There were even rumors that young Prince Michael Joseph Jackson might join Dad on stage for at least a few of the performances.

Frank Dileo later said, "I was lucky enough to work on Michael's Victory and Bad tours, which were two of his best. I never saw Michael work harder than he did in preparing for This Is It. He had that spark in his eye, and that glow on his face, that I had seen so many times before. He was completely dedicated to creating something extraordinary that not only he would be proud of, but his fans and especially his children would be proud of."

It was unanimous among those working with Michael at

these rehearsals that he was looking, sounding and moving better than ever. Some however became concerned about his stamina when he began to lose some weight. Michael Bush, Dennis Tompkins and Karen Faye approached AEG's Randy Philips with their concerns that he might not be physically ready for a series of performances. Philips hired someone who's sole responsibility was to make sure Michael Jackson ate. He was dropping weight as rehearsals continued, something that is evident in the rehearsal footage. This now makes the AEG employee, Miko Brando, Frank Dileo and Kai Chase all making sure Michael Jackson was eating.

It is debatable whether or not Michael would have wanted this rehearsal footage released, he was an extreme perfectionist and would only want the most polished, perfect look at his show to be made publicly available. He would undoubtedly however been very proud to once again dominate a new frontier, setting new records around the world for his theatrical release. He had longed to make films a bigger part of his life and now he had the number one documentary/concert film of all time. He would have certainly been pleased with the reaction to the film.

This Is It enjoyed widespread praise from moviegoers and, unbelievably, the critics. Moviegoers who described themselves as lukewarm Jackson fans came away with a deeper appreciation for Michael's talent. In a review in *The Arizona Republic*, Ed Masley wrote, "Michael Jackson wanted it to be the greatest show on Earth. And judging from the countless scenes in *This Is It* of Jackson reconnecting with the artistry that made him one of pop's essential icons in his 80's prime, his moves as fluid as the day he introduced the moonwalk to the masses on that legendary Motown special, there can be no doubt that, had he lived to see it through, that string of 50 dates in London would have been just that." Another review concluded, "It demonstrates that Jackson wasn't as detached from reality as we all figured he was. It also reminds us, sadly, that he was ready to reclaim his spot as the world's greatest entertainer." Mark Bego, author of a couple of books on Jackson, reviewed the film and concluded, "It is as if the past 16 years of tabloid headlines are being eclipsed by his sheer talent and musical magic."

The release of the movie on DVD in January 2010 added to the coffers of the estate, taking over the number one spot on the DVD sales charts and setting records for first week sales of a music film. The DVD release in Japan set sales records, becoming Japan's best selling DVD of all time. The DVD set includes ninety minutes of extra footage in the form of two documentaries: "Staging the Return: Beyond the Show" and "Staging the Return: The Adventure Begins" with great behind the scenes looks at the staging, effects, costumes, and interviews with the band, dancers and vocalists.

The *This Is It* soundtrack album was as big a hit as the movie, taking over the top spot on the *Billboard* Hot 200 album chart selling 373,100 copies the first week, not including "significant sales from non-traditional retailers." It was also the number one album on the R&B Album chart and Soundtrack album chart. The Rolling Stones were the last act to have a simultaneous number one album and documentary film with the *Sticky Fingers* album and the movie

Michael Jackson: The Complete Story of the King of Pop

Gimmie Shelter. *This Is It* became Michael Jackson's sixth chart topping album and earned his biggest opening sales since debuting with *HIStory* with 391,000 in sales in 1995. Michael Jackson was now tied with Garth Brooks at number three on the list of artists who have spent the most weeks at number one on the album chart with fifty-one weeks. Only Elvis Presley (67 weeks) and the Beatles (132 weeks) have spent more weeks on top of the album charts. *This Is it* sat on top of the album charts around the world; Canada, Japan, France, Italy, Belgium, Holland, Turkey, New Zealand, Hong Kong, Korea, Philippines, Singapore, Taiwan, Thailand, the Mid East and Columbia. It debuted in the top five virtually everywhere else. The week of November 20, 2009, while *This Is It* occupied the number one spot on the Hot 200 album chart, *Number Ones* continued its long reign at the top of the Pop Catalog album chart. Michael Jackson continued to set records around the world.

38

I am forever, I am forever
We are forever, we are forever
I am your friend through thick and thin
We need each other we'll never part
Our love is from the heart

"Best of Joy"
- Michael Jackson

In her first television interview since Michael's death, Janet Jackson talked with Robin Roberts in November 2009. The interview was to promote her new, less than originally titled greatest hits CD, *Number Ones* and her upcoming book, *True You* about her ongoing weight battle. Much of the interview however centered on Michael. Janet explained she did know of Michael's drug problem and tried to intervene, but he would not cooperate and you cannot help someone if they do not want to be helped, "You can't make them drink the water." She also spoke of her belief that Dr. Conrad Murray was responsible for Michael's death. "He was the one doing the administering... I think he is responsible." She said she thinks of Michael everyday and that she found it too soon and too painful to watch *This Is It* and did not know if she would ever see the film. *True You* was dedicated simply and beautifully, "To Mike".

Promoting her new film, *Why Did I Get Married Too"*, Janet made an appearance on *The Oprah Winfrey Show* where she further discussed the family's efforts to help Michael. "People think we were in denial but we weren't. We tried intervention several times. He was very much in denial - he didn't think he had a problem". She had become so emotional during one attempt to confront him she had to leave the room. "A lot of the relationships I've been in, they've had issues with addiction. It's difficult when you see it. (I) recognize it so quickly because I've dealt with it in past relationships."

On November 10th, Motown released some previously unreleased Jackson Five music. *I Want You Back! Unreleased Masters* is a collection of twelve songs recorded from 1969 to 1974. "Buttercup", collaboration with Stevie Wonder and an extended version of "Dancing Machine" are among the uncovered tracks included on the new album along with alternate versions of "Never Can Say Goodbye" and "ABC" that, after forty years of hearing the original versions, just sound screwed up. A reissue of *Jackson 5 Ultimate Christmas Album* hit stores the same day.

Another Motown album marked the 50th anniversary of Motown. An online vote was held in June and July to choose the fan favorites to be included on the compilation album, *Fanthology*. There were five songs total from the group and Michael on the album. Fans were also asked to vote for their favorite Motown artist of all time, the J5 came in on top.

Julien's Auction's held a Music Icons auction of rock and roll in November, 2009. Items from Elvis Presley, the Beatles, the Rolling Stones, Madonna, Prince, and many other artists were hitting the auction block along with over eighty items from the King of Pop; socks, gloves, the mold used to make his fangs for the "Thriller" video, a car, and a couple of pencil drawings. The sequined glove he wore in *Motown 25* was the biggest selling item coming in at $420,000, including taxes and fees with a bid from a buyer in Hong Kong. The pre-auction estimate for the glove was $40,000 to $60,000. The black jacket worn in "Bad" brought in a winning bid of $225,000, soaring past the pre auction estimate of $8,000. A black fedora brought in $22,000. Its pre-auction estimate was only $2,000. The glove worn in *Motown 25* was given by Michael to Commodore's member Walter "Clyde" Orange. Following his performance on the special, Clyde asked Michael for his autograph. Michael handed him the glove instead. Orange put the glove on the auction block saying, "the glove was too significant to keep…just for the world to see it, that means the world to me". Orange had hoped the glove would find a home at the Rock and Roll Hall of Fame or similar institution.

Michael Jackson: The Complete Story of the King of Pop

Premiering in December was a new A&E reality show featuring the Jackson family, "The Jack5ons: A Family Dynasty." The show centered on Jermaine, Tito, Jackie and Marlon, who each also served as co-executive producers. Randy chose not to be a part of it. The first hour of the planned six episode show was shot prior to the family tragedy on June 25th and included footage tacked on the end of the brothers recalling how they learned the tragic news.

They also attended a performance of "Thriller Live" at the Lyric Theatre. The performances earned rave reviews from each of the brothers who found it very emotional, Jackie being brought to tears. The stage production based on Michael's life was created by Adrian Grant, a long time Michael Jackson fan and associate. Grant began by publishing "Off the Wall" magazine in Great Britain and hosting the annual MJ Days (which Michael actually attended once), published a chronology of his life, *Michael Jackson: A Visual Documentary,* (for which I served as a contributing researcher) then went on to produce the *Thriller Live* shows. *Thriller Live* grew great crowds with engagements being extended due to heavy demand.

In December, 2009, the FBI released files it had been keeping on Michael Jackson from 1992 to 2005. The information was released in response to a request from the Associated Press under the Freedom of Information Act. All in all these 333 pages from the FBI files covering years of investigation of Michael Jackson resulted in no big revelations whatsoever and they never garnered any evidence of wrongdoing on his part. Tom Mesereau said these FBI files prove once again that Michael Jackson was not guilty of any wrongdoing. "He was not a criminal, and he was not a pedophile. The fact that so many agencies investigated him and couldn't find anything proves he was completely innocent."

For the American Music Awards, Michael had five posthumous nominations. As the AMA nominations are based on sales and airplay, he need not have released new material in the past eligibility period. *Number Ones* was on pace to become the biggest selling album of the year despite having been released in 2003. He was chosen as the Favorite Male Artist in both the Pop/Rock and Soul/R&B categories and *Number Ones* was chosen as the Favorite Album in both the Pop and R&B categories. Artist of the Year, the only category in which he lost, went to Taylor Swift. In her acceptance remarks she remembered the King of Pop, "To even be mentioned in a category with Michael Jackson, who we will miss and love forever, is an unimaginable honor." The broadcast was kicked off with a performance by Janet Jackson with a medley of her hits from her own greatest hits album, *Number Ones*.

Only two of the categories in which he won were presented on air and they provided bittersweet moments. Selena Gomez and This Is It guitarist Orianthi Panagaris presented the award for Favorite Soul/R&B Male. Jermaine accepted the award on Michael's behalf, dressed in a dark shinny suit and one white sequined glove. Three of his sons joined him on stage. It was Michael's fourth win in this category.

In accepting the award for Favorite Pop/Rock Male for his

brother, Jermaine reiterated Michael's message, "The message that Michael had will live on forever. He saw good in everyone and he wanted everyone to do good. He always started with love." These four wins gave Michael Jackson a total of twenty-three AMA's making him the most honored artist in AMA history. He also now held the record for the most posthumous AMA awards.

Another posthumous award came in October where Michael was named as the recipient of the Thurgood Marshall Award. Marlon traveled to New York with Steve Manning to accept the award on his brother's behalf.

For the annual year in review specials, countdowns, lists, etc, Michael figured prominently. He was the year's most searched subject on Google, Yahoo and Bing. MSNBC ranked the death of Michael Jackson as the top entertainment news story of 2009. MSN Lifestyle's Most Influential Men of 2009 included Michael Jackson. He was named not for being merely popular, but for being actually influential, "for doing something that inspires or encourages us..." When Barbara Walters unveiled her *10 Most Fascinating People of the Year* she explained they stick strictly to a rule that they only include living persons on the list. Sitting in the runner up spot for number one for 2009, behind First Lady Michelle Obama, were Prince, Paris and Blanket Jackson. *People's* annual "Most Intriguing of 2009" likewise included Michael Jackson's children as the Descendants of the Year and Michael was named as the year's Most Talked About Star. Film director Brett Ratner contributed a tribute to his friend in the special year end issue, "He was more than just the greatest entertainer in the world – he was an amazing father. He loved his kids so much, they were his entire life – he gave them his whole heart."

Entertainment Tonight aired a countdown of the Most Shocking Celebrity Deaths, which Michael topped above the airplane crash of John F. Kennedy Jr. and the car crash that claimed Princess Diana. Though not a list you ever want to top, it is an indication of the enormity of the loss.

Billboard magazine, in their year end review named country singer Taylor Swift as the Artist of the Year noting, "She sold more albums than any artist not named Michael Jackson." *Number Ones* ended the year as the biggest selling album of the year and sat on top of the Top Pop Catalog Albums for the year. He not only had the top selling album of the year, but he set a record for having four of the year's top 20 albums. Michael Jackson was also named as the number one Top Pop Catalog Artist; placing above the Beatles who were ranked at number two for the year and Michael Jackson was named the Top Digital Album Artist. The *This Is It* soundtrack album placed at number four for the year on the Top Soundtrack Albums chart. Chart Watch columnist Paul Grein noted, "His music will remain popular going forward. He has broad appeal, crossing virtually all demographic lines, to all ages and races. As great as Elvis and Frank Sinatra were, I'm not sure that their appeal is as broad."

The tributes weren't about to stop with the year end. It was announced in December that Michael Jackson was to be among the honorees for the Grammy Lifetime Achievement Award. Prince and Paris were scheduled to accept the honor for their father, which was reportedly their idea and they wrote their own speeches. It was the first high profile appearance by his children since the July 7th public memorial. The Grammy Award telecast featured a tribute to Michael, showcasing the special 3D short film made for "Earth Song" that was slated to be part of the This Is It shows. CBS joined with Target stores in distributing free 3D glasses to view the tribute. Ken Erhlich, co-executive producer of the Grammys, and who was at the Staples Center on June 24th, said "It was one of the most important portions of the concert tour to Michael and when Michael saw the film for the first time at his last rehearsal, there were tears in his eyes." It was the first time a major award show had a portion broadcast in 3D.

Lionel Richie introduced the tribute to Michael on the Grammy telecast. With Quincy Jones and Berry Gordy spotted in the audience, Celine Dion, Usher, Jennifer Hudson, Carrie Underwood, and Smokey Robinson sang along with Michael's vocals on "Earth Song" while the short film was shown on the screens behind them. Greeted with a standing ovation, the Grammy Lifetime Achievement Award was accepted by Prince and Paris Jackson. Blanket chose not to go on stage with his older siblings, electing instead to stay backstage. They were dressed alike in black suits with red armbands reminiscent of their father, and with Paris in white socks and black shoes. Accompanied by three of their cousins, Tito's sons, they addressed the audience and the world. The world

"Best of Joy"

heard for the first time from Prince Jackson:

Thank you. Thank you. We are proud to be here to accept this award on behalf of our father, Michael Jackson. First of all we would like to thank God for watching over us these past seven months, and our grandma and grandpa for their love and support. We'd also like to thank the fans, our father loved you so much, because you were always there for him. Our father was always concerned about the planet and humanity. Through his hard work and dedication he has helped many charities and donated to all of them. Through all of his songs, his message was simple, love. We will continue to spread his message and help the world. Thank you. We love you Daddy.

Paris also spoke briefly:

Daddy was supposed to be here, Daddy was going to perform this year, but he couldn't perform last year. Thank you, we love you Daddy.

These opportunities for the public to see Michael Jackson's kids and see them as well adjusted, articulate and normal helped to reshape the image some had of him as Wacko Jacko or worse, a probable pedophile. It supported the idea that much of what people thought they knew about Michael Jackson was not true.

His live performances were fondly remembered by fans when Madison Square Garden held a vote to determine the favorite live show ever at the venue. First favorites from each decade where voted on, then the number one favorite overall was chosen. Of course Michael Jackson was the number one choice, or there would be no reason to include any of this here. The 1988 performance from the Bad tour was the number one choice of fans with 36.5% of the vote. Coming in second place... Michael again. His 2001 30th anniversary special was voted as the second fan favorite with 30.3% of the votes.

The Library of Congress chooses films of cultural significance to be archived in the National Film Registry. Inducted for 2009 was the first music video ever to be chosen to be included in the national archives, Michael Jackson's "Thriller". Steve Leggett, coordinator of the National Film Preservation Board said, "Because of the way the recording industry is evolving and changing, we thought it would be good to go back to the development of an earlier seismic shift, which was the development of the music video." The library reviews hundreds of films that are "culturally, historically or aesthetically significant."

"Thriller" was also voted the most influential music video in the history of pop music by a poll conducted by social networking site MySpace. A readers poll conducted by *Rolling Stone* magazine showed the same, that "Thriller" was the favorite video of all time. Online magazine *NME* published the results of a poll of the Greatest Singers of all Time, with Michael Jackson taking the number one spot. Freddie Mercury placed at number two, and Elvis was voted as the third favorite singer with more than 10 million votes being cast.

In what seemed like an out of the blue comment to *Classic Rock* magazine, Kiss lead singer Gene Simmons said he was sure Michael Jackson was a pedophile because he knew someone who quit one of Jackson's tours because he saw young boys coming from his hotel room. Jennifer Batten, who was the guitar player on the Bad, Dangerous and HIStory tours fired back "Number one, there's no truth to it. Number two, I would guess that it was somebody who got fired. Somebody who was embarrassed that they got fired and so they made up a story." This outburst by Simmons would come back to bite him in the ass and cost his band a high profile gig.

In March 2010 it was announced that the estate of Michael Jackson had signed a record breaking contract with Sony Music Entertainment for a whopping $200 million guaranteed and a possible $250 million if certain conditions were met. The agreement called for ten new Michael Jackson projects over the next seven years. One project included in the agreement was the *This Is It* soundtrack album which was still heading up the *Billboard* Soundtrack chart. Other projects included an album of all new material, *Michael,* and a DVD collection of virtually all of his short films, *Michael Jackson's Vision.*

This new record deal dwarfed the deals of other artists like Madonna's at $120 million and Jay-Z's for $150 million, and the Jackson deal did not include royalties from the sale of merchandise. Rob Stringer, Chairman of the Columbia Epic Label group stated, "Michael has always been a treasured member of the Sony Music family. We're dedicated to protecting this icon's legacy and we're thrilled that we can continue to bring his music to the world for the foreseeable future… Both the *This Is It* movie soundtrack and DVD exceeded our expectations. We knew we had something incredibly buoyant in terms of the legacy of a fantastic artist." John Branca issued a statement reading, "During his life, Michael's contracts set the standard for the industry, reflecting his unique vision and talents that inspired and excited people in every corner of the world. By all objective criteria, this agreement with Sony Music demonstrates the lasting power of Michael's music by exceeding all previous industry benchmarks. Each new generation produces countless new fans who appreciate Michael's artistry, requiring a partner that has Sony's wherewithal, business acumen and foresight to properly and respectfully showcase his genius well into the future." Branca told *Billboard* "We have turned a lot of things down; we have been very selective. And yet we're also very aggressive about wanting to do these kinds of deals that Michael would have been proud of." Co-trustee of the estate, John McClain, added, "…We believe we have a partner in Sony that knows and appreciates Michael's artistry as well as the passion of his fans. We look forward to continuing our partnership with Sony to preserve and enhance his remarkable musical legacy." Tony Gumina, president of the Ray Charles Marketing Group, sized up the Sony deal for *Billboard,* "When you're dealing with icons like Michael Jackson and Ray Charles, their appeal in the international markets is remarkable, so you're not just selling product in North America. If there are some great Michael Jackson recordings in the Sony vaults, this should be the best catalog investment they have ever made."

Another mega deal followed. John Branca and John McClain announced the estate of Michael Jackson was partnering with the forces behind Cirque du Soleil to create projects based on the music of Michael Jackson. Plans for such a show were actually begun before Michael's death. A traveling performance of Michael Jackson: THE IMMORTAL Word Tour kicked off in 2011. A standing gig in Las Vegas, in partnership with MGM Mirage, was scheduled for late 2012. The estate and Cirque du Soleil are to share 50/50 the expenses and the profits of the shows.

Jamie King, a dancer from the Dangerous tour, was chosen as the director. Long time Jackson associate, Greg Phillinganes was chosen as musical director. The show was choreographed by Travis Payne, who worked on Bad and Dangerous with Michael as well as This Is It. Michael Jackson tour alum Jon Clark and Don Boyette were featured in the band along with drummer Jonathon "Sugarfoot" Moffet. John Branca commented, "This will not just be a tribute to Michael's musical genius, but a live entertainment experience that uses the most advanced technology to push every creative boundary as Michael always did. Having attended Cirque du Soleil performances with Michael, I know he was a huge fan. We are excited to be partners with Cirque du Soleil to give Michael's fans a truly unique way to hear, see and feel Michael's music." Katherine Jackson was also pleased with the arrangement, "Our family is thrilled that Cirque du Soleil will pay tribute to my son in such an important way." A CD was released with a collection of Jackson songs that inspired the show. The *IMMORTAL* CD debuted and peaked on the Billboard Hot 200 at number twenty-four.

THE IMMORTAL tour, with a ginormous cast of dancers

and aerialists with equally massive staging and tons of special effects, paid tribute to the King of Pop with "Smooth Criminal" and "Thriller" being the best offerings along with "Billie Jean" which featured several dancers with the lightening effects that were planned for Michael's "Billie Jean" costume for This Is It. The show closed poignantly to "Man in the Mirror" with a performer donning a black fedora and single white glove striking a pose with his hand raised in the air, lights only on the glove. The show, though at times seeming much more a Cirque du Soleil performance than a Michael Jackson tribute, is chocked full of MJ references, the gates of Neverland, a pair of giant black loafers and white socks, and even Bubbles. Michael Jackson THE IMMORTAL World Tour was ranked as the number one tour in North America in 2012 and was ranked at number three worldwide.

Coinciding with the extended stay of the IMMORTAL tour in Las Vegas was a special exhibit of Michael Jackson memorabilia at Mandalay Bay. MJ Fan Fest featured tour costumes from the 1981 Triumph Jacksons tour, the 1984 Victory Jacksons tour, and each of Michael's three solo tours – Bad, Dangerous and HIStory were all included with the costumes he never got a chance to wear for This Is It. The famous hat and glove were on display with many badges and medals from the pretend pop music military which he commanded. Sets and props from his videos were on display from "Scream", the rocket from "Leave Me Alone" (the trim around the cockpit is actually a section of garden hose), the robotic bust and car from the Moonwalker mini movie, and the giant mechanical spider to be used in "Thriller" for This Is It. Scads of awards adorned a wall fifteen feet high behind a collection of the Grammy awards he won in 1984. Neverland Valley Ranch had a huge presence with the actual gates of Neverland welcoming you to a recreation of the grounds and a recreation of his private study.

Artwork was displayed that had been created by fans. He had kept and stored these items always appreciating his fans and recognizing how important they are. Authorized by the estate, the grand display was a wonderful albeit bittersweet tribute to the King of Pop. Michael would have surely been proud.

39

Never can say goodbye
No no no no, I
Never can say goodbye

"Never Can Say Goodbye"
- Clifton Davis

As the first anniversary of his death approached, record sales were still in high gear and many new projects were on the horizon. All of this was good news for the trustees that were working to pay off the debts of the estate. *The Wall Street Journal* reported that in the first year since his death, the estate had paid off $200 million of the massive estimated $500 million debt. A $300 million loan, backed by the ATV catalog, due at year end was refinanced through Swiss bank UBS. A $75 million loan against Mijac Music had been refinanced at a much lower interest rate with royalties generated from the catalog now sufficient to pay off the loan within a year. The $35 million advance AEG paid to Michael for the string of London shows had also been repaid. Perhaps most importantly, a $5 million loan against the Hayvenhurst home had been repaid saving the home where his mother and children now lived from foreclosure. Payments on the loan had been in default as were the utilities for the home. The house was actually scheduled to enter foreclosure proceedings on June 26, 2009, the day after Michael's death. The estate later paid for renovations to the property. A Los Angeles condo, four months behind in payments, was paid up and saved from possible foreclosure proceedings. Among other creditors that were now paid up was Thomas Mesereau's legal services bill for $341,000.

All of this was possible due to the incredible earnings generated by the estate during the previous year. The June 26, 2010 issue of *Billboard*, with a wonderful Norman Rockwell style illustration by artist Mark Stutzman of a fifty year old Michael painting a self portrait of a 1983 version of himself, reported that Jackson record sales, the *This Is It* film and DVD, music publishing, merchandising and licensing and the recent landmark recording contract had earned revenues exceeding *$1 billion.*

The same issue of *Billboard* featured a special ranking of each of the top fifty hit singles spanning his entire career, those with the Jackson 5, solo hits, and duets. Each single was assigned points according to its peak chart positions, weeks at number one, weeks in the top ten, the top twenty, etc. With this point system, the biggest hit of his career was determined to be his duet with Paul McCartney, "Say, Say, Say". "Billie Jean" sat in the runner up spot. It was noted that with "I Want You Back" debuting on the charts in November 1969, Michael Jackson had graced the *Billboard* music charts in the '60's, '70's '80's, 90's 00's and 10's. He had also earned the most number one hits by a solo male artist in the chart's fifty-two year history.

A similar review of the top selling R&B songs in digital history compiled by Nielson Soundscan had Michael Jackson hogging all five of the top spots, with "Thriller" at number one, "Billie Jean" second, followed in order by "Beat It", "Man in the Mirror" and "Don't Stop 'Til You Get Enough". His other entries, he had nine of the top fifteen, included "They Way You Make Me Feel" at number eight, "Smooth Criminal" at number ten, "PYT" at number eleven and "ABC" at number fifteen.

The record setting deals secured by the estate and continued record sales that were off the charts helped put Michael Jackson at the number one spot on *Forbes'* grim list of the highest earning dead celebrities. Michael Jackson did not just out earn the other eleven names on the list, he out earned the other eleven names *combined*. The estate of Michael Jackson raked in $275 million, more than four times the second place holder, Elvis Presley at $60 million. Michael Jackson's estate earned more than the top earning live acts like U2, Lady Gaga, Jay-Z, Beyoncé, and Madonna. Continued interest in the King of Pop and more new projects kept him at the top of the list the next year too. By the third anniversary of his death, earnings of the estate were estimated at $475 million and the remaining debt was due to be paid off within a few months.

While the controversary within the Jackson family continued over the validity of the will and questions surrounded the appointment of John Branca as a trustee, publically the efforts of the estate, for which the Branca and McClain were compensated handsomely, were impressive. Tremendous headway was made in the first few months to address the massive debt and many new projects, all befitting the King of Pop, were completed and met with great success.

Meanwhile, tributes and honors for the lost King of Pop continued. The Rock and Roll Hall of Fame held a tribute to Michael Jackson with a weekend of live music at the Rock and Soul Festival in June 2010. Also set for June was Michael Jackson's induction as part of the first class of entertainers to be honored as a Legend by the Apollo Theater for their brand new Walk of Fame. Other inductees included Michael's friends, associates and idols; James Brown, Smokey Robinson, Gladys Knight and the Pips, Little Richard and Quincy Jones. Michael's friend Chris Tucker accepted Michael's award on his behalf.

Lisa Marie Presley visited Michael's grave with her daughter, Riley, not long before the one year anniversary of his death. She noted the conspicuous absence of many mementos, flowers and tributes around his plot and urged fans to rectify it. She noted on her MySpace page, "While visiting him a few days ago at

Forest Lawn, Riley and I couldn't help but notice that, while there are a few bouquets, candles and gifts there is a very large empty space around him and in front of him that could use a whole lot more." She continued, "While I am sure that the staff at The Holy Terrace [sic] do their very best to place what is sent and what is placed at the door at his tomb, I thought you might like to know that he would want and deserves more than what is there and I had an idea. Some may or may not know this but his favorite flower was the sunflower. I thought if whoever wants to bought just one silk sunflower each and sent it, the whole area around him and in front of him would be covered. We can all cause a "sun shower" if you will. He deserves to be flooded and surrounded, LET'S SURROUND HIM!" In response to her plea, a flower shop owner, Jason Levin, owner of The Sunflower Guy in San Diego County, delivered two thousand sunflowers to Forest Lawn. He in turn received a bouquet of roses and lilies from Lisa Marie Presley in thanks. For the official anniversary, one thousand sunflowers and three thousand roses were delivered to Forest Lawn to be placed at Michael's grave site.

As the one year mark neared, the well being of his children came to the forefront once again. They were said to be doing well. They were now seen periodically in public without masks or veils. Katherine had not agreed with Michael's practice of hiding their faces and now chose not to do so. Each had expressed some ambition for their future. Prince gained an interest in film making, something he shared with his father. Both were studying film direction and film making. Paris had ambitions to be an actress and

Katherine saw a lot of Michaels's musical talent in his youngest son, Blanket. Paris' first project was a role in "Lundon's Bridge and the Three Kings". In keeping with her father's philanthropic endeavors, one of the attractions for Paris in taking part in this film was that the profits from the film were to go to the U.S. school system. The guardianship arrangement worked well for about three years when suddenly – after some public Jackson family turmoil during which Katherine's whereabouts were unknown – a revised guardianship agreement was reached with Tito's son TJ sharing guardianship duties with Katherine.

Randy Jackson worked with officials at Forest Lawn to help fans gain entry to the Holly Terrace at the Great Mausoleum on June 25th. Forest Lawn officials had initially planned on closing the gates on the anniversary date. Randy issued a statement, "Michael loved his fans, and the family wants to make sure that the fans are able to celebrate his incredible life." Fans were allowed inside Forest Lawn, but were not allowed to enter the mausoleum. Thousands of fans filed in the gates to pay their respects. Other fans left flowers at the gates of Neverland.

The gates of Forest Lawn were open on Memorial Day. I visited Forest Lawn and was able to easily approach the entry of the Holly Terrace of the Great Mausoleum, though admittance inside the building was not allowed. Teddy Bears, candles, cards and lots and lots of sunflowers were left at the door.

From the a few can spoil it for all rest file, fans visiting the mausoleum wrote messages to Michael in permanent ink on the outside of the building. "Miss you sweet angel" and "Keep the dream alive" were written under window ledges and areas hidden by bushes, making the graffiti hard to spot. To help mitigate the damage and to attempt to salvage access to the mausoleum for other fans, a local fan club offered to help clean up and repair the damage. Members of the Official Michael Jackson Fans of Southern California were hoping to keep fans from being barred entry to Forest Lawn to pay their respects.

LAPD arranged for squads of officers to patrol the family home in Encino and the surrounding streets which were expected to be overrun with fans showing up to pay their respects. Katherine, Prince, Paris and Blanket meanwhile marked the anniversary in Gary, Indiana, following a few days of relaxation in Hawaii. The former home in Gary had been spruced with a new coat of paint, a new roof, new landscaping and a new wrought iron fence for the unveiling of a monument on the front lawn declaring:

King of Pop

Michael Jackson

August 29, 1958

June 25, 2009

Home town of Michael Jackson – Gary, IN

"Never Can Say Goodbye"

The monument is surrounded by a flower garden and spotlights.

Katherine also marked the one year anniversary of her son's death with the release of a photo album titled *Never Can Say Goodbye: Katherine Jackson Archives.* Available only on the

Jackson website, jacksonsecretvault.com, the book was filled with photos of her most famous son with some of Katherine's memories. There are a few errors and misspellings throughout the book. Frank Dileo's name is spelled "Deleo" and even her own daughter's name, LaToya is written as "Latoya" throughout. The photos are beautiful but not as exclusive or "never before seen" as promoted. Katherine told the Daily Mail, "I want the world to know the real Michael. I'd like him to be remembered as the loving person he was."

Katherine's partner in creating the book was Howard Mann. Mann, a businessman, had reportedly purchased some unreleased Michael Jackson tracks when Joe had failed to pay a storage bill. He was now said to be working with Katherine on plans to release the 273 songs. This was not done in concert with the estate trustees. Howard Weitzman, the attorney for the estate said Mann was not authorized to make plans to release the tracks and that the estate would take "whatever action is necessary to prevent him from unlawfully profiting." Katherine and Howard Mann were also said to be partnering to release a series of films culled from hours and hours of home video footage. The estate filed and won a lawsuit again Mann to prevent him from using any of Michael Jackson's copyrighted works.

Michael's father marked the anniversary of his son's death by filing a wrongful death lawsuit against Dr. Conrad Murray charging that the doctor withheld critical details from EMT's and emergency room personnel. A similar complaint was filed by Joe Jackson against concert promoter AEG Live. Joe was seeking up to

$500 million in damages.

The suit filed against Dr. Murray was seeking punitive damages for loss of economic support, loss of companionship and loss of consortium. The latter two being particularly outrageous claims given the well known strained and distant relationship Joe had with his son. The case ended up being tossed out of court, was refiled and tossed out again.

Joe's continued efforts to squeeze every nickel possible from the death of his son were largely blocked by the executors of the estate. One such effort included an announcement that the Jackson Family Foundation was hosting an event, "Forever Michael" at the Beverly Hilton Hotel on the anniversary of his death to celebrate his life. Not long after the grand announcement, it was learned that the "Jackson Family Foundation" was really just Joe Jackson and a "portion" of the proceeds were to go toward charity. The charity was the creation of a Jackson Family museum in Gary, Indiana, a pet project Joe had been trying to get off the ground for a decade. Howard Weitzman condemned the event stating it did not carry the approval of the estate. City officials in Gary were reported to have donated 300 acres of land to be used as the site of the Jackson Family Museum and Hotel and the Michael Jackson Performing Arts and Cultural Center and Theaters.

Legal action was also being brought against the AEG bosses on behalf of Katherine Jackson, Prince, Paris and Blanket. The suit, for unspecified damages, claimed fraud, negligence, breach of contract, infliction of emotional distress, and failure to provide life saving equipment to Dr. Murray. Attorney's for AEG responded that Dr. Murray was Michael's personal physician and was not an employee of AEG, "AEG did not choose him, hire him or supervise him." Murray was to be paid by AEG, however since Michael and an AEG representative never signed the contract AEG called the agreement not binding.

Planet Hollywood Resort and Casino played host to the Julien's Auctions Music Icons auction held on the anniversary of the death of the biggest icon of them all. More than two hundred pieces of memorabilia hit the auction block and fans grabbed up the items shattering the expected going prices and bringing in a total just shy of $1 million. A pair of worn loafers, an autograph given on June 24th, 2009, a Victory tour jacket, a drawing by Michael and his MTV Music Video award for "Scream" sold at prices soaring past their presale estimates. By far and away the star item of the auction was the Swarovski crystal studded white glove worn on the Victory tour which sold for a staggering $190,000. The presale estimate for the glove was less than $20,000. The winning bidder, Wanda Kelley, received a standing ovation from the other attendees.

Other projects being announced included the introduction of a new video game that allowed players to sing and dance to Jackson hits. Michael Jackson: The Experience, carried the seal of approval of the estate trustees, John McClain said, "It is a game that the entire family can experience and enjoy together and this is something that would please Michael tremendously."

While the estate was eager to endorse many projects in

tribute to Michael Jackson, they were just as focused on deterring efforts that attempted to cash in on his likeness or celebrity purporting to be official tributes, some even involving Katherine and Joe Jackson. Legal action was taken to block an online casino claiming to be connected with Michael and using his likeness without permission. Katherine Jackson's efforts with Howard Mann came under fire by the estate as did almost everything thought up by Joe.

    The National Museum of Dance Hall of Fame inducted Michael Jackson into their ranks in August 2010, which prompted the question, "Why the heck wasn't he already inducted?" In fact, Michael Jackson is the first dancer from the world of pop to be included, most of the other forty-three inductees coming from ballet and modern dance. He was named the 2010 C.V. Whitney Hall of Fame inductee, joining the likes of his idol Fred Astaire and Bill "Bojangels" Robinson. Marlon attended the ceremony to accept the honor. A note of thanks was read from Katherine. The museum board of director's president, Michele Riggs commented on his talent, "All his dance moves, from his robot dances to the moonwalk to all his gyrations and song and dance together, were such a unique style." A floral garden was created to honor his memory, which will become a permanent feature at the museum.

    Tributes and celebrations marking the anniversary were held around the world. In France, a weekend long celebration included a concert and tribute shows. In Japan, at the Tokyo Tower, fans gathered for a candlelight vigil and a gospel concert. Some fans paid

"Never Can Say Goodbye"

$1,100 each to sleep overnight at the tower housing Jackson memorabilia and observed a moment of silence as the sun rose. London's Hard Rock Calling featured Stevie Wonder, who paid tribute to his friend singing "We love you Michael Jackson, we love your music Michael." He also played harmonica to "Human Nature".

A plaque honoring Michael Jackson was placed at the Lyric Theater in London, where "Thriller Live" was still playing. The cast of the show performed "Speechless". The Executive Director of the show, Adrian Grant, said "The sentiment behind the song and what it now means to me in Michael's passing truly reflects the emotions one feels due to his loss – those of sadness, but also remembering the joy he gave the world as we celebrate his life."

Plans to erect a statue of Michael Jackson in the Czech Republic were met with opposition. Those criticizing the idea held that Jackson had no real connection to the Czech Republic. Prague city officials had approved a plan to place a six foot statue of Michael Jackson in Letna Park. Another statue met with similar resistance in London. Mohammed Al Fayed, father of Princess Diana's friend Dodi, commissioned a statue of his friend that he planned to place outside his store, Harrod's, which he then owned. When he sold the famed department store, the statue was placed outside Craven Cottage Stadium in London, home of the Fullham Football club, also owned by Al Fayed. Some protested the statue saying Michael Jackson had no connection to the club and it was either bizarre or inappropriate. Al Fayed responded, "If some stupid fans don't understand and appreciate such a gift this guy gave to the world they can go to hell."

Television broadcasts on June 25th were flooded with specials commemorating the anniversary. NBC's *Today Show* featured a segment live from Neverland Valley Ranch. Dennis Tompkins and Michael Bush along with makeup artist Karen Faye appeared on *20/20*. Bush lovingly characterized Michael's fashion style as "Liberace has gone to war." Faye tearfully denied he had a prosthetic tip on his nose. They spoke fondly of their association with Michael over the years and tearfully told of being asked by the Jackson family to dress Michael and do his makeup and hair one final time.

CBS' *Early Show* devoted their second hour entirely to the King of Pop with performances, interviews and taped tribute messages from many celebrities who are also fans and admirers. LL Cool J's remark struck a poignant chord, "No mater what you want to say about him, his career always mattered. You don't sell out one hundred shows in England and all over Europe because you are not relevant. This Is It would have been one of the most amazing shows you have ever seen, from probably the most amazing artist of our time."

BET, MTV, E!, Vh-1 and many other networks featured Michael Jackson specials throughout the weekend. Even Animal Planet got in on the act featuring a documentary on the new home of Bubbles the chimp and including a reunion with his Aunt LaToya when she visited the chimp in his new home at the Center for Great

Apes in Wauchua, Florida. Radio stations marked the anniversary with fans calling in with their memories and requesting Jackson songs.

Dateline landed an interview with Katherine Jackson, where Mrs. Jackson shared memories of her son and thumbed through her new photo book. She also revealed that she shares the view of many members of the family that people around Michael wanted him dead, that 'greedy people wanted him gone." She did not elaborate.

CNN featured an interview with Randy, and Jermaine made another appearance on *Larry King Live*, broadcast from outside the Holly Terrace at Forest Lawn. Randy told CNN that Michael feared for his life and feared the loss of his assets, his children and his home if he did not do what was asked of him by "the powers that be." He felt Dr. Murray was not telling the full truth and should be facing more serious charges than involuntary manslaughter. Randy also questioned the authenticity of Michael's will. He further stated his intention to continue with what Michael would have wanted, making a difference in the world and helping others in need.

Meanwhile the fate of Neverland was still in question. California assemblyman Mike Davis proposed making Neverland an official state park based on the land's historic interest. The plan was problematic for at least two reasons: then Governor Arnold Schwarzenegger had closed many state parks due to economic reasons, and the neighboring residents opposed plans to turn the property into a tourist attraction. In the meantime, the ranch was being used to hold charity events. Katherine had stated she hoped the ranch would not be sold. Later an idea was proposed by Colony Capital to turn Neverland into a music school similar to Julliard. To move forward they would need to win the approval of the Santa Barbara County officials and the trustees of the estate. The estate reportedly stated they had no objections.

CNN began a search for the top music icon in the summer of 2010. Fans were asked to rank their choices for the top five icons from a list including some international figures along with the Rolling Stones, Elvis, Aretha Franklin, Bob Dylan, James Brown, Bob Marley, Madonna, and of course, Michael Jackson. Coming out on top as the number one favorite music icon was the King of Pop.

Janet performed a concert at the New Orleans Essence Music Festival in July. Her closing song, "Together Again" was dedicated to Michael. Her Up Close and Personal tour, included her performing "Scream" with the video of Michael singing his opening lines. The performance was sadly cut short before their great dance sequence. These shows also closed to "Together Again" with photos of young Janet and Mike on the giant screen behind her.

Tributes continued from everywhere. The Smithsonian National Museum of American History in Washington, in its exhibit of popular culture, featured a fedora from the King of Pop. Artists touring at the time, and especially those playing at the O2 Arena often made a dedication to Michael Jackson. Usher's performances included a performance of, "Don't Stop 'Til You Get Enough." Carlos Santana dedicated his performance at the O2 to Michael

Jackson. Celine Dion returned to performing a standing gig in Las Vegas with a show that included a tribute to Michael Jackson, who played a seminal role in her career. "He changed my life. I saw him on TV and I wanted to sing in English because he was, so I went to learn English and met with him and I (sang) with him and he came to see the show and he had a big impact on my life."

New projects were lined up for the fall, first up was a collection of short films. *Michael Jackson's Vision* includes virtually every short film in the Michael Jackson library; with rarely seen gems, "She's Out of My Life", "Blame it on the Boogie", and the prison version of "They Don't Care About Us." The collection concludes with "One More Chance" that was never released due his legal issues looming at the time. An interesting concept, but with virtually all of the shots of Michael from behind, with barely a glimpse of his face throughout. He dances from one table top to another in a night club setting. It looks to be a compromised version put together from footage shot before the production was halted. "They Don't Care About Us" carries a new disclosure statement to combat a resurgence of the earlier controversy and help highlight the video and song's true message, "This film is NOT degrading to ANY one RACE, but pictorializes the injustices to ALL mankind. May GOD grant us PEACE THROUGHOUT the world." In addition to this DVD release, Michael Jackson was about to dominate the music charts. Again.

40

My life has taken me beyond the planets and the stars
And you're the only one that could take me this far
I'll be forever searching for your love

"(Can't Make it) Another Day"
-Lenny Kravitz

Michael, the first posthumous album of never before released material, hit shelves on December 14, 2010. Well, one track had been released before. An alternate version of "(I Like) The Way You Love Me" was included on *Michael Jackson: The Ultimate Collection in 2004.* Most of the ten tracks were said to be culled from work in the prior three years.

The album went platinum in seventeen countries; Great Britain, Germany, France, Italy, Spain, Denmark, Poland, Russia,

"(Can't Make it) Another Day"

Austria, Belgium, Czech Republic, Canada, India, China, Taiwan, Korea and the Middle East. *Michael* debuted and peaked on the *Billboard* Top 200 album chart at number three. Helping to keep the album out of the number one spot was undoubtedly the controversy swirling about that some suspected tracks had relatively little of Michael's input and were largely finished after his death. Others connected with the project assured it was the real thing including Sony and John McClain, who worked to put the album together. Three tracks in particular were being questioned including "Breaking News". Howard Weitzman countered, saying that musicologists were hired to confirm the validity of the vocals as well as former engineers, producers and musicians who had worked with Michael.

Even some family members questioned the authenticity of the vocals. Randy lashed out at the trustees of the estate and Sony claiming "some of the songs are him, and some aren't. I would bet my life on that." Tito's sons TJ, Taj and Tarryl agreed. Tarryl tweeted, "I KNOW my Uncle's voice and something's seriously wrong when you have immediate FAMILY saying it's not him." Tarryl is credited with the spoken bridge on "Hollywood Tonight". Will.i.am condemned the project being released without Michael here to put his seal of approval on it and refused to let material he worked on with Michael be released. "How you gonna release Michael Jackson without Michael Jackson here to bless it?"

Collaborators and producers each had varying opinions. Teddy Riley declared it a "masterpiece" and said "I have no doubts that these are Michael's vocals." Frank Dileo agreed, he had spoken with Michael several times while he was working on the tracks with Eddie Cascio in New Jersey in 2007. Cascio, who is credited as a musician on several tracks and at whose home some of the recording took place, was certain the vocals were genuine. In an appearance on *Oprah*, he shared, "I can tell you that it is Michael's voice. He recorded right there in my basement. It was a home studio and we worked. I was there pushing the buttons and he was there directing. That's Michael Jackson." Lenny Kravitz was proud of his collaboration, "I know he stood behind it, so I'm cool with what I did. I was proud to put it out and knew that he'd be all over it, that he'd be really with it."

The album is dedicated to "Prince, Paris and Blanket – Katherine and the entire Jackson family." The thank yous on the album are especially touching including a note Michael wrote to his children which was first printed on the liner notes for *Number Ones*, "You are my joy, the fullness in my heart is because of you. I love you beyond now and forever more." Notes from the estate to thank the musicians Michael worked with throughout his career is very much like Michael would have said, "whose talents, love and support helped Michael to achieve the many milestones of his life and career." Also just like Michael, a special thanks is included to his fans, "And especially to Michael's fans, we say thank you for you love, loyalty and endless support for Michael. – The Estate".

Rolling Stone gave the album a three out of five star rating in a review that started out harshly, "This is not a Michael Jackson album. Jackson was one of pop's biggest fussbudgets: Even when his songs were half-baked, the production was pristine. He would not have released anything like this compilation, a grab bag of outtakes and outlines assembled by Jackson's label." The review then praised several tracks with favorable comparisons to selections on *Thriller* and *Bad*. After condemning the album and the inclusion of a "grab bag of outtakes", the review continued, "There are thrilling glimpses into MJ's creative process" – noting the intro to "(I Like) The Way You Love Me."

Time praised the album as "a shockingly credible record – a carefully assembled recreation of his finest moments as a solo artist and a reminder of why we cared about him to begin with." The review concluded with, "For now, at least, Jackson receives the acceptable send-off he deserved."

Some tracks seem to bury Michael's vocals a bit, while others, most notably, "Can't Make it Another Day" with Kravitz seem, at least to an untrained ear, like a polished Michael Jackson product. While Michael's voice does seem somewhat overshadowed, or drowned out by some duet partners, the "woo-hoo's" and the reflection in his voice are unmistakably Michael. One recording artist, familiar with his work and voice, analyzed the songs and could detect tracks with splices where Michael's voice was blended with a sound-a-like sometimes in the middle of a single word, with a line beginning with Michael's voice blended into another voice, then back to Michael's. Despite the, to him, obvious splices, the real kicker was the lack of goosebumps when listening to the tracks. "I know Michael's voice and when I hear him sing, I get goosebumps. With this there are no goosebumps." With all of the controversy over whether all of the tracks were really him, or if he would have wanted the album released at all, which Teddy Riley said Michael would have loved, it is a wonderful chance to get a sense of what he had in store for his fans, much like the *This is It* movie.

In keeping with Michael's theme of "it's got to be bigger than big", a billboard promoting the album in London was officially named the world's biggest poster. The giant ad measured 29,000 square feet.

The first single, "Hold My Hand", a duet with Akon that seems to include more Akon than Jackson, is not the strongest track on the album. A sad video was produced for the single featuring Akon performing the song mixed with older footage of Michael, a sad reminder of what we had lost. "Hold My Hand" peaked on the pop singles chart at thirty-nine and at number thirty-three on the R&B singles chart. With this single making the top 40 singles chart, it set a new world record for the longest span of U.S. top 40 singles of 39 years and 2 months. Michael's solo single, "Got to be There" entered the top 40 singles chart in November, 1971, and "Hold My Hand" entered the top 40 singles chart in January, 2011. The single became a top ten hit in several other countries. According to Joe Vogel, "Hold My Hand" was chosen as the first single when a note in Michael's handwriting was found reading, "Akon song – first single".

"Behind the Mask" was released as the second single in the U.S., Canada, Japan and France. For the video, fans were invited to submit their own video footage. Entries poured in from 103 countries. The finished video project was released online in June 2011.

"Hollywood Tonight" was released as the second single in the rest of the world. "Hollywood Tonight" was originally born in 1999, when Michael first wrote some of the lyrics. He worked on the song periodically with Brad Buxer over the next several years with Michael requesting a copy of it on CD from the engineer in 2008. He never worked on it again. With many versions surfacing from throughout this period, the single differs somewhat from the album cut. The video for the single is much more a tribute and celebration of Michael than the depressing "Hold My Hand". It features dancer Sofia Boutella who was offered the opportunity to accompany Jackson for the This is It performances, but she still had a contract with Madonna's tour. Dance scenes for the video were shot outside the Pantages Theater, where "You Are Not Alone" was shot. When "Hollywood Tonight" climbed to the number one position on the Billboard's Hot Dance Club chart, it became his eighth single to do so and made Michael Jackson the male artist with the most number one hits on the chart.

The 2010 *Billboard* Year End Charts had Michael Jackson and each of his albums making a strong showing:

Top Artists
#28 Michael Jackson
Top Billboard 200 Artists
#7 Michael Jackson

Top Billboard 200 Albums

#22 *Michael Jackson's This is It*

#39 *Number Ones*

#112 *The Essential Michael Jackson*

#*137 Thriller*

Top Billboard 200 Artists – Male

#3 Michael Jackson

Pop Catalog Artists

#1 Michael Jackson

Pop Catalog Albums

#1 *Number Ones*

#6 *The Essential Michael Jackson*

#7 *Thriller*

Soundtrack Albums

#1 *Michael Jackson's This is It*

Top 100 Artists

#28 Michael Jackson

Top R&B/Hip Hop Artists – Male

#10 Michael Jackson

Top R&B/Hip Hop Album Artists

#10 Michael Jackson

Top R&B/Hip Hop Albums

#8 *Michael Jackson's This is It*

The release of a 25th anniversary edition of *Bad* and the continuing Michael Jackson THE IMMORTAL World Tour were lined up with other new projects for 2011 and 2012. *Thriller The*

Movie, an adaptation of "Thriller" for the big screen, was said to be in the works prior to Michael's death. Kenny Ortega was announced to be in line to direct with contributions also by the song's composer, Rod Temperton. Planet Michael – a multiplayer online virtual world, launched in late 2011, is a collaboration between the estate and SEE Virtual Worlds.

While these projects were officially sanctioned by the estate, others were not. Some the estate fought against. One project especially slammed by the estate was the announcement of plans to air a television program in Europe reenacting Michael's autopsy, *Michael Jackson's Autopsy: What really killed Michael Jackson*. The height of the tasteless of such a program drew the ire of fans, his family and the estate. Branca and McClain fired off a letter to Discovery Communications, Inc. expressing their outrage at the program and the equally tasteless ad which depicted a body on a gurney with a white gloved hand showing below the sheet. The letter concluded, "On behalf of Michael's family, fans, common sense and decency, we urge you to reconsider and cancel this program." This letter, perhaps in concert with a fan petition, worked to change the plans of Discovery Communications and the program was cancelled.

On the legal front, a pre-trial hearing was held in January 2011 to determine if Dr. Conrad Murray would stand trial for the involuntary manslaughter of Michael Jackson. After six days of testimony in which the prosecution seemed to lay out the bulk of its case, Judge Pastor ruled there was sufficient evidence for Dr. Murray to stand trial.

Dr. Murray surrendered to authorities entering a plea of not guilty. The criminal complaint stated that Dr. Conrad Murray "did unlawfully, and without malice, kill Michael Joseph Jackson." He was released on $75,000 bail. The judge rejected a motion to rescind his medical license, but did order him not to administer anesthetics, especially propofol, to any patients, stating, "I do not want you sedating people". He was also ordered to surrender his passport, it was feared he may try to flee to Grenada, where he is originally from, or to Trinidad, where he has a child.

Jermaine later told *Entertainment Tonight* that he felt the charges against Dr. Murray "weren't enough". Joe Jackson, along with his attorney, Brian Oxman, appeared on *Larry King Live* that evening to convey that they felt Dr. Murray "got off easy." Joe agreed with LaToya that Michael had been murdered and Dr. Murray was only part of a much larger plan. Pressed by King to name who he felt were part of this larger plan, Joe divulged that the people around Michael including Dr. Tohme Tohme and, shockingly, Frank Dileo, were "no good".

Before the start of the much delayed trial the second anniversary of Michael's death rolled around. Tributes coincided with Julien's annual rock and roll memorabilia auction and *Forbes* annual list of the highest earning celebrities. *Forbes* magazine named U2 as the highest earners for the past two year period with total earnings of $320 million. They were the highest earning living entertainers. The highest earner overall was once again the King of

"(Can't Make it) Another Day"

Pop, with two years earnings of $400 million. Total revenue for the estate for the same period topped $1 billion. John Branca commented, "The continuing overwhelming worldwide interest in Michael confirms his status as the greatest entertainer of all time."

The overwhelming interest in all things Jackson was also evident in the response to the annual Music Icons auction by Julien's. Though several items from Michael Jackson were going on the auction block, the most talked about was the original "Thriller" jacket. Michael signed a sleeve of the jacket and gave it to his costume designers to use as a template for "Thriller" jackets to be designed for concert tours. Pre-auction estimates put the value of the jacket, which Darren Julien called "the most recognized and significant piece of pop culture" at $200,000 to $400,000. The final sale price came in at 4 ½ times the highest estimate at an astounding $1.8 million. The winning bidder was Milton Verret, a commodities trader from Austin, Texas. He planned to put the jacket on display at Dell Children's Hospital in Austin then send it on tour as a fundraising item for children's charities, something that would have surely pleased Michael. As for Michael Bush and Dennis Tompkins, they planned to donate a portion of the sales proceeds to the Shambala Preserve, a wildlife preserve run by actress Tippi Hedren. Two of Michael's Bengal tigers, Thriller and Sabu, went to live at the sanctuary after being removed from Neverland Valley Ranch in 2006. Sadly, Thriller died of cancer in 2012. The other *Thriller* jacket, worn and torn for the zombie Michael in the video, is owned by the estate.

To mark the second anniversary of the passing of the King of Pop, fans gathered at locations with any MJ connection; the gates of Neverland, his star on the Hollywood Walk of Fame, his Carolwood home, the family home in Gary, Indiana. In Santa Barbara, a local helicopter pilot offered "Flight Over Neverland", and lots and lots of sunflowers were delivered to Forest Lawn. The Grammy Museum unveiled a new permanent Michael Jackson exhibit of memorabilia. Madame Tussauds in New York City featured Michael's likeness in an attraction that played his songs throughout the lobby. A customized motorcycle, featuring images of Michael, was driven through Forest Lawn in tribute to Michael. Family friend Marcell "Porkchop" Miller built the bike and made the drive through Forest Lawn on the second anniversary in honor of his friend. Days earlier, Paris tweeted pictures of herself and her brothers checking out the bike.

Marking the second anniversary of his death, Thomas Mesereau paid tribute to Michael at the Michael Jackson Auditorium at Gardner Elementary School. Introduced by Majestik Magnificant, Mesereau was treated like a rock star himself. He told of Michael's great kindness even when his life was hanging in the balance during his trial. "He wanted to use his gifts and his blessings to heal the world and as far as I am concerned he absolutely succeeded."

Frank Dileo also had plans to honor his friend. He was planned a book detailing his time working with Michael in the 80's, to "set the record straight". Sadly he never completed his memoir. Frank Dileo succumbed to complications from heart surgery in

"(Can't Make it) Another Day"

August 2011.

Another long time friend and associate of Michael's was lost just a couple of months later with the death of Dennis Tompkins. The costume designer worked with Michael Bush since the 80's when they teamed up on the set of *Captain EO*. After Jackson discovered Tompkins' talent for designing pants cut to accommodate his dance moves, they worked together making outfits for on and off the stage. Bush released his book, *Dressing Michael Jackson: Behind the Seams of a Fashion Icon* in fall 2012 with a look at the creative process and the impact Michael Jackson had on fashion and popular culture.

In recognition of the 30th birthday of MTV, *Billboard* magazine conducted a poll to find the favorite videos of each of the three decades of the 80's, 90's and 00's. Only one artist graced each of the three decades. Not surprisingly, "Thriller" topped the list for the 80's, with a whopping 65% of the vote. Michael and Janet's "Scream" came in the runner up spot for the 90's, and the number four video for the 2000's was "You Rock My World". A poll conducted by *Rolling Stone* also showed "Thriller" to be the fan favorite. The king of all videos was called "so iconic and influential that it's not exactly a surprise that it won this poll by a landslide. So much more than a promo clip for a song, this mini-movie practically invented the notion of the music video as a major cultural event."

While all of these new projects continued to be anticipated by fans, a previously unknown treasure was uncovered. An airplane hangar in Santa Monica was found to be a getaway art studio

Michael had kept for some time. The collection of Michael's own paintings and drawings was valued at a staggering $900 million. Many recurring themes in his work included chairs, he had an interest in the furniture as where he envisioned people thinking and making decisions. The number seven also featured heavily in his work. Said to be his favorite number and perhaps relating to him being the seventh child and there being seven letters in his first and last names. The collection is owned jointly by the estate and artist Brett Livingston Strong, who was his art mentor. Michael's children presented thirteen pieces of their father's art for display to the Los Angeles Children's Hospital.

September 27, 2011 saw the beginning of opening statements in the involuntary manslaughter trial of Dr. Conrad Murray. The prosecution started strong showing the jury chilling and disturbing pictures of Michael Jackson performing on stage the night of June 24th juxtaposed with a photo of his lifeless body on a gurney the next afternoon. Murray's attorney's hinted at their possible defense, which would shift throughout the days of the trial.

Deputy District Attorney David Walgreen did a stellar job setting the timeline of events the morning of June 25th 2009. At rehearsals the night before, Kenny Ortega and Paul Gongaware of AEG described him as being excited about the shows and in good physical condition, though there were concerns earlier in the rehearsal schedule about Michael's haphazard attendance.

Personal Assistant Michael Amir Williams, head of security Faheem Muhammad and Director of Logistics Alberto Alvarez as well as Chef Kai Chase testified as to the events the fateful morning of June 25th, Dr. Murray's actions, the delayed call to 9-1-1 and the arrival of the paramedics. They told of Dr. Murray directing prescription bottles and IV bags be picked up and stuffed in bags, all before 9-1-1 was called. The paramedics described the condition of the patient when they arrived and the efforts taken to revive him. His body was cold and his hands and feet were blue. They estimated he had been dead for up to one hour. After forty-two minutes of working on him, there was no sign of life. Dr. Murray divulged he had been treating him for exhaustion and dehydration and nothing else. He refused to call the death at the home and requested he be transported to UCLA Ronald Reagan Medical Center. The Emergency Room doctors recounted their efforts at resuscitation. Dr. Murray never disclosed to paramedics, or the ER doctors, that he had administered propofol to Michael. He also claimed to have witnessed the arrest.

Technicians from AT&T and Sprint deciphered cell phone activity on each of Dr. Murray's two cell phones detailing calls and texts sent and received the morning he was to be monitoring his only patient.

Medical professionals and experts each testified as to the unheard of nature of using propofol in a private home. Any use of the anesthetic outside of a hospital setting was described as an egregious deviation from the standard of care. Providing propofol outside a hospital setting, the lack of the necessary resuscitation equipment, failure to follow proper protocol in resuscitation efforts, lack of any medical records, the delay in calling 9-1-1, all added to the steady of stream of "egregious deviations from the standard of care" culminating in seventeen areas where Dr. Murray's actions directly contributed to the death of Michael Jackson. Experts testified further that even if the defense theory that Jackson helped himself to the drugs in Murray's absence was true, each of the detailed egregious deviations from the standard of care still applied.

A pharmacy owner and a representative from a medical and pharmaceutical distributor detailed the massive orders of drugs and supplies placed by Dr. Murray, all for his single patient, including 255 vials of propofol, a quantity that equals over four gallons. Prosecutor David Walgreen conducted an inventory of each drug vial and bottle found in the home and displayed them on the table in court in front of the jury. The mountain of drugs, bottles, vials and medical equipment found at the scene was a sobering sight.

Another sobering moment came when an audio recording was played in court. The recording, discovered on Murray's cell phone – was said by the defense to have been recorded by accident but was later described by Judge Pastor as Murray's insurance policy in case his relationship with Michael Jackson soured. In the recording, a heavily sedated Jackson, taped by Murray on May 10th, speaks of wanting his shows to be the best shows ever and his wish to build a children's hospital. His speech is extremely slurred and the tape concludes with him drifting off to sleep. It was startling to hear him in that state and was a vivid indication of the amount of drugs being provided to him.

"(Can't Make it) Another Day"

Dr. Murray's interview with police, which took place two days after Jackson's death, was the first time he admitted to administering propofol to his patient. The entire interview was played in court and served the prosecution's case more than add to any possible defense. During the course of the interview, he admits he had been treating Jackson with propofol for the past couple of months.

The defense had rather lame and flimsy "explanations" for Dr. Murray's actions that morning from he could not call 9-1-1 immediately as the property was gated to it was okay to administer the drugs to Michael in his home because he had asked for them. As the defense leapt from one theory to another, Dr. Arnold Klein's name was brought up time and time again as they tried to blame him for getting Michael addicted to Demerol. Of course Demoral was not detected in his system and was not the cause of death. The other one to blame for the death, according to the defense, was Michael Jackson himself. The defense team put forth theories that were found by experts to be medically implausible.

Former patients of Dr. Murray's testified for the defense that they were alive today due to his medical expertise. It was skillfully noted by the prosecution however that each of these patients were cardiac patients of Dr. Murray. He never treated them for sleep disorders and never treated them outside a hospital or clinic setting. More expert witnesses tried to refute some of the testimony of the prosecutions witnesses, but none could condone or explain the administering of an anesthetic in a home setting, the delay in calling

9-1-1 or the failure to follow standard protocol for resuscitation.

Closing arguments took place on November 3rd, and the case was given to the jury. A verdict was rendered on Monday, November 7th, finding Dr. Murray guilty of involuntary manslaughter in the death of Michael Jackson. Sentencing was scheduled for November 29th and Dr. Murray was remanded into custody immediately, having been determined to be a flight risk pending his sentencing. He was handcuffed and led from the court room.

The sentencing hearing began with a Jackson family friend and attorney reading a statement from the Jackson family for the judge to "impose a sentence that reminds physicians they cannot sell their services to the highest bidder." Prosecutor David Walgreen argued for the maximum four year state prison sentence. Due to overcrowding in the California prisons however, it was already noted that any time would likely be served in county jail. Defense attorney Ed Chernoff asked for probation arguing that regardless of what he does in the future, he will always be the man that killed Michael Jackson.

The probation request was flatly and harshly denied by Judge Pastor who delivered a litany of ways in which Michael Jackson died of circumstances directly attributable to Conrad Murray. While noting there was no intent on Dr. Murray's part, the judge relayed how Murray's deceit and lies continued for a period of time creating an astounding set of circumstances; describing the surreptitious recording of Michael Jackson – recorded at his most vulnerable point as "a horrific violation of trust" – and declaring him to be a danger to the community. At one point the Judge even inquired as to whether there was any leeway in which he could override the new Realignment Act that would allow him to sentence Murray to serve his time in State Prison rather than county jail. Judge Pastor also emphasized in his comments, in addition to the violation of his oath as a doctor and the violation of trust, the complete lack of remorse or sense of personal responsibility expressed by Murray. Murray had expressed this sense that he did nothing wrong in a documentary that aired on TV during the final days of the trial. In response to his actions on June 25th, and many aggravating factors, Judge Pastor sentenced Dr. Murray to the maximum sentence of four years. Many speculated this would be greatly reduced due to the overcrowding problem in California jails.

Murray was also ordered to pay all required fines and fees due to the court and restitution to the Jackson estate and his children for burial expenses and lost earnings. Estate attorney Howard Weitzman provided the court with expenses, receipts and itemizations of the expected revenue stream from the upcoming This Is It concert dates and other projects in the works at the time of his death. The total was an astounding $101,821,871.65. With the certain loss of his medical license greatly hindering his ability to earn a living, facing the heaping debt he already had coupled with his legal fees, his ability to pay any restitution seemed pretty much non-existent. With no hope of ever being able to begin paying such an astronomical sum, the Jackson family later withdrew the restitution request.

The estate responded to the jury verdict saying, "The estate of Michael Jackson and Michael himself has always believed the jury system works and despite the tragedy that brought about this trial we are in agreement with the jury's verdict. In this case justice has been served. Michael is missed on a daily basis but his genius and his music will be with us forever. He is 'the greatest entertainer that has ever lived'."

A tribute concert was planned for the fall of 2011 by a few members of the Jackson Family. Michael Forever: The Tribute Concert was organized and supported by Katherine and a few other family members and was planned for October 8th in Wales at the Millennium Stadium. As the timing was unfortunate, landing in the midst of Dr. Murray's trial, the tribute show was opposed by other family members. The estate also did not support the tribute show. Artists lined up to pay tribute to Michael included Smokey Robinson, Ne-Yo, Christina Aguilera, Cee Lo Green, Alien Ant Farm and Beyoncé with Jamie Foxx hosting the event. When Kiss was announced as an addition to the line up, fans were outraged given lead singer Gene Simmons' earlier comments disparaging Michael and his reputation. Fans urged Katherine to pull the plug on the event. Organizers decided to continue with the show but bumped Kiss from the lineup. The show did go on, but was less than the stellar tribute Michael deserves.

Projects and tributes authorized by the estate have a grand style that are fitting for the King of Pop. A particularly cool tribute was held in January 2012 when the IMMORTAL World tour hit Los Angeles. Grauman's Chinese Theatre's famed courtyard features the hand and footprints of stars dating back to the 1920's. For the first time in the history of the tradition, a posthumous ceremony was held to imprint Michael Jackson's black loafers and white sequined glove in cement. Prince, Paris and Blanket made the impressions. The boys each handled a shoe while Paris made an imprint with the glove from the Victory tour, using plastic wrap to prevent the priceless item from actually being coated in cement. She then wrote her father's name in the cement with a heart between Michael and Jackson. Each of the kids then added their own handprints. The imprint of the left shoe showed the regal image of a familiar crest in the sole. The King of Pop even had cool footprints.

Katherine Jackson attended with Tito and Jackie. Also participating in the ceremony was Quincy Jones, Smokey Robinson, Chris Tucker and cast members of the Cirque du Soleil IMMORTAL World Tour. Teen heartthrob Justin Beiber spoke of Michael as an inspiration and sang a couple lines of "Rockin' Robin". Prince, in a Jacksons t-shirt, spoke of the honor and what it would have meant to his father, "My dad won the lifetime achievement award. It was an award he strived and worked the hardest to get but for me, and I think for him as well, this right here is his lifetime achievement award. This is what he strived to get and this is what we are giving him now today."

In the spring of 2012 the four surviving members of the Jackson Five announced the Jacksons Unity Tour. Jackie, Tito,

Jermaine and Marlon toured together for the first time since the 1984 Victory tour, though in dramatically smaller venues. The shows included a touching tribute to their brother "who is here with us tonight in spirit" with a slide show of beautiful and touching images to Jermaine's surprisingly good version of "Gone Too Soon". Despite heavy promotion the show struggled to fill five thousand seat venues, even in Detroit, their old stomping ground.

    Meanwhile, having now fallen to become the nation's number three largest selling soft drink, behind Coke and Diet Coke, Pepsi once again pulled out the big guns for a new marketing promotion. The estate of Michael Jackson announced a new deal with Pepsi. Michael Jackson's image was featured on one billion cans of Pepsi ("perhaps a Guinness record" according to John Branca) in a newly announced worldwide deal, that also included chances to download remixes of Jackson's songs and contests to win tickets to the IMMORTAL tour and Michael Jackson inspired leather jackets. The Pepsi campaign coincided with the announcement of the release of *Bad 25*, an album celebrating the 25th anniversary of *Bad* containing remixes from *Bad* , unreleased tracks a live concert CD and, best of all, a first time commercial DVD release of a Bad tour performance from London's Wembley Area. The performance was said to be discovered in Michael's personal video library and is the only known copy.

    Warming up to the release was the re-release of the album's first single, "I Just Can't Stop Loving You" with the previously unreleased "Don't be Messin' 'Round". The limited edition,

"(Can't Make it) Another Day"

individually numbered CD single flew off the shelves. The single debuted on *Billboard's* Hot Singles Sales Chart at number one. The *Bad 25* album debuted and peaked on the *Billboard* Hot 100 at number 23, peaked at number 7 on the R&B chart and stayed for weeks at number one on the Catalog album chart.

Also marking the twenty-fifth anniversary of *Bad, was Bad25*, a documentary by Spike Lee. Lee was given complete access to Michael Jackson's vault of footage – some taken by Michael himself – of behind the scenes "stuff" said to show his great sense of humor.

The estate continues to make commendable strides toward preserving and continuing Michael Jackson's unrivaled legacy. More unreleased music from his vault, a definitive biography and hopefully more footage of performances are still to come as his fan base continues to grow with new generations.

Michael Jackson made history time and time again. He changed the music industry. He revolutionized music videos. He worked to make the world a better place. He touched and inspired people from every corner of the world. He will forever remain the King of Pop.

AFTERWORD

Ben, most people would turn you away
I don't listen to a word they say
They don't see you as I do
I wish they would try to
I'm sure they'd think again
If they had a friend like Ben

"Ben"
- Walter Scharf, Don Black

The loss of Michael Jackson affected me deeply. I have, in varying degrees, spent more than half of my life actively following his career and his life. His passing highlighted the extent to which he permeates my life, sometimes in fun, silly ways; from the tulips that leaned out from the shadow of my house toward the sun that I

Afterword

dubbed "Smooth Criminal" tulips to my usual line of "See you next Wednesday" a line from the "Thriller" video, to my mother when leaving our standing Wednesday dinner dates. I will see her again before the next Wednesday, but "See you Sunday" is not a line in any Jackson production so I cannot say that. Mom gets it.

As a kid, I watched the Jackson Five and always enjoyed their synchronized choreography in their many variety show appearances. But later on Michael released a solo album, *Off the Wall*, and I was blown away. I had a hard time reconciling that this was the same little Michael Jackson I had watched with his brothers. He had grown up and did a damn fine job of it too. But it got better.

Thriller – its singles and music videos - shown on a new network called MTV dominated airways for years and my senses ever since. He was mesmerizing. His talent eclipsed that of any other artist by a couple of light years. I wanted to know all about him. *Everything.* I began reading about him and collecting books, magazines, newspaper clippings. I recorded his videos from MTV, award show appearances, news stories and entertainment program stories. I collected a mind-boggling number of VHS tapes. I tracked each of his albums and singles up the music charts. Music award night was a major event at my house. You would have thought I was going to take home an armload of Grammys. I recorded his acceptance remarks and watched them over and over again. I loved the sound of his voice, I loved to just hear him talk.

I love to learn new things about him however trivial; like he wore a musk cologne and always smelled good, chewed lots of

Bazooka bubble gum, could snap his fingers really loud and that he made the "best french toast in the whole world". He liked to play Janet's music and dance. I would love to see that.

He seemed to have an enthusiasm or spirit – or some special quality – that made him rise above us mere mortals. It showed in his enduring love of people and his efforts to help those who needed it. It showed in his performances. Even if taking the stage with a troupe of well studied pros, you could easily spot this extra energy he brought. His steps were a little lighter, his voice exuded joy.

To this day I find myself thinking and speaking in song lyrics. At the sound of the early morning alarm I think, "I've got to get up"... then instinctively add "as jacked as it sounds, the whole system sucks" completing a line from "Scream". Shopping in the new earth friendly grocery stores where the freezer case lights go on as you pass, I of course think of the "Billie Jean" video and look down to see if the floor tiles are lighting up at my touch too.

I still won't drink Pepsi. When they fired Michael Jackson, I fired Pepsi. Even though the soft drink giant and Michael Jackson kissed and made up later rejoining for more endorsement deals, they did not include the U.S. I still haven't forgiven them though I did relax the embargo temporarily in the summer of 2012 to purchase several of the commemorative Pepsi cans featuring the King of Pop.

I am profoundly grateful for the many gifts he shared with the world and that I was at an age to fully appreciate and enjoy him. I absorbed every minute. When I hear of others recalling they were in kindergarten or elementary school during Thrillermania I find I

Afterword

almost feel sorry for them for they were not able to fully understand and appreciate the phenomenon that was Michael Jackson. My hope is that this book helps highlight some of his unmatched achievements in music and his immeasurable contributions to the world. I will forever cherish his acknowledgements of my work.

Michael Jackson's impact on the world goes much beyond his soulful voice and magic feet. An artist with his level of talent, creativity, perfectionism, originality, global reach and influence will never been seen again. He sought to make the world a better place and he did. He made my world a better place. I miss him every single day. His kind heart, generosity and love for his millions of fans in every corner of the globe will forever serve as an inspiration to others. I pray his soul rests in peace and that there is some way he knows how much he is missed, appreciated and loved. I thank him for sharing his gifts with the world, with me.

Lisa Campbell
Phoenix, Arizona

Acknowledgements

Special thanks to my husband John, for your love, encouragement and all of your invaluable help. You are a genius. I love you.

To Mom, to quote MJ, "Everyone thinks they have the greatest mother in the world, but I really do".

To Michele, thank you for your support, undertaking search missions and letting me drag you to all the MJ related events.

To Michael Firestone, thank you for being so gracious and generous with your time. You are amazing. I love you.

Special thanks to Christine Gustafson for your overwhelming generosity, understanding and advice. It helped more than you know.

Amanda Morrell, thank you for your thoughtfulness, support and technical wizardry.

Joseph Sotelo Jr., thank you for understanding my passion and all of your great ideas.

Thanks also to Misty Jones for your support at a very difficult time, making the treks with me on MJ recon missions and sharing your great photos.

I wish also to acknowledge and thank all those who supported and helped Michael Jackson throughout his life especially all of his loving and devoted fans around the world.

Made in the USA
San Bernardino, CA
04 December 2012